LACE MACHINES
MACHINES
and
MACHINE
LACES

LACE MACHINES and MACHINE LACES

Pat Earnshaw

B.T. Batsford Ltd · London

ISBN 0 7134 46846 (cased)

Typeset by Servis Filmsetting Ltd, Manchester
and printed in Great Britain by
R.J. Acford
Chichester, Sussex
for the publishers
B.T. Batsford Ltd
4 Fitzhardinge Street
London W1H OAH

Contents

Machine: a combination of parts moving mechanically, which may be operated by hand, foot, water, steam, electricity etc. Its essential feature is that it transmits force, making more effective use of it, so that a far greater quantity of work can be done than by the direct application of human energy. Speed and simultaneous replication of products are common though not essential features of a manufacturing machine.

(paraphrased from the *Oxford English Dictionary*)

'Modern mechanical lace-making bears about the same relation to simple weaving that a watch does to a wheelbarrow.'

Bernard H. Becker, *Lace-making at Nottingham*, 1884, p. 473.

Acknowledgment

My grateful thanks are due for the kindness and generosity of manufacturers, of both laces and lace machines, who have allowed me into their factories, replied patiently to my questions, supplied me with invaluable samples, and made available their archives.

Special thanks go to Roger Watson of the Lace Market, Nottingham, who produced the Schiffli lace for the Princess of Wales' wedding train, for his help and advice over a number of years; to John A. Walker of the Basford Textile Group (Lace Curtain and Raschel); Alan Moore of Birkin and Co. (Leavers and Raschel); John Ghent of Abur Pegg (Leavers); Ernest Jaffe of Malmic Lace (Barmen and Crochet machines); Stan Pengelly of Heathcoat's, Tiverton (Bobbinet); Peter Gammon of P.G. Laces (Cornely); Swiss Net, formerly Small and Tidmas, Chard (Bobbinet); the Shepshed Manufacturing Co., Loughborough (Barmen); Charles Farmer of Mapperley (Schiffli); Geoffrey Macpherson Ltd (sole agents in the UK for Barudan Multihead machines); Wiener Laces of New York (Leavers and Raschel); Forster Willi of St Gallen (Schiffli); and Firma Sandheer, Berneck (Cornely).

The laces, drafts and prints which they provided, or gave permission to be photographed, have been acknowledged in the captions of the individual illustrations, as have photographs from Spowage, Humphreys and Wyer of Nottingham; Karl Mayer of Germany; and Saurer of Switzerland.

Alan Moore was particularly helpful in identifying the now obsolete techniques of some of my older machine laces; and it was the expertise of Peta Lewis, of Ruddington Framework Knitters Museum, which discovered among my small collection of early weft-knitted nets a wedding purse of single press, and a veil of double press, point net.

I am also indebted to Alastair Thompson for labelling the line drawings, and for taking the photographs of the Schiffli machine (courtesy of Charles Farmer); to Tom Stevenson of Budleigh Salterton for sharing his experiences of Nottingham lace manufacture in the early part of this century; to Calverton Museum for documents relating to nineteenth-century stockingers; to Vibeke Ervø for information on Scandinavian laces; to Claire Burkhard for making bobbin lace copies of Barmen designs; to the Museum of London for allowing me to examine the Princess Charlotte's wedding dress with a ×30 magnifier, and thus to discover that, contrary to accepted belief, it is not a warp net but a weft-knitted double press point net, with additional trimmings of single press (see fig. 8); and to Dr Anne Wanner, and Marianne Gächter, of the Textilmuseum, St Gallen, for illuminating the identity of Swiss curtains.

Nearly all the photographs of actual laces are by Ronald Brown ARCA who has, in this fifth book, demonstrated yet again his skill in capturing the feel of lace, and his ability to reveal, in close-up enlargements, their structural qualities. An explanation of the techniques of machine laces would have been impossible without this visual addition.

Other photographic acknowledgments are to: Her Royal Highness the Princess of Wales for permission to reproduce fig. 148a. Joslyn Baker, figs. 71f, 102d, 104k(iii), 105c, 158. Chertsey Museum, figs. 11, 143. Antoinette Curzon, fig. 107i. Lise Helvard, fig. 19. Killerton House, National Trust, fig. 71b. Leicester Museum and Art Galleries Records Service, fig. 10. Doris May, fig. 136a(ii) (Barmen). Nationalmuseet, Brede, figs. 178b(i and ii). Nationalmuseet, Copenhagen, figs. 178c(i and ii). Palermo, Soprintenza alle Gallerie ed Opere d'Arte della Sicilia, fig. 176c. Phillips, Fine Art Auctioneers, fig. 45a. Science Museum, South Kensington, fig. 2. Textilmuseum, St Gallen, fig. 166. Thousand Island Crafts School and Textile Museum, New York, fig. 176b. Trent Polytechnic, Nottingham, figs. 102e, 138b, 139a, 146c. Lillie Trivett, fig. 157d(iii). Victoria and Albert Museum, fig. 168. Wollaton Park Industrial Museum, figs. 74, 111, 132e.

Machine and lace sizes have for the most part been quoted in inches, feet or yards. A simple conversion to metric measurements in the text is not possible since the whole structure of the machine – gauge, rack, shogs, needle bars etc – is built to these specifications. Inches are also used in machines of English manufacture exported abroad. For machines manufactured in continental Europe, the measurements are in cm and mm, and these can if desired be substituted in the appropriate places.

The names of the main machines – Stocking Frame, Warp Frame, Raschel, Bobbinet, Pusher, Leavers, Lace Curtain and Barmen – are printed with capital initials, to distinguish them. Names of groups of machines, however, are not given capital initials, for example: weft-knitting machines, warp-knitting machines, bobbin-net machines, twist-net machines.

Foreword

The rise, and what might be regarded as the fall, of machine laces covers a span of 200 years.

Their origin coincided with an increasing competence in the industrial field, particularly in textile manufacture. Their development followed an arduous course in which inventors pitted their wits against metal and thread, succeeded or failed, were persecuted, cheated, and physically abused. Many committed suicide, fled abroad, died of brain fever or ended their days in destitution.

The rise to dominance of machine laces resulted from the ability to manufacture a product which was attractive to wear and relatively inexpensive so that it had an immediate appeal for the millions of 'working class' women hitherto beyond that pale which enclosed the world of fashion.

The sharp nineteenth-century reactions were symptomatic of a social problem: the formerly elevated ladies clung to their formerly exclusive laces, and deliberately set out to destroy by denigration the market for a product which they made no attempt to understand. The condemnatory 'Imitation!' was only the rending *cri du coeur* of gentlewomen sucked down into the levelling quicksand of democracy.

Certainly machine laces were commercial, competitive and imitative – but so were all the fashionable handmade laces. Even the makers of those laces were for centuries treated as machines, ordered to turn out precise yardages of specific designs, within a fixed time, and for very little pay. 'Have you ever watched women making lace?' asks Natalia in Turgenev's *A Month in the Country*, in 1850. 'They sit in stuffy rooms, and never move an inch to the left or to the right.' Yet the replacement of their fingers of flesh by thin bars or spikes of metal met with the utmost resistance – from those who still wanted lace to be a status symbol of the élite.

Hand and machine laces cannot be judged against each other: each has its own world. Machines may imitate the appearances of handmade laces, but they use their own techniques for making them. In the various chapters of this book it will be apparent just how much imaginativeness was needed to translate the earlier quietly-made laces into the complex, rapid and intricately synchronized movements of the thousands of metallic parts by which machines replicated instantaneously, at vast speeds, their own noisy productions, with such tremendous power that whole buildings shuddered under their pulsating motions

The aim of this book is a triple one: to explain the basic history, structure and techniques of the major lace machines; to correlate the appearance of machine laces with the workings of the machines which made them, so that their origins can be identified; and to show how those superb feats of engineering, creativity and idealism which the lace machines represent are capable not only of resurrecting illusions of old handmade laces – and so of preserving the 'real' handmade laces from destruction – but also of producing entirely new designs appropriate to both a sentimental nostalgia and to a way of life for the present and for the future.

I

The Stocking Frame
(Métier à bas)

Lace, in its accepted definition of a slender openwork fabric made of threads, was derived from three sources: coarse functional openworks such as netting; techniques such as knitting and weaving, formerly used to construct only solid fabrics, and then adapted to the making of openworks; and surface decorations such as embroideries converted to a form where instead of being embedded in the base fabric they were made separately from it and could be added or taken off as required.

Each of these sources found expression in handmade laces through many centuries to the present day. From the mid-eighteenth century their manufacture began to be mechanized.

Essentially mechanization involves a speeding-up process. Hand movements are replaced by mobile appendages of wood or metal which can multiply abundantly the actions of one worker within the same period of time. With machine laces the first process to be mechanized was knitting. Solid fabrics could be made on a knitting machine (the Stocking Frame) from 1589. Lacey fabrics began to be produced on these machines nearly 200 years later.

This unlikely sequence is so important in the subsequent development of all the vast range of machine laces of the nineteenth and twentieth centuries that its pre-history will be explained briefly here.

Hand-knitting and the Stocking Frame

Hand-knitting uses two, four or five needles and a single continuous thread. The thread is pulled stitch by stitch through loops held on one needle – usually the left – the new loops being transferred one at a time to the other needle. The result is the 'stocking stitch', described as 'plain' on one side and 'purl' on the other. The horizontal row of loops is known as a 'course', and a vertical row of loops a 'wale'. The upper part of each loop which is held on the knitting needle is called the 'needle loop'; the lower part, which is not held on the needle but sinks down into the fabric or 'web' is called the 'sinker loop' (fig. 1).

In England, the use of knitting for everyday garments appears to have become established fairly late. One of the first clear records was in 1488 when knitted woollen

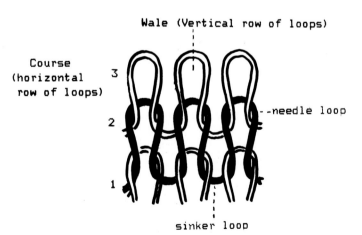

1 *Weft knitting: the terms used.*

11

caps, priced by law at 2*s*. 8*d*. (13p) by Henry VII, were made obligatory wear. Various Acts re-enforced this constraint, for example in the thirteenth year of the reign of Elizabeth I (1571):

that every person, not being gentlemen or ladies of twenty marks a year rent [that is, being plebeian], to wear a cap of wool-knit, on sabbath or holydays, except on travel, under a fine of three shillings and fourpence for every day not wearing them.

A 3*s*. 4*d*. (17p) fine, equivalent in value to two ounces of silver, seems very heavy indeed, and must certainly have been more to the advantage of the wool merchants, rapidly becoming influential nouveaux riches, than to the knitters themselves who at that time, and for long afterwards, were mainly peasants. In 1600 Shakespeare refers to the 'knitters in the sun' in the song which Clown sings to the Duke of Illyria;[2] while Celia Fiennes, travelling through England on a side-saddle at the end of the seventeenth century, gives the impression of whole counties swarming with knitters: from Norwich 'Thence we went mostly through Lanes where you meete ye ordinary people knitting 4 or 5 in a Company under the hedges.'[3]

Caps were handknitted, but stockings in the late fifteenth century were cut from woven cloth. This made them difficult to pull on, and gave them a tendency to fall into heavy wrinkles, a feature visible in many paintings of that period. The first mention of handknitted stockings in England appears in an account of 7 September, 25 H 8, that is the 25th year of Henry VIII's reign, or 1534: 'paid for 4 peyr of knytt-hose viiis [8 shillings, or 40p]'.[4] In 1537 the future Henri II of France wore handknitted silk hose. In 1561, the third year of her reign, Queen Elizabeth was presented with her first pair of black silk stockings, handknitted in England. The first pair of knitted worsted stockings is said to have been a copy of a pair brought to England from Mantua. They were knitted by William Rider and presented by him to the Earl of Pembroke. Timbs places this event after 1561,[5] Henson before, in the time of Edward VI (1547–53).[6]

The knitting of stockings was mechanized only a few decades later. Aubrey, writing in the 1670s, attributes the invention to a Rev William Lee (*c*.1556–1610), born at Woodborough in Nottinghamshire, educated at Cambridge, and rector of nearby Calverton:

He was the first Inventor of the Weaving of Stockings by an Engine of his construction. He was a poor Curate and observing how much paine his Wife took in knitting a payre of Stockings, he bought a Stocking and a halfe, and observed the construction of the Stitch, which he designed in his Loome, which . . . keeps the same to this day . . . the Art was, not long since, in no part of the world but England. Oliver Protector made an Act that it should be a Felonie to transport this Engine. This information I took from a Weaver (by this engine) in Pear-poole lane, 1656.[7]

Whether Lee's wife was knitting a tubular stocking on four, or five, needles, or a flat stocking on two, we shall never know. Certainly in Lee's machine the knitting was straight and not circular. When a circular machine was finally invented 200 years later, by Decroix, in 1798, Lee's original form of machine, which had changed surprisingly little, was distinguished as a 'straight-bar'.

Lee's machine was known as the Stocking Frame, being intended for the production of stockings, and being supported by a stout wooden frame (fig. 2). The essence of his invention was to have a separate needle for every loop, and to coordinate their action so that, the thread being laid horizontally across them, an entire row of loops was knitted at the same time instead of one-by-one consecutively.

At the time of Lee's birth, not only were knitted stockings a novelty, but so was the use of low-carbon steel. Steel sewing needles were only slowly replacing those of wrought iron.[8] The making of them was extremely tedious, every step to be done by hand, so that Lee had all the imaginative details of his invention to unravel and, in addition, all the practical difficulties of smooth wire-drawing, of bending the needle hook to the right extent and the right length, filing the groove for the tip to fit when it closed, and toughening the

(fig. 3). The needles were mounted on a short straight bar projecting horizontally in a direction away from the knitter. The weft-orientated thread was laid across them so that it could be made to enter the beards. The needle tips were then closed by pressure, and the needles moved backwards through the old loops, causing these to slide forwards over their bearded heads, forming a new course of the web.

In Lee's first attempt he used a total of 12 needles, spread over $1\frac{1}{2}$ inches. He manoeuvred the thread by hand, stitch-by-stitch, needle after needle, and produced a pair of garters. This was slow and tedious, and his next essay was to synchronize the pressing down of all the beards, by means of a presser bar, so that the old loops could be slid over all the needle heads simultaneously. The back and forth movement of the needle bar and the up and down movement of the presser bar were controlled by hand- or foot-levers. The addition of jacks reduced the force needed for each movement.

2 *A Stocking Frame, eighteenth century. Note the stout wooden frame, the bench seat, the foot levers, and the counterbalancing spring. The completed web accumulates downwards, that is, the order of knitting the courses is from the bottom upwards.*

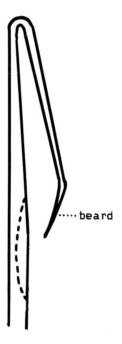

metal to withstand pressure and tension, and yet be elastic enough to spring back again the many thousands of times required to make even a few pairs of stockings.

Lee's machine worked only in stocking stitch, but his sad story demonstrates the anguish, poverty and unremitting toil which clouded his life, and that of many later inventors in the machine lace trade.

The machine's working parts consisted of needles with a reflexed tip known as a beard

3 *A bearded needle. When the beard is 'pressed' it is pushed against the hollow, holding the new loop while the older loop passes over its head.*

Lee continued to make improvements and to create his 'artificial fingers for knitting many loops at once'.[9] By 1589, after three years of exhausting work, and the dissipation of the greater part of his financial resources, his first model was completed. His Christian heart full of faith for the immense benefit which his invention must bring to all mankind, he hurried to Bunhill Fields, in London, to solicit the Queen's patronage.[10] Elizabeth, no doubt wearing her comfortable hand-knitted silk stockings, visited him, only to recoil from the pair of coarse uneven hose in thick worsted and probably weighing the best part of a pound which he offered her, and at the noise of the ugly awkward 'engine' which had constructed them. She might well have felt insulted, such garments being fit only for the lower classes. She could scarcely be expected to appreciate the almost superhuman effort they had cost the inventor.

She denied her patronage, couching her refusal in self-abnegating terms:

I have too much love to my poor people, who obtain their bread by the employment of knitting to give my money to forward an invention which will tend to their ruin by depriving them of employment.[11]

Lee was unfortunate in his monarch. Her father, Henry VIII, had been open-handed in his patronage: Elizabeth gave almost nothing to support inventions or the arts. She left open only a vague promise that if Lee would make stockings of silk, which would not affect her wool-knitting bread-eating people, and which she herself could wear, she might reconsider.

Stubbes, the passionate Puritan, in his *Anatomie of Abuses*, published in 1596, demonstrates how the personal vanity and fastidiousness of the rich and noble may have affected Elizabeth's judgment.

They have nether-stocks, not of cloth, though never so fine, for that is thought too base, but of worsted, silk, thread [linen], and such like, and so curiously knit, with open seam down the leg, with quirks and clocks about the ankles, and sometimes haply interlaced about the ankles with gold or silver threads, as is wonderful to behold. And to such impudent insolency and shameful outrage is

it now grown, that everyone almost, though otherwise very poor, having scarcely forty shillings [£2] wages by the year, will not stick to have two or three pair of these silk nether-stocks, or else of the finest yarn that may be got, though the price of them be twenty shillings or more, as commonly it is. The time hath been when one might have clothed all his body well, from top to toe, for less than a pair of these nether-stocks will cost.[12]

Worsted stockings in 1590 were recorded at 8s. or 9s. (40p, 45p) a pair.[13] All those mentioned by Stubbes would of course be hand-knitted.

For silk stockings to be made on a machine the loops had to be smaller and finer, and the needles closer together. Lee redevised his needle bar until it had 16 needles to the inch instead of the original eight and, after more arduous experiment, he eventually made silk stockings.[14] Then Queen Elizabeth died, in 1603. Under the new monarch, James I of Great Britain, Robert Cecil, later the first Earl of Salisbury, continued Elizabeth's non-supportive policy. Nor did the local hand-knitters have any sympathy for Lee's plight. With resentful atavism they were blind to all prospects except that his invention might challenge their established way of life.

A brighter vista opened as the erstwhile Protestant Henri IV, in a land where silk was abundant, invited Lee to cross the Channel and set up a workshop to supply stockings for the Court of France. By 1610 the ill-fated inventor was scarcely established when Henri was assassinated by a Jesuit monk. Marie d'Medici, Henri's widow and Regent to his nine-year old son Louis XIII, was a bigoted Catholic. She withdrew all patronage, and Lee died in the same year, it is said of a broken heart.

Within a cruelly short time the Frame was a success. William Lee's brother James returned from France and set up an industry at Thoroton in Nottinghamshire, where he was assisted by the local sheep whose fine long fleeces could be spun into a strong and flexible yarn ideal for the heavy pounding of the Stocking Frame. In 1615 a working Frame was established in France; in 1620 one was exported to Venice at a price of £500.[15]

The workers, later known as framework-knitters, were initially called 'weavers', thus making some of the seventeenth century records of the Spitalsfield area of London difficult to interpret. Timbs explains the term as follows:

The manufacture of stockings by the humble process of knitting is in strictness to be called *chain weaving*, for the fabric itself is actually produced by a series of loops . . . closely resembling those produced by tambouring.

By 1620 the Stocking Frame weavers were strong enough to form themselves into a trade association, similar to that of the Company of Pinners, Girdlers and Wiredrawers which had been incorporated in 1568.[16] Pinners were pin-makers; wire-drawers drew out wire from wrought iron either by hand or with the aid of water power, the wire being then cut and sharpened to make pins and needles; girdlers made twisted steel wire for armour, or wire links for coats of mail – all closely connected with the skill and precision necessary to make and assemble the needles, pressers, jacks and other working parts of the Stocking Frame.

By 1658 the Frame had become so important a part of English life that the Company of Framework-knitters, alarmed at the imminent vanishment abroad of some 30 or 40 Frames, petitioned Oliver Cromwell to prohibit the exportation of 'any frames and machines for knit workers of silk stockings.' The petition was granted on 14 June 1659. 'The manufacture,' it stated, 'employed great numbers of poor people such as workmen, winders, sizers, smiths etc which, if the trade left the kingdom would be thrown out of employment'[17] - a statement of fact, not belief, giving the lie to Queen Elizabeth's pious prognostication, and making the unrelieved disappointments of the hapless inventor so much more tragic.

According to the petition the Frame contained at that time some 2,000 pieces. These are all listed by Henson, down to the last sinker, locker, presser, comb, camel and slur cock.[18] Though some modifications had certainly been made in the near-50 years

since Lee's death, this list gives a vivid idea of the work which had consumed 22 years of his life, and of the depths of his despair that it had gone so entirely unrecognised.

At the restoration of the monarchy in 1661, all the Acts of Cromwell were set aside. However on '19th August, 15th King' – that is 1663, 15 years from the beheading of Charles I, though only two from Charles II's actual coronation – a new Charter was drawn up by which 'all persons having served seven years apprenticeship shall be one fellowship of the art and mystery of framework-knitters'. The embargo on exportation of the Frames 'on any pretence whatsoever' was renewed, but inadequately enforced for, in spite of the risk of seizure and punishment, Stocking Frames found their way to Louvaine, Tournay and Valenciennes; to Cordova, Seville and Cadiz; to Rome and Messina, to a total of 400 machines between 1670 and 1695.[19] It was left to William III (reigned 1689–1702) to put an effective stop to this leakage by levying a fine on any Stocking Frame that went missing from its place of work.

By that time, however, the industry was well established in France. Louis XIV's finance minister, Jean-Baptiste Colbert – better known to lace enthusiasts for his part in the development of the needle lace Point de France – had obtained specifications in 1656. With his usual thoroughness he set up a factory and also a college where machinists and framework-knitters could be trained.

By 1664 some 400 to 500 Frames were active in London, 100 in Nottingham, 50 in Leicester, 50 in Bucks. and Herts., 25 in Godalming, and 10 in Dublin. Each Frame employed two knitters, working in shifts, making a total of nearly 1,500 framework-knitters. By 1695 there were more than 1,500 knitters in London alone, and by 1727 over 2,500, with some 8,000 in the whole kingdom, of which 3,500 were in the three Midlands counties of Nottingham, Derby and Leicester.

The working of the Frame needed an accurate coordination of hand, foot and eye. 'While the hands are thus busy,' says Felkin, 'and the feet are moving at the rate of 100 yards a minute, the eyes must watch over the needles.' He adds, 'The failure of sight as evidenced by the early use of spectacles is very common, especially in the case of frame-work-knitters engaged in making hosiery of fine qualities.'[20]

In spite of the counter-weighting of the heavy movable beams of the Frame, the machines were limited in size by the strength and endurance of the arms of the workers, since shoulder and back muscles were involved in the stretch to manipulate them. Two 4ft-6in models, built about 1780 for use in Godalming, and known as Gog and Magog, languished for lack of a giant to manage them.[21] Eventually one man with sufficiently massive arms was found, and he alone made webs on Magog for 20 years, but Gog was never used at its full width, amply demonstrating how lack of mechanical power limited the size of the machine. No water, steam or electric power was ever applied to the Stocking Frame itself, though its speed was increased from 500 to 1,500 loops a minute compared with a maximum of 111 a minute by handknitting.[22] In 1808, Felkin himself, then aged 15, tried for a record production. In a single day, between 6a.m. and 9p.m. he completed three pairs of 28-gauge fashioned hose.

Why lace?

The first production of a satisfactory machine lace came when the Stocking Frame was already nearly 200 years old. During all this time it had made only solid plain-knit fabrics for stockings, waistcoats and other shaped or unshaped garments.

The adventure into openworks resulted from the interaction of a number of very important factors. Firstly, cotton wool was being increasingly imported, and its machine-spinning improved dramatically in the last quarter of the eighteenth century, providing a cheaper thread which widened the market and created an atmosphere of prosperity in which invention could flourish. Secondly, skirts were shortened a little, revealing the ankle, and hand-knitters introduced patterning such as ribs and eyelet-holes to draw attention to the lower leg, while mittens, also made on the Stocking Frame, were similarly patterned. Thirdly, handmade laces were becoming progressively narrower with less and less design until they more closely resembled a plain net than a patterned lace.

Of the possible yarns available to the Stocking Frame, the only one native to England was wool. Fine wools, culled from the sheep browsing ubiquitously over the upland pastures had been the country's main source of wealth since the Middle Ages. Flax, in spite of royal encouragement, had never achieved high quality or commercial success except in Ireland. Most linen thread was imported from Flanders, the $7\frac{1}{2}\%$ to 15% tax on its importation providing valuable revenue. Its fibres were in any case too easily fractured to withstand the crashing pressures of the early Frame. Silk had to be imported, and even the closer grouping of 24 gauge (16 needles to the inch), achieved in the seventeenth century following the application of Aston's lead sinkers in 1620, used so much silk that stockings were likely to weigh half a pound a pair.

Cotton, although requiring a far warmer climate than that of Britain, had, from 1600 when the English East India Company was founded, the advantage of preferential importation. In 1661 Charles II acquired Bombay as part of his dowry from the King of Portugal when he married Catherine of Braganza. Between then and 1684 the quantity of cotton imported increased nine times until, in 1690, it was prohibited as threatening the wool and woven linen industry of England, and the silk industry of France.

A further advantage for cotton accrued however in 1763 when, by the Treaty of Paris, India with its enormous resources was ceded by France. In the same year the first consignments of cotton arrived at Liverpool from the plantations of Carolina, named after Charles II – a trade dependent on the 45,000 slaves from Africa forcibly transported every year to the American colonies. The long staple or 'long silk' Sea Island cotton from Georgia also became available, after 1770.

Although Indian, or Hindoostan, spinners were able from 1lb of cotton to produce a thread nearly 253 miles long for weaving their gossamer-like Dacca muslins, English spinners – accustomed to longer flax, or more cohesive wool fibres – found the short staples difficult to manage, and there were only rare areas such as Tewkesbury where hand-spinning of cotton was attempted, and the thread then used for the local hand-knitting of stockings. Also, because of the tighter twist needed to bind the staples together, framework-knitters found it vexatious and, ever resistant to change, refused to work with it. Cotton yarn was in any case neither strong nor elastic enough for the weight of the jacks or for the pressures and tensions of the heavy movements needed to create fresh rows of loops. It was often lumpy and full of weaknesses so that the 'bumps and burs' caught in the beards of the needles, straining the threads, and the finished stockings were likely in no time at all to fall into holes. 'Cotton' from the mid-seventeenth to the mid-eighteenth century also referred to brushed wool.

In 1769 a patent was granted to Richard Arkwright of Nottingham for a 'Machine for making Cotton into Yarn'.[23] At the world's first spinning mill, his machinery was powered by horses. From one pound of raw cotton his Water Frame (1775) could spin a yarn 19 miles long, equivalent to 40 hanks – a record handsomely beaten in the nineteenth century, for a heavier yarn, by a hand-spinner from Norwich who converted a pound of combed long-staple wool into a thread 115 miles long which, if woven, would have made 200 square yards of wool muslin.[24] Crompton's Mule of 1779 could produce a finer and more elastic yarn than either Hargreave's Jenny or Arkwright's Water Frame, with the result that the negligible amount of cotton being consumed in hosiery manufacture before 1770 increased to 1,500,000lb in 1787, and to three times that amount by 1836.[25]

In this exciting atmosphere of invention and experiment, stocking-weavers were stimulated to begin their own innovations.

Lacey-knits: the first machine lace

The vogue for handmade lacey-knit stockings, mittens and baby caps in the mid-eighteenth century provoked an imitative response in the Stocking Frames.

In hand-knitting the appearance of openwork can involve a number of stitch modifications, for example:

1. Slipped stitch. The loop is not knitted, that is the thread instead of passing through it goes behind it and the same loop is carried up into the next course.

2. Knit two together. Two adjacent loops are knitted at the same time so that only one new loop is formed from them.

3. Pick-up stitch. The sinker loop (see fig. 1) is brought up on to the needle, leaving a small gap below it.

The problem for the Stocking Frames in copying these techniques was that their needles made new loops not singly but collectively, every needle doing the same thing at the same time. Thus no patterning of any kind was possible until a way had been found of making some of them behave differently. In the meantime the loops themselves could be manipulated by hand using a short stiff wire known as a tickler.

The first effect to be imitated in this way was not in fact openwork, but ribbing, that is the alternation of vertical bands of plain and purl stitches on the same side of the work. The web on the Stocking Frame was knitted from one side only: in effect it knitted only plain-stitch although purl would of course automatically appear on the reverse side. Thus the deliberate construction of purl stitches on the right, or face, side of the work was a challenging adventure.

It was done at first in the most laborious way. In the near-completed stocking, stitches were taken off the needles at intervals and allowed to run or 'ladder' all the way down. They were then picked up again by hand, from the reverse side.

The mechanisation of the ribbing process is attributed to Jedediah Strutt who in 1758 patented the Derby Rib machine. This machine was an ordinary Stocking Frame with an iron attachment hung at the front of it. The attachment consisted of an additional straight bar of bearded needles set at right angles to the usual needle bar, that is vertically instead of horizontally. The additional bar was so placed that its needles would enter between the horizontal needles at the points where purl instead of plain stitches were required. For example a 3:1 rib (3 plain, 1 purl) would have a vertical needle after every third horizontal needle. When the horizontal needles had been pressed, the vertical would be brought down to a horizontal position. Their beards would now face downwards instead of upwards, so that the direction of the new loops would be reversed, and purl stitches made.

Mechanised openworks were also preceded by hand-tickler manipulation of the loops, and as might be expected only small areas of lacery were constructed in a fabric which was otherwise quite solid.

But the times were full of a restless inventiveness. An eagerness to try out new ideas affected London and Nottingham equally, while the need for secrecy, to prevent both destruction and piracy, meant that completely independent workers might hit on the same inspiration unknown to each other. The precise sequence of how the hand-knit and hand-tickler effects were mechanized for the Stocking Frame is impossible to discover. Even patents are not an entirely reliable guide since both lack of money, and intimidation by wealthy and unscrupulous rivals, often forced the inventor to sell his rights. Others took the credit, and he himself remained impoverished and unknown.

The adaptations of handmade lacey stitches on the Stocking Frame took the following forms:

1. Held stitch, equivalent to the hand slipped stitch.

2. Tuck stitch, a variant of held stitch (fig. 4a). The needle loop instead of being 'knocked off' the bearded needle by the formation of a new loop was retained (as in held stitch). However the weft thread passed not across the back of it, but into the beard, which thus held two threads, and both were carried up together into the next course. This process was mechanized by the tuck presser which depressed the beards of selected needles (when the loops would be knocked off, allowing new loops to be formed) but not of others (when the loops would be tucked).

3. Stitch transfer, equivalent to knit two together (fig. 4b). A loop was lifted entirely off one needle and put onto, or transferred to, another. This process, carried out at first by a hand tickler, was mechanised and patented by Thomas and John Morris and John and William Betts in 1764 (no. 807). It was described as:

An engine or machine adapted to a Stocking Frame, for the making of oilet-holes, or nettwork in silk, thread, cotton, or worsted, as mitts, gloves, hoods, aprons, handkerchiefs, and other goods usually manufactured upon Stocking Frames, by a method entirely new.

Briefly, by this method, stitch transfer and tuck stitch were combined to produce small openings called 'eyelet-holes'. The tuck presser (for producing the tuck, or unknitted stitch) was coordinated with a bar of horizontal frame-ticklers (similar to hand-ticklers but fixed into a line of metal 'leads' on the machine). The tuck stitches instead of remaining on the needles were now taken off by the ticklers. The tickler bar was then shogged (shunted sideways), and the tuck stitches transferred to those selected needles which the pattern required should receive them, and which would already be holding their own loops beneath their beards. The double stitch would then be knocked off by the presser bar and replaced by a single new loop. The shog might carry the tickler with its tucked stitch only to the next wale, or further, so that it was possible for it to be released onto a needle which was two or even three wales away.

4. Partial stitch transfer (fig. 4c). The chosen loop was not entirely lifted off its needle, but only partly. Its lifted side was then transferred to the next needle, so that the loop was held over two needles, creating within itself a tiny gap known as a 'marking stitch', or 'knot', a technique invented by Wm. Horton in 1771 (patent no. 991).

18

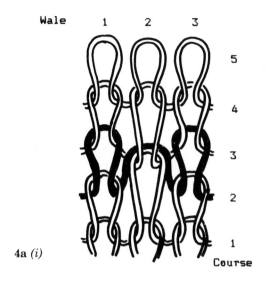

Wale 1 2 3

5

4

3

2

1

4a *(i)*

Course

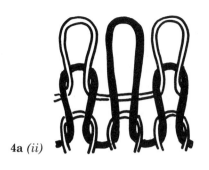

4a *(ii)*

4a *(i) tuck stitch, the middle stitch in course 2 is carried up to course 3. (ii) held stitch.* **b** *Stitch transfer (lace stitch), a needle loop from wale 3 is transferred to wale 2 in course 2, and a needle loop from wale 2 to wale 3 in course 4 (face side).* **c** *Partial stitch transfer (marking stitch), in course 2 a needle loop is partially transferred from one needle to the next so that it is stretched over two needles (reverse side).* **d** *Pelerine stitch (eyelet), the sinker loop is lifted by a tickler so that it forms an arch above two adjacent stitches in the next course, instead of lying below them (reverse side).*

5. Pelerine stitch, equivalent to pick-up stitch (fig. 4d). In the mechanical form a special tickler having a long flexible tip and known as a barleycorn was used to raise the sinker loop. The barleycorn could then transfer the sinker to the next needle, or to a further-away needle, or spread it over two needles. This stitch is also sometimes called an eyelet.[26]

1 2 3 4

5

4

3

2

1

4b

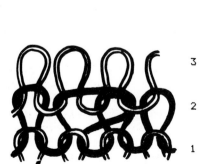

3

2

1

4c

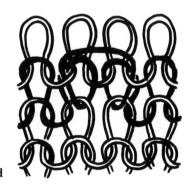

4d

The application of these newly-invented techniques to the making of patterned laces was hampered by several factors. Firstly, it was much easier for the machine to make a uniform fabric, which varied vertically over only about four courses, and per horizontal course not at all. Thus a patterned lace was a more difficult proposition, mechanically, than a plain net.

Secondly, it was also a more expensive one, since a solid fabric would necessarily use more yarn than an openwork fabric, and silk was costly.

Thirdly, the simplification of hand-made laces was drawing the attention of the fashion-conscious away from lace design and towards the fine uniform mesh or reseau which connected its parts together. The use of the term 'nettwork' in Morris's 1764 patent is interesting, for these 'aery, vaporous and intangible tissues' as Ferguson *fils* was later in poetic mood to describe them were an entirely new concept.[27] Earlier filmy veils had been of woven gauze, coarser ones of hand-knotted filet. Indeed the earliest date given by Diderot for the word *tulle*, meaning in French any fine network whether hand- or machine-made, is 1765, the year following the 'oilet-hole' patent.

A fourth influence was also at work to divert Stocking Frame productions into a new trend. The rich rewards which had opened up for framework-knitters following the popularity of ribbed stockings and simply-patterned hand-openwork, had attracted a vast mass of unskilled labour, and this rapidly brought the whole manufacture into disrepute. As much as 10*s*. (50p) a day could be earned by a skilled journeyman making hose or mittens on which floral patterns were delineated by eyelet holes, and this was a small fortune at a time when bread cost only 5*d*. or 6½*d*. (about 2½p) for a 4lb loaf, and servants might be paid, apart from bed and board, no more than £3 wages in a whole year.

'Every day men are starting up from obscurity to wealth,' observed Defoe in the 1730s[28]; and 30 years later the craving to leap from poverty to riches was even more obsessive. Greedy manufacturers used incompletely trained apprentices, instead of skilled knitters, to cut production costs, until standards had fallen so low that consumers wanted only French stockings, and even when in 1765 their importation was prohibited, Nottingham products were still rejected, until the manufacturers hit on the devious idea of working PARIS in eyelet holes around the welts. The novelty of making plain nets offered them a kind of escape route.

So it was that the eighteenth-century stocking weavers set out in search of the 'perfect net' which, idealised in the microscopic beauty of the bobbin-made droschel, was thought of as the perfect 'sexagon' (fig. 5). How the transition was made from the potential lace or net stitches to the actual production of commercially marketable nets is a long and complicated story. Very few of the older nets survive to show us their precise

5 *The perfect hexagon, the fine almost intangible net of handmade droschel, here with applied decoration.*

structure. Even when they do it needs a practised eye to distinguish them from the unpatterned warp nets which followed shortly afterwards.

The weft-knitted nets were however of immense importance, brilliantly clever and unbelievably fine. Even their looped structure is distinguishable in most cases only with a magnifier enlarging them eight times. Unfortunately the lustre of the thin silk threads obscures their clarity in photographs.

Weft-knitted nets

It was in 1768 that modifications of the Stocking Frame machine, more profound than any that occurred in all the years since it was first invented, began to transform it from a knitter of tangible stockings to a knitter of near-intangible nets. The first step was to remove the tuck presser and to convert the tickler bar to a more freely movable structure by attaching it to jointed arms called dogs in such a way that the ticklers could both be moved forwards to scoop up the loops and be shogged sideways to deposit them on other needles. This apparatus, like the old rib attachment, was fixed to the front of the machine with the ticklers so arranged that they could slip between every second needle.

A workman called Hammond was involved in this modification. He is often credited with the first breakthrough to 'lace' when, looking at the trimming of his wife's indoor cap, he suddenly saw it as a fabric the Stocking Frame might imitate. It is said that he rushed back to his machine, quickly made three lace-trimmed caps, and sold them just as quickly in the local pubs. His method was to use ticklers to transfer stitches not to the next needle but to the next needle but one, thus leaving a normal loop between each transfer. In the following course he transferred this intermediate loop two needles the other way. This diagonal crossing-over of loops was called *cross stitch*[29] and the effect was not dissimilar to the six-point star of Brussels point de Paris or wire ground made by bobbins. Just as the hand-made bobbin ground has two forms, the single and the double, so Ham-

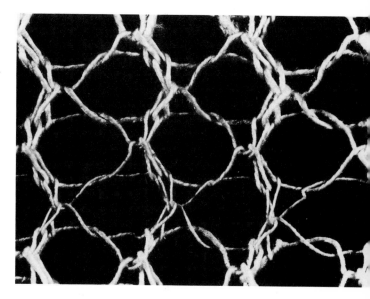

6 *A variant of Thomas Frost's square net, with alternating slack and stiff courses (× 10) (c.f. Lewis, sample 37).*

mond in a further improvement transferred two stitches at a time by tickler action two needles to the left and, in the following course, both stitches two needles to the right. This 'double cross stitch' he called *Valenciennes*.

Other experiments, in stitch transfer over variable distances, and in the spacing of ticklers one, two or three needles apart, produced Robert Frost's *tickler net* of 1769 which had some pattern areas of solid plain stitch; Frost and Holmes's *two-plain net* of 1777; and Thomas Frost's *square net* of 1781 (patent no. 1294) which was not sexangular but 'diamond-wise in squares', each mesh having four equal sides. This last made use of partial stitch transfer as well as the tuck presser, and but for its double defect of being slow to make and using a lot of silk, it might have been a good deal more successful. A broad 'spoon tickler' was used to enlarge the holes (fig. 6).

All other nets, however, were soon eclipsed in the commercial market by the products of the pin- and point-net-machines. The former was the invention of a workman called Har-

21

vey in the employ of Else who, with Hammond, had introduced the tickler bar moved and supported by dogs. Else in 1779 registered a patent (no. 1235) for the preparation of yarn for 'French or wire ground lace'; while in the same year Harvey's patent (no. 1238) was for 'Apparatus applicable to the Stocking Frame for the making of lace called Brussels, or double ground lace.' The double ground was a doubling of silk and cotton yarns together 'as the cotton thread was so very irregularly spun by Arkwright's machinery that it was quite unfit to be wrought alone.'[30] This patent was quashed as an infringement, and Harvey next proceeded to use ticklers in the form of pins 'bent in a circular form, the point upwards' to effect transfers. Though the accounts are not entirely clear, it appears from both Ferguson (p. 19) and Henson (p. 316) that it was the sinker loop which was transferred and spread over at least one needle to the left and right. Thus pelerine stitch was used to make a net of good sexangular meshes, though loose.

The machine was suppressed with bribery by the brothers Hayne, for it threatened even though it did not infringe a product of their own. The *pin machine* was thus almost completely unproductive in England. However it was pirated by the duc de Liancourt, by order of Louis XVI, and through the agency of a machinist called Rhamboult, in 1786. In France, where it had no competitors, it was improved, and it produced in Lyons and Paris large quantities of 'tulle uni' and 'tulle double' (single and double silk net). It was so successful that by the end of the century there were 2,000 pin machine Frames working in Lyons, and the net was even imported into Nottingham, where many people were employed in embroidering it. Its success was due not so much to its structural stability or perfection, for the meshes were irregular and the loops which formed them unstable, as to the French method of finishing which rendered the fabric hard, clear and shinily transparent.

As for the *point net* Frames, there is no general agreement as to the identity of the inventor(s). The most likely contender is Hiram Flint, a journeyman (i.e. itinerant)

stocking maker. Using barleycorn ticklers or points, alternate sinker loops were raised and transferred or stretched over the needle loops on either side. In the next course the intermediate sinker loops were treated in the same way. Thus a net was produced of alternating hexagonal meshes, each two courses deep, the overlaid sinker and needle loops giving to the whole a slightly three-dimensional effect. When the net was stiffened it was 'equal in beauty to the meshes of *real* plain net.'[31] But the stiffening was evanescent, dispersed even by dampness of the air, so that its shimmering aura collapsed into a ball of crêpe. The problem was that there was nothing structurally to hold the loops in position, and the smooth silk threads therefore slipped over each other and out of position the moment the support was lost. Also, as Felkin pointed out, 'the disadvantage of all these [weft-knitted] nets was that being made by the looping of one continuous thread across the machine they were liable, on being broken, to unravel'[32] (figs. 7a–d).

Flint, being too poor to market his invention himself, sold the idea to Thomas Taylor, a machinist, for £20, and subsequently died destitute in a Nottingham workhouse. Taylor patented the net in 1778 (no. 1192) but lost his nerve and sold out to Morris whose eyelet hole patent of 1764 had just expired. Morris was a tycoon notorious for his legal actions against all infringements, which had ruined many of his poorer competitors by heavy fines and confiscations.

Persecution of inventors by over-stringent patent claims – a feature of these fiercely competitive times – led some to flee the country. In 1776 the same John Morris suspecting a framework-knitter, Josiah

7 *Single press point net:* **a** *a wedding purse c.1810;* **b** *detail of the inside of the purse;* **c** *detail of the net, outer side;* **d** *detail of the same technique using a finer silk, and stretched as it would be when 'finished'.*

In this purse the use of thick silk and a small mesh has produced a fairly stable product where a fine silk and large mesh would slip. Note the snagged threads in the purse, these pass horizontally, indicating a weft-knit.

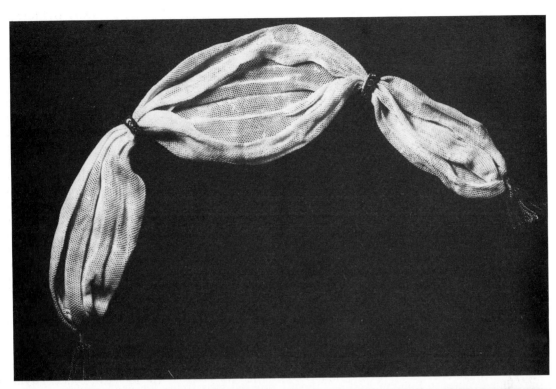

7a

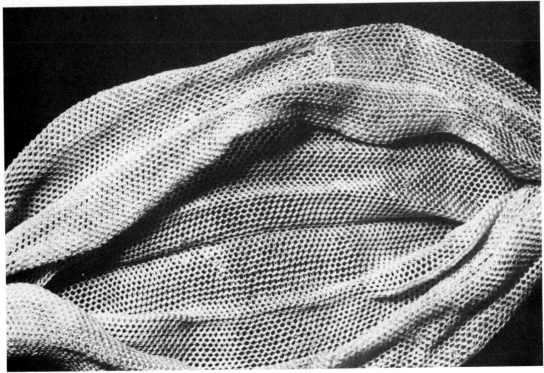

7b

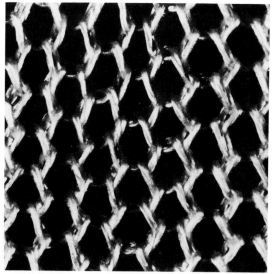

7c

7d

Branson, of infringing his eyelet-hole work, had hidden with witnesses on Nottingham's Castle Hill and spied on Branson through a telescope. The guilty Branson, in expectation of defeat and bankruptcy, secretly carried nine of his Frames to London, and had them aboard ship before he was missed from his house. His enemies moved fast: application was made to the Prime Minister, Lord North, a dispatch rushed to the coast, a revenue cutter alerted, and Branson's ship intercepted as it came within sight of France. He, the captain, crew and Frames were apprehended and imprisoned. One of his workmen, left behind, attempted to emigrate with a pocketful of ticklers, intending to show the French how they could be set up, but he was seized by a press-gang and condemned to working as a scrubber on a man of war for several years.[33]

It appears that Taylor's patent was neglected by Morris and passed eventually from him to the brothers Hayne, who were quick to appreciate its possibilities. In collaboration with a John Rogers they contrived a modification in 1786 to make the point net fast so that it could be cut into shapes without disintegrating. The main difference of technique was that each course involved two actions of the presser bar instead of only one. The sinker loop having been raised and transferred as in the earlier form was transferred again, so that it was forced over the bearded needle head in two stages before the fresh needle loop of the next course was allowed to appear. Since the new net was pressed two times for each course, it was called *double press point net*. It was known in France as 'pression double' or 'tulle anglais' (English net) presumably to distinguish it from the products of the pin-machine which the French had adopted. Flint's net (Taylor's patent) of 1778 was now referred to as *single press point net*. In double press, as in single press, the superimposed needle and sinker loops gave a shadowed effect to the meshes in the finished product. A fine extant example of this net is the Princess Charlotte's wedding dress (1816), on loan to the Museum of London (fig. 8). The metal foil which studs it is quite untarnished and may be of platinum rather than silver.

All the knitted nets were known collectively as 'patent nets', since most were patented. They were all originally made of silk, since eighteenth-century cotton was too coarse and unreliable for such fine work where the gauge might be as high as 30 needles to the inch. Bailey gives 1803 as the year in which cotton was first used on lace machines.[34] By 1805 Houldsworth of Manchester were producing good quality cotton

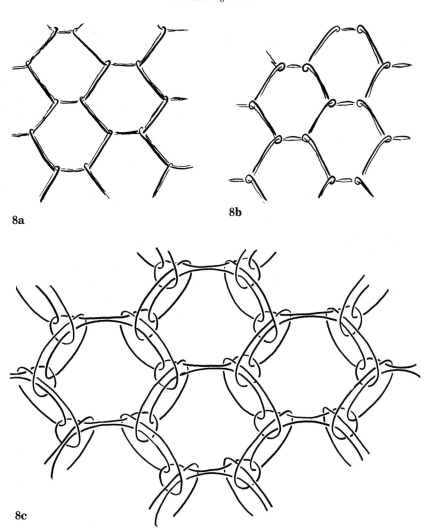

8a

8b

8c

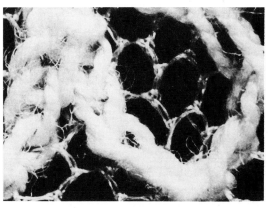

8d

8 *The Princess Charlotte's wedding dress, 1816:* **a** *a single press point net from a fragment of trimming. Note the perfect hexagon. The threads are so firmly stretched by the finishing that only an almost imperceptible looping at each angle of the meshes shows that the sides are not single strands. × 30.* **b** *the general appearance of the double press point net which makes up the fabric of the dress. × 30.* **c** *analysis of the weft course of the threads of the double press point net, as they can be made out with a microscope. The threads are shown spaced out so that their horizontal course can be followed more clearly. In fact, they lie over each other in a three-dimensional manner (see fig. 8d).* **d** *detail of a veil of double press point net, with tambour embroidery.*

broidery threads appear not on the surface but actually within the loops as if they were an integral part of the fabric (fig. 9), an anticipation of the inlay technique used with great success by the Warp-knitting machines.

Inevitably, financial success attracted fakes, and the neglected single press point net machines sprang suddenly into action, flooding the market with ephemeral imitations passed off as 'fast', and bringing the entire patent net industry into disrepute. Single press, made at one-third of the cost, was sold for 4*d*., while double press could not be retailed at less than 6*d*. or 7*d*. Customers, suspicious of being cheated, declared they would rather give 7*s*. (36p) a yard for hand-made Bucks lace than pay 6*d*. (2½p) for what might prove to be completely unstable.[36]

Later developments: warp nets and knitted laces

It was unfortunate that a period of dwindling faith in the patent nets coincided with the development of a new Stocking Frame modification, which converted it into a Warp Frame. In warp-knitting, which has no hand-counterpart, every wale has its own separate thread running longitudinally like a warp, in place of a single continuous thread running to and fro horizontally across all the wales like a weft. Early experiments with this technique in the 1770s appear to have been concerned – as the Stocking Frame itself originally was – with the creation of solid fabrics.

Warp net, like double press point net, was fast, and could be cut. It could also be made more quickly so that it cost less; it could be patterned easily on the machine; and it was more amenable to cotton thread. This last gave its production a particular boost, for during the time of the French Revolution and the Napoleonic Wars (1789–1815), when silk thread could reach England only through devious channels, the use of cotton was a great advantage. England's cotton-spinning industry was expanding rapidly, and not only the Warp Frames but the later twist-net machines (1808, 1812, 1813) were avid for its thread. The weft-nets were thus at a disad-

9 The heavy silk patterning threads have been caught within the loops of a uniformly plain net. The regularity of the design-repeats suggests that some kind of patterning device has been used.

yarns up to 300 count, though at the high price of £12 8*s*. 6*d*. (£12.42½p) a pound.[35] The first record of the use of cotton for a double press point net was in 1808 when Page of Nottingham made net with a two-ply yarn and sold his product for 3*s*. 6*d*. (17½p) a square yard – compared with £60 a square yard in 1800 for the real thing, a diaphanous droschel handmade with bobbins using the lightest flax thread.

Double press point net was so successful that demand doubled annually over the next ten years. From a total of only 20 (single press) point net machines in 1780, the number had increased to 1,500 by 1810, employing a large number of knitters and also some 15,000 outworkers who decorated the plain net with embroidery. A new embroidery technique, developed by William Hayne, made the em-

vantage. Frost's two-plain net ceased production in 1812, and double press point net in 1828. By 1830 only 30 point net machines remained in all England, most having been either scrapped, exported, or destroyed by Luddites – in 1811 their attacks were so violent that the following year the government was forced to make Frame-breaking a capital offence. The remaining machines were bought by M. Bethaud and taken to Lyons.

France and Spain, with their ample supplies of raw silk, continued to make point nets, and had between them 3,500 active machines, enough to supply all Europe with their products. Thus between the new developments in England, and the large quantities of silk point nets obtainable from abroad, England's Stocking Frames reverted to their original pedestrian purpose of clomping out plain webs for foot and leg coverings and for underwear, and this they continued to do into the 1970s when the last Stocking Frame factory, at Calverton, was closed down and the machines scrapped.

With the ending of the up-market net production, the Stocking Frame industry entered a period of depression. In 1832, at the time of the cholera outbreak in Nottingham, a mere nine-acre site near the city centre housed 947 families, comprising a total of 4,283 people. This, without making any deductions for roads, alleys, shops and tenement walls, gave a total area of ten square yards per head. 'Maggots in carrion flesh, or mites in cheese, could not be huddled more closely together,' said a report of this time. The cause of the poverty was that 'hosiery was an industry outside the orbit of steam power'[37] – or indeed any other power except that of hand and foot. Stockingers were, then, one of the most depressed groups in the country, while the twist-hands, working on lace machines originally inspired by the Stocking Frame nets, were one of the most prosperous.

Stocking Frames never returned to the making of nets. Their varied descendants – the circular knitting machine, the straight bar, and the flat bed (1862) – powered by steam or electricity, sometimes used openwork for

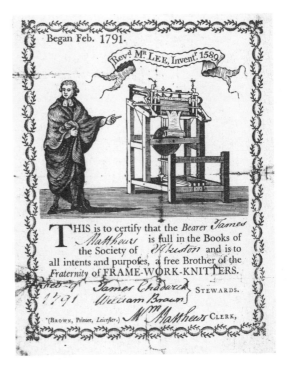

10 *An earlier association to protect the rights of the stockingers, The Fraternity of Frame-work-knitters, founded 1791.*

patterning, but the fabrics were seldom holey enough, nor the thread fine enough, to be called a lace. In 1844 the United Wool, Fall, Shawl and Antimacassar Union was founded to support the workers (fig. 10). Machine-knitted shawls in silk and wool were popular, but they lacked the delicacy of the patent nets (fig. 11). Many were made by the normal weft-knitting process, others by warp-knitting. An interesting variation was the twisted-loop fabric of the same period, made on French circular knitting frames by specially constructed twisted or 'twisel' bearded needles (fig. 12a, b).[38]

In 1847 the bearded needle for the first time in 258 years gave place to a competitor, the latch needle, invented by Matthew Townsend. Its work was coarser but also faster, and speed was of more importance than texture for the solid or sparsely-

11 *Two ways of wearing the patent nets, Promenade dresses, 1802.*

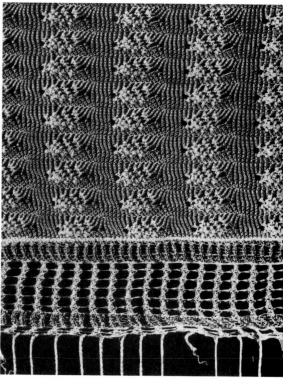

12 *Twisted loop fabric (cross-knit looping):* **a** *part of a shawl, with knitted fringe.* **b** *the stitch, showing that the yarn passes horizontally.*

openworked fabrics which the machines mainly produced.

The old variations of stitch transfer, tuck stitch, partial stitch transfer, and pelerine stitch continued to be used on the new power-driven machines to make decorated stockings, or 'fairy web' lingerie. Early pattern automation was by the organ barrel (*cylindre d'orgue*) dating from the eighteenth century and worked by putting selected ticklers out of action in each course, to make plain-knit areas. Jacquards were later applied, of a type similar to the spring-dropper Jacquards of the Leavers machine, while the computerised flat bed domestic knitting machine forms an up-to-date counterpart of the initial cottage industry.

The Stocking Frame may be regarded as a machine designed to make solid fabrics or plain webs, diverted into a brief flirtation

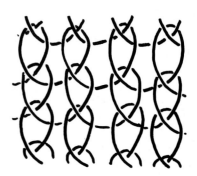

12b

with lace, and then returning to more practical productions, while a few of its derivatives occasionally continued to produce openworks, though none at all of the diaphanous quality of the late eighteenth and early nineteenth century weft-knitted nets (fig. 13a, b).

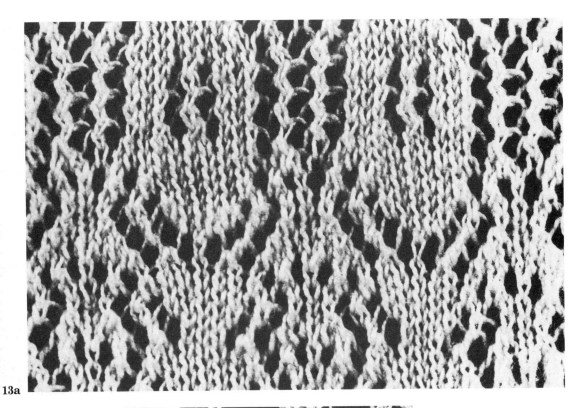

13a

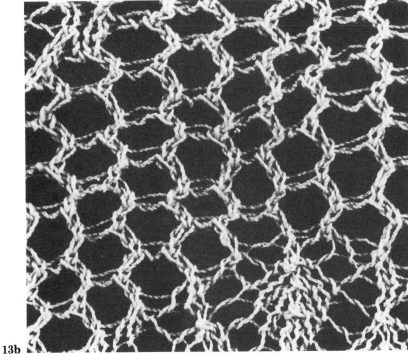

13b

13 *The problems of identification:* **a** *a stocking front, knitted by machine, detail.* **b** *detail of a hand-knitted baby bonnet. In both (a) and (b) the design parts of the work clearly show that the holey parts are weft-knitted. When there is nothing more than a plain mesh, as in fig. 7, the nature of the net can only be found by tracing the threads to find whether they run horizontally or vertically (see chapter 2).*

II

The Warp Frame And The Raschel

(Métier Warp or Métier à la Chaîne)

The process of warp-knitting is a techinque unknown by hand, but to some extent similar to crochet. It involves the use of a separate thread for each needle, instead of a continuous thread across all of them; and instead of the simultaneous formation of a complete course of loops horizontally across the web, a sequence of loops made vertically up it. In other words it knits wales, not courses. When these wales are linked together a sound fabric is formed, which can be cut without unravelling.

The evidence is uncertain, but credit for the invention is usually allowed to a mechanic called Crane, in 1775. He is said to have sold his invention to March for 100 guineas (£105). March, on the advice of his partner Horton, went to Nottingham to find suitable knitters to work it. There he met Morris, who with customary perspicacity winkled some of the details from him, and began to construct his own machine, and soon managed to give the impression that he had anticipated the technique. The first recorded letters patent for a Warp Frame was to Richard March in 1778 (no. 1186) in which individual warp threads arising from a warp on a roller, and attached to a modified Stocking Frame, were held by the eyes of guides. In 1781 Morris registered a patent (no. 1282) for 'an intire new twisting machine, for the manufacturing and making of Brussels point lace, and of all other openwork lace'. Its wording is obscure, and reference is to twisting rather than to looping or knitting, but the machine did have a row of bobbins or spools from which separate warp threads arose, instead of a single thread as in the Stocking Frame. A further

patent by March in 1784 (no. 1445) clearly refers to a method of uniting the rows of loops 'so as to form the pattern or mesh'. Blackner, writing his *History of Nottingham* in 1816, gave it as his opinion that they had 'no more claim to its originality than the man in the moon.'

According to Felkin, the first product of the new machine was 'silk hose having blue and white zig-zag stripes.' Such zigzags were sometimes known as 'vandykes', a term used for a dentate border, and it was possibly a misunderstanding of this usage which gave rise to the idea that the Warp Frame was invented by a Dutchman called Vandyke.

The Warp Frame was not, to begin with, a distinct machine but simply a Stocking Frame with a warp attachment. Like the weft knitter, it had a straight bar of bearded needles facing horizontally. Henson in his *History of the Framework Knitters*, 1831, describes the first Warp Frame which he saw, though he gives no date. It was in a pigeon loft of the 'late Mr Hardy of Twister's-Alley, London,' and was near enough an ordinary Stocking Frame 'with a warp beam appended'. The machine

was affixed to the rafter . . . having instead of ticklers a small piece of wire about five-eighths of an inch in length, called a guide, with a small hole at the end next to the needles, through which the thread from the warp was passed and made fast to the needle, each needle thus having a distinct thread.

In working, the guides were brought up above the needles. The bar which held them was then shogged the space of one needle, and the

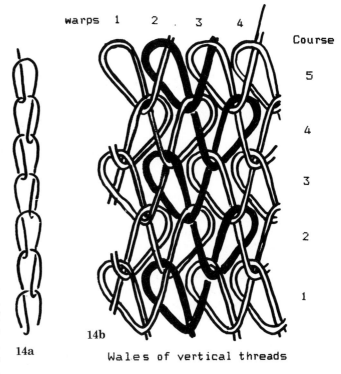

guides lowered again between the needles. In this way the thread was lapped (circled) around each needle under the beard, so that when the presser was lowered a perfect loop was brought over each needle head. If this movement alone were to be repeated, no fabric would be formed, only as many little strings of loops, like crochet-stitching, as there were needles (fig. 14). The essential cross-connections to hold the strings together were made by 'a new appendage, by which means guides were removed one needle either to the right or left at pleasure.'[1] Having lapped that needle they could, on the following course, be moved back to lap the first needle again. If this sequence were repeated row by row, the chains would be bound to each other on every course, and a very solid fabric would be formed. The successful marketing of such fabrics almost certainly preceded the commercialisation of the warp nets. The cloth was suitable for blankets, woollen jackets, 'trowsers and gentlemen's pantaloons', most especially after 1785 when the width of the machine was increased from 16 inches to 44 inches.

This method of knitting did not permit shaping of garments on the machines, so that stockings had to be cut from lengths of cloth, and stitched up the back, which made an unsightly and no doubt uncomfortable ridge. Also the material was

14 *Warp knitting:* **a** *A single line of loops, as made with a crochet hook and a single warp-orientated thread.* **b** *Four wales of vertical loops, cross-connected over five courses.*

not the least elastic, and the fashionable world found themselves attired in fabrics which, though wrought of silk, exactly resembled their ancestors' cloth hose [see p. 12] . . . it took a quarter of an hour or more to pull on the stocking . . . it was found almost impracticable to get it on in the usual manner from the top, therefore the hose was necessarily turned inside out, and pulled on in that position from the foot, this showed their lamentable defect to the tortured beaus, and as they frequently burst at the seams in the strain, before they could dress, fresh hose had to be procured, to repair the irretrievable disaster. One season saw them out of favour among the higher classes, though they still continued to be made extensively in cotton. . . . The introduction of this description of hosiery laid the foundation of making inferior goods and shaping them with the scissors, known in modern times [1831] by the dreaded name of 'cutups'.[2]

Such inelasticity might be expected to be an advantage in a net, and in theory the transformation of the solid warp cloth into an openwork was the easiest thing in the world. Wherever cross-connections between adjacent chains of loops failed to be made, holes would appear. Therefore a failure of connections at regular and quite close intervals over the whole fabric would automatically produce a net. All that was needed was for the guides to remain steadily lapping over their own needles, with cross-connections being made only every few courses, alternately to the right and to the left (fig. 15). Yet, in spite of the 1781 patent for 'an intire new twisting machine for the manufacturing and making of Brussels point lace', and the 1784 patent 'for making plain and figured lace', there are

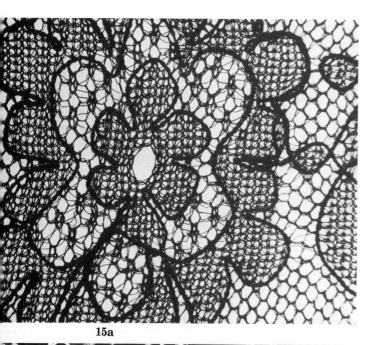

15a

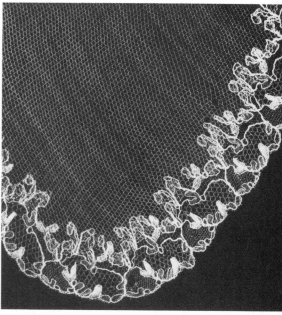

15

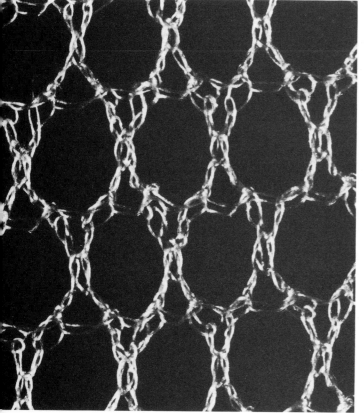

15b

15a *Detail of a warp lace shawl on black silk showing how frequent cross-connections produce solids, and less frequent connections openwork. First half nineteenth century.* **b** *Detail of a plain warp net in fine silk, imitating the wire ground, or point de Paris, of contemporary English, French or Belgian bobbin laces (× 10).* **c** *Net (b) with its added border of silk bobbin lace, similar to a Bucks point, first quarter nineteenth century.*

no records of a satisfactory warp net appearing on the market before the first years of the nineteenth century, and a manufactory of warp lace set up by Mr Ingham in Nottingham in 1784 failed within three years (Page).

The problem probably lay in the cross-connections themselves which, being made of single threads, formed very weak links between the loop-chains when the net was pulled out. Also, they tended not to stay stretched out in wear, but collapsed widthways, so that day by day the articles became narrower and longer as the wales drew closer together. Even by 1810 there were only a few hundred Warp lace Frames working compared with 1,500 point net Frames.

Experiments were made by Brown and Pindar – in 1796 according to Felkin,[3] in 1808 according to Ferguson – in placing the bearded needles upright. 120 such machines were soon producing silk net in Nottingham, the knitters being paid £2 10s. (£2.50) a week. In 1804 Robert Brown registered a patent (no. 2760) for 'A machine or apparatus affixable to horizontal warp or vandyke knitting frames' to make lace or network, using cotton thread. In the same year a patent by Samuel Caldwell and John Heathcoat (no. 2788) was for an apparatus to be attached to Warp Frames to 'render the latter capable of producing all kinds of thread lace.' The term thread meant linen or flax, of which the hand-laces were still made. The implication is not that linen thread was to be used on the machine, but that hand-laces were to be imitated.

A further modification about this time enabled the Warp Frames to produce a so-called Mechlin net, which appears to have been from the first quite excellent both in appearance and quality, and so profitable that the number of machines soon amounted to nearly 400, and the knitters were paid an average of £4 a week according to the quantity they produced. The net was made of fine machine-spun cotton costing between 15 and 30 guineas (£15.75 and £31.50) per pound weight.[4]

The structure of this net appears nowhere to be described. Ferguson says that the name Méchlin was chosen to distinguish the product from the bobbin lace Malines, but since the hand-made Malines is called Mechlin in English, the possibility of confusion is scarcely resolved. Certain of the products of the later twist-net machines were also called Mechlin (sometimes spelt Meklin, a contraction of Mechelen, the Flemish name for the city) or Malines (sometimes spelt Maleen, after the same city's French name), so that references to it in contemporary writings must be approached with caution. Nottingham's Mechlin Warp Frames ceased production in 1819, failing in competition with the newly-invented bobbinets; but they continued longer in France where the weft-knitting pin machines had already proved so successful.

A flounce of Limerick lace 'embroidered on Mechlin net' at Wincanton in Somerset c.1825 was shown at the *Daily Mail* Lace Exhibition of 1908.[5] The embroidery had taken two women two years to complete. This might well have been a warp-knitted net, made either in England before 1819, or afterwards in France.

Dawson's wheel, invented in 1791 (patent no. 1820), was first applied to the Warp Frame in 1807, and undoubtedly assisted its production of a successful net. The wheel was a carefully cut cam which could automate repetitive movements, whether of tickler bars for the Stocking Frame or guides for the Warp Frame, and so was able to make the knitters' work both quicker and easier. The attachment of the guides to a bar so that they worked in unison across the web, also helped to make the net more regular and uniform.

A modification of the Mechlin machine by Dervieu and Piand of St Etienne in 1809 produced *fond de glace* (ice-ground), also called *tulle croisé* (crossed net).[6] Both were soon suffering from the competition of Heathcoat's Old Loughborough (see ch. 3).

The wedding dress of the Princess Charlotte, who married Prince Leopold of Saxe-Coburg in 1816, has already been mentioned as an excellent example of a weft-knitted net made of ivory silk studded with silver thread and bordered with lamé (see p. 24). The recognition of machine nets by royalty was a new departure, and it seems likely that warp nets also attracted patronage. In France, in that same year, a dress of hand-embroidered bobbinet was made for the Duchesse d'Anguolême, daughter of Marie Antoinette.

Only a little later the Mechlin machines failed, at least in England, but warp-knit nets of other kinds continued to prosper, though in a fluctuating way. They suffered not only from competition with the bobbinets, but also from the silk weft-nets which continued to pour in from France to the extent of 24,000 yards a year. Napoleon I in 1802 had banned the importation of *tulle anglais* or double press point net from England and this prohibition continued. It raised the price, but created otherwise no great deprivation to the French for it continued to reach their shores as contraband transported by special longboats called Smugglers (Hénon). The restrictive effect on English trade was more depressing, and Henson, writing in the 1820s, made an angry plea for 'really reciprocal duties'. 'Posterity will judge,' he says, 'whether the English mechanic has had fair play, as while French silk net is allowed to be imported upon a light duty, not rigidly levied, British lace is vigorously and sternly seized, while the most influential and spirited of her manufacturers have been ruined and undone by confiscations.'

Early forms of plain warp net

The early Warp Frames functioned with a single needle-bar (bearded and usually placed horizontally) and a single guide-bar (each guide threaded with a warp) to make their products. Thus they were strictly limited in their effects. Only loops could be made, and all the guides had to move in unison, each either lapping its thread around its own needle, or being shogged one wale to connect with the next.

Two nets formed in this way are shown in figs. 16 and 17. In fig. 16 the guide bar laps alternately one needle to the right and one needle to the left. The mesh is completed in two courses – hence its name, *two course net* – and the hole has the shape of a small lop-sided diamond. Such tiny openings easily closed to form a solid fabric, and it was in fact only by setting the machine to a slack quality, and by using resin to stiffen and fix the threads apart, that an openwork net was created at all. The two-course net's big advantage was that it used a small amount of thread, which reduced its cost. Marketed in silk in the first decade of the nineteenth century, it is still in use near the end of the twentieth, known now as tricot net, and constructed of thin synthetic yarn as a ground for Raschel laces (see p. 47).

In fig. 17 the vertical sides, or pillars, of the meshes have been lengthened by knitting two courses straight before the guide bar is shogged sideways and the cross-connection made. This produces a hexagonal mesh where the larger hole means that it can be knitted more tightly (close quality), which makes it more stable.

16a

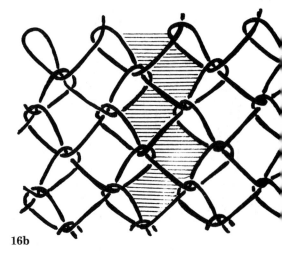

16b

16a *A warp net and double pillars from a pair of mittens, early nineteenth century.* **b** *Stitch analysis of the net of (a). The shaded areas show alternate rows of meshes.*

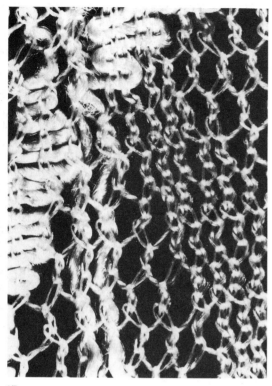

17a

Both nets suffer the weakness which results from a single thread taking the strain of making the connections at the top and bottom end of each mesh. When fine cotton was used it easily broke, leaving a longitudinal rift.

Other single-guide-bar variations were used to make solid fabrics, but a big advance in openworks occurred with the use of a second guide bar. This meant that the warp threads could be divided into two sets, which could move in opposite directions at the same time. Thus the sloping top and bottom ends could then be formed of complete loops, and the weakness of a single thread crossing was eliminated. Possible variations now included not only the length of the pillars, but also their width.

Fig. 18 shows two types of two-guide-bar warp nets dating from the early nineteenth century:

(a) is a very strong diamond-shaped mesh, made without pillars. In (b) the needles and the knitting courses have been numbered, and the action of the two distinct guide bars is clearly visible. For example, in course 3, at the same time as the thread from needle 4 is carried left to be lapped around needle 3, the thread from needle 3 is carried right to be lapped around needle 4. These opposing movements could not possibly have been made with a single guide bar, working in only one direction at a time.

In (c) the pillars are knitted by pairs of loops which cross-connect over four courses. Both in the pillars, and in the slanting ends of the meshes, the two sets of warps are all the time making similar laps in opposite directions.

The further possibilities of net-variation such as open or closed loops, full-set or half-set guide bars, and the use of laying-in threads – though recognisable in warp nets and laces of the nineteenth century – involve explanations which are better left for consideration under a later machine development, the twentieth-century Raschel (p. 37).

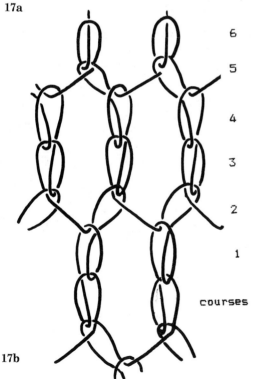

6

5

4

3

2

1

courses

17b

17a *Warp net from a silk scarf, late nineteenth century.* **b** *Stitch analysis of (a).*

35

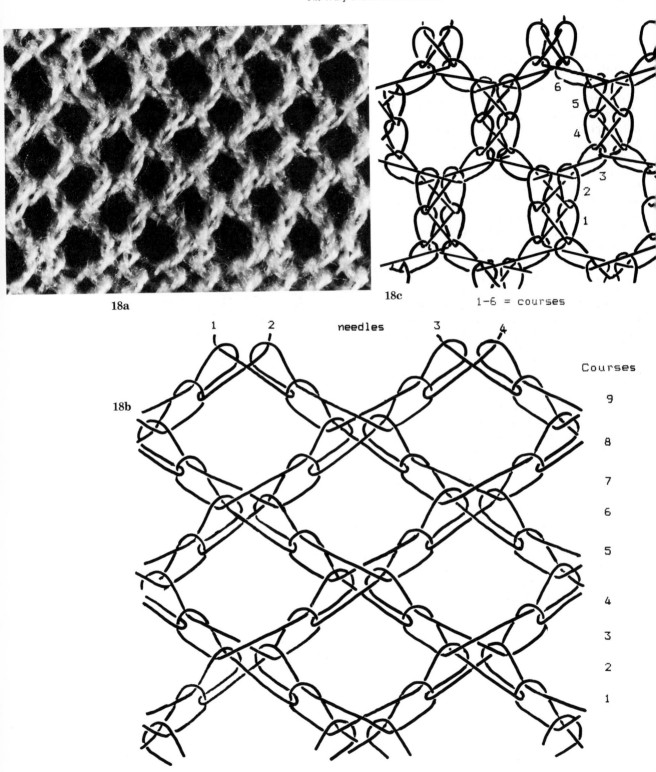

18a

18c

1-6 = courses

18b

needles

1　　2　　　　　3　　4

Courses

9

8

7

6

5

4

3

2

1

36

The early warp laces

Plain nets are linked with patterned laces by an intermediate form, the fancy nets. In spotted nets, tiny and regularly repeated motifs covered the fabric. In bullet-hole net, the design took the form of large and regularly-repeated holes. In warp tattings, narrow bands of net were decorated in a simple way with heavier inlaid threads. Since the repetition in each was completely uniform it could be controlled by a Dawson's wheel, the uneven surface of which caused the guide bars to shog in a fixed sequence.

The emergence of patterned laces, with much larger and more complex repeats, had to wait on the Jacquard apparatus. This was first applied to the Méchlin Warp Frame in Lyons (the home of the Jacquard) in 1823–4 by Colas and Delampré.[7] By 1826 M. Grégoire of Nimes was using it to make 'Embroidered warp blonde nets made up into shawls, veils and scarfs of great beauty'[8] (fig. 19). It was over ten years later, in 1837, that Samuel Draper of Nottingham successfully applied the Jacquard to the type of Warp Frame then being used in England (patent no. 7491. followed in 1840 by no. 8635). The large and elaborate designs of these early laces were entirely knitted by the use of extremely few guide bars - for the most part only two – and their patterning required great skill. The gradual increase in the number of guide bars in the later nineteenth century, and even more in the twentieth when over 70 could be manipulated, was coupled with the introduction of non-knitted, or inlay, threads which facilitated the patterning process, and enabled it to become more complex and ornate, but did not necessarily enhance its visual attractiveness.

19 *A very fine quality shawl, warp-knitted in black silk, c.1850, and imitating a bobbin lace Chantilly design.*

Later developments, and the Raschel

The Warp Frame machines were, from the very beginning of the nineteenth century, engaged in a fierce rivalry with the silk point nets coming over from France; and also, from 1809, with the cotton bobbinets from Heathcoat's Old Loughborough, and other twist-net machines. The former catered adequately for the upper end of the market while the latter, though not insensitive to upmarket requirements, were fully able to cater for the lower end. Warp Frame nets thus came to be placed uncomfortably in the middle, between two strongly competitive forces.

In the prosperity of the early 1830s when silk blondes were particularly fashionable, the width of the machines was extended to 100 or even 150 inches, and they were worked by

18a *A two-guide bar warp net, from a pair of mittens, first half nineteenth century.* b *Stitch analysis of (a).* c *Stitch analysis of a two-guide bar net, with pillars two courses deep.*

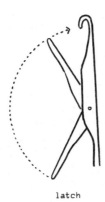

latch

20 *A latch needle. The movable 'latch' can be raised to close the hook during loop formation, thus replacing the forceful pressing in of the beard with every course, which was previously necessary.*

steam power. However the commercial panic of 1838 depressed the market, while the Warp Frame's advantage of prior facility in Jacquard patterning was brief. Between 1839 and 1841 the Jacquard was successfully applied to the Pusher and Leavers machines, and their laces – which resembled the appearance of handmade bobbin laces a good deal more closely than did the warp knits – were soon preferred. It was in fact not until 100 years later that the warp machines were again able to rise to a position of dominance in the commercial world of machine laces.

The adoption of the latch needle (fig. 20) on warp-knit machines after 1847 favoured a reversion to solid fabrics, since it knitted more coarsely and was better suited to bulky yarns. They did however continue to knit fancy and slightly openwork silk shawls in bright richly-blended colours, somewhat prettier than the contemporary weft-knitted ones. These were still being made in the twentieth century (fig. 21).

By 1947 the warp-knitting manufacture of openworks employed only 200 people, on 100 lace machines, half making hair nets, and half a coarse (10 needles to the inch) cotton lace. Neither the machines, nor even the spare parts to repair them were any longer being manufactured.[9] However, precursory developments, in the late 1930s, began to prosper after the Second World War. A fly-needle-frame (F.N.F.), developed by Morton

Sundour Fabrics and brought out in 1939, attained the high speed of 1,000 courses a minute, though its competition was with woven rather than lacey fabrics. By 1969 such warp knitters had captured a substantial share of the fabric market, namely 50% of men's shirts and 80% of women's nightwear and lingerie.[10]

The Working Party Report on lace, 1947, refers to a small plant of machines of German origin brought over from France in the spring of 1937:

The machines are narrower than other lace machines; they have a row of barbed [bearded] needles like the warp lace machine, but produce a crochet stitch and not a knitting stitch. The yarns

21 *A warp-knitted shawl of lacy design. Consecutive warps are of varying colours, and produce by their vandyke patterning a delicate intermingling of some 20 shades, ranging through turquoise, emerald, magenta, ochre, black, beige, royal blue, azure, plum, gold, grey, mauve, crimson, and violet. Early twentieth century.*

used are coarser, the products are consequently heavier. The potentialities of this type of production cannot be evaluated since the plant was not running for the greater part of the war.[11]

This appears to be the Crochet machine, which can have either latch or bearded needles, use either natural or synthetic threads, incorporate rubber for elasticated laces, work at very high speeds, and be computerized. Using weft, or laying-in, threads it can produce remarkable imitations of hand-made crochet (fig. 22). Its narrow width – less than two metres – enables it to make small quantities or 'runs' economically, which is difficult on a machine three times that width.

A far more amazing development of post-war years was that of the large (up to 240 inch) Raschel, which brought about a dramatic revival of warp openworks. The re-emergence of the technique, after a longish period of depressed obscurity, was due to a number of quite fortuitous factors. Firstly, the cost of labour had escalated to a point where it could entirely wreck the profitability of a labour-intensive lace industry such as the Leavers. Secondly, the success of warp-knitting machines in competition with the weaving looms had involved the development of new and faster techniques which could now be applied to the production of warp-knit laces. Thirdly, synthetic fibres were being developed commercially, beginning with nylon in 1938, and followed most importantly by polyesters in 1951 and 1953. Their yarns could be made as fine and lustrous as silk, but were both stronger and cheaper. They were ideal for these new, immensely fast, machines where the high tensions that were needed to keep the warp threads taut, and the continual friction of passing under and over the needle heads, led to excessive 'linting' of natural fibres and caused an accumulation of fluff which blocked the latch movements, making the machine malfunction.

The 1947 Report mentions only 50 or 60 Raschel machines making hair nets.[12] Chamberlain, in 1951, describes the Raschel as having up to six guide bars, and also two needle bars with vertically placed latch

22 *Imitation crochets made by the El Fantasy crochet machines, 1970s.*

needles cast into leads two inches wide (a length known as the English or Saxon inch) which were attached to the bars by screws. The basic needle bar and guide bar movements were controlled by cams.

The adoption of the name Raschel is ascribed to the French tragedienne Elisabeth Félix (1820–58), known as Rachel, who in the 1840s wore and popularized warp-knit shawls and pelerines of black or natural silk which were then very beautiful and the height of fashion.

Raschel machines, manufactured by the firm of Karl Mayer in Germany, became specialized for different end-uses, namely tulle (plain or fancy nets), lace and curtaining. Their patterning technique is quite different from that of the early Warp Frames which had started with a single guide bar holding a single set of warp threads, and had continued with two bars holding a double set of threads, both of them knitting. In the Raschels, the bar number was increased from 6 to 12, then 28, and within 30 years up to a total of nearly 80 (in 1985). At the same time the amount of knitting, and the size of the

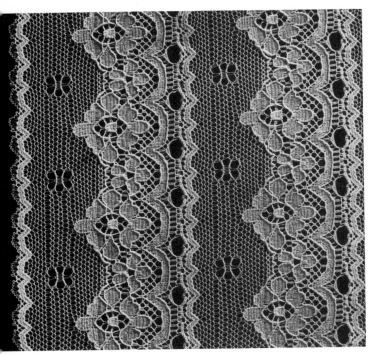

23 *Raschel lace edgings, as made on the machine, 1984. (Wiener Laces, New York).*

knitted loop, were reduced, and the patterning effects transferred to straight weft-orientated threads held down by warp pillars.

The more different threads there are, the finer, more complex and more subtle can the patterning become, until the final effect produced is extraordinarily similar to a Leavers lace in appearance (see ch. 5). Even the designs made for Leavers machines can be adapted for Raschel manufacture (fig. 23), and the lace may be distinguishable only by the thin straight lines of loops visible with a magnifier on the reverse side (fig. 24).

The parts of the Raschel machine

Fig. 25 shows the general layout of the machine. The warp roller(s) with the ground threads, and the spot beams with the patterning threads, are both situated at the top. The threads as they pass downwards interact via the guide bars and needles, and the completed web then accumulates round the cloth roller below.

In this lively and still developing machine, with its variety of openwork productions, innovations are continually being made, and one can do no more than generalize on its dimensions and capacities: width 105–130 inches; height 15–16 feet; weight 3,550–7,300 kilos (3.5 to 6.8 tons); gauge (needles per 2 inches) 28 to 48; courses per minute (c.p.m.) 300–1,200. A common average for the machines making lace is 100 inches wide and 36 gauge, that is 1,800 needles per working width. Increasing fineness of work brings increasing delicacy, not only of the lace but of the machine itself, and high-gauge machines require stable conditions of warmth (70°F) and moisture (65% humidity).

1. A single warp roller, or 'warp', may hold either as many threads as there are needles, or half that number, that is either 1,800 or 900, in the above example. This enormous quantity of separate ends has to be very carefully wound if they are to unroll smoothly. Each end may be 16,000 metres long, so that a warp roller with 1,800 ends will hold (16,000 × 1,800) metres, or a total of 28,800,000 metres (17,897 miles) of yarn, and cost several thousand pounds. There may be one warp, two or, rarely, three or four. Together they form the net or ground, and at least one will always knit. The patterning, or spot, beams hold the threads which will form the design.

2. The warp ends pass down through a sley (perforated tray) which separates them from each other and prevents their becoming tangled together.

3. They each connect with a tension rod which equalises, and maintains, the tension in every wale.

4. Each then passes through a hole or eye at the tip of the requisite guide. All the guides project downwards from their bars, over the up-pointing needles, so that guides and needles are turned towards each other like bared teeth. The form of the guides is shown

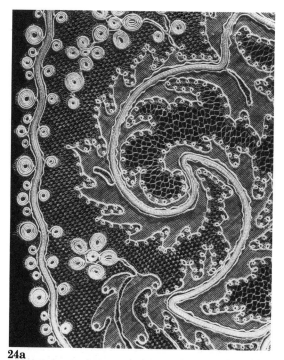

24a

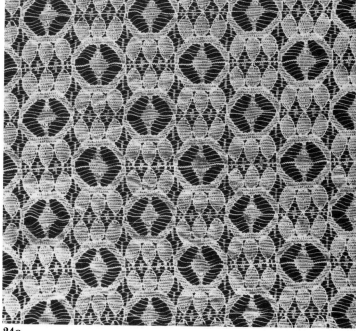

24c

24b

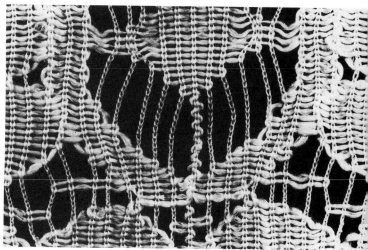

24d

24 *Variations in warp knit products, pre-Raschel and Raschel:* **a** *An elaborate cape with fancy knitted stitches and decorations of couched braid and bourdon cord, late nineteenth century.* **b** *A heavy stole with fleur-de-lys design, entirely warp-knitted in black silk, first quarter twentieth century.* **c** *An all-over Raschel lace with the knitting reduced to thin and unconnected vertical chains held together only by the inlay threads which form the design.* **d** *Detail of (c).*

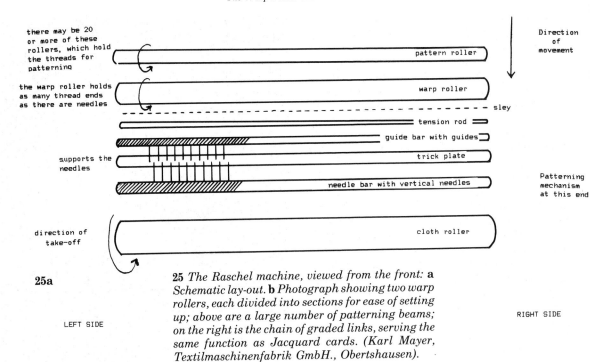

there may be 20 or more of these rollers, which hold the threads for patterning — pattern roller

Direction of movement

the warp roller holds as many thread ends as there are needles — warp roller

sley

tension rod

guide bar with guides

supports the needles — trick plate

needle bar with vertical needles

Patterning mechanism at this end

direction of take-off — cloth roller

25a

LEFT SIDE

RIGHT SIDE

25 *The Raschel machine, viewed from the front:* **a** *Schematic lay-out.* **b** *Photograph showing two warp rollers, each divided into sections for ease of setting up; above are a large number of patterning beams; on the right is the chain of graded links, serving the same function as Jacquard cards. (Karl Mayer, Textilmaschinenfabrik GmbH., Obertshausen).*

25b

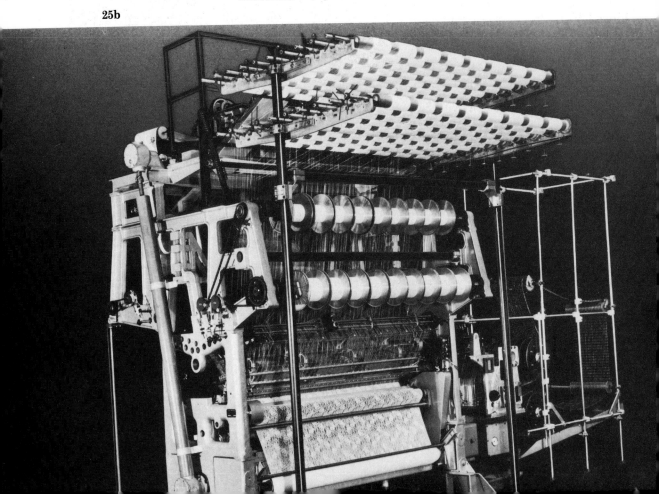

in fig. 26. They are simply individual thread-holders, immovable themselves, but rigidly joined to a bar which can be made to move forwards, backwards or sideways in either direction. 'Guide bar' is customarily abbreviated to 'bar', and machines with numerous bars (22, 52 or 78) are referred to as multibars.

5. The needles, like the guides, are rigidly attached to a bar, in this case a single needle bar – a term which is never abbreviated. When the mechanism is set in motion, the needle bar begins to move up and down, sliding in a grooved trick plate which prevents any oscillation, since misplacements of the needles could ruin a whole area of web. The hooks of the needles face the inner part of the machine and, as they rise, their latches fall open and the guides circle round them offering thread. As they sink back the latches close, and new loops slip upwards over the needles' heads.

Fig. 27a is a simple diagrammatic representation of the tips of four needles and their warp guides, viewed from the front of the machines. The guides alternate with the needles in rest, and circle around them in motion in a forward-across-back-across movement. This deposits thread within their latches and culminates in the formation of new loops. When the guides are shogged to lap around adjacent needles, rather than around their original one, the encirclement is clockwise when the shog is to the right, and anti-clockwise when it is to the left.

Fig. 27b represents a possible movement of a single guide carrying its thread over two courses, passing from one wale to the next and back again. Courses 1, 2 etc represent the time sequence of knitting.

Fig. 27c shows the same lapping or encircling movement from different views, to distinguish the terms *underlap* and *overlap* which are commonly used in describing how tulles and laces are constructed on the Raschel. Each ascent and descent of the needle bar is controlled by one complete revolution of the main crank shaft, and it is accompanied by one complete movement of the warp around the needle, the thread slotting in under the hook as it passes in the overlap. Thus any

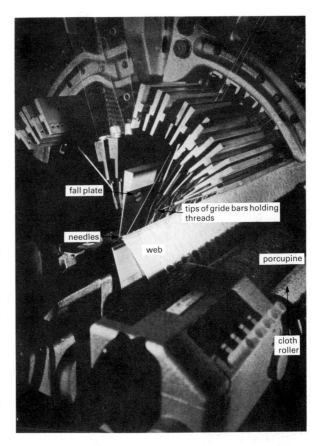

26 *The nesting guide bars on a Raschel machine (Karl Mayer).*

movement involving an underlap only, and omitting the overlap, will not result in a new loop being formed – a circumstance very important for patterning on both the lace and the curtain Raschel machines.

6. The threads, now in the form of a web, continue their downward journey. The speed at which the web is wound on to the cloth roller is called the wind-off speed. It is controlled by a tension fitment which varies according to the quantity of net that has accumulated: the more net, the bigger will be its circumference, and the slower will be the rotation of the roller. A completed web is likely to weigh between 40 and 60lb, and to be up to 100 yards long.

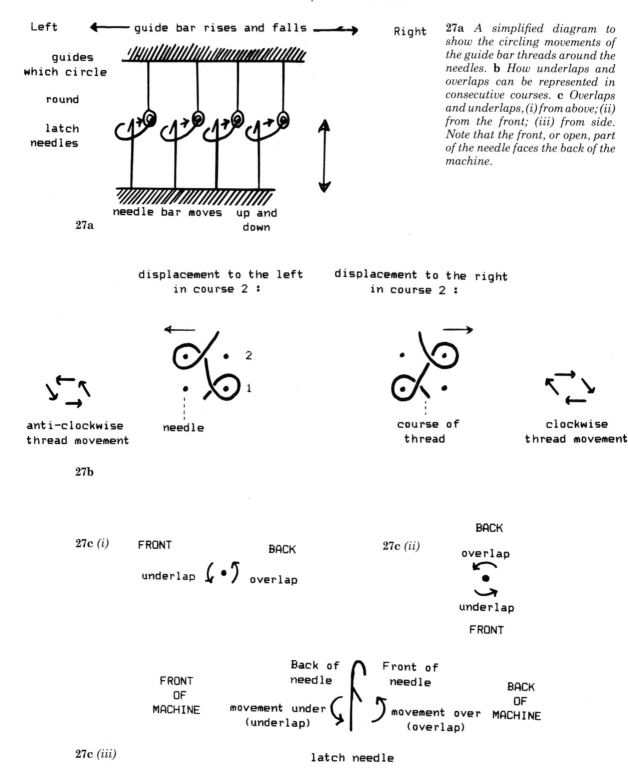

Left ← guide bar rises and falls → Right

guides
which circle

round

latch
needles

needle bar moves up and down

27a

27a *A simplified diagram to show the circling movements of the guide bar threads around the needles.* **b** *How underlaps and overlaps can be represented in consecutive courses.* **c** *Overlaps and underlaps, (i) from above; (ii) from the front; (iii) from side. Note that the front, or open, part of the needle faces the back of the machine.*

displacement to the left
in course 2 :

displacement to the right
in course 2 :

anti-clockwise
thread movement

needle

course of
thread

clockwise
thread movement

27b

27c *(i)* FRONT BACK

underlap overlap

27c *(ii)* BACK

overlap

underlap

FRONT

FRONT
OF
MACHINE

Back of
needle

Front of
needle

movement under
(underlap)

movement over
(overlap)

BACK
OF
MACHINE

27c *(iii)* latch needle

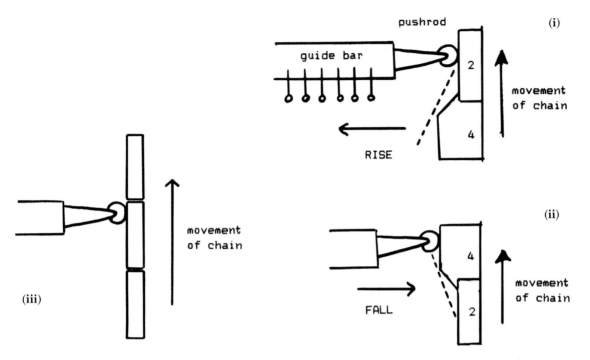

The Raschel tulle, or net, machine

Although the general information given above applies to all Raschel machines, the three main groups of end-uses (nets, laces and curtains) are associated with specific modifications. The webs produced by the tulle machines are uniform all over, and completely plain, or minimally patterned. The number of guide bars and thread sources is small.

The basic synchronization of the circling movement of the thread-carrying guides with the rising and falling needle heads, in order to produce loops, is governed by cams; while the diversion of the guides to make loops with other needles in a particular manner or at particular intervals is likely to require a more extensive patterning device. In the Raschel this takes the form of a chain located on a drum at the right of the machine.

The chain is made up of shaped links of graded sizes. It forms a continuous circle, and in fact acts in just the same way as would a very large cam. Every bulge or hollow of the chain's surface causes a movement, towards

*28a The push rod following the rise and fall of the chain surface, similar to a truck working on a cam (simplified): (i) with increase in link sizes the push rod and guide bar are deflected to the left = RISE; (ii) with decrease in link size they FALL to the right; (iii) when a series of links are all the same size there is no deflection of the guide bar. **b** The connection of chain, push rod and guide bar (after Karl Mayer) (see over).*

or away from the machine, of the push rod which rests against it; and this in turn deflects the guide bar which the chain controls so that all the threads it carries are diverted in the same direction (right or left) to the same extent.

The shaped links are of graded sizes numbered in two's, as 0, 2, 4, etc, and the deflection or shogging which they cause must be in multiples of the spaces between the needles, that is they must coincide with the gauge of the machine. Thus in a 36-gauge machine, with 18 needles to the inch, the movements must be in multiples of 1/18th inch. The links will be arranged in whatever order the net requires, which may be as simple as 0-2 0-2.

45

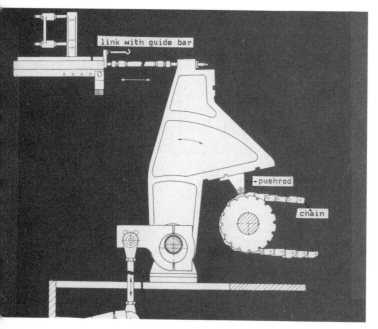

right. In summaries of Raschel movements, a fall is indicated by F, a rise by R. Every rise and fall is initiated by the revolving of the uneven surface of the chain against the end of the push rod (fig. 28b), and it is these deflections which displace the threads the guides carry to another wale, causing the ranks of loops to be held firmly together.

Some nets can be worked with a single guide bar, but two is the commonest number. Each must have its own chain of links to regulate its shogs, and two guide bars will necessitate two chains. If three bars form the net, three chains will be needed. Other possible net-variations are:

Either every guide, or every alternate guide, on a bar may hold a warp end. The first is described as fully-threaded or *full-set*, the second half-threaded, or *half-set*, or threaded one-in-one-out. The length of the pillars, or vertical sides of the meshes, can vary depending on the number of courses knitted straight and unconnected. To make a single isolated pillar a sequence of chain links of the same size must follow each other, for example 2-2 (one course), 2-2-2 (two courses), 2-2-2-2 (three courses), and so on. As soon as the number (link-size) changes, the guides will be deflected and the pillars linked together to form a mesh.

The width of the pillars may be either one or two wales. The latter is restricted to two-bar machines.

The number of loops making the cross-connections, which form the upper and lower ends of each mesh, may be either one or two. The right and left displacements or shogs caused by the chain may cover one wale, two wales, or even more, making the net extremely strong.

The net may be entirely knitted, every warp making loops; or one guide bar or more may be concerned with inlay threads (laying-in threads, or wefts). These make underlaps only so that they do not pass under the hook of the latch needle but are carried across it and lightly held in place by the knitting threads.

The individual loops may be either open or closed.

The size of the mesh holes, and the firmness or

28b The chain is moved by a rotating drum, racked by a Dawson wheel, at the rate of two links per course, one link controlling the underlap, the other the overlap. The minimum number of links needed to make a chain which will fit round the drum is 16, but if the net structure does not require so many, that particular sequence may be repeated on the same chain. It is important that smooth inclines should be presented on the surface of the chain, and that any sharp leaps which might jar the guides and cause thread breakage be avoided.

The push rod (fig. 28a) is a short stout projection which can move fractionally outwards from the machine, and back again towards it, but not in any other direction. As the hard links of the chain move against it, so the little wheel keeps in contact with the undulating surface, and is pushed gently back and forth as the chain glides past it.

If the link size rises from say 2 to 4, the push rod will be moved back towards the machine, causing the guide bar attached to it to *rise* to the left. If the link size falls say from 4 to 2, the push rod, by spring action, is moved minutely to the right to keep in contact with the chain surface, causing the guide bar to *fall* to the

slackness of the web, will depend on a combination of machine gauge (coarse or fine) and quality (close or slack). The latter is set by a wheel at the start of the work, and is related to the wind-off (also called pull-off or take-off) speed.

Permutations of these variations could produce theoretically a very large number of different kinds of net. Some will only be suitable for the grounds of patterned laces; others though firm enough to make a plain net might then be too heavy, or too expensive, for practicality. The products relevant to this book are the clouds of tulle light and aery enough for marriage veils, but Raschel net techniques can also be adapted for making stout and practical sandfly or mosquito netting, or even vegetable bags of plastic strands linked together by knitting.

Figs. 29–35 illustrate and explain a small range of Raschel nets. The reflection of light from silk or synthetic yarns unfortunately

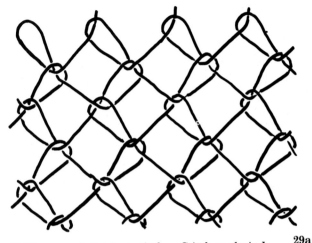

29 *Net example 1,* tricot stitch: **a** *Stitch analysis.* **b** *(i) The meaning of open and closed loops: (ii) a form of tricot net worked with open loops.*

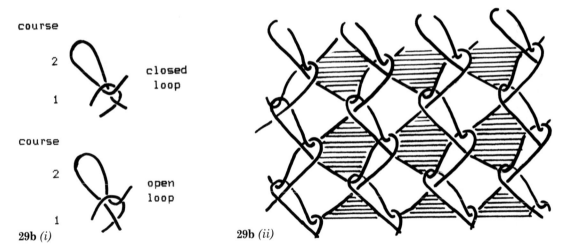

29b *(i)*   29b *(ii)*

sometimes causes a slight halation effect which reduces the clarity of the mesh-structure, in the photographs.

1. Fig. 29a shows one of the first nets to be manufactured, not very satisfactorily, by the Warp Frames (see fig. 16). It enjoyed a revival with the use of synthetic yarns since these are strong enough to overcome the defect of single-thread connections. It is sometimes called *tricot net*, and is used mainly for the

grounds of patterned laces. The meshes are small compared with the loop-size. The single guide bar is fully threaded; there are no pillars; the sloping ends of the meshes are made of a single loop on one side and a single thread on the other; shogging is across one wale only; there are no non-loop or non-knitting threads (i.e. no laying-in threads); and the loops are closed.

A *closed loop* means that the exit thread from the loop crosses the entry thread at the

47

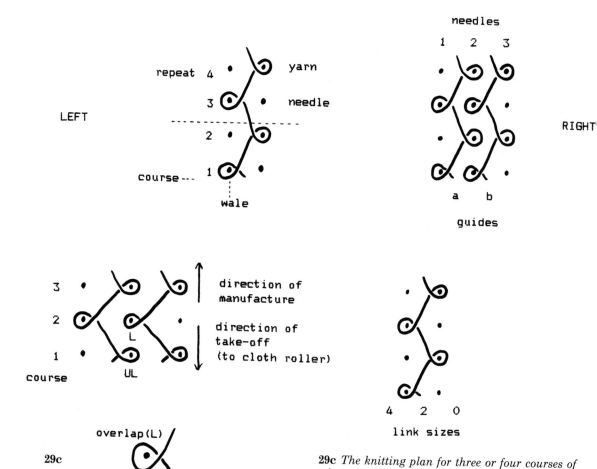

repeat 4 • yarn

3 • needle

LEFT

2 •

course --- 1

wale

needles
1 2 3

RIGHT

a b

guides

3 •

2

L

1 •

course

UL

direction of
manufacture

direction of
take-off
(to cloth roller)

4 2 0

link sizes

overlap (L)

29c

underlap (UL)

29c *The knitting plan for three or four courses of tricot net. The separate sketches analyse all the information contained in the plan.*

bottom. An *open loop* means that the exit thread does not cross the entry thread (fig. 29b).

The course of the loops can be plotted on point paper so that they are clearly visible in diagram form. The sequence of needles on the needle bar is shown by a horizontal row of dots. Each dot will represent a wale in the finished net, or lace. The horizontal rows, numbered from below upwards, represent successive courses knitted on those needles. The lines drawn in on the prepared paper are the movements of the individual warp threads as they lap around the needles, or pass across to adjacent wales (fig. 29c). On this plan of movements the work begins at the bottom (course 1), since the finished net is

carried downwards to be wound around the cloth roller.

At least one vertical and one horizontal repeat must be plotted so that there can be no doubt where any particular thread should go in any particular course. The vertical repeat of tricot stitch occupies only two courses, and its horizontal repeat two wales. All 1,800 or so threads of that net will follow these movements.

It is customary to indicate link sizes on the draft, for example 0,2,4, each number representing a fixed size of link for the particular gauge of that machine. Since displacement to the left is a rise, and to the right a fall, the smaller chain links are numbered to the right, the larger to the left.

In terms of chain sequence, tricot net can be summarised: 2-4 2-0. This means that, assuming the guide to start at link size 2, it will be caused by the next link, 4, to rise. The following link being 2, the guide bar will fall. In this example the rise and fall represent the double movement necessary for each loop to be formed, the first making the underlap, and the second the overlap. In all cases, whether the deflection is a rise or a fall, the underlap is made first.

The link-by-link clicking onwards of the chain has to be synchronized precisely with the upward and downward rhythm of the needle bar so that there is no conflict between them. The chain causes the bar threads to rise and fall so that they lap to left or right in alternation with the needle movements.

2. In the second net example (fig. 30a) the meshes are larger, and it is used for veiling or for mosquito nets. The single bar is full-set; the pillars are two courses deep and one wale wide; the sloping ends consist of a single loop on one side and a single thread on the other; traversing or shogging is across one wale only; there are no non-loop threads; and the loops are open.

On the point paper this latter feature is shown by the use of a semi-circle instead of a circle for each loop.

In this net the repeat extends not over two courses but over six (pillar two, end one, pillar two, end one) (fig. 30b). In terms of chain links, and therefore of guide bar movements, the sequence can be summarised:

0-2 2-0 0-2 4-2 2-4 4-2.

Single-bar nets are not the most stable, but they have the advantage of being cheap to produce since they use a small amount of yarn – 3.5 inches of each warp to produce an inch of fabric in net (1), and 4.5 inches of each warp for net (2). This comparative consumption of yarn per unit length of web is called the *run-in*.

3. Fig. 31a shows an example of a two-bar net. The addition of a second guide bar, or ground bar, produces a much more stable net, though often a more expensive one since more thread

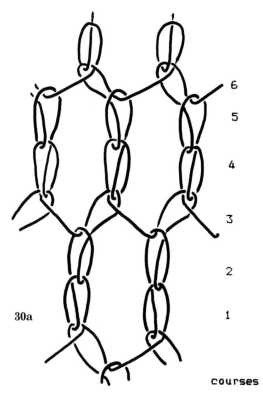

30 *Net example 2:* **a** *The stitch plan.* **b** *The point paper draft of the single guide bar movements over six courses.*

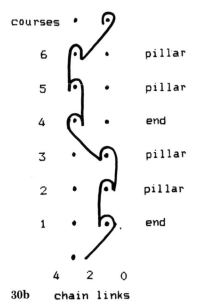

49

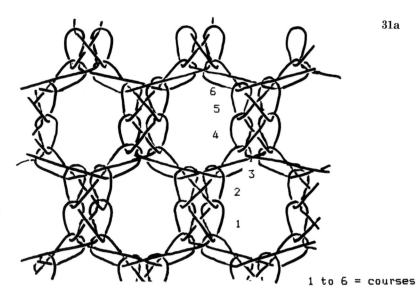

31a

6
5
4

3
2

1

1 to 6 = courses

31 *Net example 3:* **a** *The stitch plan.* **b** *The movements of the two guide bars which produce this net, separately, and superimposed over one full vertical repeat.*

31b *(i)*

guide bar 1   guide bar 2

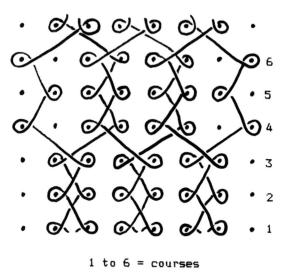

1 to 6 = courses

the lapping movements
of the two guide bars
superimposed

31b *(ii)*

(warp 1)
guide bar 1   • | • | •

guide bar 2 | • | • |
(warp 2)

is used. Each bar will be fed from its own warp roller, and directed by its own chain. One guide bar must always produce loops, the other may either knit or act as an *inlay thread*, performing an underlay only.

The two guide bars are half-set, that is threaded 1-in 1-out. This means that, in each bar, only every alternate guide is threaded

50

with a warp, the guides between being left empty. This too can be schematically represented, which may save a lot of words:

Guide bar 1 (warp 1) • | • | • | • |
Guide bar 2 (warp 2) • | • | • | • |

    where | = threaded, and • = unthreaded.

In terms of rises (laps to the left) and falls (laps to the right), the two bars have reciprocal action, every movement of one to the left being balanced by a movement of the other to the right.

    Further details of the net are clearly visible: the pillars are two courses deep and two wales wide; the sloping ends of each mesh are made of loops reinforced with a single thread; traversing is across one or two wales; there are no inlay threads; and all the loops are closed. The point paper draft is shown in fig. 31b. There is a 6-course 3-wale repeat for each guide bar.

4. In fig. 32a the mesh is small, strong, near-circular, and enclosed by four symmetrically placed loops. It is basically similar to net (3), but has a very small mesh, with the pillars omitted, and with lapping always across two wales. Both guide bars make loops and are half-set. There is a 2-course 3-wale repeat (figs. 32 b,c).

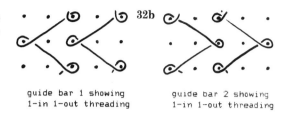

guide bar 1 showing
1-in 1-out threading

guide bar 2 showing
1-in 1-out threading

32c   the two bars superimposed

4 course
3
2
1

= position of hole of mesh

32 *Net example 4:* **a** *The stitch plan.* **b** *Its two guide bar movements plotted over a full repeat, separately, and superimposed.*

32a

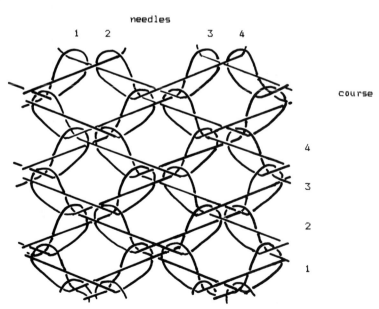

needles

1 2   3 4

course

4
3
2
1

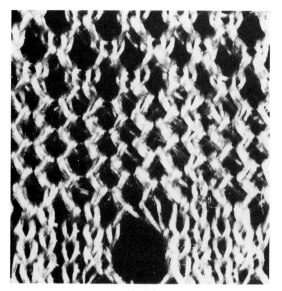

32c *The net itself, from a pair of silk mittens, first half nineteenth century. The vertical chains of loops below show clearly that this is a warp-knitted fabric but, apart from that, the zigzag appearance of the loops in the middle area shows a striking resemblance to single press point net (see fig. 7c).*

5. In many other variations the front guide bar knits while the back guide bar dispenses inlay threads. The back warps are therefore called *net-inlay* threads, and the front warps *net-pillar* threads since their loops act as pillars at the sides of the meshes. In *hex net* (hexagonal-hole net) (fig. 33a), the lapping of the front guides to form the upper and lower ends of the mesh is reinforced by the lapping of laying-in threads (fig. 33b), giving the characteristic appearance of one sloping end being made of a loop, and the other of two straight threads. This makes a very strong net and, although it looks complicated and in the finished net is not easy to analyse, the guide movements involved in its manufacture are relatively simple (fig. 33c). The front bar knits for 3 courses (2 open loops followed by one closed loop); shogs over 1 wale; knits 3 more loops; and shogs back again. That is, there is a 6-course repeat. It is in fact precisely the same as net (2). However, to this the back bar adds laying-in threads, carrying them down the pillars, and shogging them in harmony with the front bar so that the inlay reinforces the single front bar thread:

front guide bar   2-0 0-2 2-0 2-4 4-2 2-4
back guide bar   0-0 2-2 0-0 4-4 2-2 4-4

6. In *marquisette net* the role of the inlay threads is increased, and that of the knitting threads diminished. The net pillar bar in fact now forms nothing but pillars (fig. 34a), made of open loops, and it is left for the inlay threads to make all the cross-connections.

33 *(opposite) Net example 5, hex net:* **a** *Hex net in a Raschel lace, reverse side.* **b** *The stitch plan, the non-knitting inlay thread is indicated by a heavier line.* **c** *The movements of the two full-set guide bars plotted over nine courses, separately, and together.*

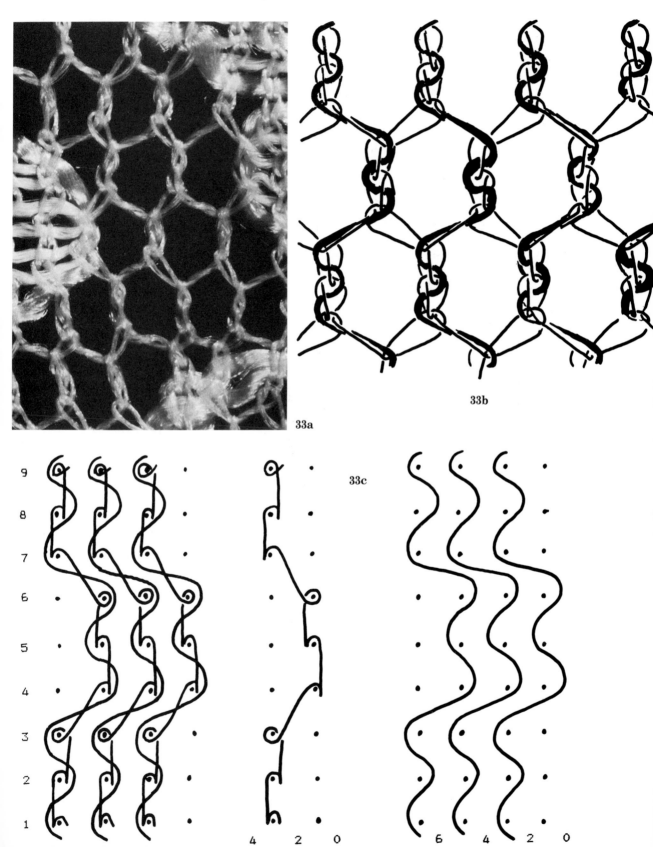

33a

33b

33c

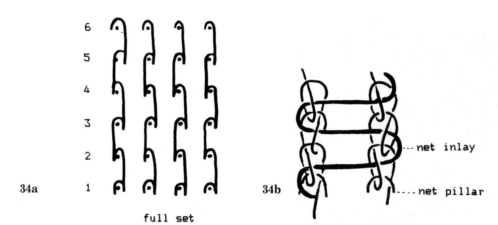

6
5
4
3
2
1

34a

full set

34b

---- net inlay

---- net pillar

34 *Net example 6, marquisette net:* **a** *A net pillar, with open loops.* **b** *Stitch analysis showing an inlay or filling-in thread crossing at every course, which would make a solid fabric when the bars are full-set, an openwork one with small meshes when half-set.* **c** *The point draft of another marquisette showing the two guide bars separately, and then superimposed, over several courses.* **d** *On the right, a marquisette* net of two guide bars, full-set, has inlay threads making a double strand at the top and bottom of each mesh. This area forms the selvage of a silk hat veil made of large meshes – on the left – which are entirely warp-knitted. Late nineteenth century. **e** Raschel marquisette in synthetic yarn, with the inlay threads shogged asymmetrically and connecting at different levels in alternate wales.

34c

2   0

6   4   2   0

Two bars superimposed
Full set

Front bar (Bar 1)
The net pillar thread

Back bar (Bar 2)
The net inlay thread

34d

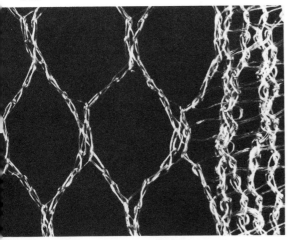

34e

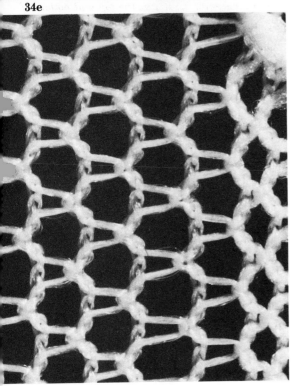

will be lapped across three wales. A simple marquisette is sometimes called *filet net*, after the square-meshed knotted nets made by hand, or after a type of net produced by the Curtain machine (see ch. 6).

In fig. 34c, the chain link repeat for the front guide (net-pillar) bar is: 0-2 2-0; and for the back guide (net inlay) bar: 4-4 6-6 0-0 2-2 0-0 6-6 or, more accurately: 4 6 0 2 0 6 since, with no overlaps, only one link per course is needed in the back bar chain, instead of two for the net-pillar bar where both underlaps and overlaps have to be produced. This necessitates a difference in speed for the two sets of threads, and for this reason the chains controlling them are separated, the former on an upper drum, the latter on a lower one.

When the bars are half-set, the upper and lower limits of the mesh are formed by single laying-in threads only. When they are full-set, as in fig. 34c, double laying-in threads will appear. Although this net is strong, it uses a good deal of extra yarn so that it has a run-in of 6.5 or 7.5, which makes it more expensive.

Marquisette can be made either fine or coarse, depending on the gauge, the denier of the yarn, and the intended end-use. Whether the bars are half-set or full-set will depend on the mesh-size required (figs. 34d,e).

7. Three ground-bars are used more commonly in laces than in plain nets, but there is a 3-bar marquisette used for curtaining: bar 1 knits pillars of open loops while bars 2 and 3 hold inlay threads. In figs. 35 and 36 all three bars are full-set, and the inlay threads connect the pillars every third course.

8. An example of a 4-bar is the elasticated *power net*. Each bar is half-set: bars 1 and 2 make courses of open loops and closed loops with laps across one or two wales; bars 3 and 4 hold an elastomeric yarn such as lycra, a synthetic yarn with the stretchable properties of natural rubber. Lycra is too thick to enter inside the needle hooks, but it can easily be applied as horizontal laying-in threads held down by the knitted loops so that it gives the fabric considerable resilience.

They run down their pillars as in hex net, and are then thrown across to the next pillar where they work for a similar number of courses, after which the guides thrust them back again (fig. 34b). The shogging intervals are usually so arranged that a square mesh is formed. For example, where the sides of the mesh are three courses long, the inlay thread

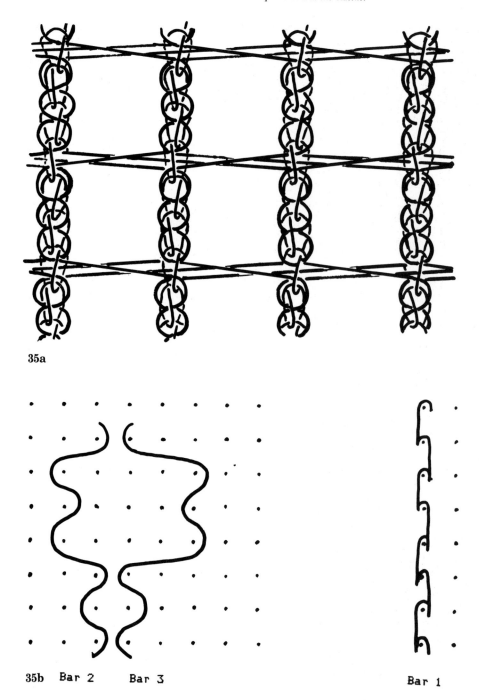

35a

35b Bar 2   Bar 3   Bar 1

35 *Stitch analysis and point plan for a three-bar*
marquisette.

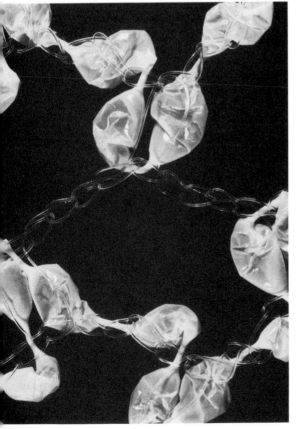

36 *Raschel marquisette closely resembling a lace made on the Curtain machine (see chapter 6).*

37 *A novelty net.*

Fig. 37 shows a novelty net in which the laying-in threads are of white plastic swollen at intervals into tiny balloons and held in place by thin warp chains of nylon knitting.

The speed of working of a Raschel machine is directly related to the complexity of the design and the number of guide bars it requires: the fewer the bars the faster the speed. Some net machines can knit up to 1,200 courses per minute (c.p.m.), and on a 170 inch wide machine, 200 or 300 square yards of net can be made in an hour, depending on quality.

The term *quality* is defined in terms of the number of courses to each inch of the completed web. Since counting the actual courses in a fine net would be difficult and tedious, the usual practice is to count the courses per mesh (eg 6 for hex net) and then multiply by the number of meshes per inch length. The relevant figure is expressed as s.p.i. (stitches per inch). The higher the number, the slower the work will be. Thirty courses or stitches per inch at a speed of 300 cpm would produce a 10-inch length of net every minute; while 60 courses to an inch at the same speed would produce only a 5-inch length. Thus the higher the quality, the longer the time taken, the greater the consumption of thread, and the more costly the lace. A poor (slack) quality will be loosely textured, a high quality closely textured

Net-production is measured in *racks*, that is the amount produced by one minute's full-speed running time of the machine, or 480 revolutions of the engine, equivalent to 480 cpm. The actual length, in inches, will vary according to the quality and can be calculated by the formula (480 ÷ spi).

The needles in the net machine have very small hooks, and make only a shallow up and down motion. This increases their speed well above that possible for the lace and curtain machines in which the needles are larger and the needle bar movements more pronounced.

The Raschel lace machine

The transition from net to lace is mainly a question of additional threads. Lace, as distinct from net, is non-uniform in density since it has heavier pattern areas (*objects* or *clothing*) separated by lighter openwork areas forming the *ground*. The net shown in fig. 30 for example can act as a lace ground by having additional laying-in threads at intervals to make a design. Such additional threads are supplied by *spot beams*. They pass from there to the patterning guide bars, which may be numerous, while the net-making threads remain restricted to two or three ground bars, threaded with warps.

In Raschels the ground bars continue to work throughout the lace, and they are always at least half-set. Patterning bars on the other hand work only in the clothing areas and so will be threaded infrequently, as the design requires, and each one differently, from its own spot-beam. Thus a patterning bar can be lapped in different directions and to different extents quite independently of any other bar, the only restriction being that their movements do not cause them to collide.

Multibar Raschels are those with a large number of spot beams, and an equivalent number of patterning bars. They began to be developed in the 1950s, specifically for the manufacture of lace. Much of the recent success of the Raschel has resulted from the increased number of guide bars which it can accommodate. In the earlier forms, a maximum of eight bars was all that could be fitted into the space available. Two or three of these bars were often taken up by the ground, leaving only six or five for patterning, which gave little scope. The actual space available for bars in recent machines has not significantly increased, but a system of *nesting* of bars has been developed.

Nesting involves the removal from the patterning bars of every guide which is not threaded, ie which for a particular design serves no useful purpose. This removal not only lightens the weight of the bars very considerably so that they can be moved more easily, but enables them to fit more closely together, in the manner of near-toothless gums. In this way several bars can be accommodated in the space formerly occupied by one, and their possible maximum increased to 78. Nested together they form a kind of rocking canopy above the needles, their pendant guides projected downwards, ready to lap or shog (see fig. 26).

For ease of reference the bars are numbered, from the front towards the back of the machine (cf Leavers, p. 117). In general the front bars make the ground, the middle the clothing, and the back the liners or outlining threads. This arrangement ensures that the emphasizing liners will appear prominently of the face of the lace, the technical back (facing the back of the machine during manufacture) being in Raschels the textural front (the surface visible as worn). Bar 1 is always a ground bar, and always knits. Bars 2, 3 or 4 may provide either ground or clothing depending on the type of lace being made. Any higher-number bars will be for patterning.

Between the pattern areas the liners have somehow to be disposed of. One method is to allow them to lie across the ground as floats. This is achieved by a succession of equal-sized links on the patterning chain, so that the outlining threads are neither diverted from a straight line nor held down by a knitted pillar. When the web has been removed from the machine these floats can be clipped away by hand, or by a machine with a clipping attachment associated with vacuum suction so that the threads are cut through and sucked away in the same instant. A more economical method is to guide the liners as unobtrusively as possible through the intervening ground so that no subsequent clipping is needed. This saves money, but sometimes at the expense of a harmonious design.

Heavy inlay patterning threads occasionally pose a similar problem. Appearing on the textural front, they give a raised overlay or overfloss effect. Since they act like wefts and are simply caught and held in place by the pillar threads, they do not have to pass through the needles' hooks, and so can be quite thick, even fluffy or crinkly, providing a novelty velvet, bouclé or chenille fabric.

The exact repetition of the design across the working width of the machine constitutes a horizontal repeat. Suppose that the repeat occupies 120 needles, and that there are 1,800 needles in all, then 15 repeats of the design will be constructed at the same time. Each sparsely-threaded patterning bar will normally contribute one thread to each repeat.

The Raschel can produce either bands or all-over laces, the latter being used as dress fabrics. Banded laces (edgings, insertions and galloons) are vertically orientated and placed side by side across the width of the machine, and linked together by special threads called *lacers* so that the web can be lifted off in its entirety instead of in a lot of narrow pieces (fig. 38). This makes handling much easier during the subsequent finishing processes of scouring, bleaching, dyeing and dressing. The essential feature of a lacer thread is that it is easily removed. This can be achieved by the use of:

1. a straight knitted pillar called a rover, which unravels when one end is pulled. The inlay threads which it held during manufacture are then left as shallow loops known as *purls*.

38 *Two bands linked by an area of lacers, and showing the border of purls that will be left when the excess material is removed.*

39 *A draft for a Raschel lace using 42 guide bars. The horizontal repeat covers 84 needles, and the vertical repeat 256 courses (Birkin, Borrowash).*

40 *A figure sheet, for a different Raschel design (Birkin).*

CARD NO. 1. BIRKIN & CO. LTD. RASCHEL DIVISION NO. 71348 / 1364

1	2	3	4	5	6	7	8	9	10	11	12	13	14	15	16	17	18	19	20	21	22	23	24	25	26	27	28	29	30	31	32	33	34	35	36	37	38	39	40	41	42
2·0	30	26	4	26	44	8	22	36	28	6	14	32	30	12	28	50	31	14	32	38	18	24	64	30	66	28	6	24	34	4	28	36	54	14	32	32	26	36	38	32	
0·2	34	28	2	28	42	12	24	48	30	8	16	34	32	6	26	52	34	18	34	48	20	18	60	34	68	32	8	28	36	2	26	52	56	16	34	38	44	28	44	40	30
2·0	30	26	4	26	44	8	22	36	28	6	14	32	30	12	28	50	31	14	32	38	18	24	64	30	66	28	6	24	34	4	28	36	54	14	32	32	26	36	38	32	
2·4	30	28	0	28	38	12	24	34	30	8	24	34	40	14	28	48	34	24	34	50	20	26	66	30	68	38	16	26	36	6	28	50	58	18	34	40	44	28	48	40	30
4·2	28	26	2	30	36	10	30	32	30	8	24	26	28	14	24	48	31	16	34	40	20	24	72	24	66	30	16	22	34	6	24	32	56	16	34	26	34	26	40	38	28
2·4	30	26	0	22	36	12	32	30	34	10	26	28	42	16	22	46	30	24	36	52	24	28	66	30	64	40	18	24	36	8	32	48	58	20	36	40	42	28	50	40	28
	26	24		20	34	6	30	28	28	8	26	26	26	14	20	40	28	18	34	40	27	26	66	26	60	26	18	20	34	6	20	28	56	18	34	26	34	24	42	38	26
	24	18		22	34	8	31	28	34	16	28	28	44	16	20	46	28	20	38	24	28	24	72	20	66	26	16	22	34	8	30	42	58	20	38	40	38	26	50	40	26
	26	16		20	32	8	30	26	26	12	20	26	24	14	18	36	24	20	38	44	24	26	66	26	58	26	20	20	32	6	18	26	54	18	38	26	38	24	42	38	24
	24	18		22	34	10	32	28	36	14	30	28	34	16	20	46	26	22	38	54	24	28	68	24	60	40	22	22	40	8	32	40	60	24	38	44	38	28	52	40	26
	22	16		24	32	10	30	26	26	12	22	22	24	14	18	34	24	24	74	18	58	30	20	18	34	6	18	26	54	20	33	22	38	26	44	38	24				
	24	16		18	32	12	30	26	36	12	30	24	34	14	18	44	26	22	36	54	26	26	68	24	60	38	22	20	44	6	30	36	60	26	36	44	36	28	52	40	24
	22	18		16	30	10	26	24	24	10	24	22	22	12	16	32	24	20	30	42	26	24	68	22	58	22	16	24	52	18	30	12	38	26	44	38	22				
	20	20		18	32	16	34	26	36	12	30	24	30	10	18	42	16	22	30	54	26	22	74	16	56	30	22	16	42	2	34	34	60	28	32	44	32	28	52	40	24
	22	22		16	30	16	34	24	34	10	24	22	22	12	16	32	24	20	28	42	24	24	68	22	58	36	22	16	32	4	16	24	50	18	28	22	28	26	44	38	22
		24		18	32	16	36	26	36	12	32	24	30	12	18	42	26	22	30	54	26	28	68	22	62	36	24	18	44	8	36	36	60	44	30	28	52	44	24		
		22		20	32	16	34	24	28	12	26	18	24	12	16	34	24	22	28	44	24	24	74	16	60	36	24	18	34	8	16	24	52	18	28	24	28	26	44	40	24
		24		14	34	18	36	26	36	14	32	20	30	14	18	40	26	20	26	52	26	34	68	22	62	38	24	24	44	14	36	40	60	30	40	44	30	28	54	44	26
		22		12	22	16	34	24	28	16	24	18	18	12	16	36	26	14	28	44	24	24	68	22	60	34	22	18	32	14	16	24	48	14	28	24	28	24	44	42	28
		20		14	28	18	36	26	34	16	30	20	28	14	18	38	28	16	30	46	24	34	74	16	62	38	22	24	42	16	36	38	60	28	40	46	30	26	52	44	30
		22		12	20	18	34	24	28	16	24	18	18	14	16	32	26	16	32	46	24	24	68	22	52	34	20	18	34	16	16	24	48	14	30	26	32	24	44	42	28
		26		14	28	20	36	26	34	18	30	20	28	16	18	38	28	18	26	48	24	38	68	22	60	40	22	26	44	18	36	36	56	30	42	48	26	26	52	44	38
		24		14	18	18	34	24	30	16	24	20	22	14	18	30	28	16	24	46	22	28	74	16	52	34	20	18	36	16	18	24	40	16	24	28	24	24	44	42	30
		22		18	26	20	36	26	34	18	30	16	30	16	20	38	30	18	24	48	24	38	68	22	60	40	22	28	42	18	36	32	56	28	42	48	26	26	52	46	40

28 courses.

2. a straight pillar knitted in a yarn which is differently soluble from the rest so that it disappears on immersion in solvent, leaving the lace intact.

3. an inlay thread worked as a draw thread using shallow laps. This can be pulled out straightforwardly.

The two edges of a band are known as the bottom edge (equivalent to the bobbin lace heading), and the sewing edge or back edge (footing). The bottom edge may be decorated with scallops, zigzags (vandykes) or purls. Shallow scallops, known as 'nipped edges' are made by the use of tensioned nipper threads. Bands bordered with deeply curved scallops have to be knitted as all-overs in which wavy rivers of lace are linked by narrow islands of net. This net is later cut away by a special machine such as the hunky molar used for Leavers laces, or by the use of heated elements which melt the synthetic yarn.

Lace bands can vary in width from 9 needles to 144 needles. In a 36-gauge machine this would be equivalent to actual widths varying between a half-inch and eight inches.

Drafts for laces are drawn in the same way as drafts for nets though they are more complicated because of the large number of patterning bars involved. When the original sketch of the lace design has been completed, it is plotted out on drafting paper of the correct quality, ie with the number of courses per inch required in the finished product, though on a larger scale (fig. 39). The movement of each guide bar in each course has to be put in on this draft, taking the thick threads first, then the gimping, and finally the warps (ground), ie working from the back of the machine towards the front.

After the draft comes the process of figuring. This consists of reading off all the bar movements, shown on the draft, in terms of the chain link heights that will cause them (0, 2, 4 etc). The numbers are arranged in vertical columns on the read-off sheet, each column representing the movements of one bar (thus 42 bars, 42 columns). Each horizontal row represents a course (fig. 40). In this example bar 1 is the stitch-forming, or knitting, bar.

Its movements are indicated by a double column of figures since it is shogged by two chain links in every course, one for the underlap and one for the overlap. The single figures for all the remaining bars indicate that they make only one movement per course, that is they are all inlay, not knitting, threads.

The vertical repeat for bars 1 and 4 is completed in six courses, requiring very short chain-lengths which will be extended by a repetition of the sequence only to the extent needed for the chain to pass round the upper drum (bar 1) and the lower drum (bar 4).

The total number of chains must equal the total number of bars, in this case 42. The number of links in any individual chain will depend on the number of courses needed to make the vertical repeat. In complex designs there may be over 21,000 links in all, and the cost of the chain alone may exceed £4,000.

The right-left shogging movements of the bars can, in theory at least, extend over two inches in either direction. The difference in height of the various chain links is equal to the size of the shogging movements so that, on a 48-gauge machine (24 needles to the inch), a rise from a number 2 link to a number 4 link would displace that bar by $\frac{1}{24}$ inch, or the distance between one inter-needle space and the next. The link sizes would all be in multiples of $\frac{1}{24}$ inch, so that at whatever actual size link 0 is constructed, each link above it will be increased at $\frac{1}{24}$ inch intervals. Thus link 2 will be $\frac{1}{24}$th inch bigger than 0; link 4, $\frac{2}{24}$ inch; link 6, $\frac{3}{24}$ inch; link 8, $\frac{4}{24}$ inch . . and link 96, $\frac{48}{24}$ inch, or 2 inches. In other words, 48 different link sizes must be available, in this example, their numbers progressing in twos from 0 to 96.

In some Raschels, the Jacquard-card apparatus is used instead of chains (fig. 41). An alternative to both is electronic patterning which, though involving initially a considerable capital outlay, ultimately saves costs, and allows for a far more rapid change-over from one lace design to another. In the system developed by the firm of Karl Mayer on their Jacquardtronic machines, the same draft as for Jacquard cards, or for a chain, can be used. The draughtsman transfers the perimeters of the design to the memory of a microcomputer using a digitising board. The thread movements are calculated by the computer, under program control, and after being checked on a print-out are transferred to a cassette tape, in terms of guide bar displacements. At the machine, the information on the cassette is fed into a magnetic bubble storage system and used to operate a selector mechanism which closely simulates a Jacquard. Thus, its six crank units, operating on the binary system, control guide bar displacements across 1, 2, 4, 8, 16 or 16 needles, via a series of electro-magnets. The total maximum displacement is across 47 needles (cf Leavers Jacquard system, p. 62).

The latch needles on the lace machines have a very long hook which, combined with the large number of guide bars, slows down the machine to a speed of about 320 courses, or needle-movements, per minute.

On the tricot machines (warp knitters other than Raschels) either solid or openwork fabrics can be produced. One of the more exotic openworks was the Moon fabric produced in 1969 on specially modified Karl Mayer machines fitted with Teflon-coated needles, and run at the slow speed of 40 cpm. The fabric was used to construct an antenna 10 foot in diameter, and looking rather like an open umbrella fixed to a tripod. The two-bar warp-knit net was constructed of gold-plated metallic yarn .0028 inches in diameter, called Chromel-R and composed of 74% nickel, 20% chromium and 3% iron and aluminium. The 14 filaments which made up the yarn were thus each only .0002 $\frac{1}{5000}$) inch in diameter. The fabric had to be both light in weight for the space crossing, and able to withstand temperatures ranging from 212°F below to 212°F above. The mesh construction was vital because the size of the apertures determined the frequency band for transmitting and receiving radio signals between the earth and the moon.[13]

Other tricot fabrics are *milanese* and the *angel laces*. The main interest of the solid fabric milanese, from a lace point of view, is that its mechanism allows two warps to traverse (pass diagonally) across the web from one side of the machine to the other, and

41 *The Jacquard apparatus of a Raschel machine, with a long stack of punched cards folded together (Karl Mayer).*

then to work back again in the reverse direction. This very stable fabric was used for milanese silk stockings before the invention of Raschel micromesh. Shorter diagonal movements are referred to as 'atlas laps' and defined in terms of the number of courses they cross, for example a '12-course atlas lap'. Such laps occur also in laces.

Angel laces are worked with only a few guide bars, but with considerable traversing so that they make simple yet pretty designs, which are mainly geometric. Frilling and ruching can be produced by a mis-lapping of one of the bars, causing parts of the lace to be gathered decoratively together. Some beautiful warp lace shawls of multi-coloured silks have been made in this way.

Elasticated nets have been mentioned earlier, worked with four ground bars. With four additional bars these nets can be patterned. Up to 56-gauge (28 needles to the inch) can be used, and 800 cpm produced.

The Raschel curtain machine

Curtains can be made on Raschel lace machines, or on Crochet machines, but the Raschel curtain machines are specifically adapted for large quantities of plain or patterned net by being able to take bigger warp rollers, and thus to make longer production runs. The needles have shorter hooks than the lace machines, and so have smaller needle movements and higher speeds. The patterning yarns come not from overhead spot beams but from a large number of spools stacked on creels at the back, each spool holding a separate thread. Widths can vary up to 240 inches, gauges between 30 and 48 needles per two-inch width, and speeds up to 1000 cpm. A 75-denier polyester yarn is frequently used, and the commonest quality is 58 spi (stitches, or courses, per inch length). Finer gauges use more thread and are more expensive.

In patterned curtains there are two chain drums, each driving the requisite number of chains, on the usual basis of one chain per guide bar. The top drum controls the knitted threads, the lower the patterning threads. When the repeat for the ground is short, the top chains are replaced by pattern wheels or cams.

The most usual curtain ground is a square mesh know as filet or *marquisette*. A two-bar form was illustrated in fig. 34. The bars may be either full-set or half-set. The pillars, knitted in open loops, are quite separate from

42a

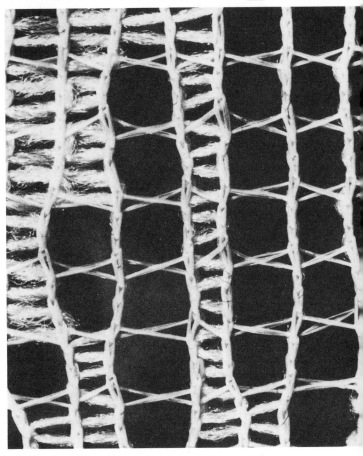

42a *A curtain Raschel showing Robin Hood in Sherwood Forest. (Lace Centre, Nottingham, 1980s).* **b** *Detail of the three-bar marquisette ground surrounding the oak tree.*

42b

43a

43a *A curtain net showing heavy inlay threads over a three-bar marquisette ground, face side, 1980s.* **b** *Reverse side of (a), detail: the lighter inlay threads are held by each knitted pillar, the heavier inlay threads only by the pillars at their extremities.*

each other except for the connections made between them by the three-wale laps of the inlay threads, every third course. Larger meshes can be made by increasing the number of courses in their sides, for example to five. Stronger horizontal connections can be made by extending the underlaps of the back bar over four wales instead of three.

In three-bar marquisettes the front bar knits as before, using a two-course repeat, while the two back bars make inlaying movements in opposite directions every third course so that their threads reinforce each other (fig. 42).

Although the basic arrangement of straight knitted pillars holding inlay thread connections remain constant in marquisette nets, considerable variation is possible. For example, two inlay bars working in opposite directions may not be completely symmetrical (see fig. 35b). Where the bars are only half-set this will show up clearly as alternate rows of empty needles. However, coarser gauges would tend to be full-set, otherwise the meshes would be too large. A 30-gauge machine, half-set, would have a distance between threads, and therefore a mesh-width, of $\frac{2}{15}$ inch.

The number of courses between cross-connections depends on the relationship of the gauge (distance between needles) to the quality (number of courses per inch length); also on whether a mesh of perfect square shape, or something more rectangular, is thought preferable.

At first, as was the case with lace, few bars were available for patterning, and designs

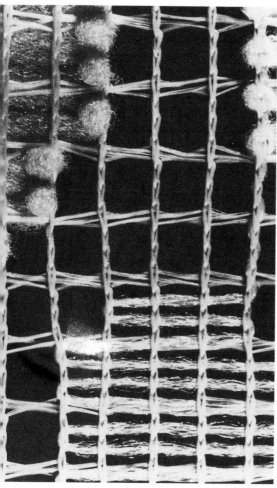

43b

caught into the knitted pillars to traverse in a graceful curve from one motif to the next, making an attractive design. In other nets the patterning threads may float between motifs and then be clipped back to give the appearance of isolated spots.

As more bars became available, there was scope for more adventurous design. One of the earlier products was the brise-bise, short curtains to be strung across the lower halves of windows, and described as a (resurrected) novelty in 1928.[14] In 1972 they accounted for 70% of Raschel curtain production.[15] In the 1950s they were produced on 12-bar Raschel machines in the form of panels of marquisette alternating with panels of fancy net. They were made vertically on the machine and connected side by side with lacers, or other means. Their lower edges – unroved, cut or ripped – could be left like that, for the raw ends would not unravel, as would a weft-knit product.

The *fall plate* is a special mechanism for producing strongly-textured patterns on the effect side (face) of the web which, during manufacture, is towards the back of the machine. The yarn manipulated by the fall plate is heavy, such as 2/200 (200 denier doubled), and it does not pass through the loop of the needle. Nevertheless it makes a full underlap and overlap, and can appear like lines of cable-stitching, or raised crochet, standing out from the fabric surface. In curtains, up to 16 bars may be used for fall-plate work, and the yarns are held to the fabric only at their extremities.

The looped openworks, weft and warp together, span the whole era of machine laces. Their story stretches from a monopoly by uniqueness, when the weft nets held their fragile sway, to a monopoly by omnipotence 200 years later, when there seems to be nothing which the warp-knitters cannot either imitate or surpass – in speed, economy, versatility and fabric strength.

were restricted to regularly scattered shapes such as circles, squares or lozenges. A five-bar net for example would have three for the marquisette ground, and two for patterning. The patterning yarns are usually heavier than the ground threads to give emphasis to the design. Fig. 43 shows a simple five-bar patterned curtain net. The inlay threads are

III

The Bobbinet or Plain Net Machine

(Métier Bobin or Métier Circulaire à Tulle Uni)

Right from the beginning of machine laces the aim of the inventors had been to imitate laces made by hand. The original influence was a double one: openwork knitting, and the popularity and aesthetic appeal of superfine nets made by a bobbin lace technique.

By 1800 the Stocking Frame had admirably copied the knitted openworks, and in this field the Warp Frame eventually added quite a number of ideas of its own (chapters 1 and 2). But attention was moving progressively towards a mechanism which could imitate the movements of bobbin lace itself – and this was a process of twisting threads, not looping them.

Bobbin laces combine a set-up of several threads held by weighted bobbins (similar to that used primitively for macramé), with a process similar to plaiting, the threads being either crossed over or twisted around each other. For at least 400 years bobbin laces have been made in the East Midlands of England. A 'continuous' technique is used, that is the threads are carried from the net-like ground into the pattern and out again, working right across from side to side of the lace. During its making the lace is fixed vertically to a padded support known as a cushion or pillow.

The appearance of this ground, commonly known as Bucks point, or half-stitch, ground in England, and *fond de Lille* in France and Belgium, is shown in fig. 44. The threads pass diagonally across from one mesh to the next

in opposing directions, producing a fabric which is strong, stable and slightly elastic.

It was this ground which the inventors now attempted to copy. Importantly, the result was the first machine created specifically for the production of openworks, both the Stocking Frame and the Warp Frame having begun by making solid fabrics. The name associated with the first commercially successful 'plain net' is that of John Heathcoat (1783-1861).

He did not hit upon the idea entirely fortuitously. His father had invested in some Warp Frame machines and Heathcoat, as an apprentice, quickly mastered their working. The first marketable net from the Warp Frame was made about 1795, when Heathcoat was 12. Continual innovations in Stocking Frame nets were still being made. All the excitement of experiment, and the euphoria of fortunes to be won, was in the air. 'I worked

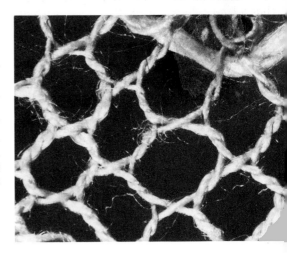

44 *A fragment of Lille, or Bucks point, ground.*

for my bread, and I tried to invent,' said Heathcoat in a later interview with William Felkin. His first patent (no. 2788), registered to himself and his brother-in-law Samuel Caldwell, in 1804, was for an attachment to Warp Frames 'whereby all kinds of thread lace [hand-made linen lace] and mitts of a lacey description may be made'.[1]

By that time warp nets made by other inventors were becoming established, and Heathcoat's attention became diverted to an even more original idea. He carefully observed a Northamptonshire bobbin lace-maker as she worked, analysing the courses followed by the various threads. He saw that they were divisible into two sets: passive threads which hung straight down, and active threads which worked over them, something in the manner of weaving except that the active threads (equivalent to wefts) followed a diagonal instead of a horizontal path.

His first machine to imitate this was invented in 1808 (patent no. 3151). He described it as for the manufacture of 'bobbin lace resembling French lace', Bucks point being known at that time as 'English Lille'. He called the circular thread-holders bobbins, and arranged them in a fan-like manner as on an actual lace-maker's pillow (fig. 45). On it he produced a band of net, three inches wide, which resembled the Bucks point ground so closely as to be indistinguishable, even to the appearance of those slight irregularities – caused by an awkwardness in the workings of the machine – which are often cited as proof that a lace is hand-made. The visual appearance of the mesh can be described as hexagonal or round with four sides twisted twice and two sides crossed over.

The Old Loughborough

Heathcoat's 1808 model never produced lace commercially, and was superseded only a year later. There was no doubt, however, that it could make a sound net. A sample from it, one inch wide, was used to decorate a baby's cap, and then washed and worn 'to test its capacity of resistance'.

Thus Heathcoat had no qualms about carrying forward his basic principles into the construction of a modified 1809 machine (patent no. 3216) which became known as the Old Loughborough after the town where, he said, 'its construction was finally accomplished'. He described it as for the 'manufacture of bobbin lace or net resembling foreign lace', and claimed that it could 'work with flax, silk, cotton or any other material of which lace or bobbin net is usually made'. But patents were often ambitiously worded. They were usually based on preliminary models, before commercial production was even attempted, and had to be broad enough to close loopholes that might permit infringement. At that time the Stocking Frame and Warp Frame nets used mostly silk, and hand-made laces linen, except for the French silk *blonde*. Heathcoat from the first used cotton, which by that time was of good enough quality for the Mechlin net made on the Warp Frames. Indeed commercial production of his nets in silk did not begin until 1824. Flax was still handspun and its thread insufficiently strong for machine lace manufacture.

The Old Loughborough (fig. 46) was 18 inches wide (that is with two quarters of working width), similar to the dimensions, and even the general appearance, of an early Stocking Frame. It was worked by hand levers, its aim being the 'beautiful idea of twisting two divisions of threads with order and regularity and without entanglement round each other'[2] in such a way that an entire row of meshes – equivalent to a course on the Stocking Frame machines – was formed at the same time.

One set of these 'two divisions of threads', namely the warps, were all arranged on a warp roller (or thread roller) at the bottom of the machine. From this they rose vertically and were attached to an upper cloth (or lace) roller around which the finished net gradually accumulated. The warp threads, although held on a single roller, were divided into two sets 'each composed of every other thread and kept apart on their way up'[3] by passing through a series of guides equidistant from each other, so that all the threads were evenly spaced. The guides were able to move each set of warps a short distance to the right or to the left.

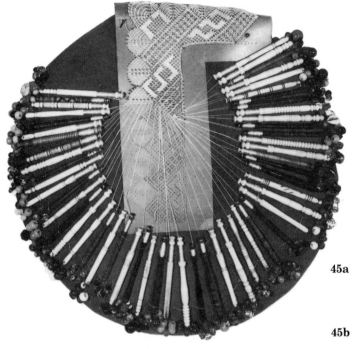

45a

45b

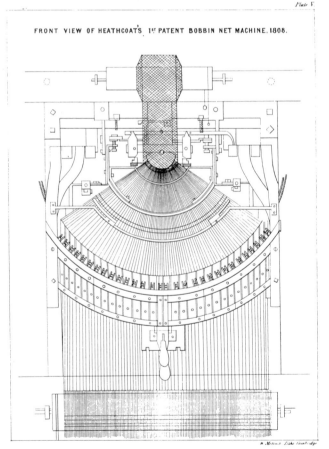

FRONT VIEW OF HEATHCOAT'S 1ST PATENT BOBBIN NET MACHINE. 1808.

The other division of threads was arranged quite differently, every single thread on a different holder, called a bobbin. These 'worker threads' were also fixed at their upper ends to the cloth roller, so that their attachments alternated with those of the warps. Bobbin and warp threads were equal in number. Heathcoat aimed, on this machine, to have the total width of the warps and bobbins equal to the width of the manufactured net, a situation impossible for the handmade lace he was copying because of the space taken up by the thread-holders.

His problem was thus to find a way of making his bobbins extremely thin. He calculated, from a piece of Bucks point lace which he analysed, that there were 40 threads to the inch. By separating the threads into two groups he now had 20 warps to the inch, which was quite simple to arrange, and 20 bobbins to the inch, which was very difficult indeed. The smiths at Loughborough could not, at that time, file down the bobbins to $\frac{1}{20}$ inch thickness. Even when Heathcoat conceived the idea of constructing them like a wafer-thin spool compressed from side to side with the two discs joined in the centre, he could not in fact manage it in a single row – as he had in his 1808 version, the fantail, by extending the row of bobbins well beyond the limits of the machine – so he arranged them in two rows, one behind the other, a situation referred to as 'two-tier'. The doubling-up, though, was horizontal between the front and back of the machine, and not vertical. Each bobbin then needed to be just marginally less than $\frac{1}{10}$ inch in thickness. The advantage of having warps, bobbins and net all occupying the same width was that, in theory at least, the machine could then be extended sideways

45a *A bobbin lace maker's pillow. The bobbins are arranged in the arc of a circle, with their threads converging to a relatively narrow area where the lace is made.* **b** *The set-up of Heathcoat's first bobbinet machine, 1808. The cross-hatched area indicates the position of the lace, the radiating lines the threads going to the bobbins, and the straight lines passing up below them the warp threads (from Felkin, plate V).*

68

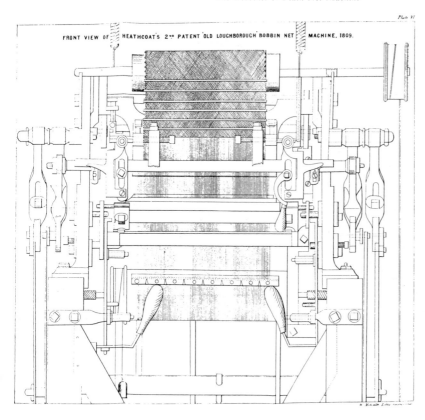

FRONT VIEW OF HEATHCOAT'S 2ⁿᵈ PATENT 'OLD LOUGHBOROUGH' BOBBIN NET MACHINE, 1809.

46 *Heathcoat's second machine, the Old Loughborough, 1809. The threads are all confined to the same width as the lace, making it possible, in theory, for the machine to be expanded sideways indefinitely. The warp roller is at the bottom, the cloth roller at the top (from Felkin, plate VI).*

almost indefinitely, to make very wide nets, while by the fantail arrangement the machine was wide and the nets very narrow.

As one problem was solved, so others were created, for Heathcoat now had to work out a sequence by which the newly-arranged threads could be twisted together. 'The mental labour was very great,' he said later. 'I was often puzzled and fatigued by attempting to overcome difficulties.'[4]

He experimented by suspending pack threads from a beam aloft across the room to represent the warps, then he 'passed the weft threads by common plyers, delivering them to other plyers on the other side, and after giving them a sideways motion, the threads were repassed back between the adjoining cords, receiving by this a twist, and the meshes were then ready to be closed by hand as upon the pillow [that is as in handmade bobbin lace]'. This sequence of movements was mechanized by transfering the action of the plyers to the bobbins; and the action of the

bobbin lace pins to points which not only 'closed' the mesh by assisting in the formation of a cross, but also tightened it and moved it upwards in the direction of the cloth roller.

Each bobbin was held in a carriage (or brass) within which it could rotate smoothly, releasing its thread (fig. 47). The carriages themselves acted as transporting vehicles which conveyed the bobbins between the front and back of the machine. They ran in thin grooves called combs, which kept their motion straight and steady. These combs were extensions inwards of the comb bars which stretched from side to side across the width of the machine, at approximately the middle of its height. Between these comb bars, arranged two at the front and two at the back, the paired bobbins, one after the other, swung back and forth 'like so many clock pendulums oscillating along the grooves', passing at every swing through the thin curtain of the stretched warp threads.

69

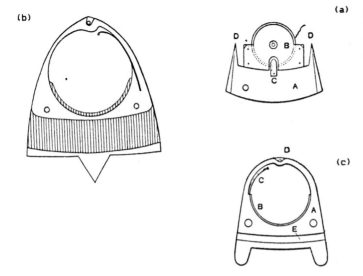

(b)

(a)

(c)

47 *Three types of carriage used on Bobbinet machines: **a** carriage with ears, which was discarded on the Bobbinet machine, but retained in a modified form on the Leavers and Curtain machines, and is still in use today.*

The momentum for this swing was provided by back and front shifting bars, or drivers, and fetchers which rested just above the comb bars and extended similarly across the width of the machine. Their supports were like stout inverted V's pivoted at their apex, and as the shifting bar pushed the bobbins through, the fetcher pulled them on the far side, and then they were pushed back again. To assist the process, the front and back of every carriage rose sharply upwards in a little notch (see fig. 47a), a shape still used in the Leavers and Lace Curtain machines today.

The backward and forward motion itself was repetitive only, not constructive. It made no provision for any interaction of threads. The technique used to twist the threads together was brought about, according to Felkin, by the front comb bar, after it had received all the carriages, making a lateral

movement or shog equal to the space between two threads, so that when the carriages were subsequently brought back to the other side (the back comb bar) each bobbin thread would have made one twist with a warp thread. 'If now the front comb bar be moved laterally till each bobbin stands opposite to the space from which it first started, and the threads be again passed through to the back and brought again to the front on the other side of each longitudinal thread, the threads will have been twice twisted.' In essence: the front comb bars make small shifts to right and left carrying the bobbin threads in unison first to one side and then to the other of the corresponding warps, thus creating twists. The repetition of this process produces two twists, and so gives the name to the product 'two twist bobbinet'. In bobbin lace-making also the four sides of the meshes are made by two distinct movements of the kind called twists. The visual effect likewise is of two small ridges on each side. Pedantically however what has occurred are two half-twists, or only one full twist; and the verbally precise French referred to the net as *tulle uni* (single net), an unfortunate duplication of the name used for one of the products of the pin machine.

The crossing of the threads at the top and bottom of each mesh is brought about differently and in a rather complex manner. Basically the paired bobbins being all at the front of the machine (in the two front comb bars which Heathcoat called conducting bars), the points were shogged one space to the left causing the paired bobbin threads, between which they entered, to cross over. The two sets of points entered alternately between the meshes, hauling them upwards in a conveyor-belt manner (fig. 48).

It was during the formation of this cross that the process of bobbin exchange, or the 12-motion shift, leading to the diagonal passage of the bobbin threads across the net, occurred. The preface to the patent abridgements says of Heathcoat's 1809 machine,

The carriages were arranged in two tiers one above the other; they traversed to the right in one

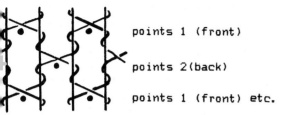

points 1 (front)

points 2 (back)

points 1 (front) etc.

48 *The entry of the points to take up, or pull up, the lace, and to help to make the crosses at the twelve-motion shift.*

tier and to the left in the other, a very ingenious arrangement transferring each surplus bobbin and carriage at one opposite extremity of each tier to the corresponding vacancies at the same end of each alternate tier.

Or, as Heathcoat describes it in his 1816 patent (no. 4076), which is 'for the purpose of making that kind of Lace commonly called or distinguished by the name or names of Bobbin Net or Buckinghamshire Lace Net':

The diagonal direction given to the bobbin threads requires that one division of the bobbins should have a progressive motion to the right and the other division to the left. It follows that when the extreme bobbin of either division arrives at the corresponding selvage of the lace, the said extreme brass [carriage] must be made to return in the opposite direction, which is done by taking the extreme brass from that division of brasses in which it has been previously employed and transferring to the other division. To effect the transfer of the end brasses from one division to the other, the fetchers have notches equivalent to the thickness of a brass cut in them.'[5]

Because the selvage was formed in this way, Heathcoat called it the *turnagain*.

He further describes how, when narrow bands of net were made on the Old Loughborough, each had to be finished on both sides with just such a turnagain. At the same time, one of the back warp threads would be diverted to make a lacer linking the bands together on the machine, but easily withdrawn afterwards to separate them. Such bands were destined to be gathered,

hand-embroidered or 'quilled', that is ruched into small cylindrical folds resembling a row of quills – not unlike the gadrooned effect of sixteenth-century ruffs – and fashionable in Regency times around the neck and head.

There is no further dependable information on the working of the Old Loughborough. Not a single machine survives, and though the principles of later machines were probably very similar, the detailed mechanics may well have involved significant differences.

Later developments

The Old Loughborough, having been created, was not allowed to rest. Almost incessant modifications were made to it, some successful, others not. Even before its patent expired in 1823, there were experiments in placing the combs straight (Straight-bolt, Morley 1812), or upside down (the Upside-down Circular Bolt, Sewell 1820), and the products claimed as new inventions. There were 156 infringements by 1816, and the number had risen to 200 by 1819.[6] Patent infringements became so rife that much of Heathcoat's time was taken up with legal battles to oppose them. Even so, inferior nets made on a variety of machines flooded the market, undercutting his prices, so that ultimately he was forced to lower the generous wages which he paid his workers to two-thirds of the previous amount, and payment for making 5-quarters (45 inches wide) bobbinet dropped from 3s.6d. (17$\frac{1}{2}$p) a rack in 1814 to 1d. in 1834, a reduction to $\frac{1}{42}$ of the original earnings. During the same period the selling price of a 24-rack piece fell from £17 to 7s (35p), a reduction to $\frac{1}{48}$ of the earlier price. Some of this reduction was certainly the result of increased efficiency. The general effect however was that although the years 1823–5 were a period of unparalleled prosperity in the trade, the market collapsed in 1826, and the mid-1830s became a period of quite acute distress.

Many of the improvements to the Old Loughborough were made by Heathcoat himself, in fact he continued to invent up to 1843 when, at the age of 60, he was turning increasingly to local politics. Some of his last experiments were concerned with improvements in patterning, namely the application of the Jacquard to the Bobbinet machine, which had never been easy (patent no. 9496); he also experimented with printing on net. Although the social events around him – the smashing of his machines by the Luddites, the fraudulent imitations of his nets, the illegal exportation of his machines – undoubtedly provided a strong stimulus to press on continually to new and better models, the main source of Heathcoat's inspiration must have lain in the energy and enthusiasm of his own temperament. His eager mind explored areas even quite unconnected with lace such as a new method of throwing silk in 1825, a way of manufacturing salt (1823), and a steam plough (1832).

In his patent no. 4078 taken out in 1816, Heathcoat describes his 10-point (10 comb-spaces to the inch) 'Bobbin-net Lace Machine', explaining in particular the details of the guides for the beam (warp) threads. They are like small wires with 'holes like needle eyes' which are attached to two guide bars carrying respectively the front and back warp threads. Both guide bars can shog $\frac{1}{10}$ inch to either left or right. Shogging of the comb bars is restricted to the two at the front. It appears reasonably clear from the specifications that the twists are brought about entirely by movements of the guide bars carrying the warps first to one side then the other of the bobbin threads, while the front comb, or conducting, bars in conjuction with the shifting bars, shogged only to bring about the 12-motion shift at the completion of each line of meshes.

The more significant improvements to the Old Loughborough culminated in a machine known as the Circular, patented in 1824 by William Morley (no. 4921). It was also referred to as the Circular Comb, or Circular Bolt, the terms comb and bolt being synonymous. This machine will be described in the next section.

The Old Loughborough, like the Stocking and Warp Frames, was an English invention but, as with the earlier machines, commercial success meant that people abroad, most particularly the French, would do almost anything to get their hands on it. The pirating of a pin machine by the duc de Liancourt in 1784, and its devastating effects on the English patent net trade, has already been discussed (p. 22). By 1812, a combination of Napoleon's blockade of Britain, and of internal chaos caused by a flooding of the textile market with inferior goods, mainly single press point nets, had brought 50,000 families in Nottinghamshire to the verge of starvation.

In the confusion of Napoleon's Hundred Days return, in 1815, an Old Loughborough was smuggled across the Channel by Cutts, one of Heathcoat's former workmen. The machine was set up first at Valenciennes but moved, when that town was under siege, to Douay.[7] Its relatively small size, probably not more than three feet, made the evasion of Customs officials, and its subsequent transport, a matter of no great difficulty. It was this machine which in 1816 produced a length of net to make a dress for the duchesse d'Angoulême, daughter of the guillotined Louis XVI, and niece of the newly-crowned Louis XVIII, who was King of France from 1814–24, except for the brief period when he had to flee before Napoleon's army.

By 1818 the penalty for exporting lace machinery had been increased to a fine of £500. Nevertheless bribery greased the way, and in that year the essential parts of a Stocking Frame found their way to Boston, Massachusetts, concealed in tubs of Yorkshire butter. The reasons for the smugglers taking such risks was not only the avarice for the rewards which lace manufacturers might expect if they could set up their industry in a country with virtually no competitors, but also the discontent, on the part of the workers, with conditions in England. There is even said to have been, at this time, a mass emigration of framework knitters to New England.

Thus, between 1818 and 1822, many skilled workmen and machinists were arriving in Massachusetts. The Old Loughborough, sometimes called the Hand Circular, had then a working width of between five and seven quarters (45 to 63 inches), and there might well have been a few surviving smaller ones. Even so, they could scarcely be smuggled whole. They were dismantled, and the small but vital parts of the Insides hidden among the effects of the émigrés. The more massive Carcases were constructed in America, from sketches made by skilled machinists. The machines were transferred to Ipswich, Massachusetts, in 1824, and powered by water. The Boston and Ipswich Lace Company was founded in that year, and a rival concern, the New England Lace Company, in 1828.[8]

England, discovering that the horse had been stolen, proceeded to lock the stable door by imposing a large duty on exported cotton thread. America at that time, in spite of having almost unlimited supplies of raw cotton, had no efficient spinning machinery. Crompton's spinning Mule was still quite young, and the Throstle Frame even younger (1800). Her own machine, The Ring Spinner, invented in 1828, was only beginning to be used in 1830. At the same time England removed the duty on Nottingham's laces, so that they easily undercut American products. Its food supply cut off, the errant horse died, in 1832. However the illicitly imported Stocking Frames were more adaptable. They reverted to the manufacture of plain hose, in thickish homespun thread.

Sophia Walker, daughter of Dean Comfort Walker who owned a power mill, records a somewhat similar story of Medway, Massachusetts, where she lived. Her father discovered *c.*1818 that two of his employees had worked on lace machines in England, and he asked them to build 'a loom of 1260 shuttles'. The machine, duly built, was worked by foot power, and the plain net it produced was sent out to neighbouring farm houses to be embroidered. The net appears to have been made in narrow bands, 'the footing woven with drop stitch to be cut, actual width, one and a quarter inch in the net'. The business moved to Baltimore in 1824, and the following year 180 yards of Walker's net, in seven patterns, was exhibited in Philadelphia, where it won a silver medal.[9]

Sophia Walker's account is not entirely easy to interpret. One of her father's English employees is described as a 'lace weaver', a

term more commonly used of framework-knitters than of twist hands; the reference to 'drop stitch' suggests a knitting technique; while the 'coach laces' illustrated in the article, and said to have been exhibited in 1825, bear a striking resemblance to velvet pile laces, made on a Warp lace machine, and patented by Dunnicliff and Dexter in 1845.[10] The '1260 shuttles' could also possibly relate to a Warp Frame: a 42 gauge machine 60 inches wide would have 1260 separate threads, as would a 36 gauge 70 inch machine, or a 28 gauge 90 inch machine – gauge being the number of needles per two-inch working width. Even 60 inches is a pretty large machine to be worked entirely by hand and foot, though it is possible that Dean Walker's machines, like those of the Boston and Ipswich Lace Company, were powered by water. To confuse the issue, the photograph purporting to show what the machine usually produced shows quite clearly a traverse net similar to Heathcoat's.

The Walker lace industry, whatever its nature, does appear to have existed contemporaneously with the New England ones, and to have failed about the same time, *c.*1830. Sophie Walker attributes its failure to excessive importations of cheap 'machine-patterned Nottingham laces' – though the Jacquard was not applied in England to either the warp machines or the twist-net machines, before the late 1830s. The patterning may of course refer to something quite simple, such as spotting, which was established earlier.

It was Heathcoat who pioneered the application of power, or the rotary principle, to Bobbinet machines. When in 1816 he moved to Tiverton, and established his factory by the River Exe, he built a huge water wheel to supply energy to drive his machines. Two years later he invested some £50,000 capital in setting up a steam-powered plant in Paris. In 1824 he invented an improved method of reeling and preparing silk yarn. He obtained £5,000-worth of very fine '3-strand 5-cocoon silk', and had the monopoly of its use for the next 20 years, for tulle made in both Paris and Tiverton.[11]

In 1826 Heathcoat transferred his machinery from Paris to St Quentin, only some 40 miles south of Douay, where the illicit Old Loughborough had since multiplied, and was busily working. Heathcoat's factory grew to 170 machines strong. It was visited, and praised, in 1849 by the President of France, Louis Napoleon, who had a passion for innovations. In 1851, by a bloody coup d'etat, Louis Napoleon established himself as the Emperor Napoleon III.

Two important names in France at this time were Ferguson and Dognin. Ferguson senior was instrumental in setting up Calais' first lace machine, purchased in England, and legitimately exported *c.*1824. He also initiated a simple patterning process, which resulted in a design of large circular spaces known as bullet holes, contrived by a modification of the cams controlling the bobbin swings. In 1838 he fled to France, seeking escape not only from a chaotic industrial situation but from the pressures of industrial espionage which made it impossible for him to keep his discoveries from spies.

Dognin *père* (1785–1848) had established the Maison Dognin in Lyons in 1805, with an extensive patent net industry. Bobbinet machines were set up there in 1825 when it was discovered that silk could be used on them. In 1826 the English government reduced the duty on imported French nets, it appears misguidedly, for it coincided with such extensive over-production at home that the English manufacturers were forced eventually to appeal to parliament. Queen Adelaide took up their cause, in the same way as she had championed the cause of the distressed bobbin lace makers. An order was issued that only English laces were to be worn at Court and, at a ball in 1831, she herself wore a dress made entirely of English silk bobbinet embroidered by hand with garlands of roses in imitation of a glowing French blonde: '... the dress was of the most brilliant description imaginable and absolutely dazzled the eye. The appearance was that of flowers of brilliant shining silk, worked upon a gossamer light fabric, having more the appearance of net made of mother-of-pearl than of any other substance ...'[12]

The Circular Machine, or, The Double Tier Traverse Circular Bolt Rotary Bobbin Net Machine (*Métier circulaire à tulle uni*)

The metamorphosis of the Old Loughborough into the Circular was completed by a series of small but cumulative mutations (fig. 49).

The use of external power, whether of water or steam, enabled much larger machines to be built. By human muscle alone, working through pedals and levers, even a 6-

49a *A section of an early Bobbinet machine showing the arrangement of the various parts and the swinging bars which propel the single-locker carriages between the front and back of the machine.* **b** *A historic Circular Bobbinet, or Plain Net, machine, built in 1853 during Heathcoat's lifetime: it shows the heavy iron carcase which early replaced the wooden frame. It was on this machine that the wedding veil of the Princess of Wales was worked in 1981 (Heathcoat's, Tiverton).*

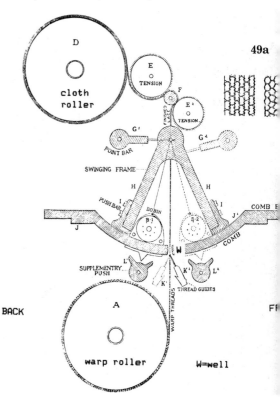

quarter (54 inch) width was hard to manage. As with the Stocking Frame Magog, a man of exceptional physique was needed to master it, and only one was found, a Mr Simpkin. Being paid by the rack, or area of net produced, he did very well: in three days he could earn £5. As demand increased, and external power was applied, the Bobbinet machines widened, to 108 inches by the 1820s, and ultimately to well over 200 inches. They seemed like symbols of an immense prosperity, but such giants were all the more a liability when demand fell sharply as it did a century later.

The general method of working remained basically the same as in the Old Loughborough, though with numerous refinements aimed at simplifying the working in order to increase the speed. The parts of the machine are here described from below upwards:

1. The *warp* ends all arose from one roller,

but were separated into two sets called the front and back warps. These were kept apart, above the roller, by a *sley* (fig. 50).

2. Each warp thread then passed through a *guide*. The guides were of two distinct types called eyelets and pigtails (fig. 51). Eyelets were described in Heathcoat's 1816 patent. Pigtails are more commonly used now, and are sometimes associated with patterning. Both types of guide are about one inch in length, the first soldered to steel *guide bars* two inches deep and $\frac{1}{16}$ inch thick, from front to back. The second are moulded into 2-inch blocks and screwed to heavier guide bars, two inches deep, but $\frac{1}{2}$-inch thick from front to back. There were always two guide bars, one for the front warp threads, and one for the back. Both could be moved by cam action one gait, or carriage thickness, from its starting position, or stop.

3. The *bobbins*, like the warps, were arranged in pairs, a row of front, and a row of back bobbins. Their total number was equal to that of the front and back warps. The bobbins were shaped like emaciated cotton reels, flattened from side to side into extremely thin circular discs. In 1824 a method had been devised for stamping them out instead of filing them as had previously been necessary (patent no. 4917). At the top of each was a tension spring so that the release of thread was constantly regulated by the pull from above. This much-improved spring allowed each bobbin to hold up to 120 yards of thread, depending on the count.

4. Each bobbin was supported in a holder which passed around it and was known as a *carriage*. The underneath of each carriage took the form of a narrow slide, not unlike an ice-skate beneath a boot. These slides slotted into grooves which lay between thin metal bars like the teeth of a comb. Held securely within these grooves the carriages were propelled back and forth, unable to diverge at all on either side. The movement was controlled by cams.

5. The metal *combs* originated in *comb bars* which, like the guide bars, extended across the width of the machine. The original Old

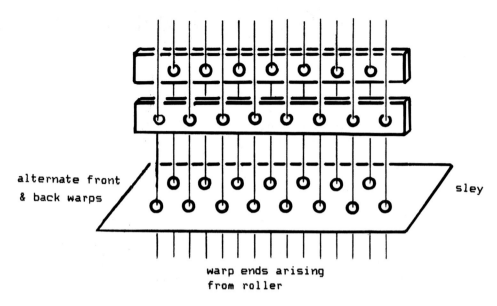

alternate front
& back warps

sley

warp ends arising
from roller

50 A sketch to show the separation of the warp ends, all from one roller, into front and back sets, and their passage through perforated guide bars.

pigtails

eyelets

guide bar

51 The guides, attached to the guide bars, which hold the warp threads.

Loughborough had four comb bars, two along the back and two along the front. Later the two were reduced to one, and the short combs which the four had supported were combined to make longer ones capable of holding the two tiers of bobbins at the same time. Formerly, with all the carriages at the front of the machine, it had been possible to shog the two sets independently. With the two front combs united, this could no longer be done (fig. 52a). The front and back combs together formed a smooth curve dipping down from the comb bars towards the central well, so that as the bobbins swung through the grooves of the combs the lengths of thread linking them to the area of interaction above, remained entirely constant. It was this pendulum swing of the carriages through the arc of a circle, on a constant radius, which gave rise to the name Circular, the carcase of the machine itself being quite straight (fig. 52b).

6. Bearing in mind that in the final net there might be 20 or more meshes to every inch of width, this area of interaction of threads where the net was made had to be crowded into an extremely small space.

7. The slots of the combs, in which the carriages swung, were of a standard size for each machine. The number of slots per inch of the comb bar was called the *gauge*. A 10-gauge machine would have 10 combs per inch width, and since each comb held two carriages, one behind the other, 10-gauge = 20 carriages per inch. Counting front and back separately, it also indicated 20 warp threads, 20 points, and 20 guides. Everything was doubled up, and a 10-gauge machine would produce 20 meshes per inch width of the net. Gauges could be 10, 12, 14 or 16, the finer ones (14 and 16) being relatively new. The actual number of bobbin and warp threads required to make net on the Circular was a multiple of (working width × gauge × 2). For example, a 10-point gauge 216 inch machine would need 4,320 threads to be wound on 4,320 bobbins; and 4,320 warp ends, to be wound on a warp

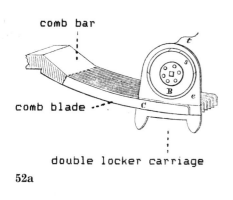

comb bar

comb blade

double locker carriage

52a

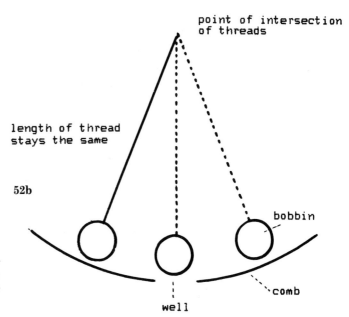

point of intersection
of threads

length of thread
stays the same

52b

bobbin

comb

well

52a *A block of nine comb blades showing their origin from the comb bar, and how the carriage rests within the comb slots* (from *Ferguson*). **b** *The pendulum swing of a single bobbin.*

roller (or beam), separated into front and back sets, passed through the holes in the sley, then through the guides, and finally attached to the cloth roller (lace roller or piece roller) above. In general, the finer the gauge the narrower the machines, for example a twentieth-century 14-gauge Circular might be 204 inches wide, a 12 gauge 222 inches, and a 10 gauge 244 inches. Although in theory very coarse nets could be made on machines up to 300 inches wide, the 274 inch is the biggest that is practicable.

8. The swing, or *motions*, of the carriages in the Old Loughborough were brought about by the drivers and fetchers of the shifting bar, which gripped into the notches of the carriage as it rocked back and forth like a swinging cradle. They could move either in unison or be split into groups, as in the making of bands. It was a rather ponderous technique, and supplementary *double lockers* were introduced by William Morley, a machinist of Nottingham, around 1818. Heathcoat's praise of him was generous. The notches on the carriages were removed, and replaced by a pair of toes or tabs which projected downwards through the comb slots, where two short arms on the locker bars

directly beneath could make contact with them (see fig. 52a). The locker bars turned regularly back and forth through a small arc, catching the toes of the carriages and sweeping them upwards along the grooves, then dragging them down again. The paired tabs of the carriages were sometimes replaced by a single tail (single locker) (see fig. 49a) which was worked in a similar manner. Another modification was introduced by Jackson and Henson of Worcester, in 1825 (patent no. 5067). It was known as the *roller locker*. In this modification, five or six further tabs were added to the carriages. They all projected down through the slots of the combs, like naked toes poking through the open end of a shoe. The tabs meshed with fluted rollers, toothed like a cog wheel, which extended widthways across the machine (fig. 53). In the same way as the double lockers, the rollers rotated briefly backwards and forwards, shooting the carriages to and fro so powerfully that the shifting bar above the combs could now be dispensed with. Both forms of propulsion are still in use today, in spite of Murphy's prediction in 1906 that the much faster roller lockers would gradually drive double lockers out of use. The double locker

77

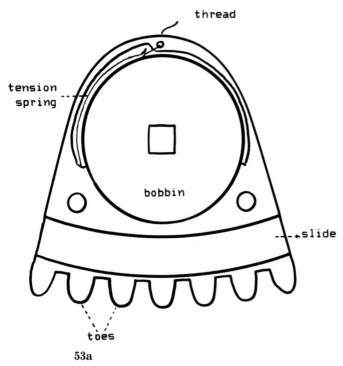

thread

tension
spring

bobbin

slide

toes

53a

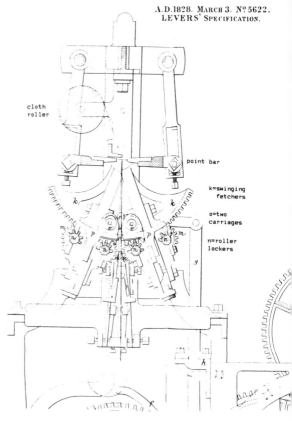

cloth
roller

point bar

k=swinging
fetchers

o=two
carriages

n=roller
lockers

53a *A rolling (or roller) locker carriage.* **b** *A machine with rolling lockers, from an 1828 patent.*

53b

could produce five racks an hour, the roller locker nine. Higher speed sometimes went along with lower quality, using quality in the technical sense of larger meshes or slacker texture, and today roller locker machines are mostly used for heavier work such as elasticated nets, patterned webs, and wig linings. Eyelet guides are associated with double locker machines and piglets with roller lockers.

9. *Twists* and *crosses.* Although in appearance the thread-movements which built up the individual meshes of the net were the same as in the earliest Old Loughborough, the mechanisms which caused those movements were transferred, in the Circular, from the comb bars to the warp guides, so that it was the moving warps which swayed from side to side around the bobbins, which themselves never deviated from their backward and forward swing. Only in making the cross at the end of the mesh was there any sideways movement of bobbin threads. In the Old Loughborough, according to Ferguson, 60 thread movements were required to make a single line of meshes.[13] Heathcoat in his 1816 improvements listed 25 actions to be carried out by the twist-hand simply to pass 'both divisions of brasses in succession between the beam [warp] threads into the comb bars and then to return them back again into the conducting bars [front comb bars]'. The total of thread movements in the Circular occupied only 12 bobbin motions, six forward and six back for each set of carriages, that is: two motions to pass the back division of carriages from the front comb bar to the back, and two to return them; a further four to repeat this sequence; and the final four to bring about

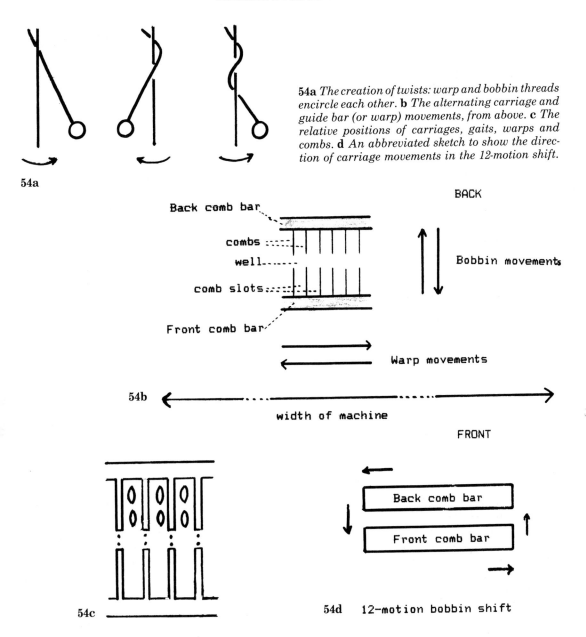

54a *The creation of twists: warp and bobbin threads encircle each other.* **b** *The alternating carriage and guide bar (or warp) movements, from above.* **c** *The relative positions of carriages, gaits, warps and combs.* **d** *An abbreviated sketch to show the direction of carriage movements in the 12-motion shift.*

54a

BACK

Back comb bar

combs

well

comb slots

Front comb bar

Bobbin movements

Warp movements

54b

width of machine

FRONT

54c

54d   12-motion bobbin shift

Back comb bar

Front comb bar

the cross. Two-twist bobbinet is thus sometimes called 12-motion net, and the mechanism of crossing the threads the '12-motion shift'. Between each motion (except for some deviation during cross-formation) the warps would sway to the right or left so that succeeding carriages passed on different sides of them, creating the twists (fig. 54a).

The two warp guide bars placed the vertical threads in a double line, the front warps and back warps, which acted in unison but independently of each other. The threads passed through the *well* at the inner ends of the comb blades, and they alternated with the carriages, in a position known as the *gait* (fig. 54b, c). When a line of warps was moved, they were pulled by the guide bar from one gait to the next, a deflection described as a 'one-gait throw'. A sequence of four motions with warp throws in between is called a 'round', and the 12-motion shift which makes the cross can therefore be described as taking place 'after three rounds'. It results in an exchange of bobbins so that a front carriage at the right moves to the back tier, and a back carriage on the left moves to the front tier (fig. 54d). The overall effect is of a movement of the front line of carriages, one at a time towards the right, and a movement of the back line of carriages one at a time towards the left, the movements onwards taking place every 12th motion. On a 216 inch 10-point machine with (2 × 2160) carriages, it will take 51,840 motions for one carriage to make the complete circuit and return to its original position – during which time several yards of net will have been produced. If the shifting motion were put out of action, no bobbin exchange would occur, the bobbin threads could not then pass diagonally, and the net would be untraversed or 'straight down'.

10. The *point bars* acted as in the Old Loughborough, slotting their thin ends inside the meshes, and supporting them briefly, as pins are used by bobbin lace makers to prevent distortion of the work by the next movements of the threads below. They also assisted with the pulling-up, or 'take off' of the completed net. The *facing bar* above the points gently pressed on the completed net, maintaining an even tension, while the *porcupine* with its spiky surface steadily wound the net upwards so that it would reach the cloth roller without any drag or uneven pull. The term 'point' is sometimes substituted for 'gauge', thus a 10-point 216-inch Circular means there are 10 points to the inch on each point bar (or 20 points per inch taking the front and back bars together). Since the number of points is equal to both the number of combs and the number of carriages, the terms point and gauge are synonymous, indeed they are often combined, as in '10-point gauge'. The number of holes or meshes widthwise across the net is always twice the gauge.

In describing the completed net, the number of holes is counted both horizontally and vertically. Horizontally it will be twice the gauge, vertically it will depend upon the quality (speed of take-off), and can vary from four to 21 holes.

Net-widths are measured in quarters, that is nine inches or quarter-yards. A 12-quarter net would be 108 inches wide, a 15-quarter 135 inches wide, and so on. Machine widths can be stated in either quarters or inches.

Net-lengths are measured in *racks*. A rack is a length of 240 meshes measured diagonally across the fabric. This rather strange unit was chosen to avoid fraudulent measurement: stretching a length of net with sufficient force can double its length, with consequent swindling as to price. Accuracy was important also to the twist-hands since they were paid by the rack. 240 meshes counted in this way are equivalent to 1440 single motions of the machine. The Circulars worked rapidly. A machine 108 inches wide could produce 1,000 meshes a minute before 1820, compared with five or six a minute for handmade Bucks point ground. By 1862 Circulars could produce 30,000 meshes a minute.[14]

The name Circular was chosen to distinguish the machine from others producing bobbin- or twist-net. As rivals failed or, if successful, acquired distinctive names of their own, the name Circular was gradually dropped in favour of the Bobbinet, or Plain Net, machine.

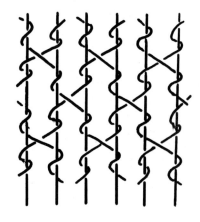

55 *Two-twist bobbinet, first made in 1808, and in production ever since.*

Plain net, and its variations

The two-twist bobbinet, first produced in 1808, was so satisfactory and so successful commercially that it has been made with little modifications ever since (fig. 55). But the restlessness which prompted machinists and twist-hands alike to experiment ceaselessly with new techniques – whether for personal satisfaction, glory or financial reward – caused them continually to attempt imitations of other handmade grounds.

In assembling a brief review of these other nets, particularly in relation to the first half of the nineteenth century, it is by no means easy to know precisely which machine they were constructed on. Early offshoots of the Old Loughborough, such as the Pusher and Leavers machines, also made plain nets for quite a number of years before patterning began. Both were frequently referred to in those days as bobbin-net or twist-net ma-

chines, since they incorporated the same principles of manufacture as Heathcoat's. Pusher nets were traversed so that they looked like Old Loughborough nets. Leavers nets, after a brief period of traversing, became untraversed, and so should be easily distinguishable from the others by tracing the threads (see chapter 5). However the Circular could also be worked as an untraversed machine, by disconnecting the shift cam and so preventing the bobbin exchange which alone determined the diagonal passage of threads.

Nor is it easy to know exactly what the nets

56 *Detail of a stole to show the similarity of the traversed two-twist net (above) and the Lille ground of the bobbin lace (below). The join is so neat as to be invisible. The sprigs on the net are made by hand, using a running stitch.*

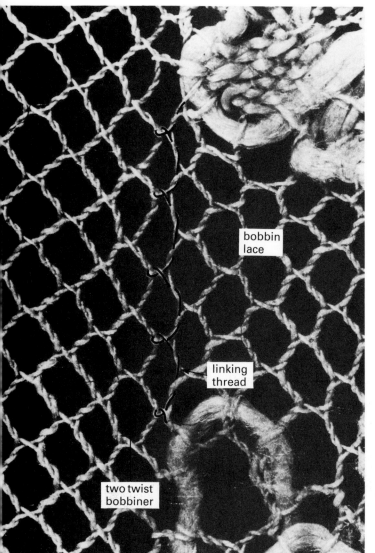

bobbin
lace

linking
thread

two twist
bobbiner

57 *Often the net was cut away behind the bobbin lace. Here, machine net and hand lace are joined by a looping stitch.*

themselves looked like. Their intriguing names – three-twist, square, platted, Brussels, fender, Mechlin, Sack Bag, honeycomb,

zephyr, Pantry Window and Grenadine – which stud the pages of nineteenth-century fashion journals and lace histories, are seldom accompanied by any adequate description of either appearances or structures.

1. *Two-twist net.* The net is named structurally by the number of twists per side made during mesh formation, and visually by the double ridges (figs. 56, 57).

2. *Tulle illusion* is a two-twist bobbinet made in silk. It only developed after Heathcoat's experiments in silk reeling in 1824 and the setting up of his Paris factories. All bobbinnets up to that time had been made in cotton. A particularly fine form of tulle illusion was created in 1828 by Dognin *père* of Lyons. The yarn was made of only two or three strands of raw silk tightly twisted to make a thin organzine thread. But names are not always to be relied on and it seems more than possible that Dognin's tulle illusion was in fact his Mechlin net, which was light and aery enough to justify that description. This makes sense of a report by Dognin *fils c.*1860 in which he said that 'the tulle illusion which his father had devised made the fortune of plain silk manufacturers in Lyons, and was copied by the English at a much later period'.[15] It would be completely untrue of tulle illusion in its usual sense, but a fair description of the long period of unuse, between 1829 and the late 1840s, for the Mechlin net described on p. 87. Heathcoat's tulle illusion was made in varying qualities at his Paris and St Quentin factories up to 1861 when, following his death, they were closed down. It continued to be made at the firm's Tiverton factory into the twentieth century for very special occasions such as the wedding of Queen Elizabeth II (1947), Princess Anne (1973), and the Princess of Wales (1981). This last veil was made on the factory's most historic machine, the 10-point 216-inch double locker Circular, powered by electricity, and dating from 1853, one of the first really large machines, and made during Heathcoat's lifetime. The silk thread used was 16 to 18 denier, the net had a 41-hole count (20 per inch horizontally plus 21 vertically). The entire veil measured 18 yards by 4

yards, and its weight, when finished, was 1.7 kilograms.

3. *Three-twist net* (Brussels net, diamond net). When the number of twists or ridges along the sides of the meshes was increased to three, 24 motions instead of only 12 were needed to produce it. The longer sides which resulted changed the shape of the holes from round or hexagonal to lozenge or diamond-shaped (fig. 58). This net was first made *c*.1831 by Thomas Sewell of Nottingham. After 1834 it was made extensively for the application of both bobbin and needle motifs, handmade in Brussels and Honiton. A resolution of 1819 'Against the introduction of mechanical machines into the lace industry of Brussels, as threatening the livelihood of hand lace-makers' followed the setting up there of eight Bobbinet machines in 1817. But Brussels and Ghent were later to become famous for their three-twist net, made of very fine cotton. Robert's self-acting (that is fully automatic) Mule for cotton spinning was invented in 1835, and its proficiency was so superb that it soon became possible to convert one pound weight of raw cotton into 1,000 miles of thread. A Mr Washer, who by the 1860s owned 16 Bobbinet machines in Brussels, used nos. 400 and 530 cotton yarns to make some filmy nets for the Great Exhibition of 1851.[16] The three-twist net was thus very light and delicate, sometimes so aerily fine as to be almost invisible and the dainty bobbin and needle sprigs, carefully stitched to it by hand, seemed to float around the head and to cascade over the train like drifting petals. It enjoyed great popularity in the second half of the nineteenth century, but the superfine cotton and the additional motions made it expensive to manufacture. In spite of the beauty of its appearance it tended to pull out of shape, and so to be less practical. It finally went out of production in the 1960s, but is being revived in India in the 1980s.

4. Another untraversed form of three-twist Brussels net was patented in 1838 by Dognin *fils*, and was called hank net. Lightly dressed it was used for violettes and toilettes, heavily dressed for hat trimmings.

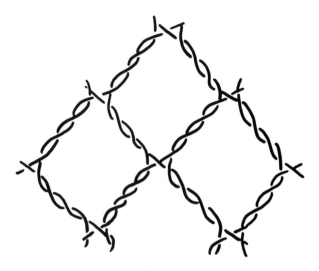

58 *Three-twist untraversed net.*

59 *Four-twist traversed net.*

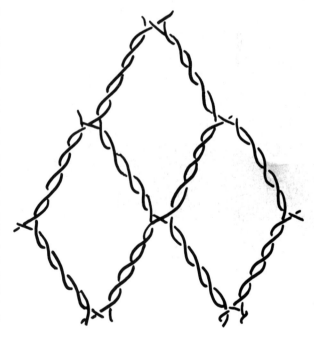

5. *Square net* (tulle carrée, tulle double, tulle de Bruxelles). The four long mesh sides had a double twist, giving the appearance of four ridges. Dognin *fils* claimed (in *Dognin*

and Co., 1913) to be the first to make this net, on the Circular machine, in 1838, though obscure references in Felkin suggest that Ferguson, Sansom of Nottingham, and Saille of Calais also produced square nets at an early date (fig. 59).

6. *Wire ground*, or point de Paris. This also was an invention by Ferguson senior in the 1820s. It imitated the handmade ground known in Bucks laces as Kat stitch or wire ground, and in the bobbin laces of northern France or the Turnhout area of Belgium as point de Paris. Examples of this fabric survive in the form of triangular capes or fichus, hand-embroidered (fig. 60).

7. *Platted net* The fabulous bobbin-made droschel, that mistily weightless Flemish ground (see fig. 5) which had inspired the early experiments in openwork on the Stocking and Warp Frame machines, was perhaps the greatest challenge to the ingenuity of machine net manufacturers. In it, each mesh consisted of a pillar of four threads plaited together. At their upper ends the pairs of threads separated, to unite with pairs from neighbouring pillars and construct new ones. The labour of working this ground by hand

was so immense that even in 1800 it cost £60 a square yard. By the 1830s with reduction in demand almost none at all was being made. A very convincing machine copy is shown in fig. 61. This net is untraversed. Platted net for the Circular machine was invented by Sewell in the 1840s, working on a 13-point machine. Though technically a triumph, its slow and tedious manufacture, when composed of a high count thread (a fine cotton), made it commercially unviable. In heavier yarns it was less expensive, and was used for curtaining. Some of the finest droschel-imitations were made not on the Circular but on other machines developed specifically for that purpose, for example the Horizontal Lace Platting machine of *c.*1810, which was in two parts separated by the length of a room, the parts drawing nearer and nearer together as the work proceeded. This machine used no. 300 cotton yarn, which then cost £16.80 a pound. It took a whole week to produce two yards of 40 inch wide untraversed net, which therefore had to be sold at £5.25 a yard. But how this could be distinguished from a platted net made on the Circular machine has not been recorded. About 1857 Waterhouse made imitation droschel on a 14-point roller locker machine. He analysed the mesh into two upright pillars each formed of two warp and two bobbin threads, and four sloping sides

60 *Wire ground:* **a** *by machine;* **b** *by hand.*

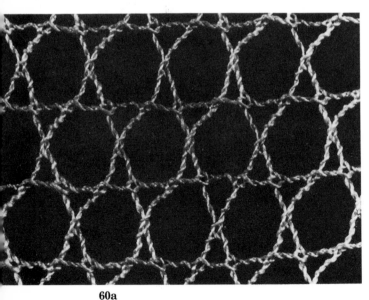

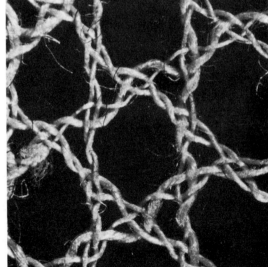

60a

60b

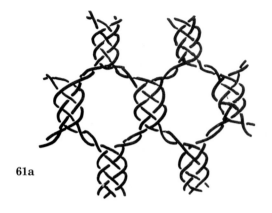

61a

61b *(i)*

61b *(ii)*

61 *Platt/platted net:* **a** *machine-made, untraversed.* **b** *a small veil, about one metre square, with sprigs of Honiton bobbin lace appliquéd onto it. In (i) and (ii), parallel streaks lengthwise down the net suggest an untraversed form, and are more clearly indicative of a machine origin than the detail in (iii) which shows a four-thread plait.* **c** *handmade droschel, for comparison.* **d** *detail of a similar machine-platted net, with a fragment of Carrickmacross muslin appliqué worked by hand.* **e** *A machine copy of a Mechlin bobbin lace with two thickened sides representing the plaits of the handmade form.*

61b *(iii)*

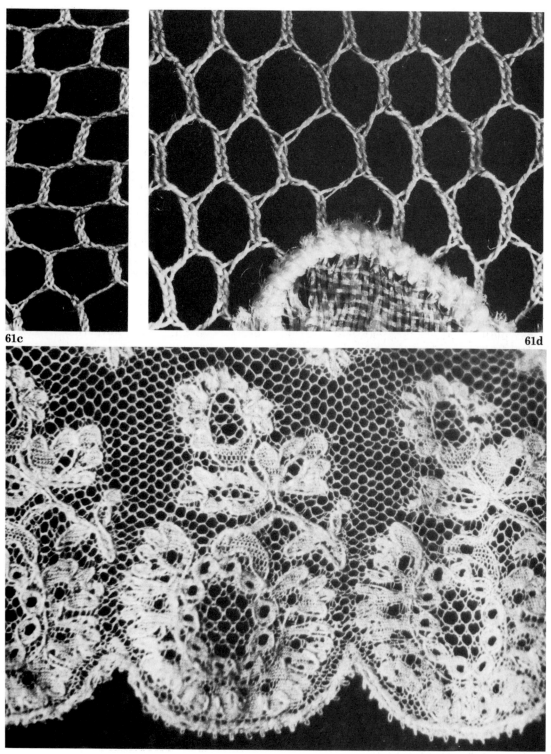

61c

61d

61e

each formed of a warp and a bobbin thread twisted together. On his modified machine, traversing could only occur over two meshes, so that the final appearance is spite of the fineness of the gauge was somewhat coarse. However it looked more or less like droschel, was patronised by Queen Victoria, and recommended by *The Times*.

8. *Mechlin* Handmade Mechlin ground is strikingly similar to droschel, the only obvious difference being that the pillars are plaited three times instead of four. Attempts by Nottingham manufacturers to imitate 'the best foreign cushion laces' inevitably included this ground (fig. 61e), but the problems of producing a clear four-thread plait at an economic price remained insuperable. It was far simpler, and cheaper, and for most purposes quite adequate, simply to give the impression of such a plait by thickening the vertical sides of the meshes without making a real plait at all. A warp-knitted net had already been marketed under the name of Mechlin, but production of this had ended in England in 1819, though continuing longer in France. 'It is now principally made on the Circular rotary machines,' said Felkin in 1867 (p. 281). This very successful and immensely popular twist net, made from the 1840s, in fact bore no resemblance at all to the handmade form. It consisted instead of straight threads linked around each other to form long diamond-shaped meshes in the manner of a wire fender, four sides each being formed of a single thread, and the other two very short sides twisted, at first with three twists, then with two, and finally with one, so that it looked 'exceedingly light and airy, and when of silk, stiffened, very brilliant. It will not,' adds Felkin, 'bear washing.' (fig. 62). This Mechlin net was in fact very unstable. It had been invented by Fox of Radford c.1829 for use of the Leavers machine, with only a single warp throwing between bobbin threads, but it made no impact on fashion until the 1840s when it was revived on the Circular. Being of such simple construction the net used little thread, and so was quick and cheap to produce. A 20-quarter (180 inch) wide Circular rotary – that is a Circular machine powered by water, steam or electricity – could manufacture enough net in a week to cover 2,000 square yards, or in a year 20 acres.[17] 'Mechlin straight-down plain cotton nets' were particularly fashionable in the 1840s and 50s in England. Few appear to have survived, but they are occasionally found as a backing for regrounded Alençon, where mesh-size and texture make an excellent match for the original *reseau ordinaire*. A Mechlin net produced by Dognin of Lyons from 1828 was made of very light silk and traversed only one mesh (Felkin p. 409).

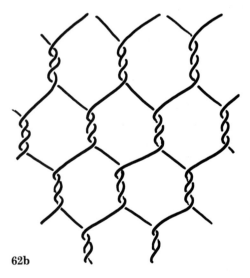

62a

62b

62a *Mechlin: the lightweight straight-down 'fender' net used to line coffins.* **b** *A very light three-twist untraversed net.*

Mechlin net made of a heavier thread was used into the twentieth century to line coffins, where the latent instability on exposure to damp would be a matter of indifference to the occupants.

9. *Grenadine* This net used a lot of silk, and so was not suitable for manufacture in England. It was made plain on the Circular machine by Dognin in 1825, in either black or white, then embroidered by hand. Its aim was to imitate the handmade Spanish pillow ground. Its silk yarn consisted of many tightly twisted singles with up to 1800 turns per metre. These were then doubled or plyed with up to 1700 turns per metre in the reverse direction. The effect was to give the yarn and its net an elastic quality, but the consequent thickness of the yarn made it rather heavy.

10. *Zephyr* was a trade name for several very lightweight nets, including the more buoyant forms of tulle illusion and Mechlin.

11. *Honeycomb* is listed as one of Croft's inventions of 1835, to be worked on either a double locker or roller locker Circular machine. It seems uncertain whether it related to a regular ground of honeycomb stitch such as occurs occasionally in handmade Bucks point, or to a simple form of patterning, since additional guide bars were required.

12. *Elastic nets.* Three patents for 'introducing India-rubber strands' into machine-laces were taken out in 1842–3, but the production of elastic nets on the Bobbinet machine appears not to have become established until the 1930s,[18] when a Lastex yarn was used, consisting of a thin core of natural rubber wound round with cotton or rayon thread. Such nets are still made on roller locker machines, mainly for intimate apparel.

13. *Mosquito nets* and *sandfly nets* were adapted by their mesh size for keeping out sandflies and mosquitoes.

The Heathcoat company's output during the 1970s included 100,000 square metres of elastic net compared with a minimal amount of cotton, 250,000 square metres of silk, and 4 million square metres of nylon net. Export,

for embroidery by the Schiffli machine (see chapter 8), was mainly to Japan, Austria, Switzerland and the USA.

Quality The fineness or coarseness of a net is determined by three factors: the count or denier of the yarn, the gauge of the machine, and the pick-up, or take-off, speed. The more slowly the net is passed to the cloth roller, the more rows the machine will have time to make per minute, and therefore the more holes there will be per vertical inch, and closer work gives finer quality. The take-off speed is controlled by toothed wheels (the quality wheel) which are set to a certain speed at the beginning of the action.

Finishing The plain net was originally sold in the 'brown' state (*pieces ecru*), that is with all its dirt, just as it came off the machine. This continued until the 1860s when it was found more economic to 'finish' it before sale. After inspection and repair it was stretched over a frame in a hot atmosphere, applied with starch and other chemicals, and fans set in motion above to dry it. More modern and mechanical processes involve scouring to remove the machine lubricant, graphite, which in spite of some problems in removing it from synthetic fibres is still, on the whole, more satisfactory than fluon or polytetrafluoroethylene. This is followed by dyeing, and stentering – the heat-application of chemical dressings, gum resins or plastic finishes which help to stabilise the nets, especially those made of silk. Dressing can be very light, allowing a bridal veil to hang in dreamy folds, or so heavy that it produces a sharp shiny stiffness like fibreglass, making an aggressive decoration, popular at one time for hats.

Patterning the net

Although the Bobbinet is described in the trade as a Plain Net machine since that is what nowadays it mostly produces, attempts to pattern it go back to its very early days, even to Heathcoat's patent of 1816 for the Old Loughborough, by which 'figures and ornaments are worked in the lace'.

The earliest patterning was by hand, after the net had been taken off the machine. The

63a

63b

63 *Embroidered net:* **a** *black Limerick lace, the design darned by hand on to a plain two-twist bobbinet, c.1830.* **b** *detail from a similar lace showing a Grecian net effect, and also a zigzagging of the needlerun stitches which is similar to the fining so characteristic of the Leavers machine.* **c** *Carrickmacross worked by hand on a four-twist bobbinet.*

63c

work took the form of embroidery, application of handmade or woven motifs, or a mixture of the two. Many thousands of people were employed in this work, mainly women and children in their own homes. It was an occupation already established with the point nets of the Stocking Frame. It involved no problems of ingenuity only good designs, time, patience and a certain skill (fig. 63).

Patterning of the net by the machine itself was a very different matter. It required non-uniform activity of selected threads, particularly of the longitudinal threads, in specific areas, where the patterning was to occur. These threads had to be quite separately guided, so that they took no direct part in the manufacture of the net, but could be moved when and where they were required to make the design.

The simplest patternings were by the addition of solid areas to produce small spots called *point d'esprit*, or larger spots called peas. Alternatively the openwork could increase in size, taking the form of large circular holes as if bullets had been fired through the net, making *bullet-hole net*. Both types had already been made on the Stocking Frame, but it was Ferguson senior in 1823 who first adapted the Circular to their manufacture (fig. 64).

A method of making spots was invented in 1831 by William Sneath (patent no. 6208) (fig. 65). His method was to hold back most of the carriages, leaving just a few working to make the spots. Another method was to use extra bars to hold some of the threads. These extra bars were operated by the organ barrel (*cylindre d'orgue*), a perforated cylinder dating initially from the eighteenth century, which made simple automatic patterning possible. It could alternatively be achieved by the use of a Dawson's wheel, working like

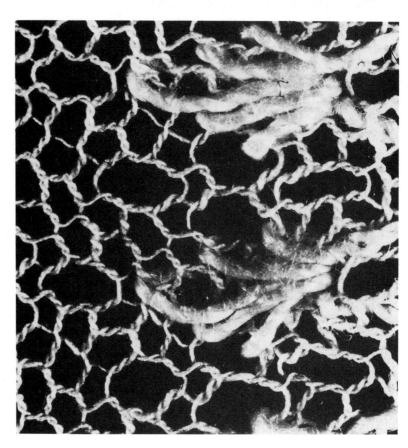

64 *An irregular net known as crackly (craquelé), with hand-run decoration and enlarged openings, showing how bullet-hole nets could be formed.*

65a

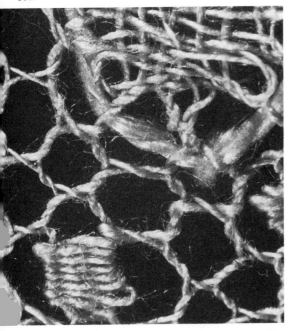

65a *Handmade bobbin lace showing a spot, or tally, in a Bucks point ground.* **b** *point d'esprit net, the Bobbinet machine copy: note the traversing of the threads.*

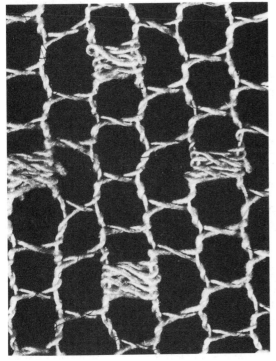

65b

a very sophisticated cam. This had been applied to the Circular in 1822.

The point d'esprit net was immensely popular. By the 1840s corsages and other garments 'of spotted tulle' were all the rage, and competition between France and England moved into the field of 'figured nets', with patents being taken out by Black of Lille, and Champailler of Calais, both in 1834. Further modifications were for larger spots such as *tulle à mouche* (literally fly net) and *tulle grain d'orge* (barley grain net).

The final truimph was the successful application of the Jacquard in 1837. In 1853 the Emperor Napoleon III offered a rich reward to anyone who could work the Jacquard by electricity. Remarkably, many of the inventions occured during the depressive years of the 1830s. By 1834 so many varied machines were in use, so many improvements being made so rapidly that narrower and slower machines became obsolete long before they were outworn. 'Many were thrown piecemeal from the windows of the upper rooms in which they had been employed into the streets below, not being thought worth the trouble of carrying them downstairs, though they had cost several hundred pounds each.'[19] Some 500 or 600 machines were broken up at that time.

In 1875 the fashion for frills, then being worn by the actress Sarah Bernhardt, favoured the putting together of little bands speckled with point d'esprit, which could be turned out by four-bar bobbinet machines, that is Circulars with four patterning bars. Spotted nets continued to be made for the next 75 years though it slowed down the work so that only four-and-a-half racks an hour, instead of six, were produced, making it that much more expensive. The demand by the end of that time was so minimal that the specially adapted machines were eventually scrapped. The knowledge of how to make spotted nets on the Bobbinet machines was at least temporarily lost, and when spot net was revived in the 1980s it was at first on the Leavers machine.

The Jacquard had opened the way for a transition from nets to patterned laces, and the Circular seemed set for a great future. But

3460

66a

66. *Patterning on the Bobbinet, the butterfly design:* **a** *the draft;* **b** *the punched Jacquard cards.*

two years later the Jacquard was successfully applied to the Pusher, and two years after that to the Leavers, both eminently more suited by their construction to the manufacture of complex designs. Thus the blossoming of the Circular into new and more exciting ventures was nipped, in the bud. Some patterns were however drafted out. In 1841 for example, Thomas Sewell of Nottingham produced patterns 'embodying ideas derived from Greek architecture' and 'in outline clothworks', that is with design areas surrounded by an outlining thread, or liner, 'throwing in beautiful openworks so as to give light and shade, and produce a rich effect

. . . This modified machine was exhibited by him in 1851, and being purchased by the Prussian government, was put to work in the public school at Elberfeld in 1852.'[20] It seems likely that his products were too expensive for marketing.

Most of the twentieth-century patterns used on the Bobbinet machines are fairly small, such as repetitive chrysanthemums or morning glory, butterflies or abstract motifs.

92

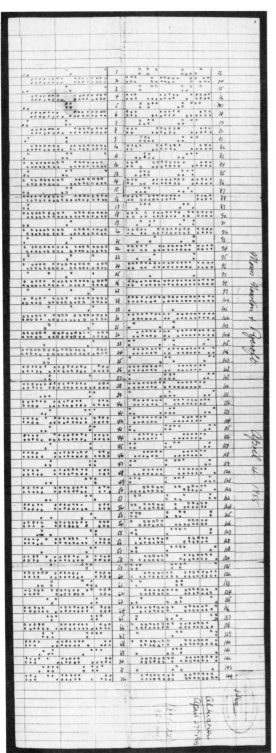

The effects are created by special thin guide bars only $\frac{4}{1000}$ inch thick from front to back, and $\frac{5}{16}$ inch high, and known as ribbon bars. These are in addition to the normal guide bars which work the ground. The ribbon bars are operated by a dropper system quite similar to that used in the Leavers, and the width of the horizontal repeat is about four inches.

Only the roller locker machines are used for patterning, the double lockers being restricted to plain net. No additional threads are used, it is the front warp ends which are separated out along the ribbon bars which each supply one thread per pattern repeat. Then a series of one-gait throws creates the pattern fillings which make the dense areas of the design. The bobbins, and the back warps, worked by cams, continue their movements as usual.

The butterfly design shown in figs. 66 and 67 was made on a 10-point machine using 40 ribbon bars punched at intervals for the patterning front warps. The ground was still a 12-motion net, and remained traversed. As indicated, 72 full motions were needed for the vertical repeat, and thus 144 Jacquard cards. Both tiers of bobbins were represented on each card, but the front and back motions were separated onto different cards. Machines used for patterning are frequently narrower than for plain net, such as 116 inches.

While Jacquard cards, and drafts, already in existence may still be used on Bobbinet machines to make patterned laces, the drafting of new designs is a forgotten art, as are the spotted nets, and the three- and four-twist diamond nets. Nor has there been for some decades sufficient demand to justify investment in experiment and research, while at the same time the rapid advances of the warp-knitting Raschel threaten to make the two-twist bobbinets permanently redundant.

The Bobbinet machines have survived many crises in the past, and there is some prospect that they may do so again. They survived their democratic popularity, which brought 'the luxury of lace to everyone's door',[21] for it did not affect their quality, nor prevent royalty continuing to patronise them (fig. 68). The English trade survived the

66b

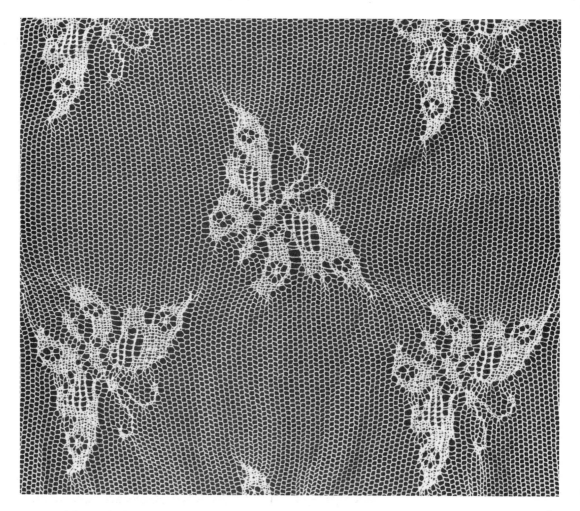

competition of the French, which by the mid-nineteenth century had developed alarmingly, with silk nets concentrated at Lyons, and cotton at Calais and Cambrai. In 1855 Lyons had a total of 500 machines, and Calais 606 which included 67 Circulars making plain net and another 122 making fancies; while at Amiens the total of net machines occupied 5,000 workers, with a further 50,000 employed in hand decoration.[22] Figures for England in 1862 give 1,797 Circulars of which 700 were in Nottingham, 500 in Derbyshire, 360 at Chard, 200 in Tiverton, and 100 at Barnstaple. Of these, 1,442 were making plain net, that from Tiverton being mainly of silk.[23]

In France during the 1860s the patterned laces, or fancies, of Calais were so successful that all plain nets were given up, and the machines transferred to Lyons, where they used silk instead of cotton – with the result that in 1890 the Minister of War found that his order for 24,000 metres of cotton two-twist bobbinet for mosquito netting, needed for military expansion in Africa and Indo-China, could not be met.

A period of prosperity around 1880 was followed predictably by over-production and slump. Another revival began about 1900 in spite of, or perhaps prompted by, those 'new chemical laces (called "burnt")' which were being made on embroidery machines in Plauen and St Gall. While these machines were a severe threat to the patterning Leavers, their ability to embroider on plain

94

Your new Dance Frock

will be dainty, durable and fascinating, if you make it of

HEATHCOAT'S "Striped Board" NET.
famous Devonshire

THESE famous NETS are the approved choice of the leading London and Paris Dress designers, and in the hands of the home dressmaker are easy to make-up with entirely successful effect. Unrivalled for their soft draping qualities and alluring simple beauty.

With free Paper Pattern. Cutting-out Diagram, and Instructions for Making-up.

25/11

SPECIAL OFFER

To bring before the notice of a still larger public the manufacturers are supplying through leading drapers, an 8 yards length (40 ins. wide) of "STRIPED BOARD" NET, the amount required to make the fashionable model illustrated. All the leading shades: Black, Ivory, Sky, Pink, Turquoise, Lemon, Lilac, Saxe, Mole, Royal, Jade, Nigger Brown, Navy, Old Rose, Peacock, are obtainable. With each length is given a PAPER PATTERN (cut by a world-famous modiste) and full particulars for cutting out and making-up this model Frock. Price, packed in box complete, **25/11.**

Ask for the NET rolled on the "STRIPED BOARD."

If any difficulty write JOHN HEATHCOAT & CO. (Dept. 2), Ironmonger Lane, London, E.C.2.

67 *The butterfly design lace.*

68 *An advertisement in* Weldon's Ladies Journal, *1921: 'to bring before the notice of a still larger public . . .'.*

bobbinet was, for the Heathcoat machines, an encouraging factor.

However by 1922 nets were again out of fashion, and now it was to be for a long time. 'One can walk down Oxford Street and Bond Street and hardly see a single lady wearing net in any form,'[24] said a Heathcoat representative of the period. In the lace-manufacturing areas of the Midlands there were spectacular bankruptcies. The industry has never fully recovered, and in 1984 the Bobbinet section of Heathcoat's Tiverton factory, founded in 1816, closed down. All the machines were offered for sale, and some went to India, where patterned cotton nets will in future be produced. Plain silk nets are now made mainly in France. In spite of the

increasing popularity, in the 1980s, of both white and coloured Schiffli embroideries on a net base, the twist-bobbinets face competition from equally fine warp-knit Raschel nets made of synthetic fibre, and of plain cotton nets made on the Curtain machine.

Gore Allen says in his closing pages: 'It was Heathcoat's desire, and the goal of all his striving, to produce by machinery an article which previously had been made by human hands, and to suffer no loss of beauty in the process.'[25] It was a laudable ambition, and it is hoped that its ample fulfilment is demonstrated in this book's account of the Circular machine and its progeny.

IV

The Pusher Machine
(Métier Pusher)

Bobbin-Net Machines and Twist-Net Machines: an explanation

It seems always to be a hazard in the study of lace not only that many different terms have the same meaning, but that one term may be used in many different ways. For anyone unfamiliar with this situation, a glance at the glossary should enlighten them.

The term bobbin-net machine is a cogent example. The Bobbinet machine of today means a traverse net machine, based on the two-tier system of the Old Loughborough which John Heathcoat invented, and its later form, the Circular, it produces a two-twist plain net as it did in 1809. However the entire period from 1809 to nearly 1850 was one of flux. In 1851 the report of the Great Exhibition commented that, in the last 50 years

'. . hundreds of patents had been taken out, and nearly as many differently constructed machines built . . It has been a matter of astonishment to see how quickly one inventor has succeeded another, and by simplifying or modifying his machines, rendered useless those of his predecessors.'[1]

These endless new developments, stimulated by people eager to make their fortunes out of the popular net, created a complex variety of machines, many of them based on an interaction of warp and bobbin threads arranged and moved in a manner similar to Heathcoat's own, and manufacturing a product often nearly indistinguishable. It was therefore quite logical for the whole lot to be called bobbin-net machines, and they were.

It was not until almost the mid-nineteenth century that any consistent attempt was made clearly to separate the various types. In the 1820s, at the time when the Circular was emerging as dominant in the production of plain net, two other models were already establishing themselves as independent producers. These were the Pusher and Levers (now spelt Leavers) machines. In the 1840s a further bobbin-net machine followed, later known as the Curtain, Nottingham Lace Curtain, or Lace Furnishing machine. Two other quite successful forms the Traverse Warp and the Straight Bolt will be dealt with only briefly here since, if any of their products do survive, outside museums, it might still be impossible to distinguish them from those of other machines.

Of the *Traverse Warp*, named because it was the warp not the bobbin threads which passed diagonally across, or traversed, the web, Felkin comments: 'this class of machines furnished few incidents of importance to the trade in after years'. Of the three men most closely concerned with its construction, c.1810–11, John Brown died in 1819 a rich man; and Mr Freeman 'resided for many years at Tewkesbury having realised considerable wealth, it is said, amounting to what is called "a plum".' The third man, the notorious Mr Nunn, transferred his machines to the Isle of Wight, where in 1833 (patent no. 6392) he made a pattern in imitation of French white silk blonde which he called Neige (snow): 'This was sold as real lace without detection during a whole season, it is said, to the amount of £60,000, of which sum probably £40,000 was profit.'[2] Unrepentant at his deceit, Nunn threatened to sue both Birkin and Vickers when they produced the same patterns and articles on other machines. However, 'the pattern had been copied originally from a foreign lace, and the threat was disregarded'. A few Traverse Warps still survived on the Isle of Wight in 1866 though the factory closed down ten years later. Mr Birkin's census of 1862 revealed 125 Traverse Warps in the Nottingham area. Heathcoat praised the machine as a great improvement on his Old Loughborough of 1809, enabling very narrow breadths to be made, which could be used as quillings. Though the machine worked slowly, the texture was excellent, and indeed perhaps superior to any other. Felkin c.1866 formulated its epitaph:

'As a machine for making plain net breadths, the Traverse Warp was unrivalled. When quillings went out of fashion, notwithstanding a simple and effective application of Jacquard apparatus to these frames, they have succumbed to the Levers and have almost disappeared. We hope one of them may make its way to the Kensington [Science] Museum before the remainder are broken up.'[3]

Traverse Warps had of course nothing to do with warp-knitting. Also, the cloth roller where the lace accumulated was at the bottom of the machine as in the Pusher, not at the top as in the Circular.

The *Straight Bolt* was named from the bolts or combs through which the carriages swung being straight instead of forming the arc of a circle, a modification invented by William Morley in 1812. Though the machine could work at a good speed, and was receptive to designs, it suffered always from the variation in length of the bobbin threads as they swung back and forth, which meant that the tension on the threads changed constantly, and the net was irregular. Several Straight Bolts were taken to Calais between 1817 and 1824, but the net was regarded as inferior, and so could not be sold and they ceased to be worked. In 1831 Draper made traversed laces which were all pattern, but 'the Straight Bolts having fallen into disrepute' he gave up his intention.

'Twist-net machines' is an even more general term, referring simply to the net being made by a twisting of threads rather than by looping them as in the Stocking and Warp Frames. All the bobbin-net machines were twist-net machines, and there was in addition a fifth type which worked on quite a different principle and made not a net but a patterned lace. It used bobbins only, had a round not a straight form, and developed as a hybrid between an everyday braiding machine, making non-openwork braids, and a complex and delicate 'Dentellière', which attempted, as it were, to mechanise the actual lace-maker's pillow. Its modern form is known as the Barmen (chapter 7).

The modification of the Old Loughborough which became known as the Pusher is generally regarded as having been invented in 1812 by Samuel Clark and James Mart of Nottingham. No specifications of the original Pusher seem to have survived, and the earliest registered patent which mentions it is dated 1825 (no. 5179). It was issued to Joseph Crowder of New Radford for 'Improvements to the pusher bobbin net machine', the pusher machine referred to being that 'commonly called Crowder and Day's improved Pusher'. His aim was to reduce the number of motions 'requisite to complete the formation of the hole or mesh' from 14 to 10.

Six weeks later another patent (no. 5207) was issued to Crowder's partner Day in collaboration with Hall. This also was for 'an improvement in a pusher twist or bobbin net machine' of a type 'commonly called Kendall and Morley's machine'. One of its suggestions was 'reversing the position of the carriage by placing the ears of the carriage upwards . . by which arrangement the pushers may be used much shorter than the usual length and much of the friction of the threads prevented'.

From this and similar evidence is seems likely that in the early Pusher:

1. The carriages with their bobbins were not worked by a continuous and uniformly-acting shift and fetcher bar as in the Circular. Instead they were propelled along the combs and between the warp threads by long prongs called pushers, equal in number to the carriages, and able to act on them either inde-

pendently or in unison according to the twisting that was required. It was from these pushers that the machine derived its name.

2. The warp beam was placed at the top of the machine so that when the warp and bobbin threads had interacted to make the net it was drawn off downwards to be wound around the cloth roller below.

3. The combs were short, and concave, so that the carriages were only held to them by the tension of the bobbin threads.

4. The carriages and bobbins were arranged in a single tier and this, with the possibility of independent motions, gave a greater potentiality for patterning. At the same time it imparted a slight irregularity to the net which made its imitations of bobbin lace more convincing.

Fig. 69 gives the general lay-out of the Pusher, 'being well understood by competent workmen in the trade' – as it appeared in patent no. 5179 of 1825. Crowder claimed that 'the inverted position of the bobbin carriages, as shown in the Drawings, moving upon single tier circular bolts, are new contrivances and my Invention, but have been used before the date of the above recited Letters Patent.' The patent gives full details, covering four pages, of all the movements involved at each single carriage motion in order to demonstrate how he reduced their number from 14 to 10. The motions are directed by a combination of lockers and pushers, both swinging from above as from the apex of an inverted V, the lockers or fetchers being similar to those 'employed in the levers bobbin net machine' and called there 'catch bars'. The function of the lockers is to slot behind the ears of the carriages as they swing, hauling them up the slopes of the combs, with the help of pusher action, until the lockers of the far side catch the carriage ears in their turn. A synchronisation of comb bar shogs and pusher bar shogs enables a traversing effect of the bobbin threads to be produced, similar to that in Heathcoat's net, in spite of the carriages being all in one row: 'after the 10th motion, at the left end of the machine, a pusher is to be removed from each

of the front comb bars in order to effect what is called the traverse'. Crosses are made twice, in alternating meshes, during the ten motions. These involve the 3rd and 5th motions, and the 8th and 10th.

The completed net is then 'taken down by the points' just as in Heathcoat's machine, but in the reverse direction.

The Pusher held considerable promise, but the complexity of the independent manipulations made it costly and slow to work, and perhaps unattractive to the workmen themselves. A further disadvantage was that the bobbins, being single tier and very thin, could not hold much thread. This reduced the vertical length of lace which could be made at a time, a serious handicap for the retailing of edging or insertion, which might be required in hundreds of yards. The web was also restricted in its width, the maximum possible being quoted as 72 inches. This compared very unfavourably with Heathcoat's machines, 216 inches wide, and upwards. Even in 1922 when a small number of the machines were still active, the largest web size was only 2 yards wide by 4 yards long.[4]

It is not surprising therefore that the ever-increasing pressures of faster and more competitive machines eventually led to the Pusher's demise. In the meantime it produced some rare and exquisite laces.

Products and history

The plain traversed net of the Pusher was indistinguishable from that of the Old Loughborough, or the Circular. On the other hand, the versatile movements of its four pusher bars, two comb bars and one warp guide bar made it more adaptable to patterning than those competitors. A bullet hole net was made on the Pusher in 1829 by John Synyer of Nottingham. The little border of loops or purls along the edge of the lace could be added by machine after about 1827, following an invention by Marmaduke Miller. To preserve the cachet of hand-finishing however the purl trimming was often put on separately when the lace had left the machine.

All sorts of inventions such as blondes

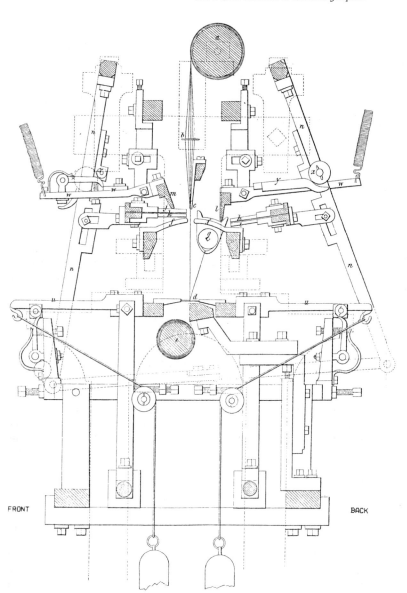

FRONT   BACK

69 *The layout of the Pusher machine, from patent no. 5179 (1825), viewed from the right-hand end. a = warp beam, b = sley, c = guide, d = points, e = work roller, ff = front and back bolts or combs, g = carriage and bobbin, h,i = back pushers, j,k = front pushers, which strike the ears of the bobbin carriages, l = back locker or fetcher bar, n = front and back arms which control the pushers.*

(1831) and spots, controlled by the organ barrel, and made initially for one type of bobbin-net machine, were quickly modified for others. This 'putting on fancies', along with tattings – nets patterned with thicker threads to make a design, and popular for the 'little ruffs à la Queen Elizabeth' during the rather precious years of William IV's reign – gave a great boost to an industry flagging from over-production. A thousand machines, says Felkin, were raised from the price of old iron (£2 to £10 each) to the value of £50 or £100.

The patterned productions of the Pusher were in a range of qualities, some quite exceptionally fine, but the machine never overcame its disadvantages of a slow method of working, limitation in size, and its failure to put in the outlining thread or liner, without which the design lacked any sharp delineation between its 'cloth work ornament' and the open effect of the net.

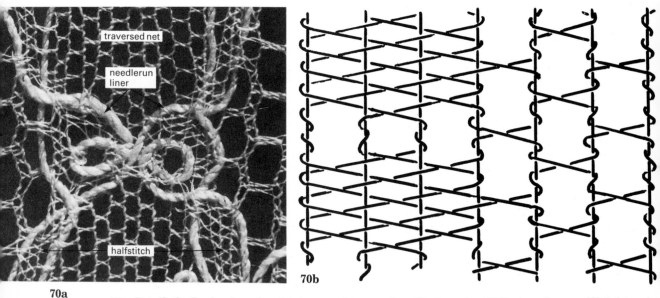

traversed net

needlerun liner

halfstitch

70a

70b

70a *Detail of a Pusher lace showing traversed two-twist bobbinet, half-stitch patterning, and needlerun liner.* **b** *Traversing of the threads in the mesh and pattern areas.*

The putting in of this thread by 'runners', using a running stitch, and working at home, gave a prestigious effect which was of value. Far less desirably it slowed down production, and a customer might have to wait weeks or even months before a really large and elaborate piece was finally completed. In the later nineteenth century it was possible to couch a fine braid (bourdon cord) either by hand or using a Cornely machine, to replace the hand-run liner. This was particularly used when needle laces were copied, such as the French handmade Alençon distinguished by a crisply raised cordonnet around the design. Imitations of Alençon and other needle laces were customarily made on fine gauge 13-point machines.

Many smaller patterns and pieces were made, but the Pusher's tour de force was the large shawls or capes, worked in a competent imitation of bobbin-made Chantilly, and sometimes of such comparable texture that a really close look is needed before its machine origin can be confirmed.

The Jacquard was successfully applied to the Pusher in 1839 by James Wright of Radford. In the large shawls which marked the great flowering of the machine, as many as 5,000 Jacquard cards might be needed for their patterning. A return of black to fashionability at this time opened up a period of prosperity, and the Pusher flourished best between 1850 and 1870 during the time of huge crinolines. Spread over those billowing silks, the Pusher shawls displayed a profusion of floral designs, back-lit by the gown's colourful lustre. Many beautifully designed Pusher shawls and capes of an exceedingly fine and light texture survive in the Western U.S.A. where, for example, the City of Paris store in San Francisco specialized in the importation of top-quality French goods.

The verisimilitude between handmade Chantilly and its Pusher imitation was augmented by the machine's replication of half-stitch or *grille* (fig. 70), an appearance of all Pusher laces, and a useful means of identifying them. It results from the traversing of the bobbin threads and can quite easily be distinguished from the conventionally woven look in many Leavers laces (fig. 71a–h).

In the statistical reports of machines working at various times and in various areas, a clear distinction is not always made between the Pusher and other minority bobbin-net machines. For example in 1833 the number of

Pusher, Straight Bolt and hand-traverse (that is non-rotary Traverse Warp machines worked by hand), averaging 5 quarters (45 inches) in width, in Nottingham, was 750. In 1836 there were 1225 Leavers and 165 Pushers. Six-quarter Pushers in 1825 cost £350 and some were sold in 1833 for only £30, when there seemed no demand left for narrow machines. A census taken by Birkin of the Devon and Nottingham areas in 1862 noted 1797 Circulars, 1588 Leavers, 125 Traverse Warps, 400 Warp Lace, and only 42 Pushers. By 1870, with large shawls outmoded, Pusher machines lost their precarious hold on the English market, they were almost entirely supplanted, their carcases smashed and sold for scrap.

A complete slump in the demand for machine laces occurred at this time. By 1875 of the total of 1400 lace machines at St Pierre (Calais), half were idle.[5] Competition with France in Pusher productions, as in nearly all other machine nets and laces, had long been acute and unrelenting. The little trail of machines drifting across the Channel from England, early included the Stocking Frame, Warp Frame and Old Loughborough. Soon after its invention, the Pusher too was caught up in this illicit trade. In spite of the penalty of deportation (to Australia) if discovered, a 36-inch wide Pusher/Traverse Warp hybrid was set up in Calais, and its manufacture of nets established in a formal ceremony before the Mayor, in 1819. In 1851, Calais had three Pusher machines out of a total of 603 of all kinds. The report of the Paris International Exhibition of 1855 says of the French productions, 'Machine-wrought lace articles are in perfect taste, and the improvements in their manufacture are such in Mechlin, Chantilly, silk blonde and Valenciennes that it is with difficulty even when examined closely that they can be distinguished from the same class made by hand.'[6]

Dognin, at Calais and Lyons, experimented in the use of woollen yarn on the Circular in 1842, attempting to make 'imitations of woollen lace like those made at Puy on the pillow'.[7] This refers to Le Puy, a centre for bobbin laces, some 65 miles south-west of Lyons. Further experiments in wool by Birkin of Nottingham in 1849–51 were on the Leavers machine, but it was the Pushers which made the most effective use of this fibre in their great soft creamy shawls, the colour of mellowed ivory. The wool might be a light worsted from sheep, or long silky mohair from goats, but the resultant shawls were described as 'lama', just as handmade woollen laces, slightly later, were given the exotic name of 'yak', and the popular cream woollen laces of the mid-1870s were advertised as 'dentelles cashmere en nuance crême'.[8] In 1852 Ferguson devised a method of winding mohair yarn on Pusher bobbins, with the Jacquard acting on the carriages rather than on the warps, and with two additional guide bars only. By 1860 Dognin had six Pushers working at Lyons making laces of mohair and silk.

The failure of the Pusher may be attributed to a number of factors: large shawls, for the manufacture of which it was so admirably suited, went out of fashion in the late 1860s; the Franco-Prussian war broke out in 1870, disrupting an important export trade; and the Leavers machine, progressing by leaps and bounds managed, as early as 1841, to put in the liner mechanically, thus saving vast amounts of time and money.

In 1875, however, a new life opened up for surviving Pushers with the invention by Leonard James of a quite different lace article. Abandoning the light delicacy of the Chantilly laces of northern France, the new product embraced the sombre richness of Spain, using Chinese silk of a special quality and brilliance. The bobbin motions and vertical thread shogs had to be specially adapted to make a thick glossy patterning in the form of dense flowers. The new laces were referred to as Spanish blondes (*blonde Espagnole*), like the handmade laces from Bayeux. Stoles, scarves, flounces and those head-coverings characteristic of the province of southern Spain around Seville and known as *andalouses*, were all manufactured in vast quantities. The manufacture of these Pusher lace blondes, in shiny black and white, continued into the second decade of the twentieth century, mostly in Lyons, though reputedly also in Spain, both supported by

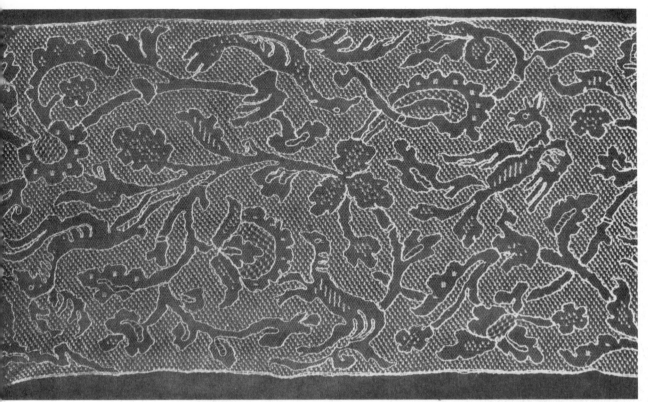

71a *(i)*

71a *(ii)*

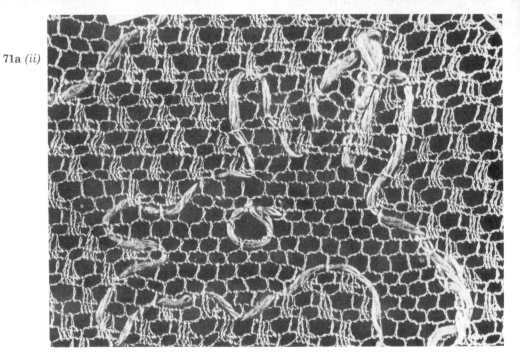

71d

71 *Examples of Pusher laces showing the variety of texture and design which is possible. In each case the clothing (design part) is halfstitch, the net is traversed, and the outline is a later addition:* **a** *(i) hunting scene with ducks, stags, pheasants and hounds; (ii) detail of the pheasant's head.* **b** *Part of a fan leaf of very fine texture.* **c** *Part of a deep edging, with craquelé net and fancy fillings. The irregularity of spinning in the cotton threads shows clearly that they pass diagonally, that is the net is traversed.* **d** *A flounce made crossways of the machine, and with an added purling; the absence of a liner in the net gives the design there a shadowy effect.* **e** *(i) Detail of a lama shawl made of mohair or sheep's wool. Such shawls were square or triangular and very large; (ii) the letter from Dickens and Jones identifies this type of shawl as Creole, and as made in Lyons c.1872.* **f** *The more densely-textured pattern of the post-*

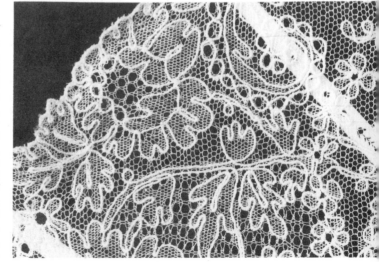

71b

103

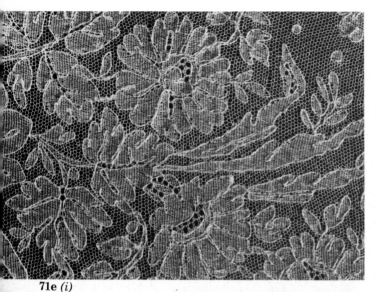

71e *(i)*

Memorandum

From
DICKINS & JONES, LTD.,
HANOVER HOUSE,
232, 234, 236, 238, 240, 242, 244, REGENT STREET,
26A, 26, 27 & 29, 30, 31, 32, 33, ARGYLL STREET,
AND 7 & 8, LITTLE ARGYLL STREET,
LONDON, W.
TELEGRAPHIC ADDRESS, "DEEANJAY, LONDON."   TELEPHONE No. 3640 (GERRARD).

71e *(ii)*

71f

1870s: a heavy shiny silk highlights the design against a finer matt ground; a liner has been used only in restricted areas, for additional emphasis.
g *The delicacy of the flowing floral design of (f) contrasts with this dense all-over design suitable for dress fabrics. The horizontal and vertical repeats are very large, and the liner (cordonnet or bourdon cord) has been put on by the Cornely machine in a continuous manner, to save the cost of hand-finishing. Width of repeat 16 inches, height $9\frac{1}{2}$ inches.*
h *Detail of a glossy black stole of a type very popular at the beginning of the twentieth century. The effect of shading around the fan leaf is achieved by an alternation of lightly- and densely-packed half-stitch. The parallel vertical lines of the warp threads are clearly visible, and help to confirm the lace's machine origin.*

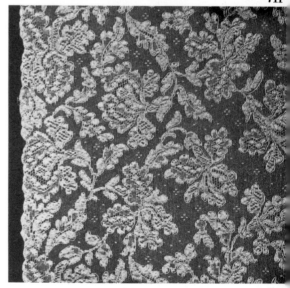

71g

local silk resources. After that, there is mostly silence.

A retailer's brochure of machine laces *c.*1920 lists 'Real Alençon' (fig. 72), and continues

This very special lace is made only in Lyons, France, on a very old bobbinet Jacquard machine. It differs from the commonly used Alençon-type [Leavers] lace in that the cordonnet is hand-run by machine around the design; the edge is turned back, hand-rolled and sewn to make a scalloped edge.

Though the Pusher is not named, the 'hand-running by machine' – presumably by a Cornely which is hand-operated – could scarcely apply to anything else at that time. Nor were there any other kinds of bobbinet machines operating solely in Lyons.

Varley, in 1959, refers to 'modern' Pushers still working at Lyons, 'specialising in a narrow range of silk nets' though none had worked in England since the late nineteenth century.

One of the people connected with the Pusher in its early days was a John Levers junior, working in association with the manufacturer, Mr James Fisher. In the boom of the 1820s he boasted that he was worth as many hundreds of pounds as the years of his age, which was 33. He invested his money in machinery, Pushers at the time costing between £480 and £550. But, no better favoured by fortune than his uncle had been, the value of his machines fell in the slump of the 1830s to a mere £120 each, and his capital dwindled away. In 1835 he took out patent no. 6778, with Pedder, for improvements to the Pusher,

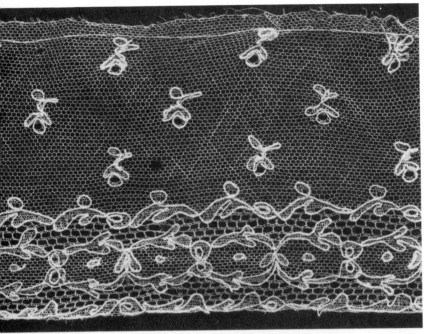

72a

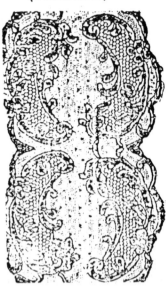

72b

72c

72a *The decadent 'Real Alençon' of the 1920s, made on the Pusher machine, with a Cornely liner.* b *Its advertisement.* c *The needle lace Alençon, made by hand since the early eighteenth century, ceased production in 1914. This example, c.1860, was copied faithfully by contemporary Pusher machines which were then at the height of their production (see fig.* 72d).

but little more is known of him except that he died two years later, in Nottingham, in poor and dependent circumstances.[9] His brother, Robert Levers, was for several years until 1847 a foreman at Fisher's factory. John and Robert were nephews of John Levers, the originator of the very eminent machine which will be considered in the next chapter.

V

The Leavers Machine

(*Métier Leaver, sometimes called Métier Jacquard*)

The Leavers machine follows the general pattern of other twist-net machines in having two main divisions of threads, the horizontal (bobbin) moving between front and back, and the vertical stretched from one or more rollers below to a cloth- or work-roller above. In the fully-developed machine, the vertical threads are divisible into two sets, the warps which make the ground, and the beams which make the patterned part. Heathcoat's general term 'beams' for his front and back warps can therefore no longer be applied.

As with the Circular and Pusher, the bobbin threads are held on emaciated spools, packed 20 or more to every inch across the machine's width. The spools are supported in carriages which have protrusions, like the ears of the Old Loughborough, by which they are gripped and hurled to and fro at vast speeds. However, the carriages occupy only a single row as in the Pusher, not a double one as in the Circular.

What particularly distinguishes the Leavers is its extremely complex arrangements for patterning, which may involve hundreds of beam rollers, and an equivalent number of guide bars to shift the beam threads to the parts of the design where they are required to be locked in by the bobbin threads before returning to their starting point, or to whatever other position the pattern requires. This complex patterning is made possible by an equally complex Jacquard system.

Another distinguishing feature of the Leavers is its immense size. Although the machine began with a width of 18 inches, it soon progressed through 54 inches to 152 inches (1862) and 166 inches (1875), and eventually to 224 inches. There was even a Goliath of 260 inches.[1] This spectacular increase was concomitant with increase in demand and, up to a certain point, the bigger the machine, the cheaper the product. However, in a falling market, the large machines quickly became an impediment, and today most Leavers machines in England have a working width of between 186 and 202 inches, with an overall carcase width of 360 inches. In general, the narrower machines can work more quickly. They have a height of about 120 inches, and a weight of 17 tons, with some 40,000 moving parts. The total number of threads varies between 12,000 and 50,000 according to the size and complexity of the design, and can be sufficient in total length to stretch half way round the world. The working widths are always in multiples of 9 inches since the lace, or web, is measured in quarters (quarter yards).

History

The Leavers was initially a modification of the Old Loughborough, and only later became a quite distinct machine. According to tradition and William Felkin, the Leavers machine was invented in 1813 by a Mr John Levers, a framesmith and setter-up of Sutton-in-Ashfield.[2] Ferguson and Hénon both give the date as 1814. Levers' labours were 'carried on in a garrett at the top of a building situated in a yard on the northern side of Derby Road [Nottingham]; and so quietly and secretly as not to be seen by anyone, even of his own family'. We have Felkin's and Ferguson's word for it that the original idea was to make the 18-inch wide machine horizontal rather than vertical, in order to avoid any infringement of Heathcoat's 1809 patent.[3] In 1817 Levers 'altered his machines from a horizontal to an upright position, and built many of them yearly.'[4]

There has been from time to time a good deal of speculation and controversy over the spelling of the inventor's name. The trade name of the machine, and its products, now and for a number of years past, has been Leavers, but all the patent specifications up to at least 1930 give Levers. Felkin, in his invaluable *History*, published in 1867, uses 'Levers' throughout, although Ferguson, writing in French in 1862, already has doubts and refers to 'the system Lever or Leaver'. Henri Lemaire in his complex technical handbook for the machine manufacure of Valenciennes lace, published in 1906, consistently uses 'Leavers'. So does Hénon (1900), while Murphy who edited *The Textile Industries*, published in 1910, uses 'Levers'. It seems a reasonable assumption that the inventor's name was Levers, and that the commercial transition to Leavers dates from the twentieth century, and may have originated in France. According to Varley, the Lace Working Party of 1946 came to the firm conclusion that an 'a' should be included. 'The trade association thereupon adopted it,' he says, though he himself retained serious doubts in the matter.

Ferguson says that there were three John Levers: father, son and nephew.[5] According to Felkin, Levers had no son but two brothers and a nephew John.[6] There is in short no general agreement, and insufficient is known about any of them for the roles they may have played in the machine's invention to be uncompromisingly defined. The first patents bearing the name John Levers were issued to the nephew in 1828 (nos. 5622 and 5741, followed by no. 5940 in 1830) (fig. 73a). The first two relate to the application of rotary power to the Circular and Levers machines; the third is for using a roller locker on the Levers.

The Leavers machine abandoned the origi-

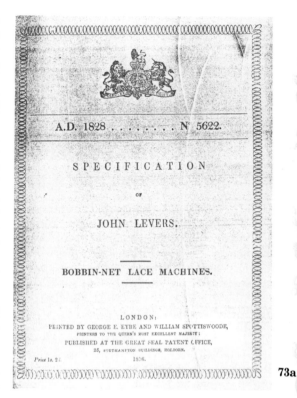

73a *The title page of John Levers junior's patent specification of 1828 (no. 5622).* **b** *Thread paths in one form of untraversed net. The bobbin threads run straight down, and the front warps alternately loop and pillar. There is no reverse warp to tie the loops, and they would tend to slip making the net unstable, 1840s.*

nal two-tier system of carriages but continued to produce traversed net by separating its single tier into back and front sets of carriages at the appropriate moment. These sets were then shogged one gait before being brought back again to their single row. This technique was replaced in the 1830s by straight down or untraversed, nets (fig. 73b). A restricted traversing of front warp threads was developed a good deal later, and was called the Lyons technique.

A feature particularly mentioned in the 1828 patent was an 'improvement in the reciprocating action' which would cause the machine 'to drive the bobbin carriages at

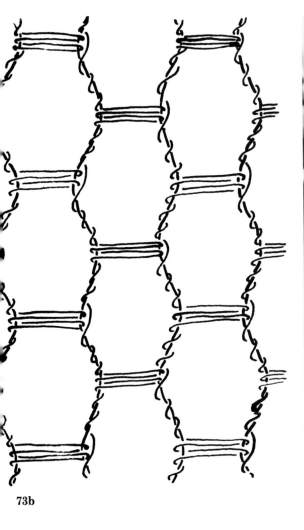

73b

74 *A knob Jacquard: each 'card' has raised knobs of wood which activate droppers and direct the liner.*

intervals, thereby leaving time between each movement [motion] for the shogging of the guide bars.' This was subsequently of great importance for patterning.

The putting in of the thick thread or liner on the machine was first achieved by Wragg in 1841 using a knob Jacquard (fig. 74). Knobs of wood were used instead of holes in the 'cards' to act on guide bars

forcing them to greater distances, and thus got gimp threads around the flowered patterns, which had before been put in by the needle. This was a great discovery, operating however to displace the labour of many embroiderers . . This was not an unmitigated evil, for the labour was unhealthy,

and of late years ill-paid for long hours and close application.'[7]

The Leavers, in the same way as other machines, suffered intermittently from over-production and slump, and the Nottingham trade suffered from competition with Calais and Lyons. Inventors and manufacturers continued to emigrate – as they had to France in the heyday of the Warp Frame, and to America in the 1820s. Ferguson *père* left England for France in 1838 at the time of the American commercial crisis. However during the French revolution of 1848 when Louis Philippe d'Orleans was deposed, many ex-Nottingham twisthands fled back again, arriving destitute. 'A public subscription was commenced on their behalf which amounted to a total of £600' and 'the greater portion of them were removed to Australia'.[8]

Russia, like France, had her eyes on the apparent gold mine of Nottingham lace. In the autumn of 1833 a Russian agent arrived 'for the purpose of filling a secret factory on the steppes with smuggled lace machines' which would constitute a 'source of danger to the textile industries of England'. The export of lace machinery was still illegal not only in England but also in France, where any person caught was liable to ten years imprisonment with hard labour and, in addition, 'had to stand for one hour after being sentenced with an iron collar round his neck in the public market-place'. Yet with no great delay this agent acquired 13 'tulle looms' (five Bobbinet and eight Leavers) at amazingly low prices, and with none of the expected resistance from the Customs men. Unknown to him, his surreptitious activities had coincided with a period of depression, and manufacturers were only too delighted to unload onto him their many useless machines, 400 'infinitely better machines having been broken up for old iron' only a few months previously.[9]

In 1862, at the time of the American Civil War, an acute shortage of cotton advanced the price of yarns by 75%. At the time of the world slump in 1926 the number of Leavers in use dropped dramatically, 'insurance fires' were rife, and many machines were sold for scrap at £50 a piece. The Working Party of 1947 reported 'The Leavers section has encountered violent slumps in the last forty years.' The current cost of a Leavers machine is £110,000. The danger for Leavers has perhaps never been greater than in the past two decades, with the rapid development of Raschels in the field of openworks. In 1970, W.R. Evans wrote: 'In the last two years the whole of the trade in lace has declined

slightly, about 4% overall, while in the same period Raschel products have grown 40%.'[10] Even Leavers' advantage of working well on natural fibres, while the Raschel is largely restricted to synthetics, is being eroded by the development of spun polyesters which look and feel remarkably like cotton. Its designs too are being copied, so that Raschels are converging on Leavers laces, and the two techniques have become very hard to distinguish, except when a magnifier pinpoints the tiny lines of chainstitch which in Raschel hold the whole thing together.

The parts of the machine (figs. 75a,b)

The long threads which extend from the bottom to the top of the machine are of two types:

Warps There may be two, one or no warp rollers. Where there is one, its threads have an S-twist, that is their fibres have been spun in a clockwise direction. Where there are two warps, the second has a Z-twist, its fibres having been spun in an anti-clockwise direction. The two warps are distinguished as: S-twist or front warp, right warp, warp; Z-twist or back warp, reverse warp, left twist, left warp, or reversed thread.

Both front and reverse warps are equal in number to the bobbin threads. For example if the machine has 3,000 bobbins, there will be 3,000 front warps, or front warp ends, all arising from one roller. When a reverse warp is present it will also have 3,000 ends arising from one roller. All the warp ends pass through a grid called a sley so that they are kept apart from each other and there is no possibility of tangling. To accommodate them, 6,000 separate sley-perforations have to be made.

All the 3,000 front warp ends must be of the same count, and so must all the 3,000 reverse warp ends, but there is no need for them to be the same as each other, and the reverse warp may be either finer or coarser than the front. The terms 'front and back warps' are not comparable with those on Heathcoat's machine where both sets come from the same roller, and so have identical threads.

The main function of the warp threads is to

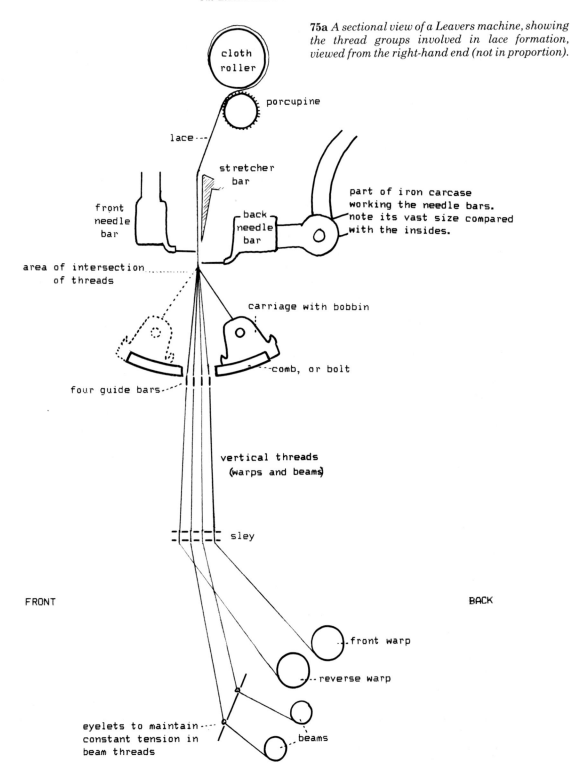

75a *A sectional view of a Leavers machine, showing the thread groups involved in lace formation, viewed from the right-hand end (not in proportion).*

cloth roller

porcupine

lace ---

stretcher bar

part of iron carcase working the needle bars. note its vast size compared with the insides.

front needle bar

back needle bar

area of intersection of threads

carriage with bobbin

comb, or bolt

four guide bars ---

vertical threads (warps and beams)

sley

FRONT

BACK

front warp

reverse warp

eyelets to maintain constant tension in beam threads

beams

75a

111

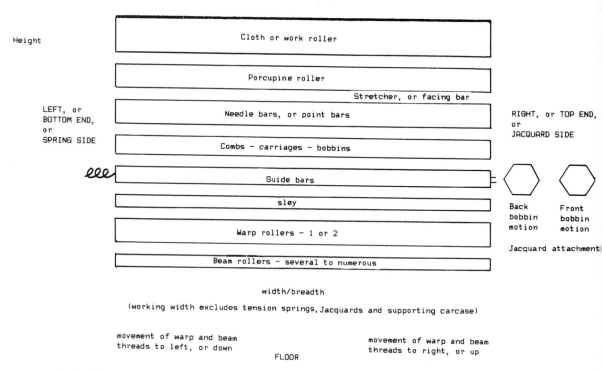

Height

LEFT, or BOTTOM END, or SPRING SIDE

| Cloth or work roller |
| Porcupine roller |
| Stretcher, or facing bar |
| Needle bars, or point bars |
| Combs – carriages – bobbins |
| Guide bars |
| sley |
| Warp rollers – 1 or 2 |
| Beam rollers – several to numerous |

RIGHT, or TOP END, or JACQUARD SIDE

Back bobbin motion   Front bobbin motion

Jacquard attachment

width/breadth

(working width excludes tension springs, Jacquards and supporting carcase)

movement of warp and beam threads to left, or down

FLOOR

movement of warp and beam threads to right, or up

75b *A schematic front view of a Leavers machine.*

interact with the bobbin threads to form the openwork ground which links together the parts of the design (known as solids, gimping, fining, platting, objects, motifs or set clusters). A ground formed of only two sets of threads, front warps and bobbins, is unstable, as the threads tend to slip and slide. Reverse warps were introduced in the 1830s to lock the front warps against the bobbin threads, thus creating an untraversed net. To keep all the threads taut the tension on them is set by a spring at about six pounds, though this can be varied in different techniques.

Beams These are primarily patterning threads, and they achieve their versatility by being independently controlled. They act mainly in the patterned areas, and each beam contributes one thread to each horizontal repeat (fig. 76). The simplified diagram is intended to explain what is meant by a horizontal repeat, a vertical repeat, and one design motif. Probably 30 or more beams would be involved, each contributing one thread to the pattern area in each repeat, whether an all-over fabric or a series of bands is being produced. Thus while the number of warp ends per warp roller is equal to the number of bobbin threads, the number of beam ends per beam roller is only equal to the total number of horizontal repeats.

The total number of beam rollers required is determined by the size and complexity of the design. In theory, and sometimes in practice, 400 may be needed. More usually the number is far less, say between 50 and 150, and even this makes for a complicated drafting and setting-up procedure.

The independence of movememt of the beam threads means not only that an almost unlimited range of designs can be produced, but also that endless artistic variations of colour, texture and fibre are possible. On each roller, the beam threads must be the same, but if there are 50 rollers these could in

112

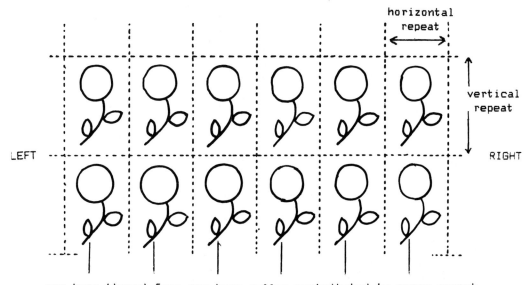

one beam thread from one beam roller contributed to every repeat

76 *Vertical and horizontal repeats.*

theory at least all be different. Like the warp ends, the beams must pass through the grid of the sley so that they are securely held and at the same time isolated from their closely crowded neighbours.

Sley The sley is simply a strong wire mesh full of thousands of tiny holes. It stretches across the entire width of the machine, and extends about 12 inches between front and back (fig. 77a). Its function, as already mentioned, is to prevent entanglement of front warp, reverse warp and beam threads by separating them into different holes. It also serves a secondary function of holding their roots in a constant position. This is important since not far above the sley the threads begin to interact and lock together, shifting this way and that as they do so, so that there is a recurrent strain as though a strong but erratic wind swept through them, and only their fixed and stable base enables them to regain their natural position. The beam threads from one roller are uniformly threaded and can act only in unison, but beams from different rollers can and do act independently.

The order in which the threads are passed through the sley, every one by hand, is called the *set-out*. It will vary with the pattern to be created, and also with the particular Leavers technique which is to be used. Fig. 77b shows a possible set-out, from back to front of the machine, in a technique known as Centre Gimp. It requires in all: 80 reverse warps; 24 beam threads; 80 front warps; 4 backs and fronts (additional beam threads to stabilize the heading and footing of the band, and including lacers and purls); 28 liners (thick outlining threads); and 4 selvage threads, for all-over laces only.

The set-out needs to be drawn only for one repeat. If there are eight repeats widthwise then this sequence of threading will be repeated eight times across the width of the machine. If there are 40 repeats, it will be repeated 40 times, and so on.

As soon as the manufacture of one design has been completed, the machine must be dismantled, and rethreaded for another design. Then the holes pricked in the sley have to be blocked in, using soap and lampblack with a covering of varnish. The dark colour makes the threads more easily visible, while the varnish gives a firm surface. The pricking of the new set-out can then begin.

*77a The sley, showing how all the warp ends and beam threads, rising up from the warp and beam rollers below, are slotted through meshes pierced in the wire grid. Each repeat is separated by a narrow path. **b** The sley plan for threading a single repeat of 144 bars on an 80-carriage centre gimp set-out. The odd numbers are arranged on the left, the even on the right (Abur Pegg, Long Eaton).*

Suppose this to be as in fig. 78. A simple calculation will show how many holes have to be pricked. If the width of the design is two inches, and the width of the machine 224 inches, the set-out will have to be pricked in its entirety 112 times (i.e. 224 ÷ 2).

Here, each repeat involves 128 beam threads, making a total of 14,336 holes (i.e. 128 × 112). Subsequently 14,336 threads will have to be passed one through every hole, by hand, a time-consuming process which adds considerably to the cost of the lace.

Fig. 78, as drawn, indicates not only the origin of the threads but their destination, a set of guide bars which can slide between right and left of the machine, displacing by their movements the yarns which are threaded through them, that is they guide those threads to the particular spot which the pattern at any moment requires them to occupy. Warps and beams, moved by bars, are sometimes referred to collectively as 'bar threads'.

Guide bars, or *bars* The guide bars are similar to the ribbon bars of the Circular machine.

Originally the threads passed through little eyelets, but in 1849 a patent (no. 12897) was taken out by James Oldknow to replace the soldered-on eyelets with holes punched equidistantly (fig. 79a, b).

The guide bars must extend beyond the working width of the machine since their movements are controlled by the Jacquard apparatus which lies to the right, and by springs which lie to the left. The bars form part of the *insides* of the machine, which are of extreme delicacy, in contrast to the hefty iron *carcase* which weighs many tons. In the early days of the twist-net machines smiths were hired to make the frame – Levers himself was a frame-smith – while clock- and watch-makers were in demand for the manufacture of the delicate precision parts. In the set-out shown in fig. 78 the slender bars which hold the beam threads are only .01 inch thick, and made of watchspring steel. They have to be tough enough to survive the endless strong tugs in opposing directions to which they are subjected, and to do this without either expansion of fatigue.

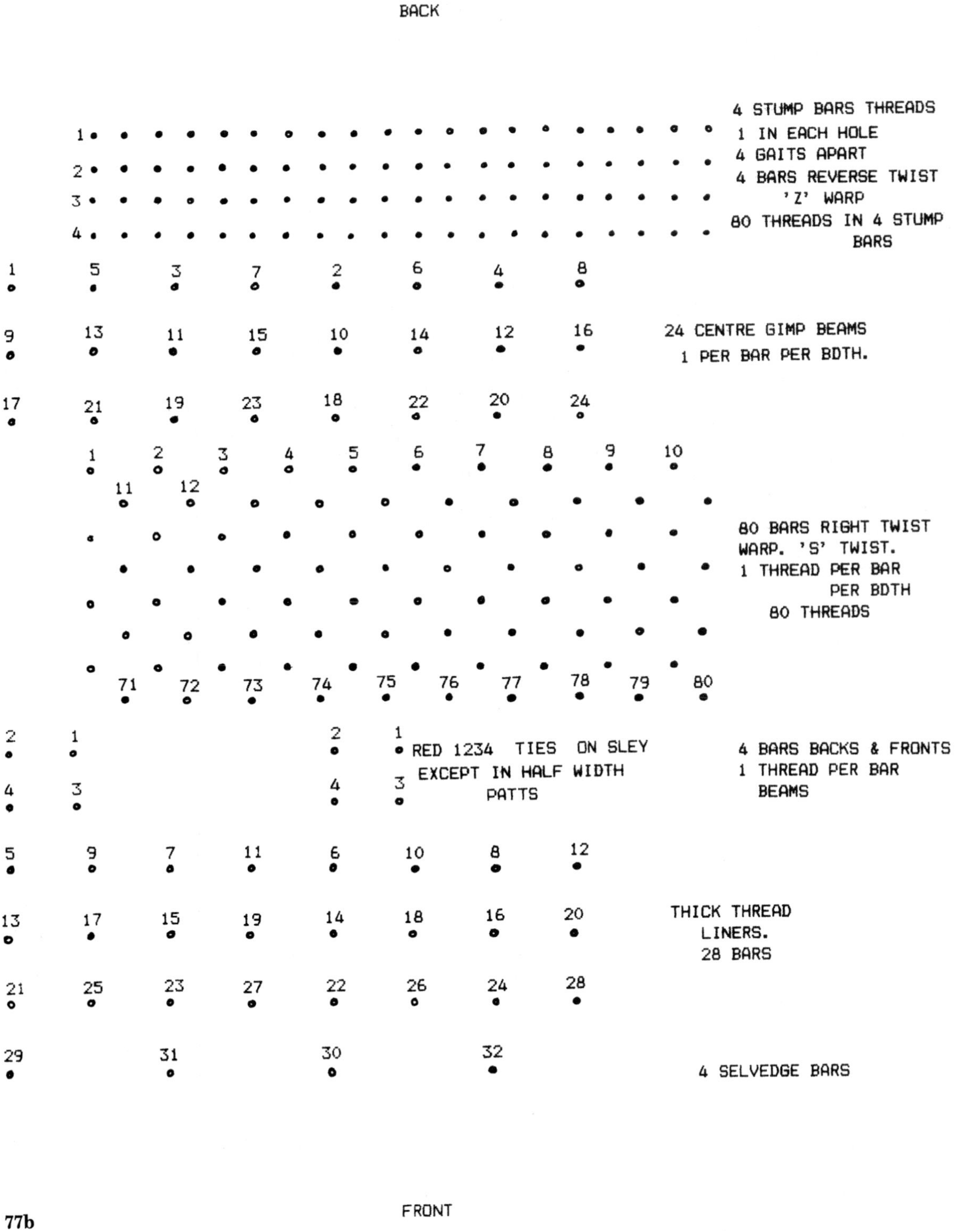

The Leavers Machine

BACK

4 STUMP BARS THREADS
1 IN EACH HOLE
4 GAITS APART
4 BARS REVERSE TWIST
'Z' WARP
80 THREADS IN 4 STUMP
BARS

1   5   3   7   2   6   4   8

9   13   11   15   10   14   12   16   24 CENTRE GIMP BEAMS
1 PER BAR PER BDTH.

17   21   19   23   18   22   20   24

1   2   3   4   5   6   7   8   9   10

11   12

80 BARS RIGHT TWIST
WARP. 'S' TWIST.
1 THREAD PER BAR
PER BDTH
80 THREADS

71   72   73   74   75   76   77   78   79   80

2   1   2   1
   RED 1234 TIES ON SLEY   4 BARS BACKS & FRONTS
4   3   4   3 EXCEPT IN HALF WIDTH   1 THREAD PER BAR
PATTS   BEAMS

5   9   7   11   6   10   8   12

13   17   15   19   14   18   16   20   THICK THREAD
LINERS.
28 BARS

21   25   23   27   22   26   24   28

29   31   30   32   4 SELVEDGE BARS

77b

FRONT

115

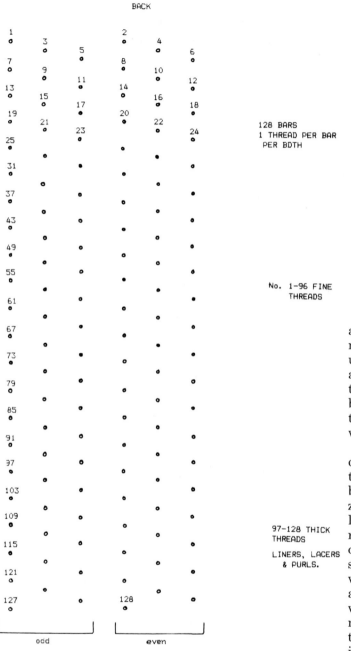

BACK

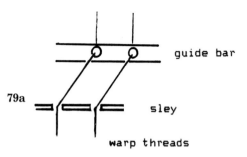

guide bar

79a

sley

warp threads

128 BARS
1 THREAD PER BAR
PER BDTH

No. 1-96 FINE
THREADS

97-128 THICK
THREADS

LINERS, LACERS
& PURLS.

79 *The holes punched in the machine's numerous guide bars allow the passage of warp and beam threads:* **a** *threads rise from holes in the stationary sley to pass through holes in the moving guide bars.* **b** *the arrangement of the bars, simplified. The staggering of the threads, so that adjacent sley threads do not go through adjacent bars, has been omitted.* **c** *the guide bars from above, showing the order of numbering.*

odd   even

78 *A sley plan for a single repeat of a 48-carriage independent beam set-out. The dots are angled to prevent friction between the bars which hold the vertical threads. The numbers are those of the guide bars (Abur Pegg).*

Every beam roller has its own guide bar, and the number of bars will vary with the number of rollers, which in turn is dependent upon the design – in the above example 128 are present. Each beam roller supplies one thread per design repeat (i.e. one thread per breadth), thus its bar will hold as many threads as there are horizontal repeats, which in fig. 78 was 112.

In the set-out fig. 77b, each front warp end, or thread, also has its own bar. In this case there are 80 front warp bars, plus 24 beam bars, each contributing one thread per horizontal repeat. Such individual threading allows great versatility of movement. The 80 reverse warps on the other hand are allocated only four bars, known as *stump bars*. Each stump bar will hold a quarter of the reverse warps – 20 in this example – for every repeat, and therefore across the whole working width each stump bar will carry (20 × the number of repeats) that is 20 times as many threads as each patterning bar. The labour of its displacement will thus be 20 times greater, and the stump bars have to be stronger and heavier than the others. As will be seen later they are a means of increasing the possible width or complexity of a horizontal repeat by removing the back warps from Jacquard control.

116

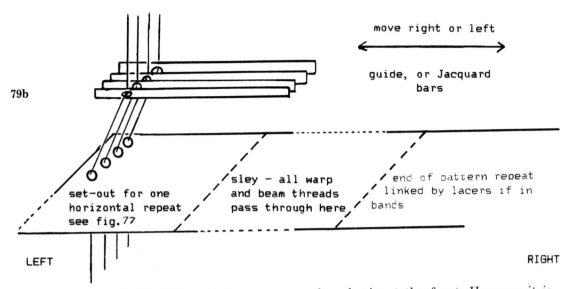

79b

move right or left

guide, or Jacquard bars

sley – all warp and beam threads pass through here

end of pattern repeat linked by lacers if in bands

set-out for one horizontal repeat see fig.77

LEFT

RIGHT

All the bars are held side by side in a bar box or casing which lies in the *well*, immediately below the inner ends of the front and back combs. The bars are kept apart from each other only by the minutest of metal brackets. These enable each bar to slide freely in either direction, without friction.

As the various threads leave the sley they do not pass vertically upwards, but instead slope off to the right, sometimes for as much as two inches, before finding their hole in the appropriate bar and ducking through it to emerge on the other side and pass straight upwards again. This angling ensures that the threads actually rest against the lower left hand side of the guide bar hole, which steadies them and prevents their floating uncertainly about as the bars slide.

The bars are numbered in arithmetical sequence from back to front of the machine (fig. 79c) in contrast to Raschel where the

numbers begin at the front. However it is clear from the two examples of sley set-outs that consecutive beam threads on the sley do not pass through adjacent bars. The object of this separation is to reduce the hazards of friction and entanglement which might result from a too-close proximity of moving threads. Thus the beam threads in the first row of the fig. 77b set-out are separated to go through bars 1, 5, 3, 7, 2, 6, 4, and 8 respectively.

The distinct right-left movements of the many guide bar threads enables them to interact with different bobbin threads on successive motions, and so to form an intricate and extended design.

Bobbins, carriages, combs and *gaits* All these terms have the same meaning as in the Circular machine, and the structures are basically similar, although the Leavers machine has only one set of bobbin threads instead of two, and the method of their propulsion is to some extent different (fig. 80a).

The number of carriages per half-inch width of the machine is known as its gauge. In Leavers the gauge usually varies between 9 and 16, with 12 being the finest used today. A $4\frac{1}{2}$ gauge was used by Messrs William Fletcher in the early twentieth century to imitate a Barmen lace; while a 14-gauge machine was

79c

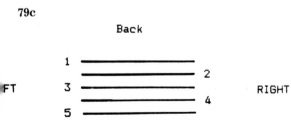

Back

1

2

3

4

5

FT

RIGHT

Front

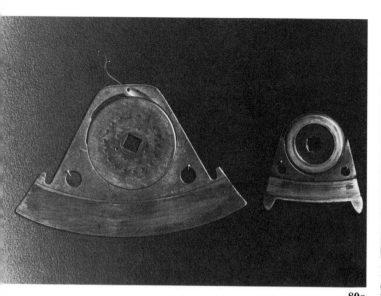

80a

8

80a *A twentieth-century Leavers machine carriage, left, and a double locker Bobbinet carriage, right.* **b** *The caravelle of Christopher Columbus, R. West, 1893 (Hénon, p. 445).*

sold to Japan in the 1970s. A coarser 10-gauge is used for many classes of work. Fig. 77b is described as an '80-carriage set-out', meaning that the horizontal repeat involves the action of 80 bobbin threads. On a 10-gauge machine there would be 20 carriages, or bobbin threads, per inch. Therefore 80 carriages would represent a 4-inch wide repeat. Thus, if the machine is 224 inches wide, it would hold 4,480 carriages (i.e. 20 × 224).

By the same token, 56 repeats, four inches wide, could be fitted into this working breadth (i.e. 224 ÷ 4 = 56).

In movement, the row of carriages hurtles down the curved slope of the comb slots, across the well, passing between the ranks of warp and beam threads, and up the other side. In the momentary hiatus before they return the vertically stretched threads are swayed by the gliding bars to right or left so that they can pause, quite still, at another gait before the carriages whoosh past again.

The speed of the bobbin swings is fixed by the crank shaft at a pace of around 120 to 140 motions a minute, where a motion is defined

as the swing of a carriage from the front to the back of the machine, or vice versa. Even 180 motions a minute were achieved at Lyons in 1890,[11] when Leavers machines were at their peak, before the competition of the Schiffli machines started them on a slow decline (see chapter 8).

In the heyday of the end of the century, gauges as high as 18 were worked at Calais,[12] but obviously the higher the number, the closer the threads movements to each other, and the vastly greater the hazard that, swaying and crossing over distances a mere $\frac{1}{36}$ inch apart, more than 100 times a minute, they would collide. The 18-gauge machines were in consequence extremely delicate, and proportionately costly to run. The slightest expansion of the steel of the guide bars must throw the warp and beam threads out of position so that the carriages crash through them, cutting all the threads down, and ruining the web. Nevertheless an example of a 'Chantilly' lace worked on an 18-gauge Leavers machine survives in the Museum at Calais. It was made by Robert West for the Chicago Exhibition of 1893, and shows the caravelle of Christopher Columbus, with billowing sails (fig. 80b).[13]

In Nottingham, only four 16-gauge machines were ever made, for Birkin and Co., but they were scrapped in 1939 as too complicated for use. Even for 12-gauge, a certain temperature is needed to start them, and any higher gauge would be that much more critical. Also the fineness of the work of the high gauge machines requires extremely fine thread, such as top quality Sea Island cotton, itself expensive. Even then, the smallest irregularity in the spinning would stop the machine, while any dryness of the air would cause the threads to snap. In the last quarter of the twentieth century, only the lower gauge machines are economic.

For convenience, the direction of the carriage swings are described as *front motions*, or the movement of the carriages from the back combs to the front combs; and *back motions*, or the movement of the carriages from the front combs to the back combs. Back and front motions combined make one *full motion*.

The direction of the guide bar movements, or throws, are described as to the right, a *rise*, or going up; and to the left, a *fall*, or falling back. Warp and beam threads may throw to either the right or to the left on either the front or back bobbin motion.

It is the meticulous alternation of these two sets of movements, at right angles to each

FROM ABOVE:

BACK

LEFT   RIGHT

FRONT

81 *Throws and motions: the movements of carriages and guide bars at right angles to each other in a horizontal plane.*

```
1-4=back and forth bobbin swings (motions)

X and Y = side to side(right-left, left-right)
          warp and beam deflections (throws or shogs)
```

```
FROM FRONT OF MACHINE:
```

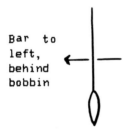

Bar to left, behind bobbin

Front motion(bobbin at front of comb)

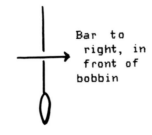

Bar to right, in front of bobbin

Back motion(bobbin at back of comb)

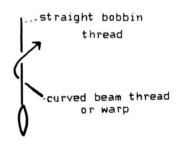

...straight bobbin thread

-curved beam thread or warp

Result

119

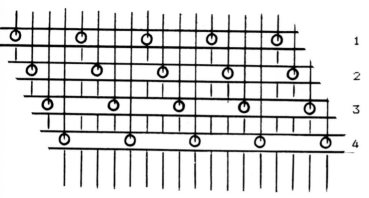

82 *Diagram to show the threading of a set of four stump bars.*

other, which enables the threads to twist together, with a variety of partners, and so produce the lace:

front motion – throw – back motion – throw – front motion . . . (fig. 81).

Since the resting places of the warps and beams, during the bobbin motions, is at the gaits, their throws are described in terms such as a 1-gait, 2-gait or 3-gait throw, referring to the number of comb-slots or carriage-positions which they cross in going from one gait to another.

Similarly, the bars which hold the warps or beams are punched with holes at the gaits, since this is where they stand when the machine is at a stop, or not working. The punching is usually at 4-gait intervals, but the bars will be threaded only as the pattern requires: in fig. 77b for example at every 80th gait for both front warps and beams. The 80 reverse warps, however, being allocated only four bars (stumps), must be threaded every fourth gait if they are to cover the total number of gaits in the machine (fig. 82). Thus, working together, they are responsible for the close uniformity of movements which constitutes the net or ground of the lace.

In setting up the machine the gaits are not numbered in sequence across the whole width – which would make for clumsiness where 4,000 or 5,000 gaits are involved – but in terms of the displacement of warp or beam threads from their starting point. Thus the numbering for each thread begins at zero or dead

stop, which is its resting position when not being pulled in either direction. The first displacement of a thread, for example across three carriages, would then be from gait 0 to gait 3 (fig. 83).

The throws of the guide bars are controlled by the Jacquard through a complex device which includes a set of droppers reacting with a pulsating drive blade which, via a lever, operates a draw bar. The Jacquard causes displacement of the guide bars to the right, while counterweighting springs draw them back again to the left.

It is however the catch bars, driven by the crank shaft, which hurl the carriages in their headlong swing, and set the rapid pace of the machine, meticulously synchronizing the guide bar throws, the bobbin motions, the rotation of the Jacquard cards, and the pulse of the drive blades so that they follow one after the other without pause or break in the relentless rhythm.

What the catch bars do is to catch the ears of the carriages, and pull them first in one direction and then in the other (fig. 84a,b). They can however work in two quite distinct ways:

1. *Landing Bar*. This was the earlier form, which consisted of two brass bars, one beneath each set of combs, running the width of the machine. These landing bars worked in unison with the catch bars, above the combs, and supplemented their propulsion. The catch bars themselves worked on a pusher and fetcher principle, catching the carriages by their ears, or nibs, on their upward swing, then in effect running forward a little to shoot them back down the curved slope of the comb to be caught by the catch bars on the other side; rather in the manner of two grown-ups alternately pushing and catching a child on a swing, so that their hands come up once full, and once empty.

2. *Go-through* (fig. 85). This was invented in 1835 by Thomas Alcock, but was not perfected, or commercially productive, until 1875. It was further improved in 1904. It dispensed with the landing bars, and could control two bobbin motions by a single turn of the crank shaft. The two catch bars, at the same time,

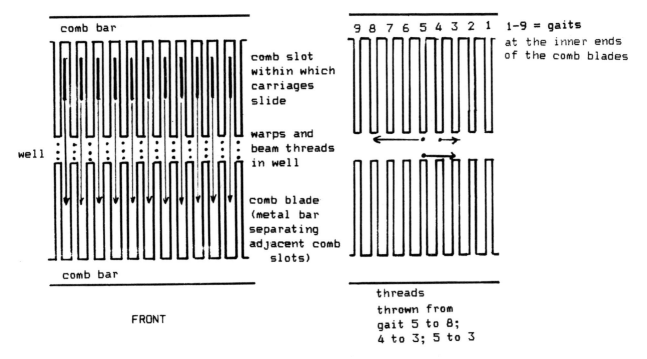

BACK

comb bar

comb slot
within which
carriages
slide

warps and
beam threads
in well

well

comb blade
(metal bar
separating
adjacent comb
slots)

comb bar

FRONT

9 8 7 6 5 4 3 2 1   1-9 = gaits
at the inner ends
of the comb blades

threads
thrown from
gait 5 to 8;
4 to 3; 5 to 3

83 *Combs from above, showing the throws (right-left movements) of warp and beam threads, always starting and stopping at a gait.*

were replaced by a single carriage bar. This, instead of pushing the line of 3,000 or so carriages away, hung on to them, going forward with them the full extent of the rather short combs, and then bringing them back again, as if the carriage bar were a very very long hanging cradle, rocking an attenuated baby backwards and forwards in its arms with immense speed. This fast, short movement was gentler than the Landing Bar, and enabled the machine to turn out four racks an hour compared with the Landing-bar's three, for the same quality.

The two types of machine are now sometimes referred to as the Leavers and Go-through, that is the term Leavers is used only of the Landing Bar, though apart from the variation in the drive mechanism the two are very similar. Landing Bar machines are now obsolete in England, but still used in Calais. Their more leisurely pause at the end of each motion enables longer throws – up to 12 gaits – to be made, to the great advantage of the design.

The bobbin threads are not affected directly by the Jacquard, and so lie straight while the warp and beam threads pass across or around them. In many Leavers techniques the bobbin threads give a strong effect of parallel lines passing lengthwise in the finished lace.

Points, racks and *quality* As the lace is made, so warp, beam and bobbin threads steadily unwind, deflect and interact. The area of interaction lies just above the well, and here the twisting of the threads together is completed. It simply remains for the threads to be tightened, and the lace web pulled upwards towards the cloth roller. Both processes are carried out by a double set of 'points' which operate as in the Circular machine, one at the front and one at the back, in alternation with each other, pulling the web upwards as it were hand over hand.

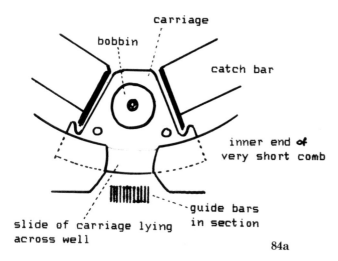

84b

84a *A carriage showing the catch bars interlocking with the nibs.* **b** *The catch bar raised to show the close packing of the carriages, in their extreme front position, with half their slides protruding beyond the comb slot.*

85 *A Go-through machine, from the front (Birkin, Nottingham).*

The lace passes first over a stretcher or forcing bar which presses against it, providing a tension which helps to maintain the even upward flow, as well as presenting to the twist-hand, or machine operative, an inspection-area where defects can be marked out to be attended to later.

From the stretcher bar, the slowly-revolving porcupine digs its short spikes into the fabric, hauling it up onto the cloth roller. The speed of turning of the porcupine determines the ultimate firmness or slackness – that is the quality – of the work: the greater the speed of take-off, the looser will be the lace.

Lace production is measured in racks. This, in the Leavers machine, is the amount of lace wound onto the cloth roller by 960 revolutions of the porcupine, as the result of 960 full carriage motions, or 1,920 single ones, front or back. The fewer inches there are per rack, the better will be the quality, since it will mean the lace has been worked more closely, the same number of motions being compressed into a shorter length. Thus '12-inch quality', or 12 inches of lace made by 1920 motions, is superior to '18-inch quality', or 18 inches of lace made by 1920 motions. The terms 18-inch rack, or 12-inch rack, are sometimes used to express the quality.

Finishing It will be noted that in the above account the word 'completed' is used of the lace as it accumulates, rather than 'finished'. In the lace trade, finishing has a special meaning, and refers to the processes to which

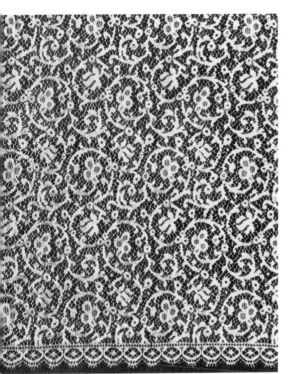

86 *An all-over lace made crosswise of the machine: note the vertical and horizontal repeats, and the cut warps at the lower edge where this piece was separated from the next.*

Vertical and horizontal repeats, drafts, figure sheets and the Jacquard

Leavers laces may be made as *all-overs* which stretch across the full working width of the machine, and can be as many yards long as required up to about 40 or 42 the maximum that the cloth roller can hold. The term all-overs is applied to patterned webs, or laces (fig. 86). Unpatterned webs are called plain nets; while nets with a tiny regularly-repeated design such as dots or squares may be referred to as spotted nets, fancies, or novelty veiling.

Alternatively they may be made as *bands*. These are edgings, insertions or galloons, placed side by side across the width of the machine, and also capable of being made in 40 to 42 yard lengths. The bands or breadths are linked together by lacers which can later be withdrawn to separate them (fig. 87).

Flounces are all-overs made crosswise of the machine, but of limited length. They are separated from each other by cutting across the warps at the point where a particular vertical repeat ends and before the next begins.

The width or breadth of a band, or of a horizontal repeat in an all-over, is measured in carriages, for example an '80-carriage set-out' (see fig. 77b). The actual width, in inches, of such a set-out will vary according to the gauge of the machine, for example a 10-point 80-carriage set-out would be four inches wide, while a 12-point 80-carriage set-out would be 3.3 inches wide.

The height of the vertical repeat is measured in carriage motions: a 120-motion set-out would involve 60 carriage swings to the front (front motions) and 60 carriage swings to the back (back motions) to complete it, before it began again. The wider the band, and the longer the vertical repeat, the higher the cost. Today the maximum practicable width is eight inches, and a greater width makes it difficult to maintain a constant tension in the beam threads. The maximum practicable height is limited only by the wieldability of the Jacquard apparatus, a longer repeat meaning more cards, greater weight, and greater space occupation. 700 to

the 'grey' or 'brown' web, removed in its entirety from the machine, is subjected before it is marketed. These processes include repairing, washing, bleaching, stretching, stiffening or dressing, and the removal of lacer threads so that the web is separated into bands. In the nineteenth and early twentieth centuries such work was carried out in vast rooms where the entire lace had to be blotted inch by inch by hand to remove excess water or starch, and then was dried by fans turning slowly in the ceiling above, circulating the air. Modern methods, more mindful of the health of the workers, send the web through wide shallow stentors, covered over to prevent leakage of fumes. Within these, every process takes place: the web goes in limp and dirty, and comes out stiff and white or, if required, tinted.

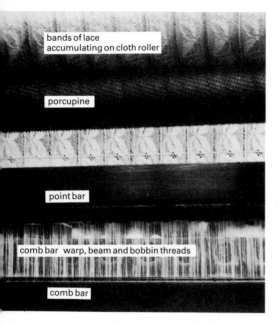

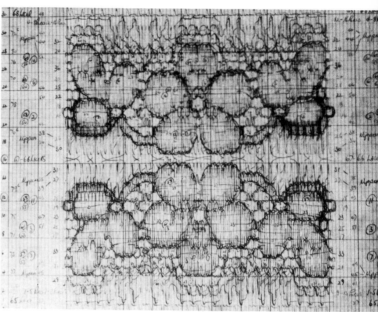

87 *Detail of a machine, showing the lace bands linked together vertically by lacers (Abur Pegg).*

88 *A Leavers draft for a pair of narrow edgings (Abur Pegg).*

1,000 is a quite adequate number. This, depending on quality, would give something like a nine-inch vertical repeat.

In designing patterns for the Leavers machine, only one repeat in a horizontal and a vertical direction needs to be drawn. This is enough to indicate all the throws of warp and beam threads needed to create the net and the solids. It also gives all that is required to calculate the sley set-out, to determine the arrangement and threading of the guide bars, and to work out the number of Jacquard cards needed, and how precisely they should be punched.

The number of guide bars which a Leavers machine can use is a question of both expense and practicality. At a simple economic level, the more guide bars there are, the longer the draft will take to draw, and the more time-consuming will be both the pricking of the sley and all the subsequent sley- and bar-threadings. On a practical level, every Jacquard card must be able to control every guide bar. Therefore the more guide bars there are the bigger the Jacquard cards have

to be. Beyond a certain point they would be so heavy and cumbersome as to make manipulation difficult, even if they are split into two sections as they sometimes are for the sake of stability. In practice therefore the number of guide bars is kept below 400, though if cost, and speed of working, were no object, the theoretical limit would be a good deal higher.

The *design* is sketched to show how the lace will appear when complete and ready for use. The *draft*, which plots every thread movement needed to create that design, often follows the same arrangement. Thus the carriage motions needed for the vertical sequence will in fact be numbered along the top from left to right; while the number of carriages needed to cover the horizontal repeat will be arranged at the left side, from below upwards. It follows that every horizontal space will stand for a bobbin thread, or carriage, position, and every horizontal line for a gait.

Fig. 88 shows a 32-carriage 144-motion 80 guide bar draft orientated in this way. The various short lines that zigzag up and down

124

are the bar throws, which will always begin and end at a gait. In the original draft they are shown in some half-dozen different colours which makes their individual movements stand out more clearly.

The function of the draft is to enable the design, drawn on paper, to be effectively transferred to Jacquard cards motion by motion. The cards then create the design in the lace by manipulating the vertical threads. Historically, the Jacquard patterning mechanism for woven fabrics was invented by Joseph Marie Jacquard of Lyons in 1801. In spite of initial violent opposition from the silk weavers who were afraid of being made redundant by the new development, the process was a success. By 1812, it had been applied to 11,000 weaving looms in France. However its application to lace-patterning proved unexpectedly difficult, even though simpler automatic patterning devices such as the organ barrel and Dawson's wheel had been in use since the eighteenth century. After many attempts, and sundry patents, a really successful break-through was made by Hooton Deverill in 1841 (patent no. 8955), for 'improvements in machinery for making and ornamenting lace commonly called bobbin net lace'. the invention consisted 'in the application of the Jacquard apparatus . . for the purpose of shogging the guide bars . . in producing ornamental figures or devices' upon various

kinds of lace. 'By this invention the Dawson's wheels commonly employed are dispensed with.' By the time of the Great Exhibition in London, ten years later, the most complex and beautiful designs were being produced, some of which have never since been surpassed.

In constructing the draft, the squared paper used will be some multiple of the gauge, since actual size, for example 20 bobbin threads to the inch, would be too small for clarity. A ×4 enlargement spreads 20 bobbin threads over four inches, which is much more visible. In figs. 89 and 90a, the structure of a small part of a draft is analysed to show how it is built up, and how the numbering of the various parts is arranged. The orientation used here is that of the lace while on the machine. This saves that mental rotation required to link draft to figure sheet.

The gait is the part of the well at the end of each comb blade, the well being a gap about two inches wide stretching across the machine in the hollow between the down-slop-

89 *The meanings of the terms, and arrangements, used in a Leavers draft (after Lemaire). Here, the motions and gaits shown on the draft are arranged as made; more usually, in England, they are arranged on the draft as the lace will be worn (see fig. 90c).*

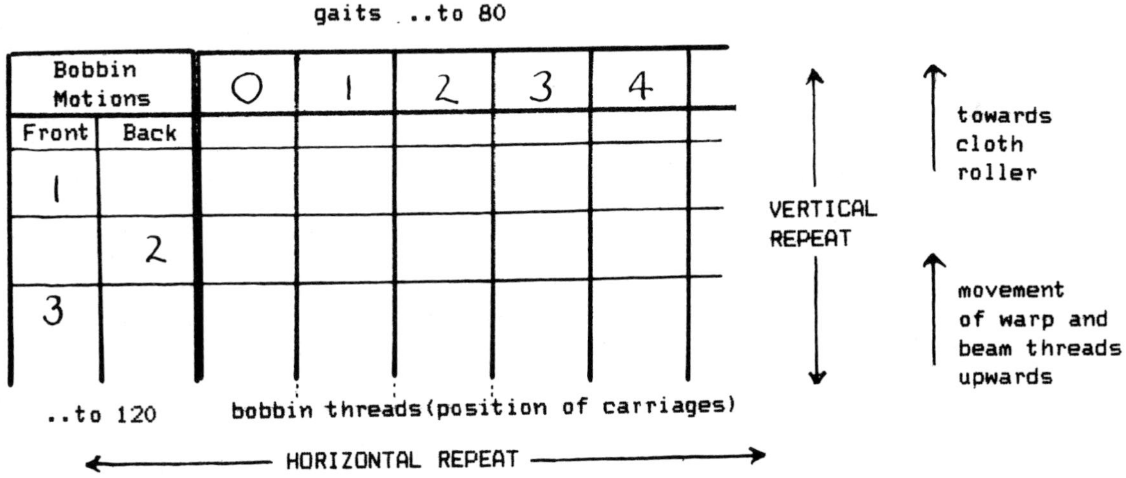

125

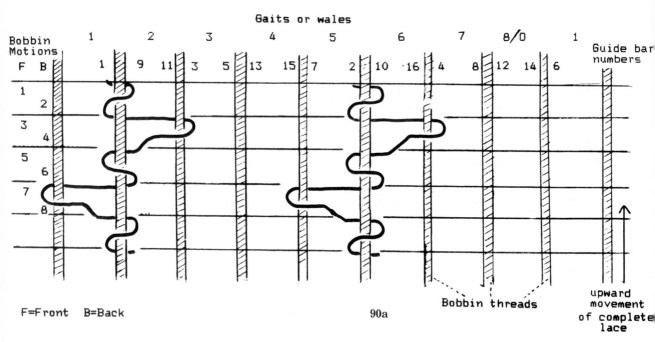

Gaits or wales

Bobbin Motions

F=Front B=Back

90a

Bobbin threads

upward movement of complete lace

ing front and back combs (see fig. 84a). During a carriage swing, up to seven or eight warp and/or beam threads may be lined up motionless at each gait, between the front and back of the machine, waiting to be diverted by their guides. As the carriages pause momentarily at the limit of their flight, the guide bars leap into action and throw their threads to right or left, then stop instantly at the new gait as the carriages prepare to swoop again. When the carriages reach the limit of their new motion, the bars glide swiftly again, to right or left, geared so that throws over one gait or eight gaits, or any distance in between, will all occupy the same instant of time. The 8-gait maximum on a 12-point machine would represent a throw of one-third inch. Beam threads can be carried over considerably longer distances, in a series of steps, even up to two inches, but this puts some strain on them, being deflected so far from their point of origin. In the *belle époque* of the Leavers machine, just before the first World War, single throws of 23 gaits were not unknown (see cover illustration). But it is unknown, now, how such throws could be achieved, since no gearing could effect them within half a second, which was

90a *A draft paper showing two guide bars making identical throws over eight motions, arranged as on the machine.* b *A draft and figure sheet showing the throws of 16 guide bars over eight motions, for square net called Valenciennes. Here the bars are paired at intervals of eight: 1 with 9, 11 with 3, 5 with 13 etc. The course of only one thread in each pair is shown. F = front, B = back ((a) and (b) after Lemaire).* c *The 90° clockwise reversal between a normal English draft (on left, as lace is used) and a figure sheet (on right, as lace is made).*

all the time available between bobbin motions. Possibly the upward movement of the web was arrested by disconnecting the porcupine, so that throws could be made in slow motion.

Fig. 90a shows the front and back bobbin motions clearly separated, the front being always represented by odd numbers, the back by even. If the theoretical thread movements of a single guide bar are plotted, it can be seen how all the complexity of fig. 88 was built up.

The completed draft gives an admirable idea of the movements necessary to make the lace. It does not however explain how to transfer the information to the Jacquard

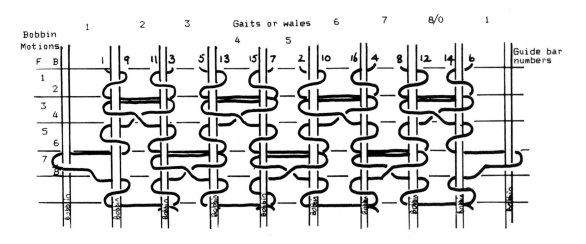

throws of guide bar 16
during eight bobbin motions

16 bars, numbered from back to front, as
on the machine, and on the Jacquard cards

90b

Front motions	Back motions	16	15	14	13	12	11	10	9	8	7	6	5	4	3	2	1
1	2	6 7	4 5	8 9	4 3	8 7	2 3	6 5	2 1	7 8	5 4	9 8	3 4	7 6	3 2	5 6	1 2
3	4	5 6	3 4	7 8	5 4	9 8	1 2	7 6	3 2	9 7	3 5	7 9	5 3	5 7	1 3	7 5	3 1
5	6	7 6	5 4	9 8	3 4	7 8	3 2	5 6	1 2	8 7	4 5	8 9	4 3	6 7	2 3	6 5	2 1
7	8	8 7	6 5	10 9	2 3	6 7	4 3	4 5	0 1	6 8	6 4	10 8	2 4	8 6	4 2	4 6	0 2

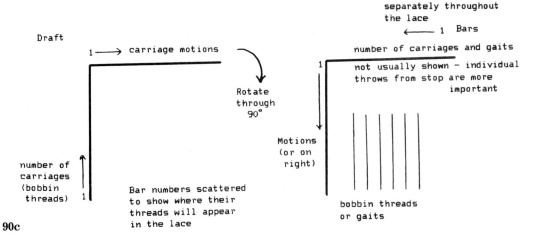

90c

91a

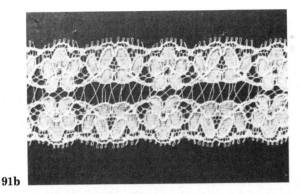

91b

91a *(previous page) The full figure sheet of the draft shown in fig. 88.* **b** *A piece of lace made to this draft (Abur Pegg).*

cards. An intermediate stage is necessary, one known as figuring, or reading-off. The *figure sheet* which results represents a clockwise rotation of the draft through 90° (fig. 90b, c). The carriage motions are now numbered at the side from above downwards, motion 1 being the first to move upwards to the cloth roller. The numbers of the carriages and of the gaits is now no longer significant, and straight vertical lines with intervening spaces adequately represent them. The bars which in the draft appeared scattered are now numbered from right to left along the top. The figures in the columns are gait throws per motion per bar, from the stop points, higher numbers being to the right of each stop.

To describe what happens in fig. 90b one could say:
After the first bobbin motion the threads in bar 9 move from gait 2 to gait 1;
after the second bobbin motion they move from gait 1 to gait 3;
after the third bobbin motion they move from gait 3 to gait 2 . . which is very tedious and verbose and even so not entirely clear. The information is better summarised:

Bobbin motions		Movements of bar no. 9
Front	*Back*	*Gait sequence*
1	2	2 1
3	4	3 2
5	6	1 2
7	8	0 1

It is not even necessary to put in the front and back motions separately since these can be taken for granted. Fig. 91a shows the full figure-sheet for the draft, fig. 88. Although it looks much more complex, it is to be interpreted in exactly the same way as for fig. 90b.

In this example, the draft represents two bands (fig. 91b), so that although, in all, this involves 32 carriages, numbers 1–16 are repeated, to make the subsequent double punching of the Jacquard cards easier.

The reading-off, though it requires considerable patience and concentration, is quite straightforward once the thread-following technique has been mastered. The creation of a draft from a sketched design, on the other hand, requires skill and experience to determine how the many threads can be most conveniently allocated to produce the desired effect without any risk of cotting (thread tangling) as would happen if adjacent bars were too similarly threaded.

In the completed figure sheet shown in fig. 91a, each vertical column of figures gives the various gait positions occupied by one bar throughout the 144 motions of the vertical pattern repeat. Each horizontal line of figures gives the movements of every bar at a single bobbin motion.

The Jacquard One horizontal line, or one bobbin motion of the lace, is constructed at a time. At each line, or between each motion, all the guide bars have to be moved as indicated on the draft and the figure sheet. It is the work of the Jacquard to automate these movements. The information given in the horizontal lines is converted into a series of holes punched in a series of cards, with a new card to represent every line. The cards are numbered 1, 2, 3, 4 etc corresponding to the bobbin motions, and the cards and motions must be equal in number, for example a total of 144 in figs. 88 and 91a.

Front and back motions must have their own cards, and these are separated into two distinct sets, mounted on two separate six-sided cylinders at the right-hand side of the machine (fig. 92). Both act in precisely the same way, though alternately with each other. The odd numbers are front motions,

92 *The right-hand end of a Leavers Go-through machine showing the two Jacquard cylinders with their cards, and the bottom bar cylinder, not in use, but pierced with holes for receiving the dropper probes. The main part of the machine is to the left (Spowage, Humphreys and Wyer).*

and the even numbers back motions.

Two distinct aspects of the Jacquard have to be considered: the activating mechanism; and the code-punching of the cards which determines the effect of the activating mechanism.

Broadly, the activating mechanism is a drive blade which shoots back and forth above the front and back motion Jacquard cylinders, in rhythm with the bobbin swings. If they swing 100 times a minute, 100 cards will have to be turned, 50 front and 50 back, to coincide with 50 pulses of the front motion drive blade, and 50 pulses of the back motion drive blade – which is pretty rapid.

The cards work indirectly, by placing an obstruction in the path of the drive blade, which results in a deflection of the guide bar attached to it towards the right. The obstruction takes the form of selected dropper heads, and it is the position of holes or blanks on the Jacquard card which determines the selection. These positions, in turn, are set by the numbers on the figure sheet which themselves represent the length of throw of every guide bar at every motion throughout the design.

The cards Every guide bar must have a fixed place allocated to it on every card. A simple example of 16 bars can be taken since a greater number poses no additional problems but only needs a greater width of card to accommodate it (fig. 93).

On the figure sheet the guide bars are numbered from right to left. On the machine they are numbered from back to front. Their corresponding positions on the Jacquard cards are marked in the same way, that is the right of the Jacquard card represents the

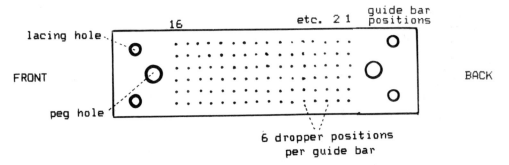

Space allocation for 6-dropper 16-bar set-out

93 *A line drawing of a Jacquard card showing the positions allocated to each of the 16 guide bars for a 6-dropper set. When the card-repeat is very short, as here, a further four identical cards will be punched to carry on, making a cycle long enough to go around the cylinder, and to reduce wear.*

back bars of the machine, and the left of the card the front bars.

Droppers The length of the throw of each of these 16 bars, on both front and back motions, is controlled in a mathematical manner. The graduated droppers provide a variable obstruction to the drive blade, resulting in a variable displacement of the buffer. The buffer displacement deflects a lever which pulls a draw bar, causing the guide bar attached to it to be pulled to the right, or to rise.

The arrangement of the Jacquard cylinder

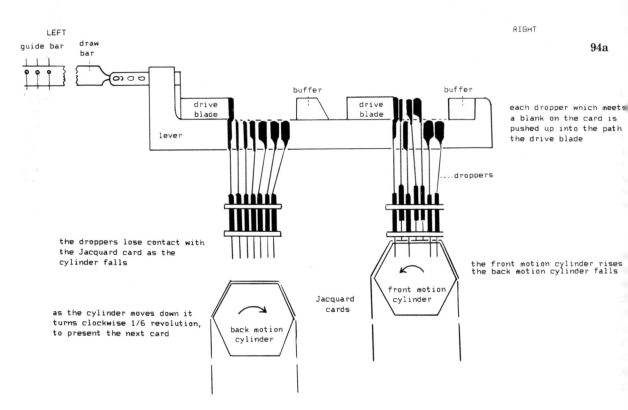

94a

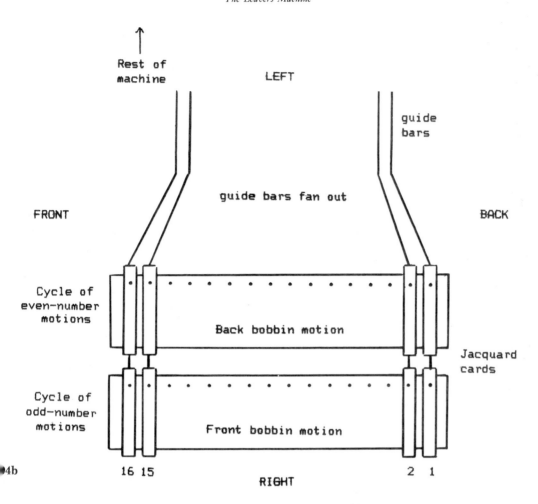

↑

Rest of machine

LEFT

guide bars

guide bars fan out

FRONT

BACK

Cycle of even-number motions

• • • • • • • • • • •

Back bobbin motion

Jacquard cards

Cycle of odd-number motions

• • • • • • • • • •

Front bobbin motion

4b

16 15

2 1

RIGHT

4a *The Jacquard end of the machine from the front (not in proportion).* **b** *The arrangement of the drive blades and dropper boxes over each guide bar position, from above, with bars 1, 2, 15, 16 only shown. Right, left, front and back refer to the machine as a whole.*

and cards, droppers, lever, drive blade, buffer and draw bar in relation to each other and to a guide bar is shown in fig. 94a. Each guide bar has to be connected with two dropper boxes, one over the front motion cylinder, the other over the back (fig. 94b). Sixteen guide bars therefore require (16 × 2) dropper boxes. A more sophisticated example, say with 200 guide bars would need 400 dropper boxes, making the escalation of expense with more complex designs very obvious.

Each dropper box contains a set of 6, 7 or 8 droppers, depending on the maximum length of throw required by that design. Each individual dropper is a nine-inch steel pin, with a rigid probe below, which contacts the card, and a flexible shaft above, terminating in a toughened head. The heads are precision-shaped to be exactly equivalent in width to $\frac{1}{2}$, 1, 2, 4, 8 or 16 gaits, though the latter size is not now used. Their actual thickness will depend on the gauge of the machine. On a 10-point gauge, with 20 gaits to an inch, each gait will represent $\frac{1}{20}$ inch. A $\frac{1}{2}$-gait dropper head will then measure $\frac{1}{40}$ inch across, a 1-gait $\frac{1}{20}$th, a 2-gait $\frac{1}{10}$th, and so on. The dropper heads are so shaped that they will fit with each other in any combination (fig. 95a).

133

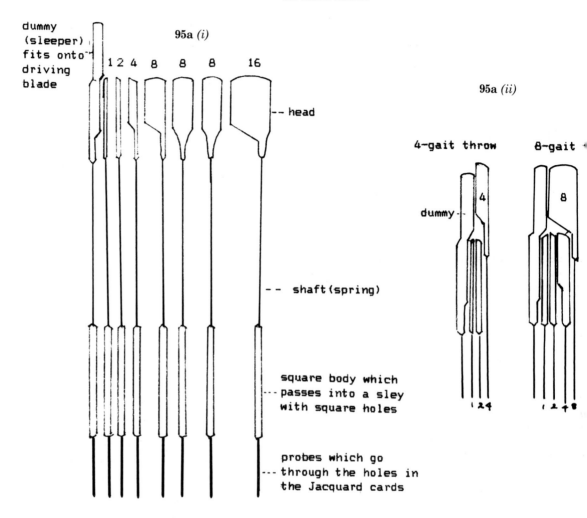

95a (i)

dummy
(sleeper)
fits onto
driving
blade

1 2 4 8   8   8   16

-- head

-- shaft (spring)

--- square body which
passes into a sley
with square holes

--- probes which go
through the holes in
the Jacquard cards

95a (ii)

4-gait throw   8-gait

dummy

4   8

ı 2 4   ı 2 4 8

Interaction of cards, droppers and guide bars

To move the bars, the droppers must provide an obstruction to the drive blade. The extent of the obstruction, and therefore of the bar throw, has to be read from the Jacquard card, and is determined by the precise way in which it is punched. Every guide bar is allocated six or seven dropper positions of fixed value on each card (fig. 95b), the numbers of the dropper positions corresponding to the sizes of the dropper heads.

For example if, on card 2, the figure sheet requires guide bar 2 to be thrown six gaits to the right on the back motion, the card must ensure that dropper heads to the value six ar pushed upwards to obstruct the drive blade a the required instant. There is no single hea of the value six, and heads 2 and 4 will b selected to work together.

It is the blank surface of the card whicl brings about the upward push of the heads The remaining droppers are rendered ineffec tive by sinking into holes in the card' surface, and on into the face of the cylinder Each face of the two cylinders is bored witl row after row of six (or seven) holes, ove which the guide bar positions shown o fig. 95b must fit exactly. The cards are held i place by a series of ratchet holes which fi over pegs on the cylinder surface.

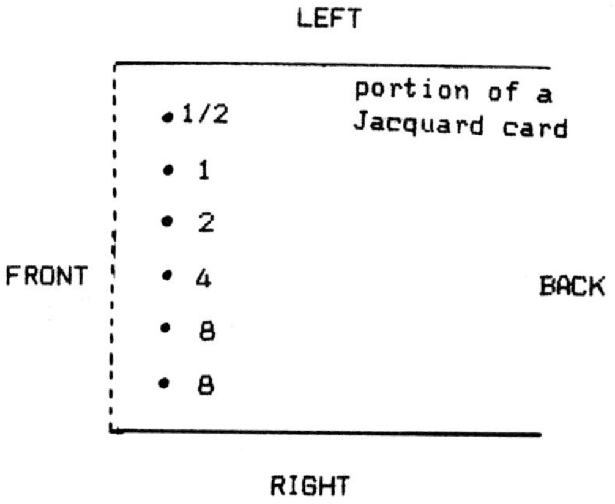

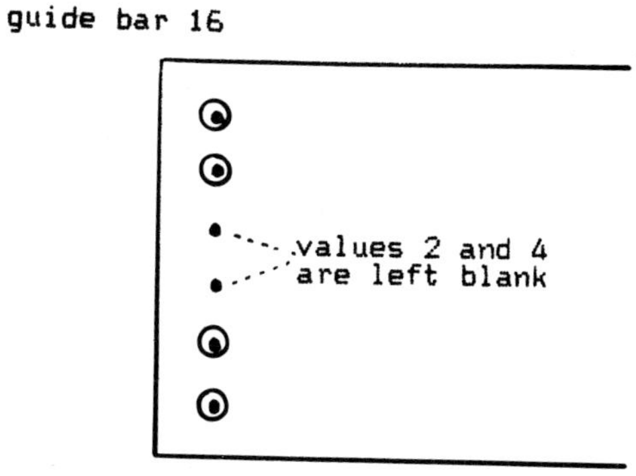

LEFT

guide bar 16

portion of a
Jacquard card

• 1/2

• 1

• 2

FRONT   • 4   BACK

• 8

• 8

⊙
⊙
•····values 2 and 4
•···´are left blank
⊙
⊙

RIGHT

95b   **95c**

The dots indicate possible positions of holes.
1/2 to 8 indicates the value of the position
if blanked.

95a *A set of droppers: (i) the position of the droppers at dead stop, the numbers indicating the number of gaits per throw which the intervention of the droppers will initiate; (ii) how the shape of the dropper heads enables them to fit together when raised.* **b** *The arrangement of the dropper values over the card: some cards have seven dropper positions for longer throws, an additional 8, making a possible total of 31½ gaits. Note front, back etc relate to the position of the card in relation to the rest of the machine.* **c** *A combination of blanks and holes producing a value of six gaits across which that guide bar will be thrown.*

The holes in the cylinder are fixed and permanent, but the Jacquard cards must be punched for every motion of each particular design. In effect if motion 2 requires guide bar 2 to throw six gaits to the right, dropper positions 2 and 4 will be left blank while the remaining dropper values are holed (fig. 95c).

The series of movements by which blanks produce guide bar throws can be summarized as follows: when the carriages swing to the back of the combs, the back motion Jacquard cylinder turns anti-clockwise to present card 2 on its upper surface. The whole cylinder rises upwards and so comes into contact with the six or seven steel probes of the dropper box above it. Droppers ½, 1, 8, 8 and 8 will enter

the holes that have been prepared for them. Droppers 2 and 4, meeting a blank, can go no further. As the cylinder continues to rise, their heads are pushed upwards into the direct path of the drive blade where they cause a 6-gait obstruction. The drive blade, to cover its fixed distance, has to push them out of the way, and this in turn forces the buffer further from the machine, towards the right. The buffer as it is displaced, pulls on its lever, which pulls on the draw bar, which pulls on the guide bar attached to it. In this ingenious way the bar is pulled six gaits to the right, that is it rises through six gaits (fig. 96).

This done, the carriages swing to the front of the combs. The back motion cylinder, its work done, sinks down, rotating as it does so through 60° to bring the next card on to its surface. This releases the raised droppers which fall down into their dropper box. The guide bar moves marginally leftwards, drawn back by a spring fixed at its opposite end, the whole width of the machine away.

As the back motion cylinder lowers, the front rises, presenting its card to the dropper sets above it. The whole process begins again, affecting every guide bar . . . and so on at every bobbin motion throughout the entire vertical extent of the design.

Fig. 97 illustrates part of a Jacquard card

135

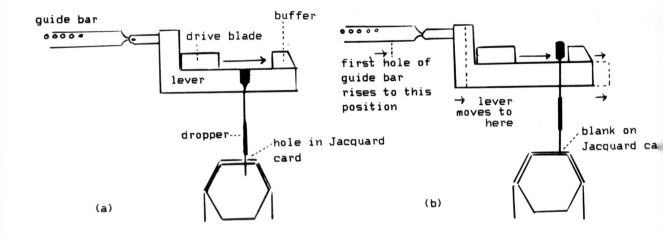

(a)

(b)

96 *The hole versus blank reaction of the dropper probe to the Jacquard card, a simplified diagram of dropper action:* **a** *the dropper passes through a hole in the Jacquard card, and sinks into the corresponding hole in the cylinder. The dropper head remains below the level of the drive blade and so no movement of the attached guide bar occurs.* **b** *a blank on the Jacquard card forces the dropper to rise into the path of the drive blade. The thrust of the drive blade must still carry it through the same distance, therefore it pushes against the dropper and buffer until this distance is reached. This deflects the buffer with its attached lever, draw bar and guide bar, to the right. Thus the guide bar threads rise, or are thrown, to the right.*

97 *How throws of two to six gaits are represented on a Jacquard card: their effect passes via the droppers to the guide bars.*

97

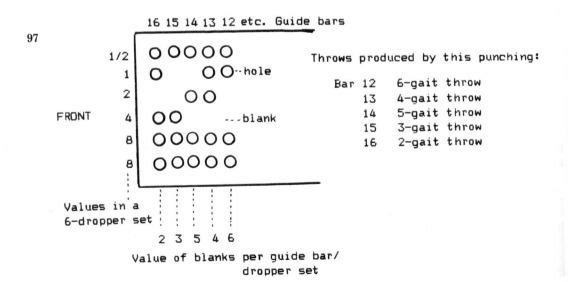

96

punched for five bars. It shows the arrangements of holes and blanks necessary for
throws of 6, 5, 4, 3 and 2 gaits respectively.
Although 8, or even 7, is the largest single
throw now practicable, the dropper system
has the theoretical capacity to cope with
much larger ones. For example $(1 + 2 + 4 + 8 + 8 + 8)$ gives 31 gaits; and $(1 + 2 + 4 + 8 + 8 + 8 + 16)$ gives a total of 47 gaits. The $\frac{1}{2}$ is
always present, representing a sleeper or
dummy (*dormeuse*), and is omitted from these
comparative calculations.

As the guide bar moves, so every thread
along its entire length will be thrown by the
same amount simultaneously.

It is the droppers, reacting to the cards,
which determine the *length* of the throw. The
direction of the throw is the product of two
interacting factors: the value of the blanks on
consecutive cards, and the counterweight
pull of the guide bar springs from the left.
Thus:

Front motion: the first throw of any guide
bar, when the machine is initially set in
motion, is inevitably to the right, since the
droppers act that way. At rest, the spring is
relaxed and the bar threads at stop.

Back motion: if the following card, on the
other cylinder, gives a higher dropper total
than the first, the drive bar must push the
buffer further away, and the bar will rise even
more. In other words, there will be a second
movement of its threads to the right.

Front motion: if the next card gives a lower
dropper total, for the bar under consideration, than did the back motion, then the bar
will fall, or throw to the left. For example, a
sequence of four cards giving blanks valued
at 1, 2, 3, 1, for the same bar, would result in
three consecutive 1-gait rises followed by a 2-
gait fall.

When an alternating series of 1-gait rises
and falls (e.g. 0-1 0-1) occurs, the result is
pillaring: the bar thread rises across one gait
with the bobbin thread in the front position,
and falls across one gait with the bobbin
thread in the back position, so that a twist is
made around the bobbin thread. Pillaring
may be either clockwise (reverse warps) or
anti-clockwise (front warps) (see fig. 104d).

The complete transformation of the original sketched design into the full set of Jacquard cards ready to go on the machine may
take four or five weeks and cost several
thousands pounds.

Punching the cards is an art in itself. A small
'piano puncher' is used, with matching right
and left 'keys' so that two cards (front and
back motion) can be punched at the same

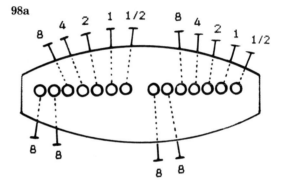

98a

98a *A piano puncher. The hands fit over the
machine, fingers at the back, thumbs at the front.
The right hand is used to punch the throws associated with the front bobbin motions, and the left
hand for those associated with the back bobbin
motions.* c *A Jacquard card punched for 122 guide
bars, and using six droppers only: above, detail;
below, the complete card (Abur Pegg).* **98b,c**

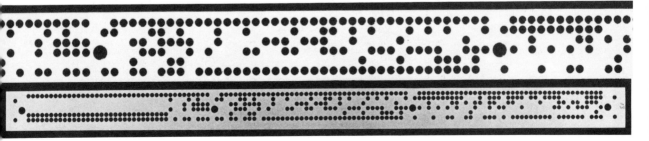

time, the odd numbers (front) with the right hand, and the even numbers (back) with the left. The figure sheet is fixed on a stand above the puncher, with a ruler marking the motion being punched, while a moving bead on a cord, stretched across the sheet, automatically marks the bar position reached. Each column of the sheet may have two numbers, the left representing the front motion, the right the back motion. In a 7-dropper system, the keys for droppers $\frac{1}{2}$, 1, 2, 4, and one 8 are at the back of the puncher, the keys for the remaining two 8s at the front (fig. 98a,b). Alternatively all three 8s may be at the front. Power is provided through a foot pedal.

Leavers laces

The varied effects possible in Leavers are almost unbelievably complex. In the past something like 400 different ground effects alone could be produced. Grecian nets had larger holes surrounded by a series of smaller holes; crackly (craquele) was irregular and the meshes sometimes coffin-shaped (fig. 99a); filet was square; pin-hole filet had a tiny hole at the corner of each square, making a delicately pretty effect; duchess was a guipure; hexagon a large and rather rough-looking mesh produced by thread tension; while Valenciennes was round or diamond-shaped. There were in addition guipure bobino, crazy, Tenerife effect, wire ground, Genoa point, point de Paris stripe, and Malines. Many of these date from the last decade of the nineteenth century when fancy hat veilings, produced prolifically in France, had such names as violette (fig. 99b) and friquette.

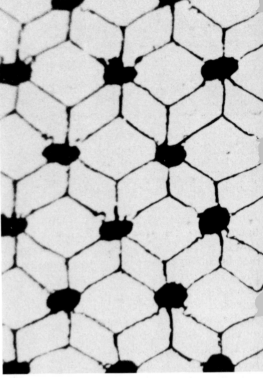

99b

99a   **99c**

99a *A mesh of crackly or craquelé net.* **b** *Tulle violette (Hénon, p. 560).* **c** *A Leavers flounce with a basket of flowers design, imitating a bobbin-made Chantilly.*

138

The frequent use of the names of bobbin or needle laces, made by hand, was and is based on simple distinctive features such as the raised outline in Alençon, the form of the design in Chantilly (fig. 99c) and, in Valenciennes, the mesh shape, the lack of an outlining thread, and the presence of small holes or 'ticking' around the clothwork. These are accepted trade names for machine laces, though inspired initially perhaps by a wish to deceive or to sound prestigious.

The Leavers machine has several distinct techniques, but two features likely to be found in all of them are liners and lacers.

Liners are outlining threads, arising from beam rollers. They are threaded in such a way that they can be held around the border of the motifs only by the bobbin threads. This makes the liner more obvious on the face than on the reverse side where it is crossed by the two warps, or other vertical threads (fig. 100a,b). As the lace web moves upwards, the liners are carried as floats between one motif and the next, that is they are not attached at all to the lace surface in that area, and so can be clipped away afterwards. If clipping is done by hand it is a time-consuming and expensive job, and was only possible on an extensive scale while labour was cheap. The cutting-shaving-vacuum accessory described on p. 59, shortens the time enormously, but is a big capital outlay. There are various alternatives to the use of floats and clipping:

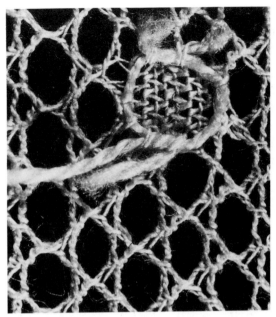

100b

100 *Liners:* **a** *to show how the heavy outlining threads are carried down over the surface of the lace as floats without forming part of the fabric, then are later clipped back.* **b** *detail of a clipped float, badly finished.* **c** *detail of a needlerun liner.* **d** *liner threads cleverly drafted so that they carry on in continuity around the motifs and do not need to be clipped.* **e** *when complete continuity is not possible floats will appear on the face and must be clipped during finishing. (See over).*

100a

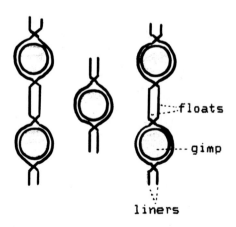

floats

gimp

liners

floats cut away, leaving clipped ends above and below gimping.

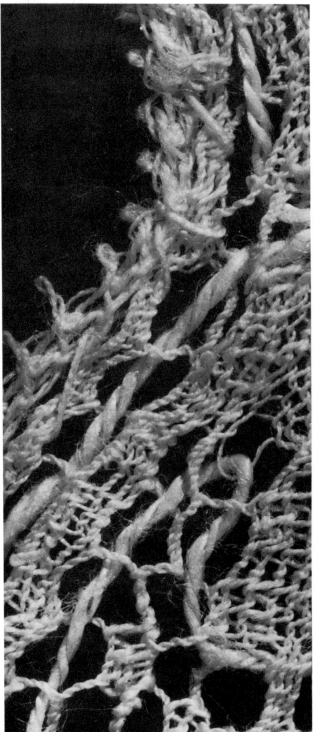

100c

a. the liner may be run in by hand (fig. 100c). This was common practice on all nets and laces until 1841 when Joseph Wragg invented the technique for putting in the liner on the machine;

b. it can be added by the hand-operated Cornely machine, after the lace is finished: 'having no clips the goods resemble real laces very closely'.[14]

c. the design can be so arranged that the liners, though put in on the machine, continue on from one part to the next without floats, so that no subsequent clipping is needed (fig. 100d,e). This is a method much in use today, but unless care is taken it tends to emphasise the liner at the expense of the pattern, which gives a displeasing effect.

100d

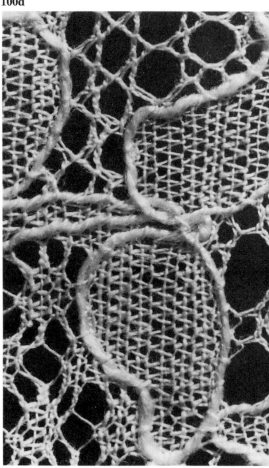

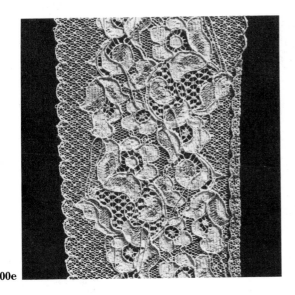

100e

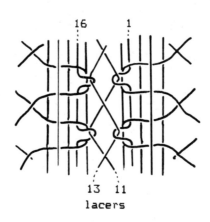

101a

Lacers The function of a lacer, or the linker-together of two widths of edging, or bands, on the machine, is to stabilize them during manufacture, to facilitate their handling during the finishing process, and then to allow them to be separated with the minimum of effort when they are ready for retailing. This separation can be done in various ways:

a. the bands are arranged with their two back edges together. Bobbin threads 1 and 16 are under tension, so that when the lacers on bars 11 and 13 are withdrawn, 1 and 16 sink back into the fabric, leaving a straight edge (fig. 101a).

b. the bands are arranged front and back edges facing, and a row of purls is to appear along the front edge. A bobbin thread along the back edge is brought under tension by a heavy lacer. When the lacer is withdrawn, the bobbin thread sinks back, leaving a straight edge at the back, and a purled edge at the front (fig. 101b).

c. a deeply scalloped front edge inevitably means a certain wastage of space and fabric. The bands are usually placed back to back and front to front (see fig. 91b).

d. galloons, with both borders scalloped, are linked by narrow areas of net rather than by lacers. During finishing the net is cut away

101 *Lacers:* **a and b** *Two methods of linking vertically-arranged bands together until they have been removed from the machine and finished.* **c** *a galloon, produced in yardages and then cut apart, made without lacers. Here the outer circular decorations have been embossed to give the appearance of raised spots. (See over).*

101b

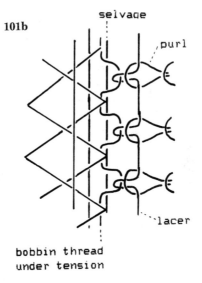

along each curving border, either by hand or by a special machine such as the Perfector or the Hunky Molar. The edge will then appear slightly ragged (fig. 101c).

141

101c

The major techniques of Leavers laces are:

1. Bobbin Fining, with Single Warp variant;
2. Centre Gimp;
3. Independent, with Back and Front Gimp (Spanish Gimping) variant;
4. Lyons.

All may be found in surviving examples of nineteenth and early twentieth century laces, but only centre gimp and independent are at all commonly made today. In all techniques, thick threads are placed at the front of the lace (future face side) and reverse warps when present at the back (future reverse side).

1. Bobbin Fining (figs. 102a–i, 103 a–g). In this very ingenious technique there are no beam threads except for liners and lacers, the entire patterning and many varied nets being made simply by the interaction of bobbin threads with front and reverse warps. In the net the reverse warps pillar on the bobbin threads and the front warps throw to make the meshes; but in the patterned areas heavy weighting of both sets of warps pulls them into parallel lines alternating with each other, while the light springing of the bobbin threads allows them to run out in a zigzag manner around them. The original throws produce a 3-1 3-1 muslin effect of the front warps, in fact a warp fining, but as shown in fig. 102a the special weighting immediately pulls them into a vertical position, dragging the bobbin threads outwards until they twist like a spiral stairway between one front warp and the next.

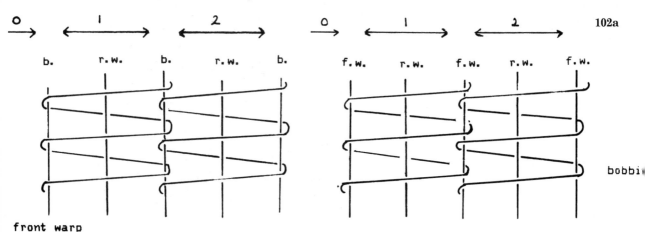

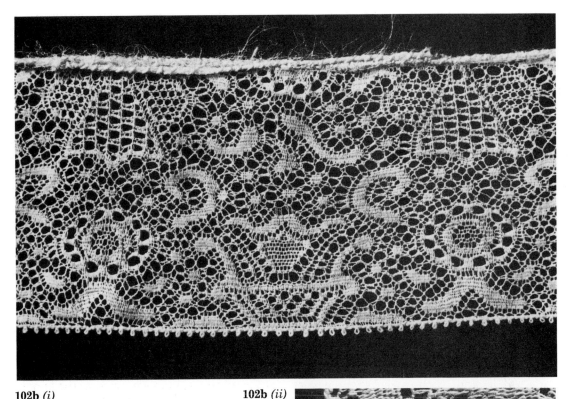

102b *(i)*

102b *(ii)*

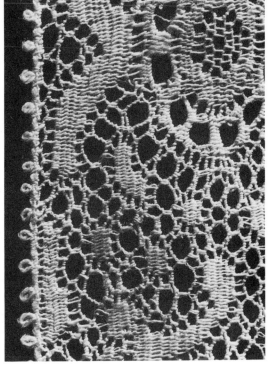

102 Bobbin fining *laces, made with three sets of equal-thickness threads, and densely worked:* **a** *the identity of the various threads and how they arrive in that position:* b = *bobbin;* fw = *front warp;* rw = *reverse warp.* **b** *(i) a convincing representation of eighteenth century Binche bobbin lace, arranged as worn, c.1880; (ii) detail, arranged as made.* **c** *(i) a collar imitating a fine eighteenth century Flemish lace, the varied fillings all made on the machine, c.1847. (ii) detail.* **d** *An imitation of a Flemish 'opaque' lace of c.1700, orientated as on the machine.* **e** *The Comet Val, a representation of Halley's comet, 1910.* **f** *Russian lace: dentelle russe dated by Hénon, 1877.* **g** *(i) a mat made for the Paris Exhibition, 1900. (ii) detail.* **h** *A design of dancing figures, with liners made from beam threads, dated by Hénon, 1883.* **i** *The courses of the patterning threads in dense, and less dense, areas of laces (a) to (g). (i) is similar to Mechlin (Malines) net (see fig. 104f(ii)). (iv) is similar to half-warping, made by the front warp. In the net, the bobbins lie straight with the reverse warps pillaring on them, while the front warps alternately pillar and throw to make the meshes.* b = *bobbin;* f = *front warp;* r = *reverse warp.*

143

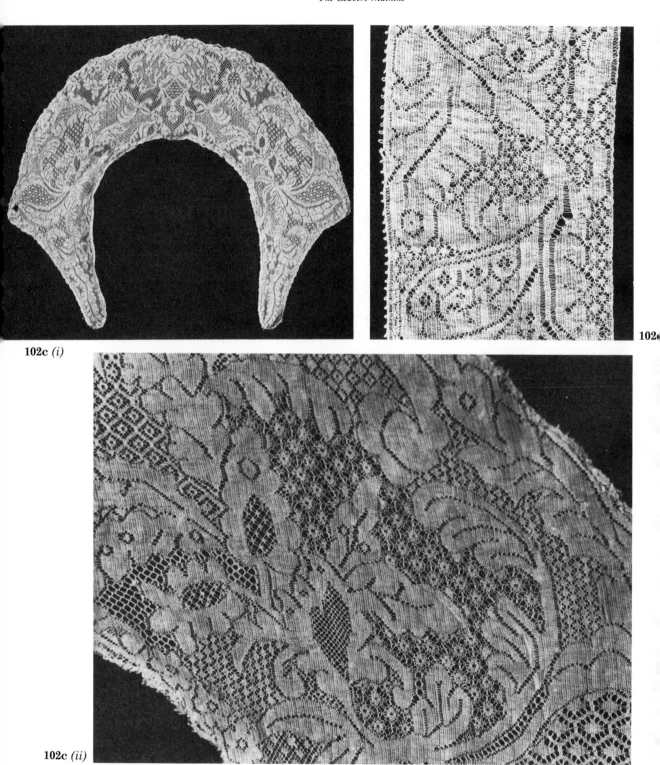

102c *(i)*

102c

102c *(ii)*

102e

102g *(i)*

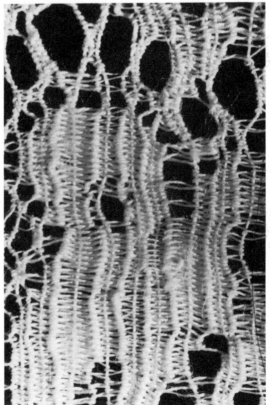

102g *(ii)*

102f

102h

The separation of front and reverse warps into alternating parallel lines, instead of coinciding pillars, makes the lace appear twice as fine in gauge as it actually is; while the large quantity of expensive bobbin thread which it consumes makes it truly prestigious.

Figs. 102b–i show a series of bobbin fining laces worked densely in heavy threads to intricate patterns; and figs. 103a–g some of the lighter forms with varied fillings – many of them described in Lemaire's *Silk* – indicating the great range of widely different end-products of which this technique was capable.

Single Warp – or Fining Lace or Warp Fining – is generally regarded as a variation of bobbin fining in which the warp weighting is not strong enough to bring about the reversal shown schematically in fig. 102a, though a slight slackness of the bobbin threads may allow them to be pulled away

from the reverse warps which pillar around them, giving an effect of front warps linked on either side to the bobbins (fig. 103h).

2. Centre Gimp (figs. 104a–k). In this technique, a fourth group of threads, the gimps or patterning beams, regularly appear, situated centrally while the front warps occupy a forward, and the back warps a rear position in the well.

Two notable pattern effects, which frequently appear together, are flossing and gimping. In *flossing* the gimps are in front of the front warps, held to the lace surface only by the bobbin threads. They are of heavier yarn – originally floss silk – producing a strikingly dominant raised effect. In *gimping* the front warps are in front of the gimps, that is the gimps are truly 'central' between back and front warps, so that the pattern appears

i   f   r

b

ii   f   r

b

iii   r   f

b

103a

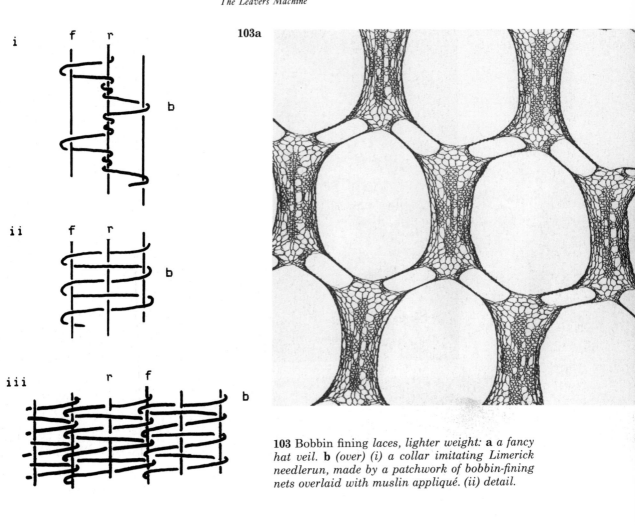

103 Bobbin fining *laces, lighter weight:* **a** *a fancy hat veil.* **b** *(over) (i) a collar imitating Limerick needlerun, made by a patchwork of bobbin-fining nets overlaid with muslin appliqué. (ii) detail.*

iv

102i

103b *(i)*

103b *(ii)*

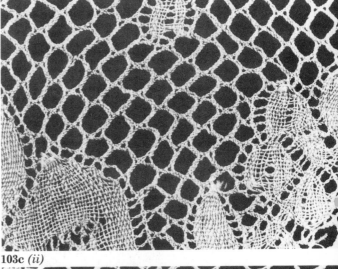

103c *(ii)*

103c *(i)*

103c *(iii)*

103c *Valenciennes lace: (i) above, handmade bobbin lace; below, a machine copy of the same design. (ii) detail of the bobbin lace. (iii) detail of the Leavers lace, with ticking around the clothwork and round Valenciennes ground* (mailles rondes). *(iv) (over) a swatch of samples of* maille ronde, *c.1900.* **d** *(i) an imitation of either a filet lace, or of a curtain lace with a filet ground. (ii) detail.* **e** *an imitation of that point lace made from machine tapes linked by buttonhole-stitching which was a popular pastime of home embroiderers in the second half of the nineteenth century.*

103c *(iv)*

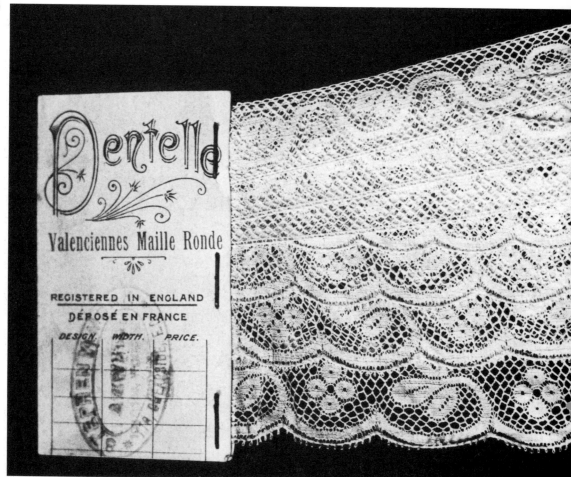

103d *(i)*

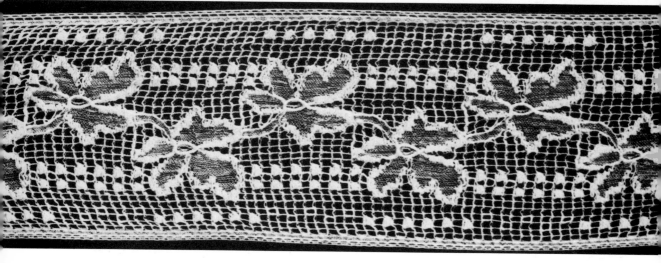

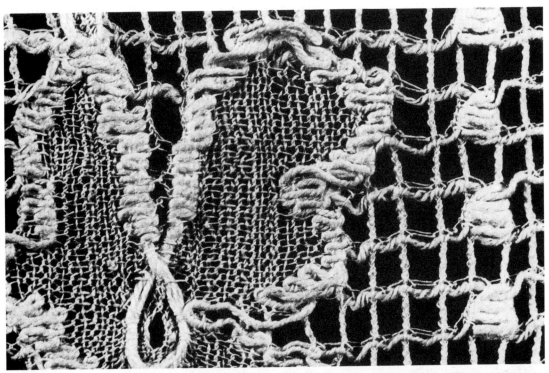

103d *(ii)*

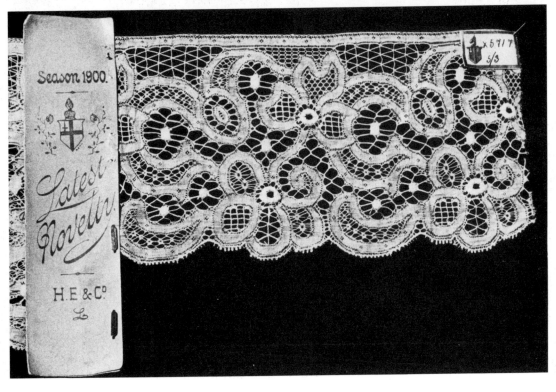

103e

103f *(i)*

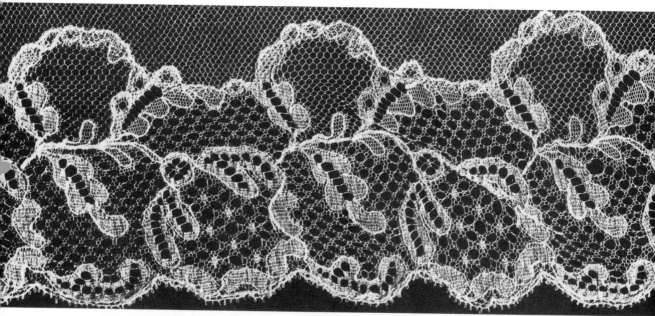

103f *(ii)*

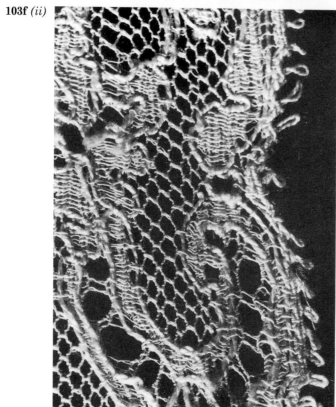

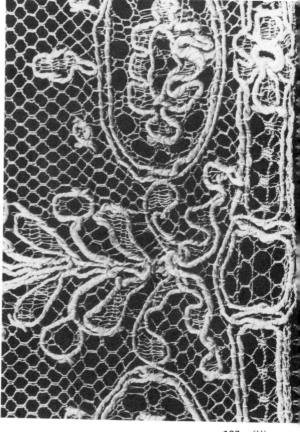

103g *(ii)*

103g *(i)*

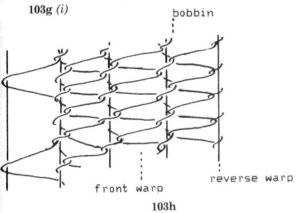

103h

flatter and less obtrusive (fig. 104a). In both, the throws are over three to six gaits. In *double gimping* two gimps work together over the same area, sometimes throwing in opposite directions over as many as six gaits, to produce an effect of much greater density (fig. 104b). Another possibility is two-motion gimping, or *half-gimping*, in which the beams instead of throwing right or left at every motion throw only on the front motions.

There are sometimes areas of warping or warp fining within the pattern, giving a touch of lightness to the inner portions of flowers. Here, there are no gimps, and the front warps throw in a 3-1 3-1 manner between twisted pillars of reverse warps and bobbins, as described in bobbin fining, though the bobbins remain tight-sprung (fig. 104c). Thus, flossing – gimping – warping, correspond to heavy – medium – light densities, adding richness to the design.

In flossing and gimping, both warps are restricted to pillaring on the bobbin threads, the reverse in a clockwise, the front in an anti-clockwise direction (fig. 104d), and their function is to clamp the passing gimp threads to the pillar so that they cannot slip. In the ground, where the gimps cease to function,

103f *(i) an imitation Bucks point lace attached to a plain bobbinet with as much care as if made by hand (reverse side); (ii) detail, showing the imitation round Valenciennes mesh.* **g** *(i) machine Alençon, an imitation of a handmade Alençon design, with raised liner; (ii) detail, arranged as on the machine, the pillaring in the fancy net shows the presence of two warps, and the liners with their clipped ends are beam threads.* **h** *Bobbin fining (Nottingham School of Art sample book c.1850).*

the front warps open out forming the top and bottom connections of the meshes, while the reverse warps continue to pillar in a 0-1 0-1 manner. Thus, while the reverse warps behave uniformly throughout the lace, and can with advantage be threaded through stumps, the front warps do not behave uniformly since in the clothing they pillar, or do warp fining, and in the ground they make meshes. They therefore have to be differentially threaded, each group being allocated its own bar.

A typical stump bar net is six-motion or *Ensor net*, devised by Frederic Rainford Ensor between 1854 and 1865. It was intended to imitate the round plaited mesh, or *maille ronde*, of early Flemish and Valenciennes bobbin-made laces, but using only three threads (bobbin and two warps) instead of four as in the handmade. The holes are 'perfect hexagons' achieved by compacting the crossing of the warps at either end so that they look like a straight bar (fig. 104e). A patented improvement of 1896 claimed to have achieved 'a perfect imitation of the true lace.'

Another common centre gimp mesh is *loop net*, also known as 3-1 2-1, or four-motion, or over-the-top-and-twist net (figs. 104f, g). The loops can be made to either the right or the left.

It is seldom possible for reverse warps, front warps and beam threads all to be allocated their own bars. For example in the fig. 77b set-up, warps alone would occupy 160 bars, and since 150 is nowadays the normal maximum for economic convenience, there would be no bars left for the patterning gimps. One solution already mentioned (p. 116) is to split the reverse warps into four groups which are then confined to four heavier *stump bars*. The advantage of this is that it leaves more guide bars available to accommodate a greater number of patterning threads; the disadvantage is that the mesh-formation cannot be stopped when the patterning begins (fig. 104h).

A compromise can be reached by the introduction of another set of bars lying below the first, and hence referred to as *bottom bars*. Their position means that they are not restricted to a mere two inch well-space between the back and front combs as are the *top bars*.

The number of bottom bars, in the absence of space restrictions, can be quite enormous, such as 600 or 1,000,[15] though 400 is about the maximum used today. These large numbers need have no adverse effect on the size and manageability of the Jacquard cards since the bottom bars have their own set of cards, and a separate cylinder which deals with both

104a *(i)*

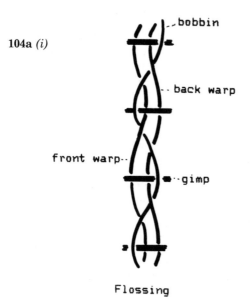

Flossing

104a *(ii)*

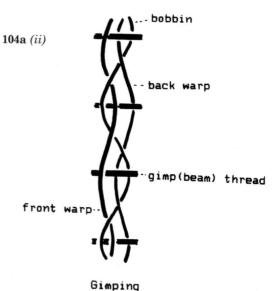

Gimping

154

Single gimping 2-0
2-0

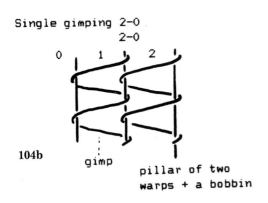

104b   gimp   pillar of two
warps + a bobbin

Double gimping 3-0
3-0

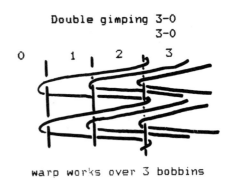

warp works over 3 bobbins

104c

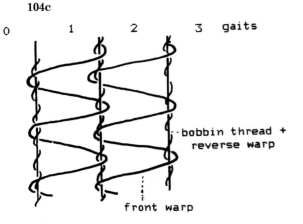

0   1   2   3   gaits

bobbin thread +
reverse warp

front warp

104 Centre gimp *laces, made with four sets of threads of variable thickness:* **a** *(i) flossing: the gimp lies over both warp threads so that it appears prominently on the surface of the lace; (ii) gimping: the gimp (patterning beam thread) is central between the front warp which goes over it and the reverse warp which goes under. In both, the bobbins are lightly sprung so that the two warps are pulled almost straight while the bobbin threads appear to circle around them.* **b** *outline sketches to show single and double gimping, and the gait throws involved in their manufacture.* **c** *Warp fining, or muslin: compared with bobbin fining, the reverse warps pillar instead of lying centrally, and the fining threads are front warps linking pillars instead of bobbin threads linking front warps.* **d** *the direction of warp pillaring, clockwise on the reverse warp and anti-clockwise on the front warp, the bobbin threads being held straight by tight springing which increases the tension.* **e** *(i) the structure, and (ii) a draft (after Lemaire) of Ensor net – note how the front and reverse warps lock each other to the bobbin*

thread. In the actual lace (iii) the cross is less conspicuous, and the mesh appears as a clear hexagon. **f** *(i) 3-1 2-1 net with throws made by the front warp, the reverse warp pillaring; (ii) 3-1 2-1 net, made with front warp only, and known as Mechlin or Malines (maleen) net.* **g** *a centre gimp lace showing flossing, gimping, pillaring and a 3-1 2-1 net.* **h** *a stump bar net, continuing through the pattern area, the decorative filling in the flower centre is Grecian net.* **i** *the Jacquard apparatus with an auxiliary bottom bar cylinder on the left, and the normal front motion Jacquard cards on the right of the photograph. Above the cards are the dropper boxes and, beyond them, the fanned-out guide bars (Birkin, Nottingham).* **j** *two examples of bottom bar work showing the subtle design effects of which the machine is capable, the very long throws of the gimp threads, and the crosses at the upper and lower ends of every mesh of the bishop's net. (i) was made on a 9-point gauge machine with two-motion gimping, both warps and beams making fancy net effects.* **k** *(i) an imitation of the seventeenth century needle lace Venetian gros point; (ii) detail: the raised work has been added by hand and buttonhole-stitched over, the lower liner is a bourdon cord stitched on by hand, the centres of the flowers enclose maille ronde and other nets some of which have been separately inserted; and the guipure 'bars' are made of warp, beam and bobbin threads tightly twisted together. (iii) all the tiny fragments of the design in this lightweight silk lace, orientated as made, have needed two clips of the liner on either side. (iv) in this imitation silk blond (blonde de soie, Hénon, 1870), the entire edges and some of the enclosures have been cut by hand, while the row of small ovals has been opened by the removal of lacers.*

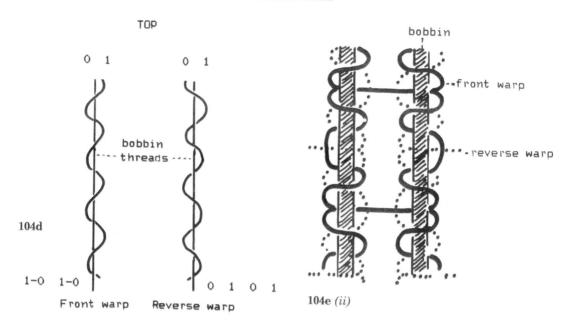

TOP

0 1   0 1

bobbin
threads

104d

1-0   1-0   0 1 0 1

Front warp   Reverse warp

bobbin

front warp

reverse warp

104e *(ii)*

104e *(i)*

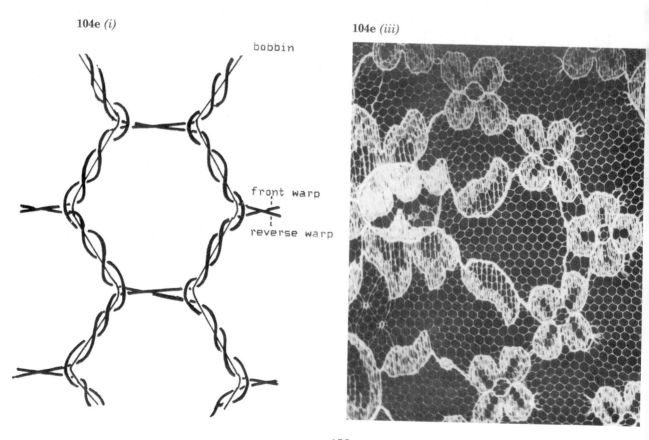

bobbin

front warp

reverse warp

104e *(iii)*

3-1 2-1 Net

3-1 2-1 Net (no reverse warp)

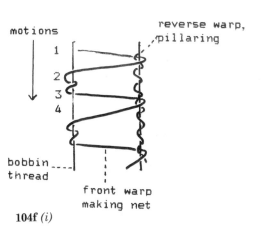

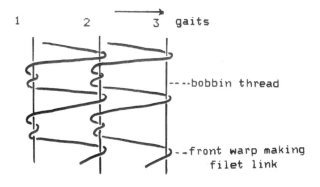

104f *(i)*

104f *(ii)*

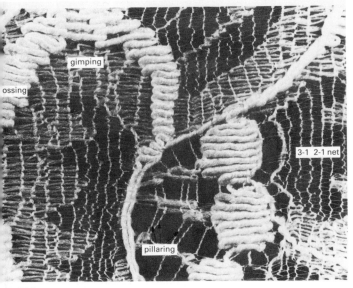

104g

104h

104k *(i)*

104i

104j *(i)*

104k *(i)*

104k *(ii)*

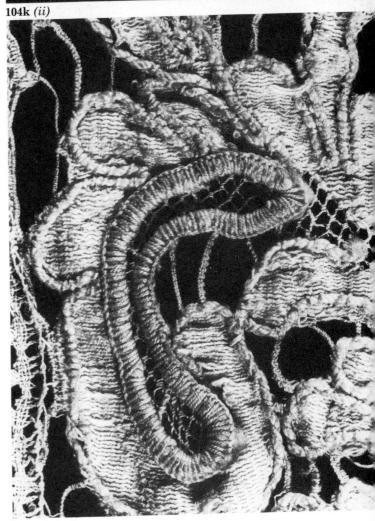

back and front motions simply by rotating at twice the speed of the top bar cylinders (fig. 104i). The dropper system works in the reverse direction to that of the top bars, the rise of a dropper causing a guide bar to fall.[16]

Although the bottom bar threads are independent of each other, the length of throw which each can make is strictly limited, since they pass not directly upwards but via four stump bars. These have sufficiently large holes so that as a bottom bar is moved to left or right, its threads can be displaced, within the stump bar, through one or two gaits, according to its Jacquard control, and so it can change from pillaring to fining and back again.

In single bottom bar work, the front warps are in bottom bars, the reverse in stumps only, and the beams in top guide bars of the usual kind. In double bottom bar work, the reverse warps are also in separate bottom bars, though they pass upwards through the same stump bars. The general effect of all this is an immense freedom of movement for an enormous number of individual threads, and even though each warp throw itself is limited, the illusion of much wider throws can be created, especially by the top bars. Calais in particular can still make bottom bar laces of excellent detail with illusions of 21-gait throws created by a close addition of three seven-gait throws, and with subtle light and shade effects produced by an intermingling of double gimping and warp fining (figs. 104j(i) (ii)). The very numerous vertical threads give the lace a richly substantial texture.

A distinctive ground of double bottom bar laces is *bishop's net* which, though untraversed, has a cross at either end of each mesh. Bottom bars, Ensor net and bishop's net are found only in centre gimp laces, and loop net is also found mainly in this technique.

Figs. 104k(i–iv) show centre gimp effects which were possible only when labour was cheap. The cost of machine laces has always been proportional to the amount of handwork involved. In 1860 the total cost of the product was made up 70% by yarn, 15% by capital overheads, and only 15% by wages, which at that time were seldom more than 18s. (90p) to £1 15s. (£1.75) a week.[17]

104k *(iii)*

104k *(iv)*

3. Independent (figs. 105a–i). There are no warp threads, only beam and bobbin, to construct both ground and pattern. All the threads are S-spun. Each beam thread has its own guide bar, giving considerable flexibility of patterning, without any stump bars to impose a uniform repetitiveness on the net. In the arrangements and movements of the threads there is a closer approximation to weaving than in either the centre gimp or bobbin fining techniques, and they could quite easily be mistaken for woven laces (see chapter 9).

The beam threads are separated into three groups known as back, middle and front gimps, which are threaded through back,

middle and front groups of guide bars respectively (see fig. 78). The back bars work on the back motion (while the carriages are at the back of the combs), and the back gimps therefore pass in front of the bobbin threads. The front bars work on the front motion (while the carriages are at the front of the combs) and the front gimps are therefore thrown across the back of the bobbin threads. The sleepers, threaded through the middle bars, remain still, and in the finished lace they lie parallel to the bobbin threads, alternating with them. The sleepers are thus like the warps used in weaving, while the back and front gimps appear like wefts passing between right and left, over and under the

160

sleepers to give the appearance of a plain weave, very similar to the wholestitch of a bobbin lace. Both pillaring and fining are rare in independents, and the patterned areas are commonly known as platting, matting or weaving.

105 Independent beam *laces:* **a** *the woven look characteristic of this group, and how it is produced.* **b** *(i) the typical woven look of a Valenciennes bobbin lace imitated by the independent technique, c.1920; (ii) detail* **c** *(i) a provincial bonnet with Antwerp bobbin lace imitated by the independent technique; (ii) detail which shows its machine origin in the*

105a

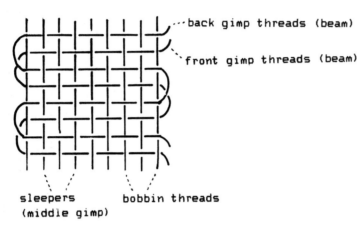

back gimp threads (beam)

front gimp threads (beam)

sleepers (middle gimp)   bobbin threads

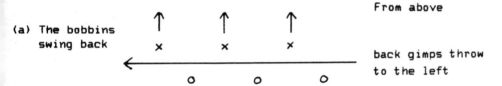

From above

(a) The bobbins swing back

x=bobbin

o=sleeper

back gimps throw to the left

sleepers (at gaits) stay still

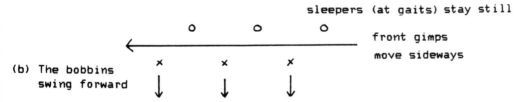

sleepers (at gaits) stay still

front gimps move sideways

(b) The bobbins swing forward

As lace is compacted:

(a) becomes

Back gimp in front of bobbins and behind sleepers

(b) becomes

Front gimp in front of sleepers and behind bobbins

105b *(i)*

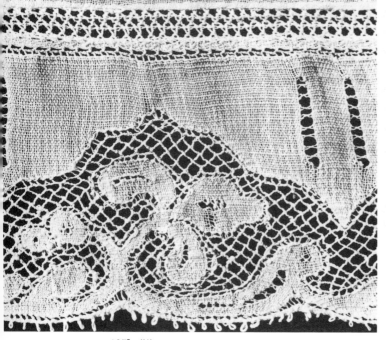

105b *(ii)*

105c *(i)*

*lack of clarity of the five-hole ground (*fond de vièrge*) and of the purled border. **d** (i) an imitation of a Lille bobbin lace; (ii) detail. **e** (i) above, handmade eighteenth century Lille bobbin lace; below, Leavers copy c.1898; (ii) detail of handmade Lille; (iii) detail of Leavers Lille, arranged as made; (iv) detail of net in (iii). **f** (i) imitation of a Belgian point de Paris lace, dated 1922 in Birkin's archives (no. 7241); (ii) detail of the central area, arranged as on the machine, showing the clips of the liners. **g** (i) imitation of 'point lace' by the independent technique; (ii) detail showing continuity of thread between the 'tape' and fillings. In the prototype the tape would have been woven, and the fillings made of buttonhole stitches worked by hand. **h** (i) imitation of a filet lace; (ii) detail: in the handmade original the square mesh would be knotted at every corner. **i** a fine copy of a black silk Spanish bobbin lace, with the very delicate net ground scarcely visible. The wholestitch, halfstitch, honeycomb and fond simple of the handmade form are all convincingly represented, until seen through a strong magnifier.*

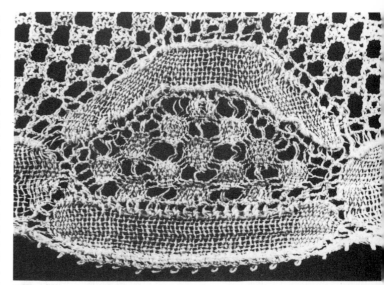

105c *(ii)*

105d *(i)*

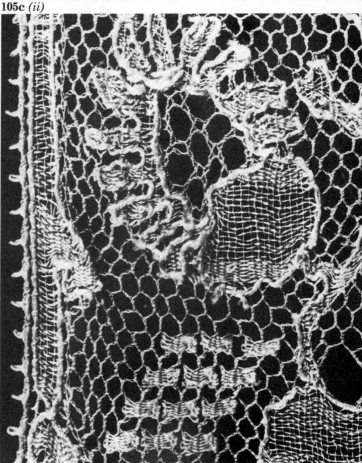

105d *(ii)*

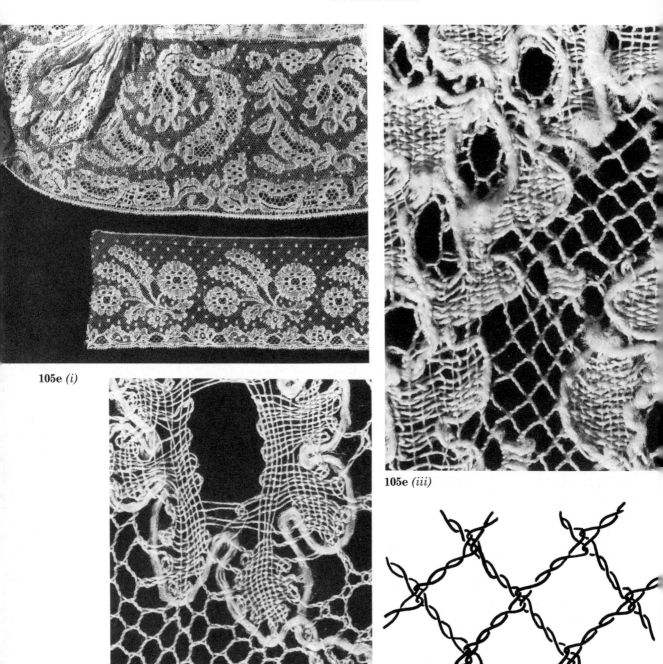

105e *(i)*

105e *(iii)*

105e *(ii)*

105e *(iv)*

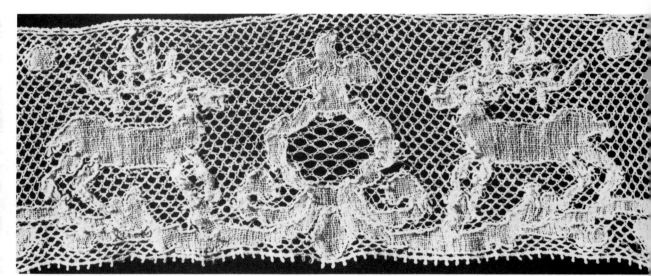

105f *(i)*

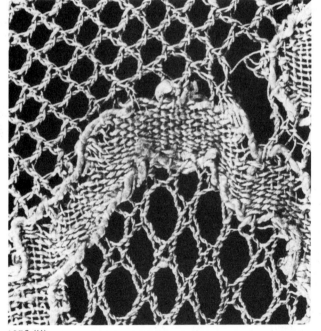

105f *(ii)*

105g *(i)*

105g *(ii)*

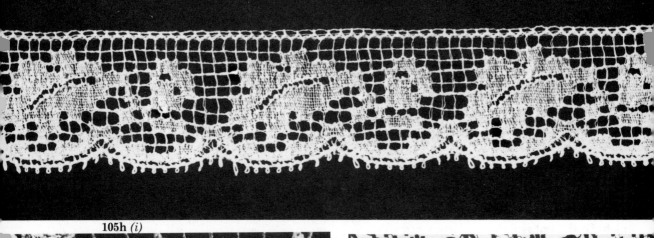

105h *(i)*

105h *(ii)*

166

105i

In Spanish gimping, warps are present, sandwiched between the front and back gimps.

4. Lyons (pronounced lions) (fig. 106). The distinctive feature of this technique is the traversing or diagonal passage of the patterning threads. The reverse warps are held in stump bars and produce pillaring. Patterning can take the form of single or double gimping (see fig. 104b).

Yarns used

Leavers machines can make use of almost any natural or synthetic fibre with a smooth finish. Of the natural fibres, cotton and silk are the most useful, though the former has the disadvantage that it may shrink when washed, and the latter that it is comparatively expensive. Silk threads can be as fine as 16 to 18 denier, or as coarse as 44 to 48. Cotton works best with a high twist such as 30 or 40 per inch. Between 80/2 and 220/2 Egyptian or Sea Island cotton was being used in 1950, with a tendency towards finer singles. Today, 40 denier nylon is quite common. The bobbins, having the least amount of space, hold the finest yarns – up to 120 yards of low denier nylon. The coarsest yarns, know as T-threads or thick threads, are used for liners and lacers, and for the fronts and backs where additional strength is needed. For these, in 1950, 60/3 cotton was used, that is, count 60 plyed three times. Of the vertical threads used for nets and gimping, the reverse warps are usually the finest, then the front warps. The beam threads are coarsest since this gives greater emphasis to the design. Lastex or lycra threads may be used as reverse warps in elasticated laces (fig. 107a). For shiny novelty effects, trilobal or tetralobal synthetics, with a triangular or square cross-section, may be used, their flat surfaces being highly reflective.

106 A Lyons *lace (Abur Pegg).*

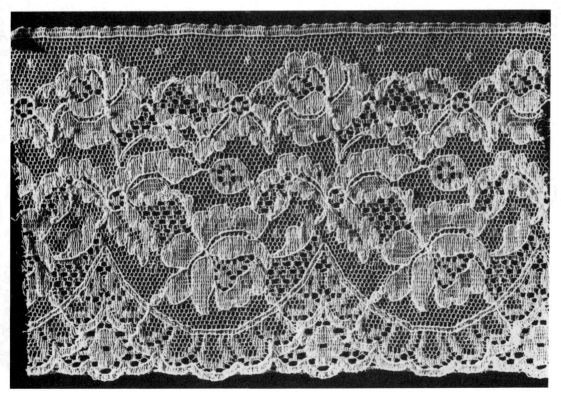

Special effects

The Leavers during the nineteenth century was, like most other lace machines, primarily concerned with the imitation of handmade laces. Particular attention was given to small details such as *ticking around the clothwork*, which referred to the line of tiny holes or net encircling the pattern motifs in handmade Valenciennes (see fig. 105b). A method of copying this was invented by Bagley in 1838.[18]

The structure of handmade *clunys* or 'leaves' is most easily carried out by a bobbin fining technique, in which the bobbin threads are pulled outwards by the front warps, while a reverse warp rests down the middle. An independent technique can also be used (fig. 107b–d). A furnishing lace known as Cluny is made in a coarse yarn (80 to 100 count cotton) on 7, 8, 9 or 10-point machines.

Imitations of bobbin laces such as Beds Maltese and Le Puy were given a guipure effect of *bars with purls*. These purls had to be supported by special threads, just as in the needle lace Alençon the purls or picots had to be constructed around a horsehair so that they were all of uniform size. In Leavers such support threads have to be removed slowly and carefully by hand, which would, now, make them too expensive (fig. 107e).

Decorative purls along the front edge of the lace are less troublesome since they can be supported by lacer threads which have in any case to be disposed of. Front edge purls may be made of one or two threads (fig. 107f). *Spiders* were also imitated (fig. 107g). *Flossing* was sometimes added by hand to laces other than centre gimps, a form of employment which continued into the 1930s (fig. 107h).

Two Leavers laces fashionable in the early twentieth century were angel skin or *peau d'ange* (fig. 107i), and *cut-out* lace. The latter was intended to be cut into separate motifs and stitched on or into underwear.

The last of the major twist-net machines, the Lace Curtain, is described in the next chapter. It set out on a path of its own, and was imitative only of that small group of craft laces known as netting, or filet.

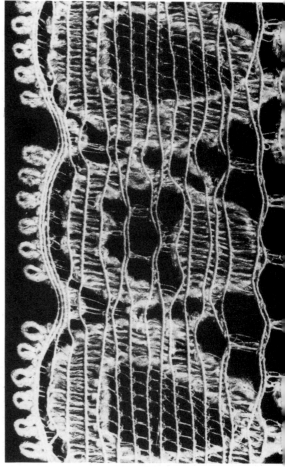

107a

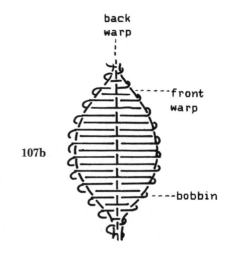

107b

168

107a *In this centre gimp lace, lycra replaces the reverse warp (reverse side of lace).* **b** *The arrangement of threads in a bobbin fining cluny.* **c** *Above, an imitation of Beds Maltese; below, the strong contrast between thin and thick threads makes the woven look less obvious. Both, independent beam.* **d** *(i) raised motion spots: the clawker comes out so that the porcupine and the Jacquard cylinder cease to turn, the web stays still, and a spot is constructed using just a few threads. Here, 'halfstitch' petals enclose a central area of clunies. (ii) detail, showing the large-meshed hexagonal ground. Independent beam.* **e** *(i) a black silk guipure lace, the ground formed of prominently purled bars (called* guipure soie, *1884, Hénon). (ii) the numerous supporting threads needed to produce good clunies and purls, 1912 (Abur Pegg).* **f** *A two-thread picot, or 'turned over' purl: the two bobbin threads are held in place by heavy lacers as the purl is made.* **g** *(i) spiders, characteristic of bobbin-made torchon laces, here copied by the independent technique (ii) detail.*

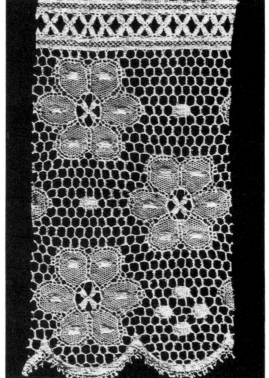

107c

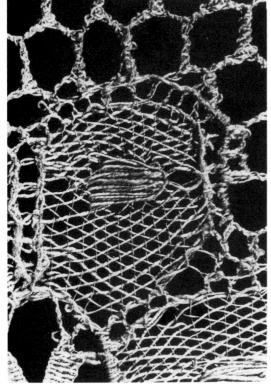

107d *(i)*

107d *(ii)*

107e *(i)*

107e *(ii)*

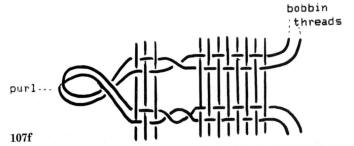

107f

107g *(i)*

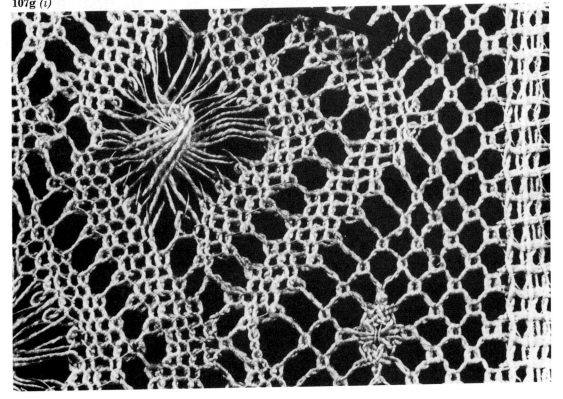

107g *(ii)*

107h

107h *An imitation Binche, the flower centres high-lighted with hand-flossing.* **i** *Peau d'ange; the shiny white silk flossing yarn floats across the invisibly fine net from one motif to the next, 1950s.*

107i

VI

The Nottingham Lace Curtain Machine

or Curtain, or Lace Furnishing Machine

History

The features which distinguish the Lace Curtain from any other bobbin-net machines were reputedly invented in 1846 by John Livesey, of Nottingham. No patent is registered in Livesey's name before 1851 (no. 13750) and that, along with subsequent ones, appears more closely connected with plush finishes and fringing than with any modification directly connected with the production of curtains.

Felkin, and Hénon, both credit Livesey with a kind of 'straight down loop' (*boucle verticale*) in which instead of the bobbin threads traversing across all the warps as in bobbinet, they passed across two warps only, making square meshes in which only adjacent warps were encircled by the same bobbin thread.

This must have been very difficult to arrange on the machine, indeed Felkin says, 'this plan was not at first thoroughly successful.' However, after certain improvements, 'a second warp, serving for weft, placed behind the machine, and wound on large bobbins [spools] was added, and placed under Jacquard control . . the ordinary bobbin threads served for joining together the straight down ranks of meshes'.[1] This would produce a mesh made up of three groups of threads – one to lie straight and parallel (warps), a second to loop between these warps (spool), and a third to bind or tie loop and straight thread together (bobbin) (fig. 108).

Although Leavers nets or grounds are also known as straight down, meaning untra-versed or passing vertically instead of diagonally, the final appearance is not the same: the sides of the Curtain machine meshes actually remain straight, while Leavers meshes tend to seek a hexagonal form.

It is upon this arrangement that curtain nets and curtains are principally made. The tissue is not solid or fast, and will not bear too much stress in wear; nevertheless cloth [pattern areas] worked of single, double and three-fold texture can be introduced at pleasure; and intermixed with openworks, form elegant designs in the network, by the application of Jacquard apparatus to one set of threads, and a separate one upon another part of the threads, so as to produce the effects of light and shade in floral and geometric patterns. These are much admired for their beauty when hung up so as to intercept the light. (Felkin p. 381).

The usage of lace for curtains was at that time a novelty. Its application to other household, and church, linen had long been established, but these huge white designs silhouetted against the brightness of tall sash windows must have had tremendous charm. In 1851 there were 100 Curtain machines at work in and near Nottingham. In France, by 1856, various firms were making 'lace looped curtains upon Livesey's system'.[2] With the easing of the restrictions on the exportation of lace-making machinery, in 1842, Curtain machines travelled as far afield as America, Poland and Russia.

With the exception of two references by Felkin to 'curtain net machinery' and 'curtain machines', neither the name Curtain machine nor Furnishing machine, appears in

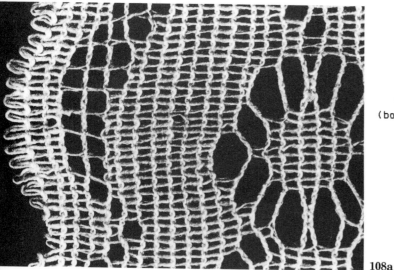

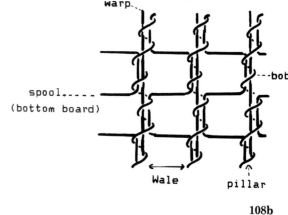

108a

108a *Detail of a characteristic Curtain machine net. The strong parallel lines running vertically make it look straight-down, or untraversed.* **b** *A simplified diagram to indicate its structure. The warps are in fact reinforced by a top board thread which makes them look even heavier.*

patents or elsewhere before 1880. It is then mentioned several times during the 1890s. This tardiness would seem to indicate that for quite some time the Curtain machine was thought of less as a machine in its own right than as a modification of the Circular. Felkin himself says the invention was produced upon 'circular machinery'; and so does Ferguson, 'On Circular machines are made guipure curtains, but the tissue is weak and does not survive many washings.'[3] A further quotation from the 1850s reports that, 'A new manufacture has been introduced since 1846, consisting of good imitations of Swiss curtains and blinds, which although so recently commenced employs a hundred machines of the kind called Circular.'[4]

No further details are available of Livesey's machine except that, like the Pusher and Leavers, it was single tier (all the carriages in one row) and, like all the bobbin-net machines, produced its effects by the interaction between laterally-moving verti-

cal threads, and to and fro bobbin swings in a direction at right angles to them. Distinguishing features of the twentieth century Curtain machine, apart from its straight-sided meshes, are the use of interceptors to act on the threads and make 'figured or ornamental lace'; and the animation of the Jacquard effect not via droppers and driving blades, as in Leavers, but via cross-needles and strings.

Both these features appear to have been at least to some extent anticipated by two patents registered in the name of William Crofts, in 1842 (no. 9467) and 1846 (no. 11,334). Crofts was acknowledged to be 'one of the quickest and cleverest hands working in the Levers' frame', and, 'upon the exit of Mr John Levers jun. from Mr Fisher's manufactory, Crofts took his position as principal mechanician of the establishment'.[5] However, like Levers senior, and so many other innovators, Crofts lacked that practical business acumen and ruthlessness needed to profit from his own creativity. Retired, in 1867, he was not, according to Felkin, 'in the enjoyment of those pecuniary results which his mechanical talents have undoubtedly deserved'. Nor did Livesey fare any better: other people made use of his ideas and eventually, tired of England, he emigrated to Australia.

The Curtain machine appeared long after other bobbin-net machines were established

174

and producing patterned laces. It thus had the advantage of being able from the start to make use of the Jacquard apparatus. At the Great Exhibition of 1851, some fine store curtains were on display, each five yards long by two yards wide, covered with spacious designs so elaborate they required between 12,000 and 15,000 Jacquard cards. They were valued at £1 10s. (£1.50) a pair. Felkin says, 'The speed of the machine is such that a pair of curtains, each four yards long, may be produced on one machine in two hours . . The business in these goods is intermittent; during the season [summer] some tons' weight of cotton curtains leave Nottingham weekly.'[6]

As for who was responsible for the more magnificent designs, contemporary opinion varied but gave a general pre-eminence to England's main rival, France. 'In England they work for quantity and to keep the price down,' wrote Ferguson junior. 'They do not keep up quality nor cultivate taste. Cheapness is a fatal rock, and cheating one another of designs will ruin any manufacture. We do not agree that English designs are equal to those of France. If an English maker has not a French designer, then he purchases patterns in Paris or Calais.'[7] Working conditions in England were also far from ideal. Recurrent industrial depression, with fluctuating wages, had led *c.*1846 to the formation of the Amalgamated Society of Operative Lacemakers.

In general, however, the curtain industry prospered as long as windows remained large and the predominating mood was one of *arrivisme*. By the early twentieth century developing American manufactures, such as the Quaker Lace Company of Philadelphia, began to provide serious competition. 'Lacecurtain' even became a new adjective meaning 'having social or economic standing; often used to imply ostentation or pushing parvenu traits' (Webster's Dictionary 1976). By 1914, 21% of the world's Curtain machines were in the USA, and exports from Nottingham and Scotland to America consequently fell, from $752,775 in 1891 to $53,774 in 1922.[8] Britain, in 1924, had 800 Curtain machines, half in Nottingham and half in Ayrshire.

Curtain machines had been intended from the first to make very large pieces of lace, and their working width grew to astounding proportions, varying between 144 and 420 inches wide until, by 1928, 300 inches was regarded as the minimum that could function economically. They could make not only vast and intricate designs, but also much smaller imitations of handmade filet, as well as a range of plain or patterned nets trade-named Padlock, Cranford, Ariston and Lacitex.[9] But, shaken by the severe and widespread economic decline which began in 1929, lace curtaining was further threatened by the advent of the art deco period, with houses becoming shorter and rounder, ceilings lower, and tall sash windows turned into short bowed casements so that it was necessary to encourage the entry of light rather than to obstruct it with suspended patterning, however holey. The lace curtain's elaborate magnificence was thus reduced to simple coloured strips of net harmonising with 'spreads for beds' and duchesse sets littering the tops of dressing tables. In 1939 the machines were diverted into the manufacture of surgical, camouflage, sandfly and mosquito netting, as well as anti-scatter netting for windows – totalling in all 65 million square metres from Nottingham alone.[10]

The Curtain machine suffered little competition from other machines until about 1900 when Schiffli embroideries on bobbinet began; but by far the fiercest competition was 50 years later from the Raschel which, exploring the relatively new artificial silks and synthetic fibres, and working with immense speed, could produce curtains far more quickly and cheaply. It was the fortuitous nostalgia of the late 1960s which brought a reversal of fortune, kindling a mild passion for floating cupids levitating amid garlands of flowers, bullrushes and drifting swans languidly enmeshed in rivers of net, and Oriental figures seated beneath tufted pines (fig. 109). The vogue for natural fibres which followed gave another advantage to the Curtain machine, for the Raschel's rapid warp knitting sheared from the cotton yarn vast quantities of 'lint' and for it the smooth tough filaments of synthetics were much more congenial.

175

109 *A half-curtain, or* brise-bise. *Note the square-meshed ground and the tunnel across the top to hold the curtain rod. Though the design does not attempt to imitate a handmade lace it may well have drawn inspiration from eighteenth-century silk designs, such as those by Pillement.*

The parts of the machine

The front view of the Curtain machine is similar to that of the Leavers (figs. 110a, b), and the terms used – rise, fall, right, left, sley, carriage etc – are for the most part identical. However, it always has only one warp roller; its patterning threads are not arranged in the same way; and its patterning mechanism operates on a quite different principle.

There are four groups of threads: warp, top board, bottom board (sometimes replaced by a beam), and bobbin. All are equal in number, thus on a 360 inch 10-point machine there would be a total of 14,400 separate threads. Their activities are:

Warp – passes down the lace in straight lines;

Top board – pillars on the warp in the ground, and gaits (throws or shogs) in the pattern areas. That is, it can act alternately as a warp or as a weft;

Bottom board, or beam – acts as a weft, making, for example, two-gait throws in both the ground and the pattern;

Bobbin – ties the bottom board or top board threads to the pillars.

The earlier machines had only three groups of threads, the bottom board spools being a later addition.

Warps The ends, or separate threads, arising from the single warp roller pass upwards through a sley, and then through holes in a single guide bar. This warp bar is controlled by a cam so that every one of its threads will be displaced to the same extent by each of its sideways movements. The warps therefore cannot pattern – which means behaving non-uniformly – and they form instead a kind of skeletal support for the entire fabric.

110a *A diagram of the end view, after patent no. 16280, Birkin and Goodley, 1906.*

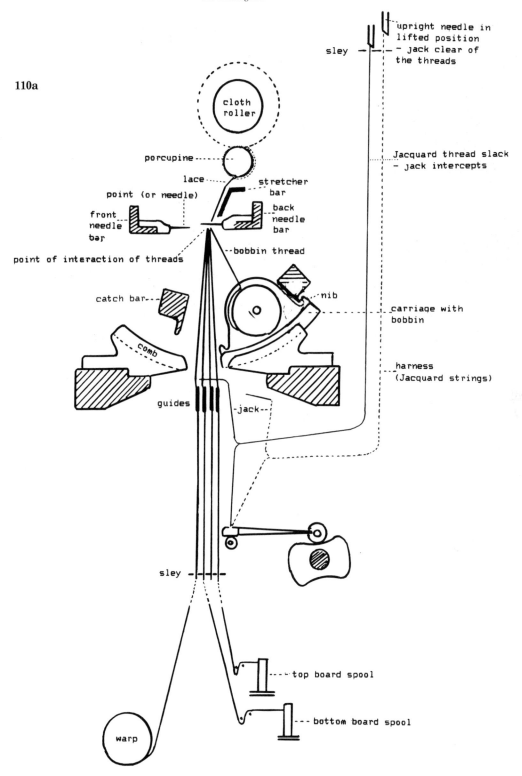

110a

upright needle in
lifted position
— jack clear of
the threads

sley

Jacquard thread slack
— jack intercepts

cloth
roller

porcupine

lace

stretcher
bar

point (or needle)

back
needle
bar

front
needle
bar

bobbin thread

point of interaction of threads

nib

carriage with
bobbin

catch bar

comb

harness
(Jacquard strings)

guides

jack

sley

top board spool

bottom board spool

warp

110b *A curtain machine, from the front. Twentieth-century models may be 612 inches wide and weigh 30 tons (Spowoge, Humphreys and Wyer).*

Top board These are held on upright spools at the back of the machine, each spool carrying approximately three to four ounces of yarn. The threads pass through small tension springs which help them to unwind evenly, then through a sley, and then through the holes in the back guide bar.

The *beam* when present acts as a second warp with all the ends coming off the same roller. Its ends are passed through the front bar, while the warp ends are transferred to the middle bar.

A *bottom board* holding spools was a later development, and serves as an elaborate replacement for the beam. It is sometimes known as the second board, or Swiss board, and its spools hold finer threads. These, like the top board spools, go through tension springs, and finally through holes in the middle guide bar. The use of a single beam gives greater uniformity of tension than thousands of separate spools from which the release of each thread is individually controlled. However, when extensive and intricate patterning is required, spools must be used since only they have the necessary individuality to release, through Jacquard control, constantly varying amounts of yarn (fig. 110c).

Guide bars Three bars – front, middle and back – are needed to hold the three groups of threads. The front bar is at the front of the machine, and normally holds the warp threads. It is also known as the first bar, warp guide, or combination bar.

The middle bar holds the bottom board spool threads, and may be called the second

110c

110c *From the back, showing the top and bottom boards, with spools, and the ladder which leads up to the Jacquard apparatus in the roof, from which the harness rays down (Batsford Textile Group Ltd, Nottingham).*

111

111 *A set of seven cams, made by Birkin and Co. in 1840 for the Leavers machine, but similar to those used for lace curtaining. The seven trucks with their levers rest on the uneven cam surface.*

bar, Swiss bar, or fine spool bar, referring to the finer yarn.

The back bar holds the top board spool threads, and is also known as the third bar, coarse spool, or back spool bar. A fourth bar can be added to separate the fine spool threads into two groups when more intricate Jacquard-controlled patterning is required. All three bars are made to work uniformly across the width of the lace by *work cams*, so that every thread in a particular bar behaves in precisely the same way. The cams are like circular wheels of uneven circumference which, as they revolve, alternately bulge and recede. The edge of the can moves against a truck which is attached to a lever, connected to a guide bar. The effect of a bulge on the cam is to push the truck away, causing it to 'rise' to the left. As the bulge passes, the truck sinks back, following the circumference of

the cam, and its lever and guide bar 'fall' to the right. The fall is reinforced by a spring at the far left-hand end of the guide bar which, compressed by the rise, pushes back through the whole 360 or so inches of the working width against the truck, clamping it constantly to the undulating circumference of the cam (fig. 111).

Thus the basic action of the guide bars, and therefore of the threads which they hold, is a series of relatively small movements to right or left, each bar having its own cam, and acting independently of the other two. The

179

rises and falls may be across two, three or four gaits. In theory the maximum is seven, in practice four, since longer throws stretch the guide bar thread at a very acute angle to its fixed position in the sley, putting a greater frictional strain upon it, as well as increasing the speed of throw necessary if collision with the bobbin threads is to be avoided. After each rise or fall, the gaiting thread returns to its original non-working position.

The regular cam movement cannot itself be stopped while the machine is working, but the sway of individual spool threads from the middle and back bars can be interrupted by the Jacquard mechanism.

Combs and carriages The basic structure of the combs, carriages and bobbins is similar to other bobbin-net machines, though the carriages are larger to accommodate an adequate length of coarser thread, and the carriage slide almost fills the depth of a comb so that the to-and-fro swing is very short. These bobbins are sometimes called brass bobbins to distinguish them from the wood bobbins which hold the spool threads (see fig. 80).

The *gauge* is defined in terms of the number of carriages per inch width, not per half-inch as in Leavers. Thus a 420-inch 10-point machine would have 4,200 carriages and bobbin threads, and the same number of warp ends, top board spools, and bottom board spools when these latter are present. The gauge may vary between 6 and 20, though 10 is most commonly used.[11]

The carriages are swung by front and back catch bars. These connect with the nibs of the carriages in a pushing and catching ritual similar to that described for the Leavers landing bar.

The term *gait* does not mean precisely the same as in Leavers. It is still the distance across a bobbin thread, but the appearance in the finished lace is quite different. In most Leavers laces the bobbin threads lie straight and parallel, and the gait positions are clearly the spaces between them. In the Curtain machine however the warps are weighted so that it is they which give the appearance of lying straight while the bobbin threads circle

around, binding the spool threads to them. Thus warp and bobbin threads appear superimposed, and the gait becomes the space between two warp threads or, to be quite precise, between the inner and outer borders of two separate bobbin thread ties (fig. 112a). The carriages are not of course deflected during their swing, the straight back and forth movement along the rigid combs is as undeviating as ever, while the warp guide bar gaits to right or left as required. However, as the threads interact, the warps are at once pulled straight by their weighting, and the lightly sprung bobbin thread, gradually released, is made to encircle it – a process not unlike that which occurs in bobbin fining.

Thus *pillaring*, created as shown in fig. 112b, may be defined as 'two or more threads, warps or spools, encircled and bound by one bobbin thread'. Pillaring is controlled by the pillar cam.

In *net formation*, the pillars must be connected together, and this is done by one or other of the spool threads making short gaits. Fig. 112c makes it obvious that while this

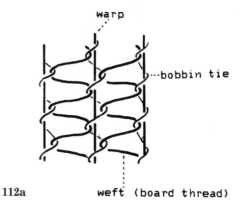

112a   weft (board thread)

112a A two-gait tie. **b** *Bobbin pillaring: as the warp thread is pulled straight, the looser bobbin thread is made to pillar around it.* **c** *Detail of a Curtain machine net showing the weakness of the bobbin ties. Above, links made by the spool threads are the same in every wale; below, the links alternate in adjacent wales.* **d** *Quality, compared simply by the number of meshes per unit length of lace, a fine four and a coarse two.* **e** *Simplified cam action showing its effect on a lever, via the truck which makes contact with its surface.*

TWISTING OR
PILLARING   Successive 1-gait
throws from
gait 0 to gait 1,
and return

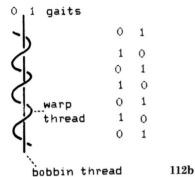

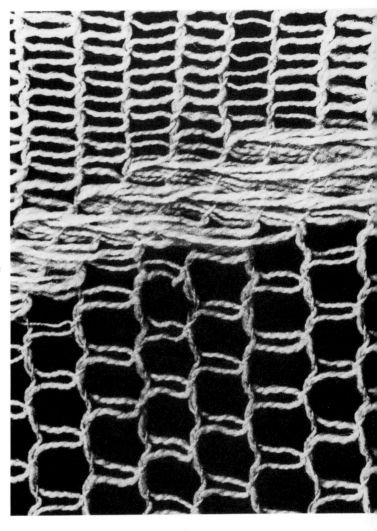

0	1	gaits
	0	1
	1	0
	0	1
	1	0
warp	0	1
thread	1	0
	0	1

bobbin thread   112b   112c

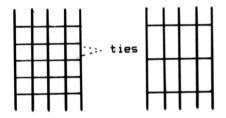

:::- ties

Stiff quality   Slack quality 112d

112e   From front of machine   Simplified diagram of cam effect

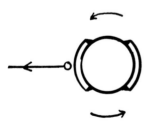

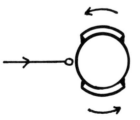

Truck and lever displaced to the   Truck and lever fall to the
left by bulge.   right as cam flattens.
Guide bars rise.   Guide bars fall.

181

technique ensures that the cross-bars of the net are simply and economically formed, they nevertheless introduce a serious weakness, in being held in place only by the bobbin thread ties. Further, this sort of straight-down net is rigid, lacking any of that pliancy which the traversing of the bobbin threads in the two-tier Circular machine gives to its nets, when the paired bobbin threads, passing diagonally in either direction, encircle each warp in turn across all the meshes of the web, locking the fabric together in an easy flexibility. The square meshes of the early lace curtains were easily broken, causing long splits to appear between the pillars so that the whole thing fell apart. There were continual improvements, and advertisers always made a point of stressing the 'unequalled for durability' aspect of their products.[12]

Patterning, also known as clothing, gimping or filling-in, is brought about by longer and more frequent gaiting of the spool threads in specific areas. As in the net, the gaiting threads are tied at every new position by the bobbin threads before they return.

Points As the rows of work are completed, the 'points enter to take up the ties'.[13] In other words, the upward-sweeping point-bars work alternately at the back and front of the web, inserting their tips to carry the lace upwards, past the facing bar to the spiky porcupine, a steel roller covered with wire bristles, which turns the smooth cloth roller on which the work accumulates.

As in the Leavers, *quality* refers to the speed of take-off which is set by the porcupine. A slow take-off gives a stiff quality with many meshes per unit of vertical length. A rapid take-off gives a slack quality with few meshes per unit of vertical length (fig. 112d). For the Curtain machine, quality is defined as the number of complete bobbin motions (front + back) required to produce three inches of lace. For example, 60-quality means that 60 complete motions produce a three-inch length of lace across the width of the machine; 20-quality means that 20 complete motions produce a three-inch length, and so on. The greater the number of motions, the closer the work and the higher the quality.

The quality can be calculated from a finished piece of lace by counting the number of bobbin thread turns (one complete turn = one full motion) per three inches, or alternatively the number per inch ×3.

A *rack* is the measurement of length used, as in other lace machines, as a basis for piece-work payments. In the Curtain machine it is defined as that length of lace produced by 1,440 bobbin motions (720 front + 720 back). The higher the quality therefore the shorter the actual length of a rack will be, but the unit is fair enough as a basis for pay since the time and skill of the twist-hand is more closely related to the number of carriage motions than to any actual measurement. For a 60-quality curtain, 60 motions would by definition give a three-inch length of lace; 720 full motions, the length of a rack, would then give 36 inches. For a 20-quality lace, 720 full motions would give 108 inches; and an 80-quality rack would measure a mere 27 inches (80 motions produce three inches, therefore 720 would give nine times as many, ie 27 inches).

An average take-off speed is five racks an hour, needing the completion of 3,600 full motions, or 60 forward and backward swings every single minute.

Although there are a number of different types of cam – pillar, bar ground, combination, jack – they are no more than uneven wheels, each complete rotation of which represents at the most two full bobbin motions (fig. 112e), and they produce uniformity rather than variety of effect along the three bars. The complex non-uniform patterning of which the Curtain machine is capable has another source. In a sense it is a negative process, consisting of an interruption of the cam-controlled gaiting in selected areas. Where this happens, gaiting in those areas cannot occur, the adjacent pillars will not be linked, and holes will appear.

Jacks The interrupting device is called a jack, or interceptor. What it does is to stand in the way of the thread movements so that they cannot take place – rather like a policeman stepping into the road and holding up his hand to stop the traffic (fig. 113). In technical

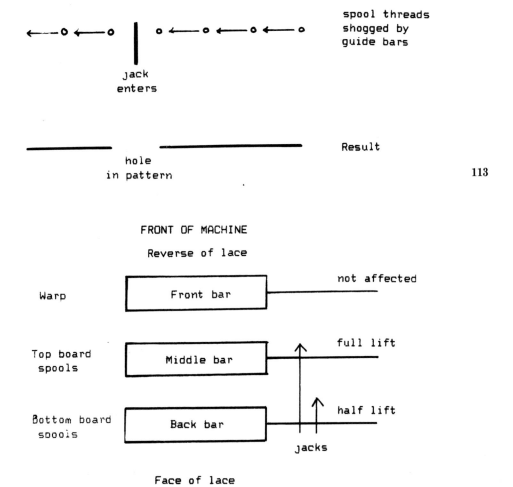

113 *The effect of jack intervention in preventing the shogging of specific spool threads.*

114 *The relation of jack action to the vertical bar-threads. The back of the lace as made (technical back) is the front of the lace as used (textural front). The parallel warp threads form ridges on the reverse side of the lace.*

language, the jacks can cause the guide bar threads 'to either place, or leave off, the ties.' The ties (encirclement by the bobbin threads) are placed when the spool threads stop at a pillar; and are left off when, at that point, they go beyond. Here, in the actual lace, the spool threads will pass over the warps and not be held down to them.

Jacks are equal in number to the carriages, and their effect is only on the spool threads. Each jack is a hardened steel wire, the outer thin end of which can enter between the vertically-stretched threads and stop their sideways movement. When not in use, the jacks are drawn back into a series of slots called tricks, which also serve to prevent any lateral oscillation. The jacks shoot up and back in the same plane as the bobbin swings, acting individually and not in unison, to enter between the threads or to be held back from them, as the Jacquard determines.

Each jack can affect only those threads immediately on either side of it. Jacks do not affect the warp threads at all, and may affect the two sets of spool threads either together or separately. A partial interception of the thread movements, affecting only the back bar (top board) threads, is called a *half-lift*, and results in lighter areas of patterning sometimes called brights. A *full-lift* takes the jack across both back and middle bars, so arresting the gaiting of both top and bottom board spool threads, and causing a hole (fig. 114).

The control of the individual jack movements is the work of the Jacquard. The basic structure of the Jacquard is similar to that of the Leavers: sets of cards are punched in a differential manner so that they control the movements of the patterning threads. The set of cards in each is joined into a circle, representing one full vertical repeat of the design; and mounted on a pair of cylinders which, between motions, advance towards or retreat from a selective mechanism which, card by card, transmits the required design to the patterning threads. For the most part, in both machines, each card represents the gaiting to occur at each bobbin motion, so the speed of turning is very rapid. The Curtain machine has the additional complication that some of the jack movements require two bobbin motions, front and back, to complete them.

Apart from all this, Leavers and Lace Curtain Jacquards differ in their size, in the number of cards needed, and in the agents through which they produce their effects. Although both have two Jacquard cylinders, each holding a set of cards, those of the Leavers move up and down alternately in a vertical plane, one controlling the front bobbin motion patterning, the other the back. In the Curtain machine the advance and retreat is in a horizontal plane, and the two cylinders do not move alternately, but together, one controlling the top board spool threads (back bar), the other the bottom board spool threads (middle bar). In some classes of work the bottom board threads gait only on the front motion, and its cylinder will then turn at only half the speed of the top board Jacquard which works on both back and front motions.

The Jacquard cards

Each top spool Jacquard card controls the gaiting of the patterning threads at every bobbin motion. So, the cards must be the same in number as the bobbin motions required to complete the design, even up to 12,000.

In Leavers, the horizontal extent of the design was defined by the number of carriages involved, for example an 80-carriage set-out. Only this much needed to be punched on the Jacquard cards since the repetitive threading of all the 100 or so guide bars automatically carried the repeat across the web. In the Curtain machine, the situation is rather different. For one thing, the threads to be manipulated are crowded into only two bars, so that differential threading is no longer possible. For another, the Curtain machine has to be capable of constructing not only narrow bands but also huge designs intended to cover a large proportion of the entire web. This means that every single patterning thread must be allocated a position on the card, even when their total number tops 4,000. Related to this, is the mode of operation of the jacks. They are not, and cannot be, operated in unison, like the threads of a Leavers guide bar. Each is quite individually pulled, or not pulled, by strings.

The problems of Curtain machine card-punching are simplified by four things:

a. Each jack has only a single, simple movement, that of going between, or not going between, selected spool threads. Jacks do not initiate gaiting, which is cam-controlled, but arrest its effect where the pattern requires it.

b. It follows that no arithmetical device, such as a graded set of dropper heads, is needed, as it is in Leavers, to calculate the length of throw.

c. Therefore only a single hole position, per spool, is needed, not six or seven positions.

d. This simplicity enables the spool thread positions to be arranged in rows, of 16 at a time, on the cards, numbered from the bottom upwards, the numbers corresponding to those of the actual spools on their boards (fig. 115a). Thus the length of the card is

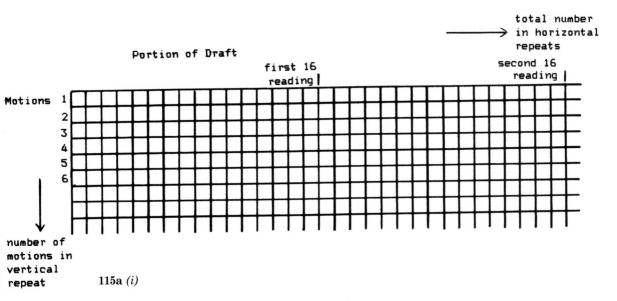

Portion of Draft

total number
in horizontal
repeats

first 16
reading

second 16
reading

Motions 1
2
3
4
5
6

number of
motions in
vertical
repeat

115a *(i)*

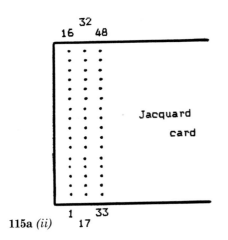

115a *(ii)*

The numbers represent the spool threads

115a *(i) numbered spool positions as arranged on the draft, and continuing for the width of one horizontal repeat; (ii) how their positions are transferred to the Jacquard card, 16 at a time.* b *(i) a theoretical draft which plots jack interceptions of top and bottom board spools over two bobbin motions; (ii) an actual draft for an 8-point 45 quality single action combination all-over lace: the darker squares are red for top board spools, the lighter blue for the combination ties (Basford Textile Group).* c *The information on draft b (i) transferred to the two sets of cards, top board and bottom board.*

reduced to $\frac{1}{16}$ of what it otherwise would be. For example, a machine with 4,200 top spool threads would need, if their positions were marked out side by side with an allocation of $\frac{1}{4}$-inch apiece, to have cards 1,050 inches, or nearly 30 yards, wide. By arranging the positions in rows of 16, the required width is reduced to 66 inches, or 1.8 yards. This is still pretty hefty, especially considering that two sets of cards that size are needed. They occupy, in fact, far too much space to be placed at the side of the machine, and the whole thing – cards, cylinders, and the mechanism which they operate – is hauled up into the roof of the factory from where, high above the massive carcase, thousands of strings ray downwards, fanning out from an aperture in the ceiling to become attached, in a very specific manner, to the jacks in their tricks below.

The draft The design which is to be made is drawn, and then drafted to show the action of the patterning (spool) threads. The draft is quite different from Leavers since it shows not left to right gait-throws, but back and forth jack movements. A horizontal row on the draft still represents the activity, or non-activity, of all the jacks for a single bobbin

185

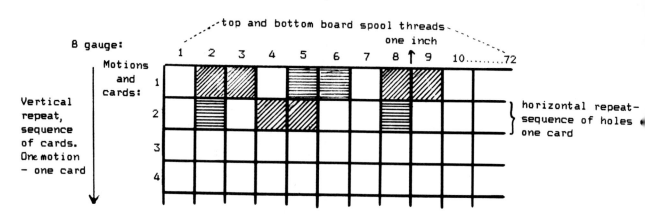

red: instructions for jacks controlling top board spool threads.

green: instructions for jacks controlling bottom board spool threads

115b *(i)*

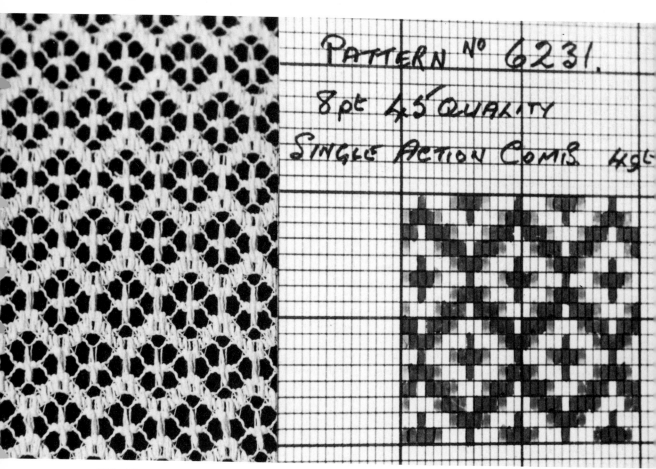

PATTERN Nº 6231.
8pt 45' QUALITY
SINGLE ACTION COMBS. 45g

115b *(ii)*

186

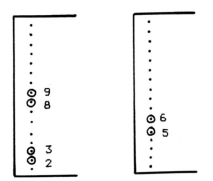

Card 1.
top board spools.

Card 1.
bottom board spools.

115c

motion. However, a vertical row represents not a gait but a position of a spool thread. The patterning is represented by a series of squares drawn of a scale which is a multiplication of the machine's gauge.

Instructions for top board spools are indicated in red (solids), and for bottom board spools in green (Swiss ties). White indicates pillaring, producing holes or meshes, but this is not entered on the Jacquard card since it is controlled by a cam. Blue may be used for combination ties (nips), involving the warps and a combination cam, rather than the Jacquard. More complex codes may at times be used: red, green and blue may have alternative meanings, or additional colours may be added, such as orange and black.

Where the design across the web is divided up into identical repeats, only one of these need of course be drafted, but the cards themselves must still be punched or blanked for every thread. Fig. 115b shows a small portion of a draft, indicating by varied shading the red and green infillings.

Punching the cards When the draft has been completed, all the information which it gives has to be translated from red and green squares into holes or blanks on Jacquard cards, the red making one series, the green another.

Since the potential hole positions on every card are in rows of 16, the squares have to be read off in this way. For example, in the fragment illustrated:

Motion 1 – red squares are shown for spool numbers 2, 3, 8, and 9. Holes must be punched in these positions on card no. 1 of the set controlling the top board spools in the back guide bar. Also in motion 1, green squares are shown for spool numbers 5 and 6. Holes must be punched in these positions on card no. 1 of the second set, controlling the bottom board spools in the middle guide bar.

In fig. 115c the small dots represent spool thread positions according to their numbers. The small circles represent holes punched. The areas between the holes are blanks. Suppose that the design which has been drafted has an actual breadth of 10 inches, and that the width of the machine on which it is to be worked is 300 inches, 10-point gauge. This means that the draft shows 100 threads out of a total of 3,000, and its instructions must be repeated 30 times in order to cover every spool thread across the machine. The punch-operative, therefore, having got to the end of the first horizontal row of the draft must begin once again at the beginning of that row, continuing straight on the same card. When the draft instructions have been represented 30 times on the first card, its punching is complete, and the operative can proceed to the second row, and the second card. So the punching will continue, line by line of the draft, 30 times over for every card, and two cards for every line, one for the red squares and one for the green.

When the last card of the vertical repeat is reached, the punching is finished. Each set of cards can be joined into a circle and mounted on the appropriate cylinder. When this has gone round once, it will begin to go round again, and then again, automatically repeating the sequence until it is stopped.

Press-offs: how the cylinders work

The two cylinders are four-sided, and made of wood or brass. Each side is pitted with holes arranged in rows of 16, to a total of 3,000 or whatever the number of top or bottom board spools for that particular machine may be.

The cards are held on the cylinder face by small pegs which slot into the card's peg-holes. The cylinders act in unison, making quarter-turns in pace with the bobbin motions. This continues, step by step through the card sequence, until the lace is completed. In certain classes of work the top spool cylinder turns twice as fast as the bottom spool cylinder.

All the holes which have been punched in the Jacquard cards must rest precisely over the holes present on the cylinder. As the cylinder turns, it advances to offer its card towards a doffer plate. This is attached by springs to a needle plate from which project exactly as many needles in exactly the same arrangement as there are holes in the Jacquard cylinder, and spool thread positions on the card. There is a separate needle plate for each cylinder, and in a position of rest the doffer plates cover the needles.

As the machine is set in motion, the cylinders advance in unison towards their doffer plates, moved by an eccentric cam driven by the machine's main drive shaft. Projections at the side of each cylinder push back the doffer plate exposing the thousands of needles neatly arranged in their ranks of 16. As the cylinders continue to advance, the needles are pressed into the holes in the cylinders in every position where they are able to pass through the card, that is wherever the card has been punched. Where they cannot pass through because they come up against blanks, their further advance is halted, and in effect they are pushed back. This differential effect on the needles is called the *press-off*. It is the basis on which the jacks are motivated to intercept or not intercept the spool threads (fig. 116).

The horizontal needles, against which the cards are pressed, are called 'cross-needles'. Attached to them at right angles are 'upright needles'. When a cross-needle passes through a hole in a Jacquard card, and on into a cylinder hole, the upright needle is pulled forwards, or 'lifted'. This pulls on the Jacquard string attached to it, tightening it. The pull is transmitted to the jack to which the other end of the string is tied, with the result that the jack is held clear of the spool threads,

it cannot be activated by the jack cam, and so cannot interfere with the work cams which automate the gaiting of those threads. This allows clothing, or patterning, to be produced.

However, when a cross-needle meets the resistance of a blank on the card, its upright needle is pushed back, or rejected. Its string remains slack, and this allows the jack to be driven by the jack cam. It springs between the relevant spool threads, arresting their sideways action, and causing pillaring and the formation of openwork to occur. In technical language,

the action of the jack or interceptor, entering the back spool [top board] threads, causes them to change from weft to warp [ie from making horizontal connections or cross-ties to vertical movements or pillaring]. When the jacks are held back on the other hand, the back spool threads cease to be warps [passing vertically] and commence gaiting [passing horizontally] in the form of weft threads [ie they are subject to throws across wales, or gaits, which can produce solids].[14]

Or, alternatively,

the holes in the card are non-action areas, and there cloth continues to be made. If the needles go through a hole in the card it pulls a jack out from the tricks and allows patterning through the spools. A blank however causes the impact of needle and card to knock a string down and cause the jack to come through separating the threads and making a hole in the cloth.

As so often happens with lace, a superabundance of synonyms confuses accounts of this machine. Thus 'the jacks enter' can be rendered 'the jacks press in, or are turned in, or are allowed to go in, or to come through'; while 'the jacks are held back' can also be expressed 'held out, right back, pulled out, or retire'.

As soon as the press-off has been completed, the Jacquard cylinder retreats, and the doffer plate, released from the pressure against it, moves forward again to cover the needles. As it does so, each cylinder makes a quarter-revolution by means of a clawker, and the next cards click into the presentation position. The cylinders advance once more, and another horizontal row of patterning begins.

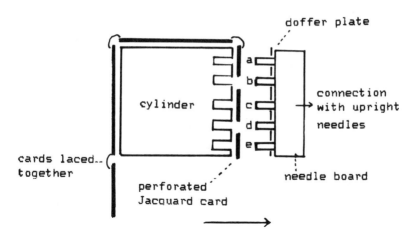

116 *A simplified diagram to illustrate the structures involved in the Jacquard press-off: a–e are needles; as the cylinder advances, needles b and d penetrate holes in the Jacquard card, while needles a, c and e are halted by blanks.*

The tie-up

The set of strings which links the thousands of upright needles with the thousands of jacks constitutes the 'harness' (see fig. 110c). The strings are made of heavy linen or, more recently, of polyester. The disadvantage of this arrangement is that the strings are vulnerable to changes of humidity, which in a factory are not easy to control. Such changes may cause the strings to extend, or to shorten, and this is unfortunate since their entire patterning effect is completely dependent on their slackness or tightness. Any aberration can be corrected by frequent adjustment, but it all adds to the cost of production. Another obvious danger is friction between the strings during their constant movements, but this can be obviated by the use of a sley.

Since there are two cylinders, each jack must receive two strings, one to relate it to the middle spool (bottom board), and the other to the back spool (top board), threads, so that it has an opportunity of intercepting either, according to the instructions record-ed on the card (fig. 117a). Then the full 6,000 spool threads (in the example on p. 187) can produce their effect through 6,000 strings attached in pairs to 3,000 jacks.

On large curtains, mirror image designs are often required, either to make a matching pair, or to make a single very large curtain with the pattern arranged on either side of a central motif. In this case, even more complex tie-ups are needed: to each upright needle double strings must be attached, which separate and extend to opposing sides of the web, so that each needle controls the two opposite sides of the work. In this way right and left sides can be produced simultaneously, in reverse to each other, making possible an exact symmetry. This sort of arrangement is called 'universal tie-up' (fig. 117b).

In constructing the draft for such a design, only half of it needs to be blocked, and each card needs to be punched for only half the width of the web, since every hole, or blank, will produce its effect twice over, on the right and on the left side of the machine.

The very centre string of the mirror image, at the point where the designs reverse, will be not a double but a single one, from one needle to one jack per Jacquard cylinder. This odd one is called the 'turnover string'. However, if there is to be a central decorative area, such as a coat of arms, between the mirror images, then this has to be punched separately, at the far end of the Jacqard card (figs. 117c, d). The larger this single-string, or non-repeat, area is, the more holes need to be punched, the

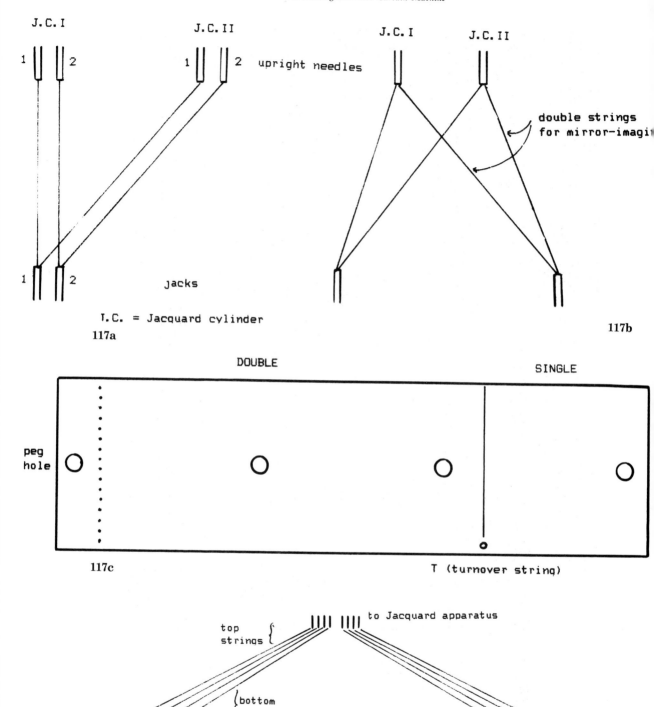

J.C. I

1 ⊔ ⊔ 2

J.C. II

1 ⊔ ⊔ 2   upright needles

J.C. I

J.C. II

double strings
for mirror-imagi[...]

1 ⊔ ⊔ 2   jacks

J.C. = Jacquard cylinder

117a

117b

DOUBLE

SINGLE

peg
hole ○   ○   ○   ○

117c

T (turnover string)

top
strings {

to Jacquard apparatus

{ bottom
strings

jacks

117d   double stringing   single stringing
to allow turnover   double stringing

190

117e

117a *The double stringing of the jacks: JC I and JC II indicate the two sets of cards, one for each spool board.* **b** *The universal tie-up which makes simultaneous mirror-imaging possible: one upright needle from each Jacquard, and one jack at the right and left sides of the machine, are shown.* **c** *A Jacquard card with double-stringing on the left-hand area for mirror-imaging, and single-stringing in the right-hand area for the central non-repeat part of the web.* *The single row of dots represents the first 16 potential hole positions.* **d** *The double and single areas in relation to the harness, simplified.* **e** *A curtain with central 'single' design flanked by mirror imaging* (Pharoah by Anna's Choice, Ayrshire). **f** *Comparison of fine and coarse gauge effects: (i) 8-point double action work; (ii) 14-point with much greater intricacy and delicacy of detail* (Basford Textile Group).

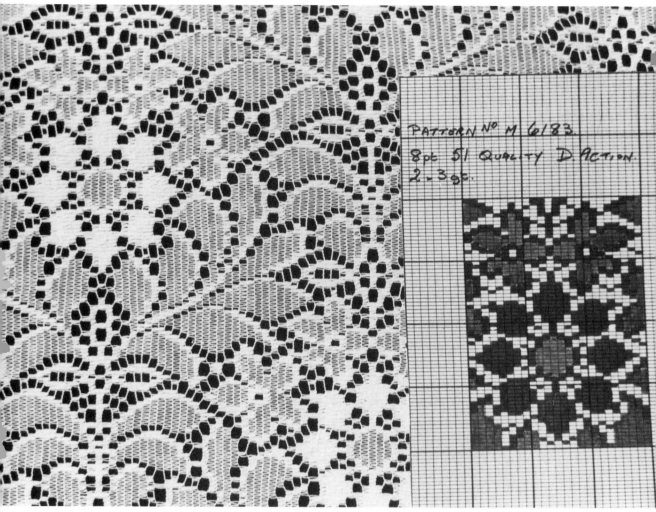

117f *(i)*

longer the card, the greater the number of needles required, and the more costly the work (fig. 117e).

Classes of work

The set-up of the Curtain machine allows complex patterning, which is reinforced by variations in thickness, or colour, between the four sets of threads:

bobbin – bottom board – warp – top board
FINE ⟶ COARSE

Either cotton or synthetics can be used.

The gauge of the machine is proportionate to the detail required in the design. Fine detail requires a fine gauge such as 14, while a bold design needs a low gauge to accommodate thicker thread (fig. 117f). Higher gauge machines are for the most part smaller than low gauge machines, and they produce smaller quantities of finer work.

Grounds Curtain machine grounds or openwork parts are broadly distinguishable into Madras, filet and Swiss nets. Apart from varying in whether or not jacks are involved, they can also differ in whether two, three or four gaits are thrown; in whether all the

117f *(ii)*

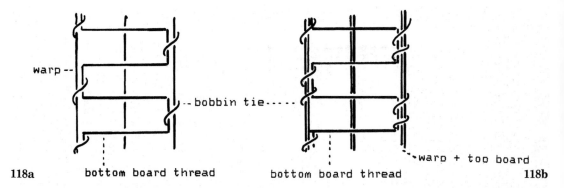

bottom board thread   bottom board thread   **118b**

gaiting is to the left, or whether right and left throws from the original pillar alternate; in the extent to which the middle and back guide bars are involved; and in whether there is special weighting to produce nips, or combination ties, between adjacent warps. A summary of the main types is discussed below.

1. *Bar grounds* are sometimes called independent ground since they function independently of the Jacquard apparatus, using work cams which control each bar as a whole producing either a uniform pillaring of the warp, or regular two-gait throws of the spool threads to form the tops and bottoms of the meshes. Inevitably the groundwork runs right through the area of patterning. Basically, bar grounds are all variations of square net or filet. Worked with only three sets of threads (warp, top board and bobbin), the result is thin and unstable, producing a net known as Madras. In this, the bobbin ties which lash the gaiting threads to the pillars form points of weakness, and Madras net's only advantage is its low cost, resulting from the small amount of thread used. It is no longer made. The normal sequence for a work cam is that it rises on the back motion and falls the same number of gaits on the front motion.

A three-thread net can be made stronger and heavier by:

a. extending the gaiting;
b. making the gaited threads overlap;
c. using double instead of single ties;
d. using bottom board threads to make a fourth set, with the top board pillaring on the warp while the bottom boards throw every

118a *Single tie filet, or 2-and-1 filet: the beam (bottom board) throws across two wales in one motion, and the vertical side of each throw is held by a single tie.* b *Double tie filet.* c *'Lockstitch net' described as 'new' in 1908: (i) the overlapping of the gaited threads adds strength and durability. (ii) an actual lace with a small motif imitates the appearance and design of hand-filet. (iii) detail.*

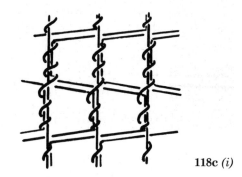

118c *(i)*

third motion. In filet ground, a beam is used instead of bottom board spools.

In *single-tie filet* (or 2-and-1 filet) the beam thread crosses two wales in one motion, and the vertical side of each throw is held by a single tie (fig. 118a).

In *double-tie filet*, the throws are on the front motions only, instead of every motion, therefore the vertical side of each throw is held by two ties (that is the gaited thread remains by the pillar for two motions) before returning (fig. 118b, c).

2. *Jacked grounds* introduce an independence of movement for the spool threads which can add considerable variety to ground ef-

118c *(ii)*

fects, since adjacent threads may either throw or pillar, under Jacquard control, instead of all doing precisely the same thing at the same time. Three-thread jacked grounds can produce an inexpensive *mock filet*, but this tends to be unstable through inadequate cam control.

Other jacked grounds can be grouped under the name *Swiss* because of the greater involvement of the middle or Swiss guide bar with its bottom board spool threads. In these, although the sides remain straight, the meshes are not quite square, and the ends are like horizontal arrow-heads pointing left or right and sometimes called V-ties. The Swiss tie can be made as a bar ground in which the back bar throws every notion, but it can just as well be intercepted by a jack, to space out

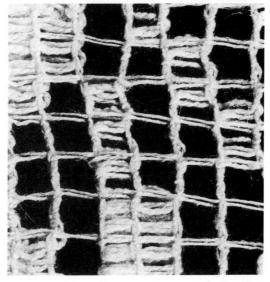

118c *(iii)*

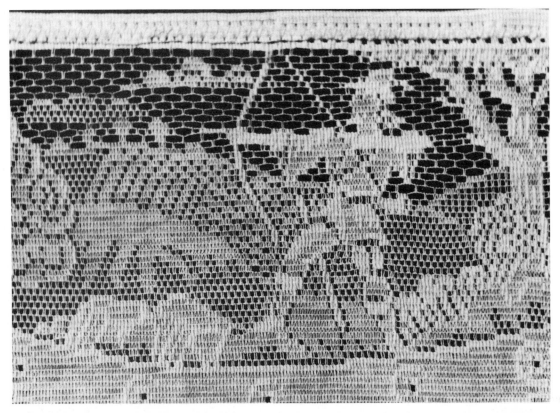

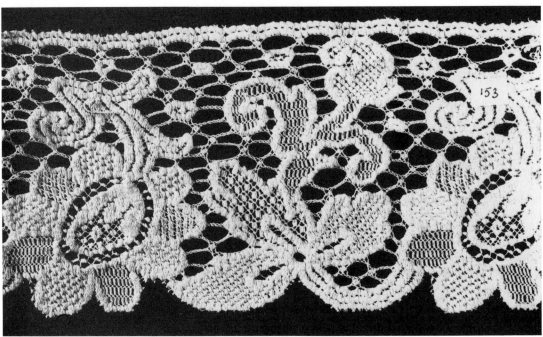

120a

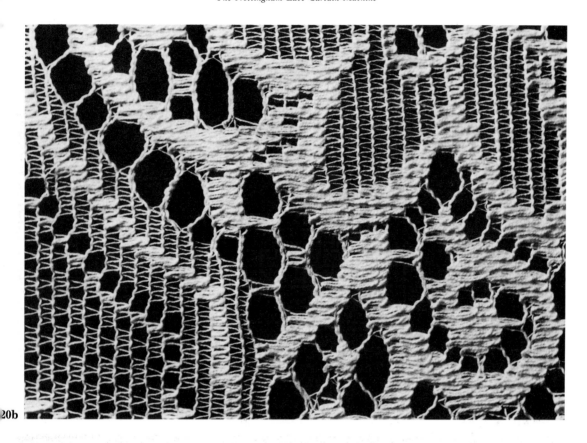

120b

119 *Jacked grounds in a commemorative panel similar in design to those produced by the Raschel (see fig. 42a). Robin Hood is made of two-gait throws spaced out by jacks to give variable density; the sky is made of Swiss net, 1982.*

120a *Combination effect.* **b** *Detail of modern curtaining: the lighter effect is made by two-gait Swiss ties, the denser by top board throws over four gaits, with the Swiss board threads continuing beneath them; in the mesh ground the top board pillars, giving an effect of heavy straight-down threads; the guipure areas are achieved by combination ties (Basford Textile Group).*

the ties and make a bigger hole, which gives decorative effects (fig. 119). Swiss ties can be used to make a plain net, or the ground of a patterned lace. Possible variations of both Swiss, and filet, nets are numerous, and complex, but the main ones are determined by whether two or three gaits are thrown, and

whether the ties are all in one direction or in opposite directions on alternate throws.

3. *Combinations* In the combination effects, two or more pillars (warp + spool threads) are pulled or nipped together (combined) by the bobbin threads, making large and irregular holes which give a guipure effect (fig. 120a, b). Combination can be described as a 'two-gait Swiss tie with the weight on'.[15] The weight pulls the pillaring threads together until they meet and become one.

Patterning (a) with one set of spool threads (top board), the variation is limited. In *single action* all the spool throws are the same, all three-gait or all four-gait. However by the use of jacks, the top spool threads can vary sufficiently to pillar in the ground, and make regular throws in the pattern areas.

In *double action* work, either two-or four-gait throws can be made by the same threads depending on the Jacquard instructions. The

121a

121b

121a *A typical large scale curtain design of the late nineteenth century. The delicacy of effect results from variations in the length of throws and in the size of the holes.* **b** *A narrower edging made on the Curtain machine. It demonstrates the dramatic impact of a large design in heavy top board thread.* **c** *Detail.*

198

121c

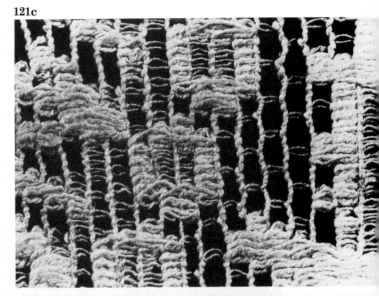

top board spools gait at every motion, and their cylinder has to work at twice the speed of the bottom board Jacquard where gaiting is only at every second motion. The making of the clothing (flossing or pile) is the function of the top board spools. Their heavy thread gives an impressive contrast against the openwork ground (fig. 121a–c).

122a *A flouncing of lightweight silk with a square-meshed pinhole-filet ground. While parts of the patterned areas strongly suggest Swiss ties, the clipped liners are far more characteristic of a Leavers technique. c.1850.* **b** *Detail.*

123a,b Store *curtains and* brise bise. *These engravings of c.1906 illustrate the meanings of the two terms, though the technique used here –* guipure renaissance, *or point lace – is quite different (from Charles and Pagès).*

2a

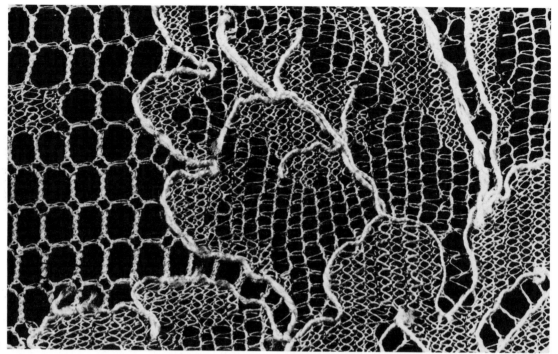

122b

123a

123b

(b) with two sets of spool threads, various different classes of work are possible such as Swiss, Swiss Madras, Swiss and Combination, Swiss Madras and Combination.

Comparison with Leavers laces

While certain types of Leavers and Lace Curtain laces may be confused (figs.122a, b, see also figs 103i and 112a), they are for the most part easily distinguishable, bearing in mind the following points:

a. The ground, or net, of Curtain machines is often square-meshed, or with strong vertical lines linked by horizontal Vs. Such nets are rare in Leavers, where the meshes tend to be hexagonal or round.

b. The Curtain machine, with a maximum throw across three or four gaits, has nothing comparable to Leavers' independent technique with its neatly woven appearance.

c. In Leavers, gimp or beam threads are often restricted to the patterned areas (especially in centre gimp laces). In the Curtain machine, because of the full threading of each of the two or three bars, every thread has to be present in every part of the lace although, if subject to Jacquard control, they can be made to behave differently.

d. The Curtain machine can make huge pat-terns, for example six feet wide and 24 feet high. Leavers could never manage more than about one foot square.

Curtains

From the time that lace curtains were first invented in the mid-nineteenth century, they were hung down the length of high windows, flanked on either side by heavy drapes of wool or silk. In the second half of the century, store curtains and brise-bise came into popularity. *Stores* (French = blinds) hung centrally over the recesses for perhaps three-quarters of their length, hovering over rows of ornamental plants placed on low tables to catch the sun. The short curtains, later stretched horizontally to cover this gap, were known as *brise-bise* (French = *briser* to break, *bise* a light cold wind). They provided privacy, and held back the draught when the windows were opened (fig. 123).

Though frequently named after this class of production, the Curtain machine is not exclusively connected with it. At the patterned level it can make tablecloths, antimacassars, place mats and even fashion accessories (fig. 124). Its nets can be coarse and utilitarian, or fine enough to be used for surface embroidery by for example the Cornely machine, at a time, now, when cotton bobbinets are much in demand and very short in supply.

124 *Part of a mantilla of heavy black silk.*

201

The Barmen

or Circular Braiding Machine

History

This machine, unlike the bobbin-net machines, was not English in origin, and although it produced laces by a twisting technique similar to that of handmade bobbin laces, it has a completely different origin from the Bobbinet, Pusher, Leavers and Lace Curtain. For one thing, it was never concerned with the making of quantities of net. It began instead as a maker of twill-weave braids, some of them of the type used for that point lace which is otherwise known as renaissance, braid or tape lace. In short, while the bobbinet laces were derived from nets later enlivened with patterning, the Barmen laces were derived from solid braids later pierced with openwork (fig. 125a, b).

Since Barmen machines began as braiders, their natural method of manufacture was a diagonal weave. This meant they could easily be adapted to make the crosses and twists of continuous bobbin laces, especially those of fairly simple designs, such as torchon.

The braiders had for the most part a relatively small carcase, of circular form. The threads arose from tall bobbins carried on upright spindles. From here they converged on a central point, where the completed lace was drawn off. In contrast to the warp, beam and bobbin threads of the twist-net machines which have a static, or severely restricted, point of unwinding, the spindles of the braiders could glide swiftly and freely around the circumference following a sinuous course.

The lace braider was a development of the second half of the nineteenth century. In 1858

Brooman patented a hand- or power-operated machine in which 'the bobbins are rotated on their own axes by means of spindles' to make 'Brussels, Val, and Mechlin lace' (no. 2592). The most influential development however was that of Malhère in 1872 (patent no. 852). It was followed by more detailed specifications in 1873 (patent no. 2121). Malhère's machine, known as *La Dentellière* (the Lace-maker) aimed to imitate more closely even than Heathcoat had done the movements and products of bobbin lace-making. Heathcoat had concentrated on analysing the thread movement into divisions (passives and workers) which could be applied to a machine. Malhère instead concentrated on the actions of the lace-maker's hands. He classified them into three:

a. a half-turn of the hand to bring about twists or crosses of the bobbin threads;

b. a horizontal push to select and bring into contiguity the threads which were to be crossed or twisted;

c. the placing of the pins to hold the work as each set of twists and crosses was concluded.[1]

The lay-out of the machine which resulted is shown in fig. 126a. The first action (a) was brought about by 'discs' which 'turn a half-revolution [180°] at determined moments, consecutive discs turning in opposite directions'; the second action (b), the *twist* of the threads 'by turning the discs when they are carrying two bobbins', and 'the *crossing* of the threads by moving the bobbins from one disc to another' – a principle very similar to

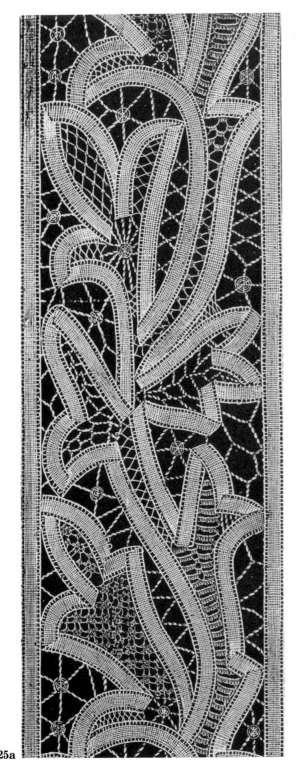

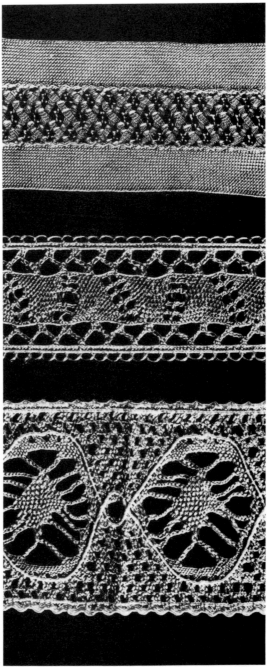

125b

125a *Machine tape-braids similar to those made in Barmen, Germany, but using a plain weave, and forming a tape- or point-lace. Young Ladies' Journal, 1869.* **b** *Fancy openwork braids.*

126a La Dentellière *of Malhère, as seen in 1881* (from *Hénon*).

small piece was completed; and the take-off was equivalent in position to the lace formed over the pricking on a bobbin pillow. A.S. Cole, referring to the machine in 1880, described it as resembling

the pillow of a lace-worker with the threads arranged over the pillow, something like a large semicircular frame-work of iron, with thousands of threads from the outer semi-circle converging to the centre . . The cost of producing lace in this manner is said to be greater at present than by hand.[2] The remarkable similarity of the movements described here to those of bobbin lace-making can be illustrated in a series of simple diagrams (fig. 127a).

La Dentellière could make use of the Jacquard, as could Brooman's 1858 machine, but, elaborate and ingenious as it was, it still fell far short of Malhère's ambitious expectation. In his 1872 and 1873 specifications he illustrates a form of net, and describes the movements necessary for it to be made (fig. 127b). In 1880, a German named Büdenbänder took out a patent (no. 1236) for 'improvements in a combined lace and braid machine', which explains in detail all the levers, plates, axles, rails and cams needed to move the bobbins in the required manner. In it Malhère's fan-shaped arc of a circle was closed, making a circular machine, while his arrangements for twisting and crossing the threads underwent only minor modifications. Two years later Busche produced his 'Braiding machine for the manufacture of real Torchon, Valenciennes and similar lace' (no. 3357), followed in 1883 (no. 5990) by 'a braiding machine for making imitation handmade lace'.

Further patents by Malhère's sons, for example no. 11411 in 1894, attempted to overcome the negative economic aspect of their father's invention by adopting the circular machine form, resulting in a fusion of Dentellière and Braider closely similar to the Barmen of today. It was a good deal smaller, faster and more practical than the Dentellière, but it was still limited in the type (simple) and the width (120mm or eight inches) of lace which it could produce – limitations which it has never overcome. It

that still used in Barmen machines where a pair of spindles (or bobbins) can circle through 180° around each other, or slip from one pair to the next, causing the threads they release to pass over each other.

Malhère, obsessed with verisimilitude, aimed to make his machine not only perform like a lace-maker's pillow, but also to look like one, though on a vast scale (fig. 179, p. 284). His 1,800 to 2,000 bobbins were held in a fan-shaped frame, arranged in a single row round the arc of a circle, so that all their threads were of equal length. The third action (c) consisted in the placing of between 250 and 300 pins to hold the work temporarily as each

(i)

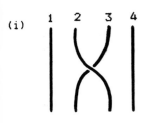

CROSS
Left thread of
inner pair laid
over right thread
(pairs are
        interchanged)

127a *The main bobbin lace-making movements: the twist and the cross (i) from above; (ii) end-on view. The discs must be capable of moving the bobbins in the same way as do the lace-maker's hands.* **b** *The making of a plain twist net, patent no. 852, 1872.*

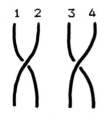

TWIST
Right thread of
each pair laid
over left thread
(pairs stay
        together)

(ii)   The movement   The effect

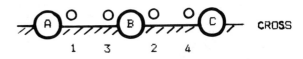   CROSS

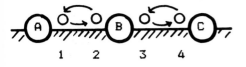

   TWIST

A, B, C = discs (or plates)
1, 2, 3, 4 = bobbins

▨ = surface of pillow in bobbin lace-making

has a firm place in the commercial market, is an admirable producer of furnishing laces and, through its scope for using an extensive melange of thread, colour and textures, a lace with its own very special niche in the world of fashion.

At what point the name Barmen was first used for the machine is uncertain. Barmen is one of the centres of the Wuppertal industrial area in Germany, and both braiding and ribbon machines were firmly established there in the mid-nineteenth century when narrow tapes used in 'point lace' were being made.[3] Patents up to the twentieth century referred to 'Lace-making Braiding machines'; in the *Daily Mail* Lace Exhibition of

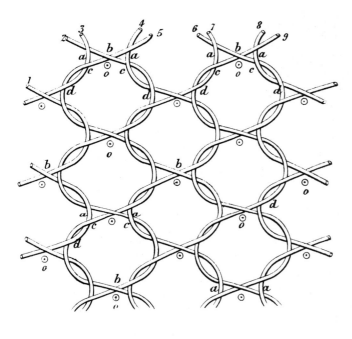

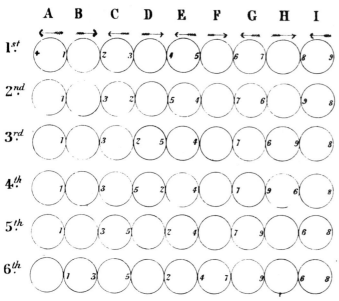

1908 it was called the Patented Circular Machine; and some writers as late as 1930 used the term Circular machine,[4] thus opening the way for all sorts of confusion.

The English franchise was taken up by Birkin and Co at the end of the nineteenth century, and patents registered in their name in 1899 (no. 1127) and 1905 (nos. 3873 and 3874) relate to inventions by the Malhère brothers. By 1914 there were five factories in Le Puy.

The structure of the machine

The general structure of one of the present-day Barmens is shown in fig. 128a. As far as general appearance goes, this compact machine resembles far more closely the circular hosiery frame invented by Brunel in 1830 than it does the vast multi-ton edifices of the twist-net machines. The idea of circularity may indeed have been borrowed from Brunel's invention, though the details are quite different. In the round knitting machine of the 1870s, the circle of latch needles huddled along the outer border like hungry fledgelings while an endless worm of thread was distributed among them, slipping one after the other new loops over their heads as the latches gaped open, and closed, swallowing the yarn to regurgitate it rapidly in the form of loops.

In the Barmen, the active units are not latch needles but spindles, each supporting a large bobbin of thread. Instead of one continuous thread circling in turn to every needle, the bobbins each carry quite separate threads. Instead of needles waiting passively for the thread to be brought to them, the spindles are capable of independent movement, and they whiz round the running plate at high speed, like upright robots, alternately rotating on turntables, and shooting jerkily off along interlacing tracks so that their threads twine together in a complex manner, building up around the apex as around a maypole a compact and intricate fabric.

This tip of the 'maypole' is known as the mandrel. Its cylindrical commencement becomes, as it rises, flat and blade-like so that what started as a tube of lace becomes a

For making the plain net shown in Fig. 1, the discs A . . . I, Fig. 2, are arranged as shown in line 1, and they are then rotated, bringing the threads 1 to 9 into the position shown in line 2 to produce the crossings *a*, Fig. 1. The carriers are then moved to the position shown at line 3 and rotated to the position shown in line 4, to produce the crossings *b*, the other crossings *c*, *d* being produced in a similar manner.

127b

128a

128a *The Barmen machine showing the circle of bobbins around the circumference of the running plate, with their threads converging towards the centre. The tube of lace rises up above the machine and is collected on the right. The Jacquard cards are just visible at the left of the photograph (Karl Mayer).* **b** *From above: the arrangement of the bobbins on the running surface, and on either side of the plates which move them, in a two-thread Barmen.* **c** *Seven plates, shown here in a straight line instead of an arc, with odd numbers 3 and 5 turning anticlockwise to reverse the position of their two spindles, indicated by dotted lines.*

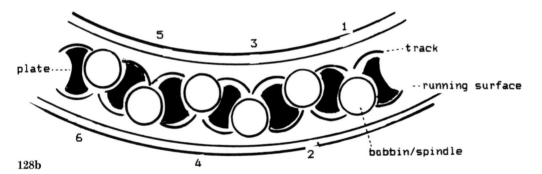

128b

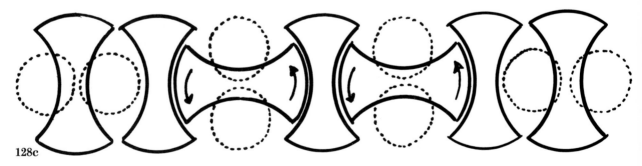

128c

straight band of double thickness. Upon this mandrel the threads converge, and the completed lace is drawn up by a rough 'thorn' made of emery paper (originally shark or dogfish skin), and equivalent to the Leavers porcupine. By this means the lace rises above the machine, and then coils downwards into the waiting basket like a lazy snake.

The present day Barmen exists in a number of varying forms, but the general specifications are approximately 1.8m long by 1.5m wide by 1.7m high. Its diameter varies according to the number of spindles, which may be 44, 52, 56, 64, 72 or 96, even, rarely, 124, each machine being constructed for a fixed number. It can work at a speed of up to 400 movements, or Jacquard cards, a minute, though 240 is more usual – the disadvantages of a very high speed in terms of basic design and fineness of product being greater than the advantages of a very rapid production. The lace has a maximum width of four inches doubled over, or eight inches opened out. Either natural or synthetic fibres can be used, the latter varying from 80 to 3,000 denier. The take-up speed is regulated according to fineness or coarseness of yarn and design, at between two and 12 metres an hour.

Thread movements

The bobbins, or thread holders, are somewhat like overgrown cotton reels, each mounted on a metal spindle with a tension spring attached at the top, and with a large foot at the bottom. They can hold up to 214 metres of yarn apiece.

The domed top of the machine has a flat outer rim where the spindles are equally spaced along the circumference. When the machine is still, or 'dead', the spindles stand in pairs on either side of biconcave discs, or *plates*, each capable of rotating around its central point through 180° or 360° (fig. 128b). The plates are numbered in a clockwise direction, and consecutive plates rotate in opposite directions, the odd numbers anticlockwise, the even clockwise. The bases of the spindles, below the flat rim, are connected with the patterning mechanism. In the earlier Barmen this took the form of a complex

system of levers, (see fig. 132e), but it is now more compact, consisting of cogs meshing with those of the plates to bring about their half or full turns which set the spindles in motion and add force, speed and direction to their mobility.

The rotations of the plates are like a series of overlapping circles: each as it turns passes close against the concave side of its neighbour. Thus, as one plate turns, the next, on either side, must always be still (fig. 128c).

The overall effect is of two main movements, broadly equivalent to the twist (*tourne*) and the cross (*croiser*) of bobbin laces: the first a half-rotation which reverses, through 180°, the positions of the paired spindles which flank the plate; the second, a sequence of vigorous pushes from alternating plates which shoot single spindles off with great rapidity along a sinuous track, passing as it were in and out of adjacent plates as from one partner to another.

In older machines, there was an actual running track incised in the metal like a sunken monorail, or rather two monorails meandering neatly around the outside of the plates and intersecting between them. The tendency has been for more and more of the mechanism to disappear below the working surface so that now only the spindles stand above, and even the plates lie in hollows, flush with the surrounding metal.

The meanings of cross and twist, in reference to hand lace-making, was shown in fig. 127a. Each cross and twist represents in effect the movement of a thread and its holder through 180°. In bobbin laces the work is done in a horizontal plane. Visualized in slow motion, the bobbins are lifted through the air, to right or to left, and then put down again on the pillow: this was the action that was imitated by the Dentellière. In the Barmen, the bobbins stand vertically, instead of lying flat, and so are not limited by a pillow surface but can in effect go below it (fig. 129a). Nevertheless, allowing for this right-angled difference in position, and for the additional latitude of the machine's spindles, the movements remain very similar.

However it would be dangerous to oversimplify. Though odd- and even-num-

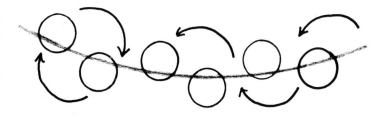

Twist   Cross

129a

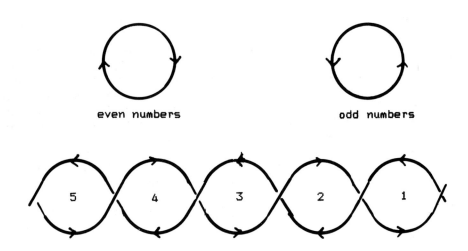

even numbers   odd numbers

129b

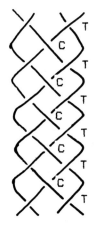

129c

129d

129a *A simplified diagram, from above, to show the similarity of Barmen and bobbin lace movements. Twist: a clockwise turn of the plate through 180° reverses the positions of paired bobbins. Cross: the bobbins are pushed on from one plate to the next. Compare fig. 127a(ii).* **b** *(i) Half-circling: the arrows indicate start and stop positions of the two spindles, and their direction of movement. (ii) The sinuous passage: the arrows show alternating clockwise and anti-clockwise turns of the plates needed to produce this movement, and how the spindles can pass in either direction.* **c** *A halfstitch plait formed by a series of twists and crosses.* **d** *A two-thread twist.* **e** *A good quality Barmen lace with wholestitch constructed mainly without warps, though possibly with two supporting strands at either edge.* **f** *Wholestitch with the warps more crudely tensioned. Five warps are clearly visible passing down through the lace, and holding the L-shaped blocks which form the design.*

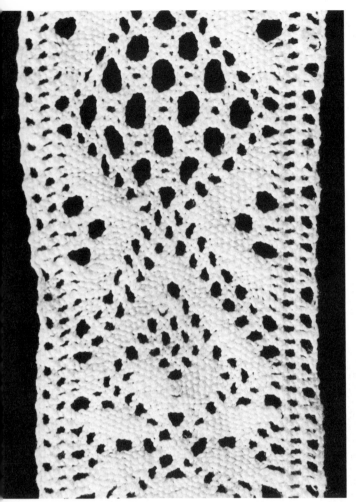

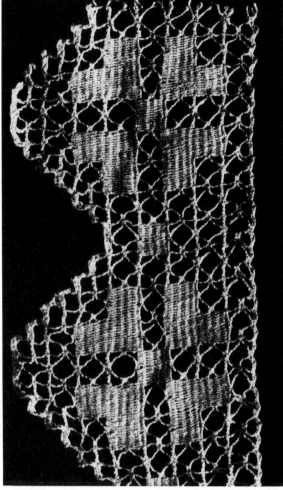

129e

129f

bered plates are consistent in their directions of turning, the half-circling of the spindles, and their sinuous passage, can be made in either direction (fig. 129b). The extent of each spindle's movement is determined by the Jacquard apparatus, and as it reaches the end of a particular run it is turned firmly through 360° and shot back again in the reverse direction.

Moreover, the twists and crosses of individual spindles do not take place in isolation, as in bobbin lace-making, but coincidentally, and very fast. In bobbin laces, never more than four threads (two workers going over or under two passives) are handled at one time. By machine, any threads around the circum-

ference can work simultaneously, and the terms passive and worker are not applicable in anything like the same sense as in handmade laces.

It should be noted that it is not the bobbins themselves which revolve, except for that minimal amount necessary to release more thread. It is the fixed plates which flick repeatedly through half or full turns, and so produce the lateral progression of the spindles.

As in bobbin laces, the twists and crosses have to be distributed sequentially among different bobbin threads if anything like an orderly pattern is to emerge in the lace. When four bobbins are taken alone, for example, continued repetition of even numbers rotating clockwise, and odd numbers rotating anti-clockwise, would give a half-stitch plait (fig. 129c). A repetition involving only a pair of spindles on a revolving plate would give a two-thread twist (fig. 129d).

The effect of *traversing*, or diagonal movements of the threads across the entire width of the lace and back again, is achieved by the Barmen as in continuous bobbin laces, by one set of threads weaving in and out of the others across the width of the band. The angle of working is likely to be 45° as in torchon laces.

The effect of *wholestitch* or clothwork, in other words the appearance of a plain weave, requires a cross-twist-cross repetition which is well within the capability of the Barmen machine. However the convergence of the Barmen threads towards the centre makes the appearance of two sets of parallel threads intersecting at right angles far from easy to achieve. Differential tensions on the relevant bobbin threads can help, and so can the

laying down of static *warps*, or pillar threads, which may be few, or so numerous as to equal the spindles in number. The warps were originally strung from the top of a hollow immobile rod towards the spindle threads in the centre, the rods being about the same height as the spindles and arranged at the circumference of the machine so they are clear of the running track. Yarn is fed into them from below, and can be of any colour or texture (fig. 129e, f).

This type of arrangement, now largely obsolete, is called a two-thread Barmen, because there are two sources of thread, above and below. In the more recent one-thread machines all the threads come from the

130 *The convergence of threads from the tips of the spindles to the mandrel. The beaters or 'knives' are shown moving up from the slots around the dome to compact the series of right over left twists which have been made.*

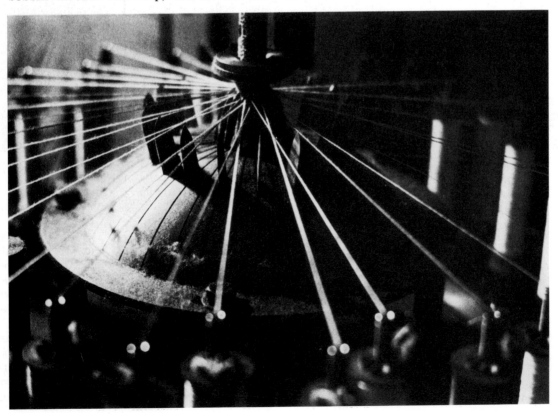

211

spindles above. Here the so-called warps are fewer in number and wound on spindles, just like the other threads, the difference consisiting in their strictly limited movements, only with adjacent threads, but it is enough to reduce the harsh effect of the two-thread warps' rigidity.

The *lacers* or draw threads which link the bands together during manufacture have similarly limited movements, and are mounted on coloured spindles so that they can easily be distinguished.

No pins are used to hold the threads in Barmen laces, as was attempted in the Dentellière. Instead two sets of *beaters* rise up through slits in the dome compacting the lace as it moves towards the thorn (fig. 130). They are equal in number to the spindles, and correspond in function to the back and front point bars of the various bobbin-net machines. The beaters work in rhythm with the Jacquard cards which control the plate and

spindle movements, rising and falling 240 times every minute. In a working machine the movements are so fast they appear as a blur.

Patterning and the Jacquard

Although the Barmen is restricted to a maximum lace width of eight inches, these narrow pieces, off the machine, can be inconspicuously joined to make reasonably sized tablecloths or even bed covers. When a single width at a time is made, it is at first a cylinder with its front and back edges seamed together with nylon. On removal from the machine, the lacer is easily withdrawn, and the band opened out. As many as four narrower bands can be made at the same time (fig. 131a, b), all linked together by lacers to form a tube, but the maximum diameter must never exceed four inches, and may be only half that distance, depending on the size of the mandrel which has been chosen.

The Barmen can copy almost any cross-twist sequence found in continuous bobbin laces of geometric type – halfstitch, wholestitch, fans, leaves, spiders and plaits, as well as grounds such as torchon, valenciennes and cinq trous (rose or virgin

131a *A series of four narrow bands. One lacer has been removed so that the tube can be opened out.* **b** *Detail of the nylon lacer.*

131a

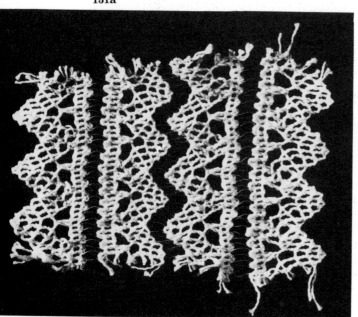

131b

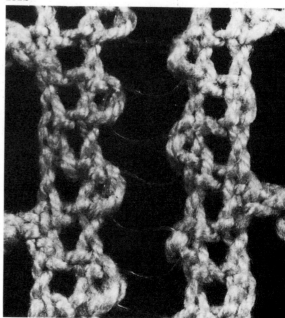

ground). How machine- and handmade products can be distinguished will be discussed later. Unfortunately, the more competent the copy, the more expensive, and many subtle nuances which enlivened the Barmen laces of earlier decades have had to be abandoned. A good wholestitch for example needs extensive Jacquard patterning. Decorative picots within the lace need supports of some kind to prevent sinking back into the other threads under the tension of the bobbin movements. In handmade lace, every picot loop is held in place by a pin so that it cannot slip. Since the Barmen has no pins, an auxiliary thread has to be used. This is often of nylon monofilament, the smooth surface of which enables it to be easily withdrawn when the work is finished – as horsehair was withdrawn from the picots of the needle lace Alençon. Nevertheless setting up such threads needs time and skill, and the addition this makes to the cost may be out of all proportion to its utility.

All the Barmen threads, with the exception of the warps in two-threads machines, are movable, and subject to Jacquard control. Their movements are brought about by cogs which rotate the plates, and it is these parts which the Jacquard has to act upon – just as in the Leavers it acted on the guide bars, and in the Curtain machine on the jacks.

Since alternate plates act in different directions, anti-clockwise and clockwise, their odd and even numbers must be separated on the Jacquard cards. They are arranged in two rows, one above the other, across the card, with as many potential hole positions as there are threads. This will vary according to the capacity of that particular machine. The odd and even rows on the cards are staggered (fig. 132a).

A draft is made to plot out the design, as it is for other machines. In fig. 132b the plate or glider numbers go from right to left along the top, and the card sequence is numbered from above downwards along the right-hand side. Thus each two horizontal rows represent one Jacquard card, and each vertical line represents a bobbin thread. On the cards, as on the draft, odd numbers represent crosses, and even numbers twists. These twists and

crosses have therefore to be marked on the draft in the appropriate squares. This may be done in various ways: by making an X; by breaking one of the X sides so that it indicates the direction of thread movement; by putting in just the relevant diagonal to indicate right over left (right top to left bottom) or left over right (right bottom to left top); or simply by blocking in the squares, since Jacquard stimuli to odd or even numbers automatically produces a constant effect (fig. 132c).

The sequence shown in this part draft would produce an area of half-stitch. Half-stitch plaits can be made by continuing this pattern over sets of just four threads at a time. Other groupings, still using the cross-twist-cross-twist (CT CT) sequence can produce a torchon ground (fig. 132d).

Wherever a square is marked, a hole will be punched in the corresponding number position on the Jacquard card. In the Barmen, a hole initiates movements, blanks are non-movement areas, that is, the spindles in blank positions will remain stationary. The interpretation of the cards is brought about by horizontal probes, which may enter the holes or be rebuffed by the blanks. This differential movement causes hooked wires either to engage with two lifting bars (for odd and even), or to be knocked off. The displacement of the lifting bars is transmitted via springs to the mechanism beneath the running surface. This connects with cogs at the bases of the plates, resulting in an instantaneous flick which propels the spindles in the appropriate direction (fig. 132e).

The cards are mounted on a four-sided cylinder which advanced horizontally towards the probes, activates them, and retreats again, allowing the probes to recover and the next card to be turned up on the cylinder face (fig. 132f). The odd and even numbers on the card are dealt with at the same time, by two sets of probes. On machines with a large number of plates and spindles, say more than 60, the Jacquard cards are split at about the halfway mark, since shorter cards are more stable. The second set – plates 49 to 96 for example – have to have their own cylinder, and their own probes. Fig. 132g shows a Barmen draft and accompanying

One Jacquard card

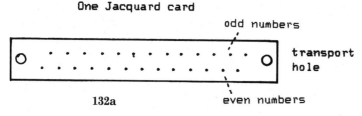

odd numbers

transport
hole

even numbers

132a

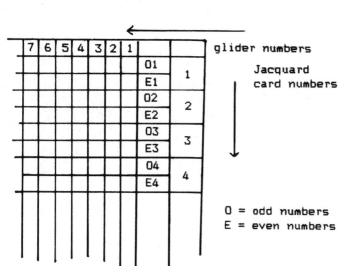

glider numbers

Jacquard
card numbers

O = odd numbers
E = even numbers

132b

132a *The potential position of punch holes on a Jacquard card.* **b** *The setting out of a draft.* **c** *Three possible methods of marking the draft. The numbers refer to positions of plates on the running surface. Broadly, where O = odd number, a thread movement left over right, or right bottom to left top (a cross) is indicated; and where E = even number, a thread movement right over left, or right top to left bottom (a twist) is indicated. However the draft sequence cannot be followed through in the same way as in bobbin laces where crosses and twists refer directly to threads, and pins are used to clarify the thread positions as the work proceeds.* **d** *(i) A Barmen lace of torchon style. (ii) Detail to show torchon ground and halfstitch. Warps are visible to the left and right.* **e** *An early Barmen machine, showing the separation of odd and even numbered Jacquard cards on to two cylinders, and the upright hooks engaging with the lifting bars. The complex lever system below links with the bases of the spindles.* **f** *A modern Jacquard attachment on a Karl Mayer machine showing the odd and even row on every card, and the square cylinder meeting the probes.* **g** *A Barmen draft, the punched cards made from it, and the lace produced (p. 216).*

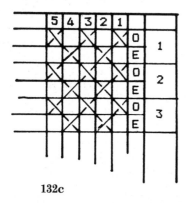

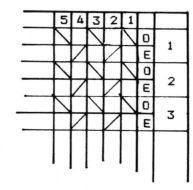

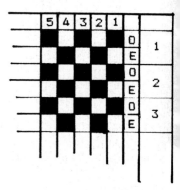

132c

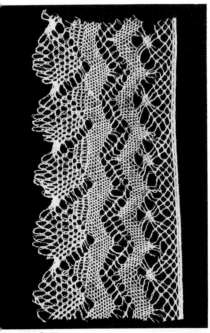

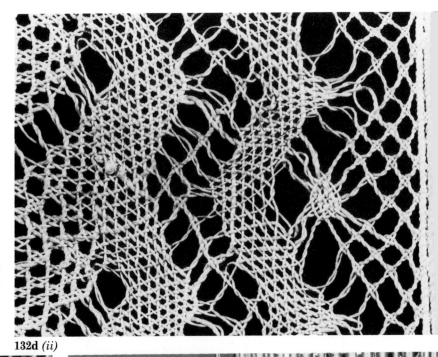

132d *(i)*

132d *(ii)*

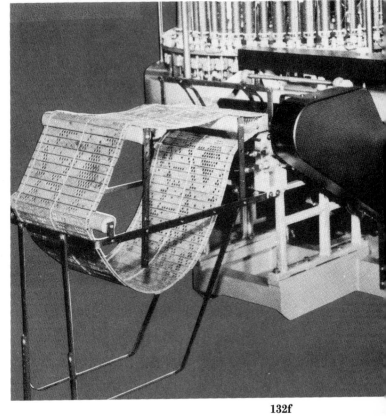

132e

132f

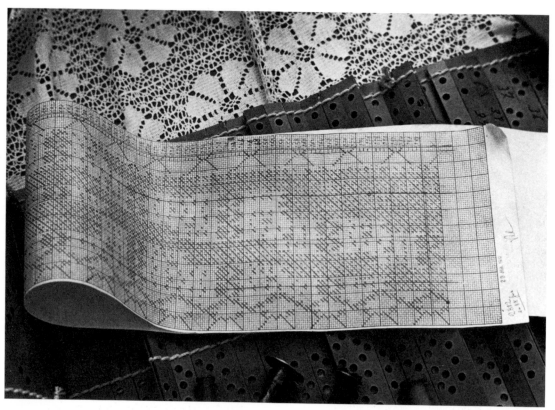

132g

cards. The lace, which comes off the machine in narrow strips, has been joined to make a wide fabric.

Comparison of Barmen and bobbin laces

The drafts used for Barmen laces are to some extent equivalent to bobbin lace prickings. For example in fig. 133a, which represents a pricking for *torchon ground*, the numbers along the top indicate the pairs of bobbins – five pairs, or ten bobbins. The draft- or grid-paper comes ready drawn with lines at the required angle, so that only the pin positions need to be marked in. Here the angle of working is 45°.

The positions which the pins will occupy are numbered in sequence on the draft, through 1 to 29. A small part of the resultant thread formation is shown in fig. 133b. To produce this effect on the Barmen, the draft would be marked as in fig. 132c. The connect-

ing of the lines on either side indicates the limit of the bobbin threads used in that particular effect. The torchon ground which results will be identical. The variation in technique – that the bobbin lace proceeds pair by pair diagonally, while the Barmen does the entire width horizontally at the same time is not, here, visible in the result; while a not-too-heavy tension in the Barmen threads can even give the appearance of a minute gap or pinhole in the centre of each cross, though pins themselves have not of course been used (for a horizontal technique, without pin-holes, but made by hand, see p. 267).

Bucks point ground (Lille ground) is rarely found in Barmen laces, but it sometimes occurs over small areas (fig. 134a). In bobbin laces, the same draft as for torchon ground can be used, with the addition of two dashes along the sides to indicate two twists (fig. 134b). The shorthand representation of the movements then becomes CTTT CTTT, with the supporting pins placed beneath the

216

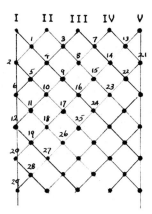

133a

*133a A pricking for handmade torchon ground. The dots represent pins, and the numbers the order in which they are put in. **b** A diagram of torchon ground, with twists (T) and crosses (C) marked in. The pinholes are represented by small circles.*

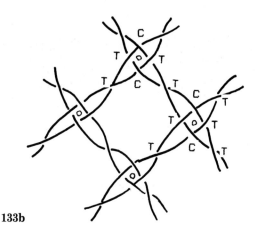

133b

cross, which is now more sharply defined as the point where the pairs separate to form the twisted sides of the meshes. To accommodate the extra length of the sides, the angle of working is commonly adjusted to 52° or more, so that the holes can enlarge into a rounded shape, instead of being compressed into an angular form.

For the Barmen, the angle of working is less significant, since it can easily be adjusted by differential tensioning of the threads, or alteration in the pull-off speed. What does happen, is that the draft becomes elongated in relation to the finished work, since every

additional twist has to be punched on its proper line on a separate Jacquard card, and in all, $3\frac{1}{2}$ cards will be needed to cover each CTTT sequence, which adds quite considerably to the expense of production (fig. 134c).

Halfstitch and wholestitch In bobbin laces, the same pricking can be used for either, with pins placed only at the outer border, in the sequence indicated (fig. 135a). What differs is the thread movements, halfstitch being a CT CT repetition, wholestitch a CTC CTC repetition. The constant change of partners which makes possible the passage of the single, or paired, worker bobbins across the passives can, if necessary, be written out in full, but it is not shown on the draft or the pricking.

On the Barmen draft, everything has to be spelt out for the machine, and nothing can be implied. Every twist and cross must be unequivocally punched on the cards, so that the required spindles can be moved as necessary. Fig. 135b shows a halfstitch strand worked through a group of eight bobbins. When a particular bobbin is 'resting' its thread stays still while the others work round it. This situation is indicated on the draft by straight lines linking the relevant X's, and it accounts for the fact that in the Barmen halfstitch parallel lines run lengthwise whereas in bobbin laces they pass horizontally (figs. 135c, d. see also fig. 132d (ii)).

Summary

Barmen laces can be distinguished from bobbin laces by:

a. The lack of pinholes: though some can be simulated, others are always missing (fig. 136a(i)). However, not all bobbin laces have pinholes, for example the peasant laces of Scania in Sweden are made without prickings, and the only pins used are along either side, to hold the lace to the pillow. A Barmen firm near Gothenburg made excellent copies of these laces, before the second world war. The imitations, made of linen thread like the originals, were identical in colour, texture and design, and only a sceptical examination reveals a slight awkwardness of tension within the wholestitch

217

134a *(i)*

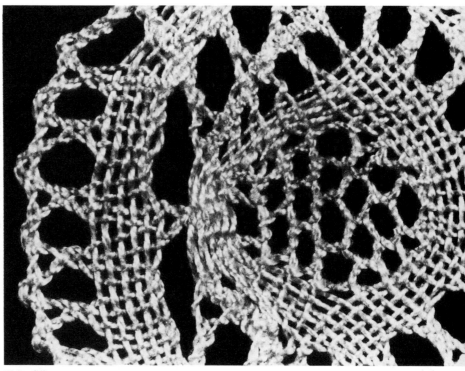

134a *(ii)*

134 *Bucks point, also known as Lille, tulle or net ground.* **a** *(i) The mesh used as a filling in Barmen lace. (ii) Detail. (iii) A sketch of the thread movements.* **b** *A bobbin lace pricking for seven vertical meshes of Bucks point ground. The pairs of dashes represent two twists, and the dots pin positions. I to IV = eight pairs of bobbins.* **c** *A Barmen draft for a single mesh of the same net.*

I   II   III   IV

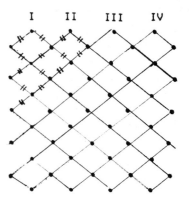

134b

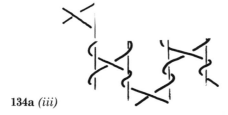

134a *(iii)*

134c

218

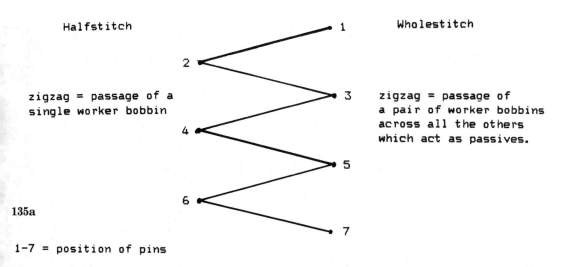

Halfstitch   Wholestitch

zigzag = passage of a
single worker bobbin

zigzag = passage of
a pair of worker bobbins
across all the others
which act as passives.

135a

1-7 = position of pins

135a *A bobbin lace pricking which can be adapted for either halfstitch or wholestitch.* **b** *A Barmen draft for eight bobbins making a halfstitch strand.* **c** **and d** *The distinction between Barmen and bobbin lace halfstitch, where horizontal and vertical refer to the lace as it is worked.*

135b

135c

135d

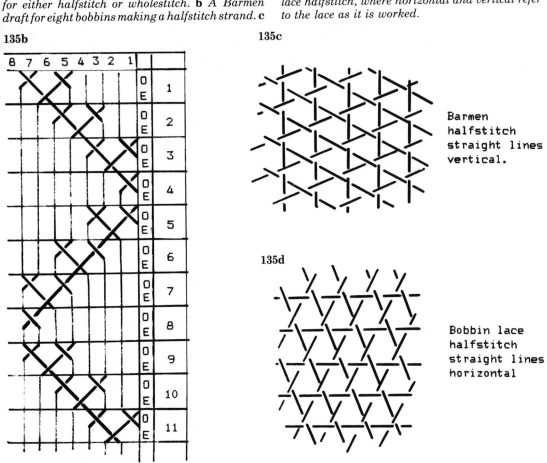

Barmen
halfstitch
straight lines
vertical.

Bobbin lace
halfstitch
straight lines
horizontal

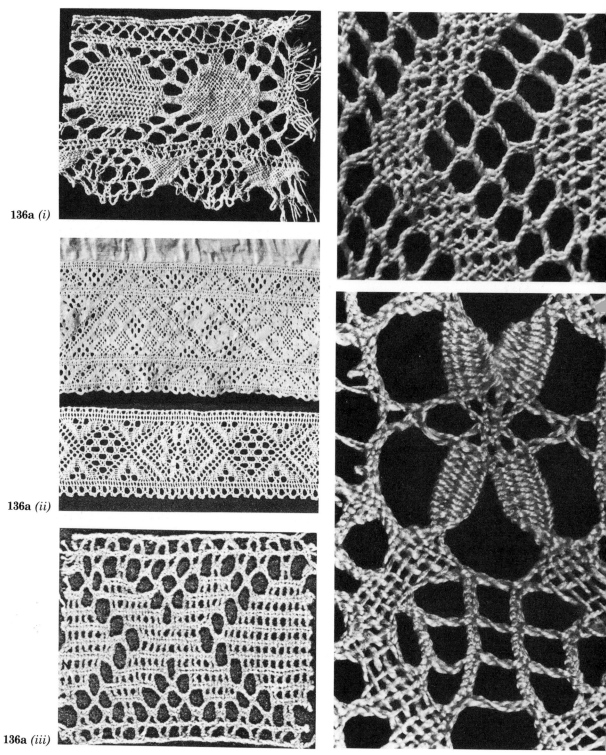

136a *(i)*

136a *(ii)*

136a *(iii)*

136c

areas (see p. 211), and an over-tight twisting around the holes (fig. 136a(ii)), and see (e) below. Pinholes are also lacking in the woven openwork fringes of Hedebo which have a superficial similarity to Barmen laces (see p. 267, and fig. 178c), but their method of construction clearly distinguishes them, being continuous with the fabric on the one side, and with plaited or knotted warps on the other.

b. Irregularities of tension: these can to some extent fake not only pinholes, but also that fallibility which is often regarded as the hallmark of a handmade product.

c. In halfstitch: the parallel lines usually run lengthwise of the lace in Barmen, widthways in handmade, though the direction may at times be reversed in either (see figs. 135c, d).

d. In wholestitch: the paired passage of worker threads, so clear in most bobbin laces, cannot readily be copied by the Barmen.

e. A strong vertical line effect: this occurs when static threads (warps) are used (see fig. 129e). They are an economy measure. Since they do not move, they do not need to be drafted. Thus they reduce the complexity of the Jacquard cards, and the cost of the lace. Some Finnish bobbin laces, which do not use prickings, and so lack pinholes, have in addition a parallel line effect. This is in fact produced by plaiting, but nevertheless gives a close approximation to Barmen warps (fig. 136a(iii)).

f. Additional twists: which would not occur in bobbin laces are often necessary in the Barmen because of the horizontal or all-round method of manufacture, as opposed to the bobbin laces' one- or two-at-a-time diagonal passage (fig. 136b).

g. Doubled thread: the impetuous speed of the machine generates considerable tension, and the threads often need to be thicker than in handmade lace, or even doubled, to make them more durable (see fig. 137a(ii)). This is not entirely definitive: in some Flanders (Antwerp) laces of the early eighteenth century for example, two, three or even four linen singles might be worked together without being plyed; and strands of silk in eighteenth-century blonde might be similarly treated. But this is not common practice.

h. Fluff: the continual lashing up and down of the beaters between the threads fluffs out the cotton fibres so that they contrast with the smooth texture of the more gently-used threads in bobbin laces. Tougher fibres such as jute can preserve a more clean-cut appearance.

i. Plaits: in the Barmen, plaits may be worked with only three threads instead of two pairs as in bobbin laces (fig. 136c).

j. Footing: in the Barmen the same pair of threads comes out of the footing as goes into it; in bobbin laces a different pair comes out.

k. A slight error in working in the Barmen is likely to appear at exactly the same point in every repeat, but not in a bobbin lace.

As with other machine laces, increase in the cost of labour, and decrease in demand, have caused the Barmen machines to produce less convincing copies of bobbin laces than they once did (fig. 137a). A patent by Birkin of Nottingham, with Malhère freres, in 1899 (no. 1127) relates to the forming of a halfstitch diamond, and scalloping. Another, by W.H. Price and the Shepshed Lace Manufacturing Co., in 1908 (no. 18804) relates to

136a *(i) Barmen lace: the crossing plaits show no pinholes, the left halfstitch area has vertical straight lines, the threads in the right wholestitch area are not at right angles to the edges of the lace but run diagonally, which is easier for the Barmen to do*[5]. *There are two heavy warps along the sewing edge, or footing. (ii) Above, Scania bobbin lace from a peasant headdress, c.1830. The fine thread is cotton, at that time a luxury in Sweden. The lace has been heavily starched, and polished with a rub-stone, which makes it look less handmade. Below, a copy of a Scania lace made on a Barmen machine by the firm of A. Marks, of Gothenburg, Sweden, c.1930. (iii) Finnish lace worked with 16 bobbins, showing the warp-like effect.* **b** *Barmen lace showing a tightly twisted effect.* **c** *Rigid Barmen plaits which look more machine-made than the well-formed cluny.*

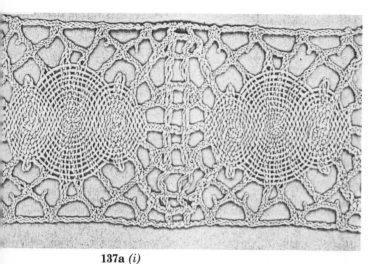

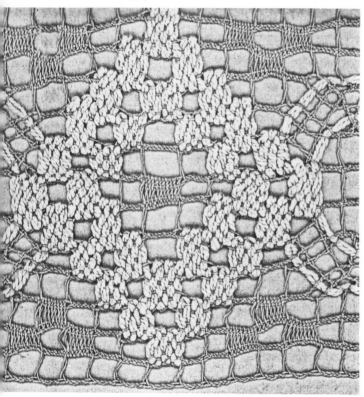

137a *(i)*

137a *(ii)*

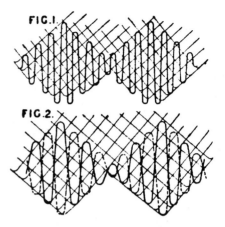

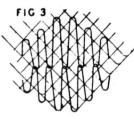

Lace and lace-making. — Relates to the manufacture of torchon lace on the machine described in Specification No. 11,411, A.D. 1894. In the ordinary method, a pattern is formed by traversing a single thread to and fro as shown in Fig. 1. To increase the speed of production, two or more threads are made to work simultaneously, as in Fig. 2, or, instead of traversing the whole distance, the threads may meet and interlock, as in Fig. 3.

137b *(i)*

18,804. Price, W. H., and Shepshed Lace Manufacturing Co. Sept. 8.

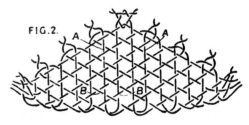

Lace.—The production of scallops in torchon lace on braiding-machinery is expedited by causing half the threads A to travel vertically from the base to the edge of the scallop and return obliquely, the other half B travelling obliquely and returning vertically.

137b *(ii)*

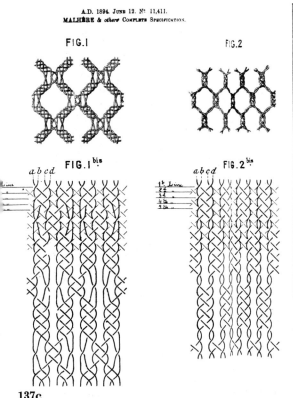

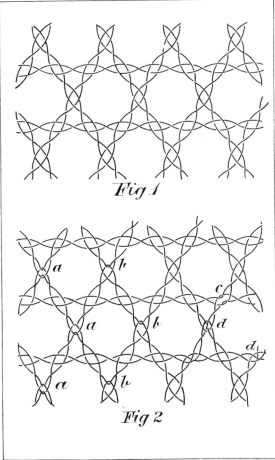

137c

scalloping, again in halfstitch (fig. 137b). The term 'vertically' in this patent refers to the position of the threads after removal, as the lace will be worn, not as it is made on the machine.

Again, early forms of plaiting may have been more deceptive. The Malhère 1894 patent for a plait (no. 11411) is amazingly like bobbin-made Valenciennes or Mechlin grounds (fig. 137c). The curved lines indicate the limit of the plait, and though the patent drawing does not make it precisely clear, the holes or mesh openings have been indicated here by a straight line, so that the joining and separation of the vertical plaited sides is more obvious. In this type, two pairs of threads are involved. Note the direction of

137d

7459. Birkin, O. W., [*Malhère, E., Malhère, L., and Malhère, A.*]. April 8. 1905

Braid ; lace.—The net shown is made on the machine described in Specification No. 11,411, A.D. 1894, by arranging the bobbins in three sets. Each set works in pairs which twist together and form lines straight up and down the fabric or inclined to the right or to the left. At the meeting places of four threads, each may go on and form a plain crossing, or one or both pairs may turn back, or an inclined thread may be caused to twist with a vertical thread as shown at *a, b, c, d*. The formation of the net may be discontinued at any place, and a patterned fabric made instead.

137a *Two Barmen laces showing clear threads, picots, and an effective use of double thread to give a more dramatic design. c.1910. In (i) the threads in the centres of the circles of clothwork turn back on themselves: this is rarely found in bobbin laces. (Birkin archives).* **b** *Two methods of producing halfstitch on a Barmen machine, patented in 1899 and 1908 respectively.* **c** *Four-thread plaits, described in patent no. 11,411, 1894.* **d** *Point de Paris, or wire ground, patented in 1905.* **e** *Cluny spots, patented in 1902.* **f** *Spiders, patented in 1906.*

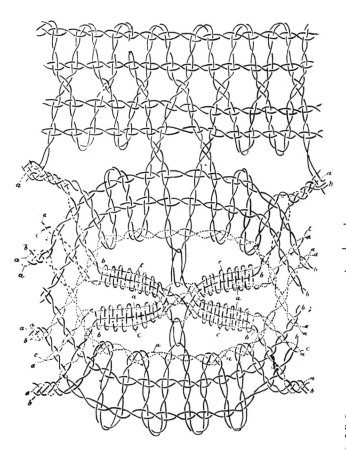

137e

A.D. 1906. Jan. 12. Nº 872.
TRECKMANN & *others'* Complete Specification.

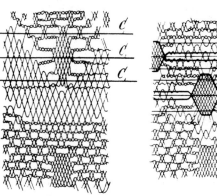

Fig. 1ª.

Fig. 2.   *Fig. 3.*

137f

Lace and lace-making.—Relates to the manufacture of Torchon, Cluny, and similar laces on machines of the kind described in Specification No. 11,411, A.D. 1894, and has for its object the production of Maltese cross, Maltese, or Cluny spots or effects produced by combinations of Cluny or Maltese spots. One or more lightly-weighted thread or threads *c* are interwoven in the manner indicated with heavily-weighted threads *a*. The heavily-weighted threads twist together at the commencement or end of a spot.

Braiding-machines.—Relates to a method of making "spider-net." This fabric is a loose open braid having at intervals spots or "spiders" of close braiding, Fig. 1, connected to the rest of the fabric by twisted threads B. In order to make the spider as nearly circular as possible, the intersections of the threads B of each spider are made round wires *c*, Fig. 3, on which the fabric slides and is finally drawn off by the take-up rollers. In conjunction with the wires, heavily-weighted bobbin-threads *i* are used to enclose each spider and reduce the breadth thereof. The effect of the wires used in conjunction is to increase the length of the spider.

movement of the intersecting threads, indicated by broken Xs.

Most of the modern laces made on the Barmen machine are guipures, but torchon-type grounds do occur, as well as rose ground, Bucks point ground, and kat stitch otherwise known as wire ground, point de Paris or six-point star (fig. 137d). Guipures, as in bobbin laces, use less thread, take less time, and are cheaper to produce.

The representation of point d'esprit ovales (leaves or wheatears) was patented by Birkin and others in 1902 (no. 10544) (fig. 137e, and see fig. 136c). On the machine these structures are known as Maltese cross, Maltese spots, Cluny spots or Clunies, indicating yet again that machines and their laces have a language all their own. Nowadays the Cluny construction is less faithful, and its appearance less sharply defined.

Spiders too were the subject of a patent (no. 872) in 1906 (fig. 137f). The use of supporting wires such as those described here, and the intermittent use of increased tension by weighting some of the threads, adds greatly to the cost, and Barmen spiders sometimes look as though they have been worked in two halves, while the wide curvature of their threads destroys conviction.

The Shepshed Lace Manufacturing Co. first produced E-lace-tic in 1934 at their factory in Loughborough, the lastex yarn being threaded through static warp feeds (fig. 138a).

Bewildering as some Barmen laces may appear at a quick glance, a careful examination is likely to reveal that there is not a single Barmen lace which could not with certainty be identified as such, given a little patient analysis of its technical features, one by one. Nor can it make any venture into complex patterning: its threads are limited to a maximum of some 120, while handmade bobbin laces can use over 1,000. Similarly it cannot imitate non-continuous bobbin laces, or needle laces, or craft laces, or those with an extensive net ground or, economically, those with a representational design as of animals or flowers.

Some geometric Leavers laces could possibly be mistaken for Barmen because of the diagonal passage of their threads (see fig. 107g) – indeed Messrs William Fletcher and Sons of Derby, in the first half of the twentieth century, pronounced one of their products 'a splendid example of Leversmade BARMEN' (fig. 138b) – but the almost invariable contrast between thin bobbin, and thicker warp and beam yarns, is an easily identifiable Leavers characteristic. Also, the Barmen machine has, apart from the occasional use of warps, only one source of thread, while Leavers always has two, sometimes three, and most often four. Thus the pillaring which is such a common feature of Leavers laces is absent in Barmen products.

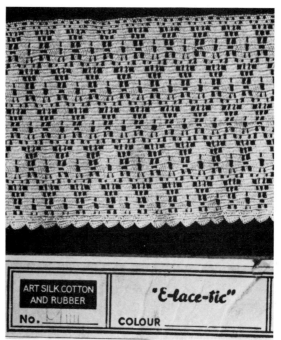

138a

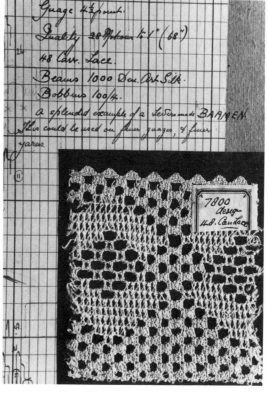

138b

138a *E-lace-tic made by the Shepshed Lace Manufacturing Co., 1930s.* **b** *'A splendid example of Levers-Made Barmen'.*

VIII

Embroidery Machines As Lace-Makers

Handmachine (Métier à Bras), Schiffli,
Multihead, Bonnaz, Cornely

Hand-embroidery as a means of decorating plain nets began at the end of the eighteenth century, when the emergence of single and double press point nets provided a new means of livelihood for increasing numbers of women and children.

Two techniques were mainly used: chainstitch or tambour work using a miniature steel crochet hook attached to a wood or ivory handle; and a running or in-and-out stitch using a blunt-tipped sewing needle. Neither was entirely new: the first, on silk or muslin, had been a popular pastime of leisured ladies from around 1750; the second had been used at least from the sixteenth century, for patterning knotted filet and woven gauze. Neither however had previously been in the nature of a commercial enterprise, as they now became. With the marketing of the firmer, more stable, and less expensive cotton bobbinets, from 1809 on, hand embroidery became a major industry in Nottingham, Ireland, Switzerland and Austria, giving employment to tens of thousands of people.

It was not long before attempts were made to mechanize the process. They proceeded along two parallel lines: large embroidery machines from five to 21 yards in width (from right to left) and with 300 to 1,500 needles; and modified sewing machines of relatively small size, mainly one to two yards, and with a maximum of 24 needles. Some worked with a single set of threads; others, notably the Schiffli, with two sets (needle and shuttle) to make a lockstitch.

I. Handmachine or Handloom (*Métier à bras,* Handstikmaschine)

As with the lace machines, so many experiments were going on at the same time that it is hard to isolate the first commercial success. Credit is usually given to Josue Heilmann, of Switzerland, for his invention of 1828. His work is recorded in a patent registered in London in the name of Henry Bock, in 1829 (no. 5788) for

machinery for embroidering fabrics by the use of a large number of needles formed with an eye in the centre and a point at each end; which needles are passed through the fabric from opposite sides alternately by means of pincers. An arrangement of apparatus upon the principle of the pentagraph [an erroneous spelling of pantograph] is employed for changing the relative positions of the fabric and the needles. It is likewise proposed to apply this apparatus to machines in which tambouring needles are used. (See p. 256).

Heilmann's machine had developed that pre-eminent quality of industry, replication. It could produce not one design, but many repetitions of it all at one go, by using a number of needles all doing the same stitch at the same time across a breadth of fabric, instead of, as the hand embroiderer must do, one needle making one stitch at a time in one part of the material. The name given to the machine had a double significance. Firstly, it was motivated solely by human hands and feet, and no non-human power – water, steam or electricity – was ever applied to it. Secondly, it was able to copy the stitches of hand embroidery, with the sole exception of the knot, so perfectly that they could not be distinguished when only a single motif was examined (fig. 139a). However, the consequences of simultaneous repetition by many needles produced its own distinctive features. Controlled by the pantograph, stitches had to be of the same length, in a corresponding position, and of the same number, in every repeat, and threads would be carried over from a stem to a leaf in precisely the same way every time – unless there was some inequality in the lengths of thread used (fig. 139b). When, later, reversible work in satin stitch (*broderie au passée*) was done, even this distinguishing feature was absent.

The general form of the handmachine was as follows: a stout iron carcase supporting above it a frame on which the fabric to be embroidered – a woven cloth, or machine net – was tightly stretched; on either side a row of pincers (sometimes called nippers or finger-pieces), lined up at equal distances facing the cloth, and immediately opposite each other; a row of needles clamped in the jaws of one of the rows of pincers, and pointed towards the fabric; the needles fine, sharpened at both ends, with an eye in the middle; each thread a little more than a yard long, fixed at one end to the fabric, and at the other inconspicuously knotted through the eye (figs. 140a–c).

The original machine was small, and held only 20 needles. However it could still work at 20 times the speed of the hand embroiderer. Later the machines enlarged, to 15 feet wide, with over 300 needles set some 4cm apart from each other, or a variable distance, depending on the pattern required.

The patterning device, or pantograph, was placed to the left of the machine. It consisted of a line drawing which was an enlargement of the actual design, traced in ink on pasteboard, and having the positions of every stitch marked on it. The drawing was fixed to an upright display stand and connected with a jointed lever which could be moved from stitch to stitch by the operative. As the lever was moved, so the frame which held the fabric was made to glide smoothly in a horizontal or vertical direction.

As soon as the frame reached the position

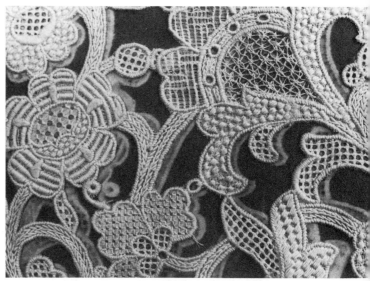

139a

139b

139a *Drawnwork effects, and other stitches, produced by the handmachine. A lace sample photographed over a blueprint.* **b** *Detail of the reverse side of handmachine embroidery with eyelet work, showing carry-over of threads.*

140a

140b

required for the next stitch, the operative manipulated foot pedals causing the row of needles to advance towards the stretched fabric, and pierce it. The needle tips were then gripped by the pincers on the other side, the first set released its hold, and the second set retreated in unison, pulling the needles back with them so that the thread was drawn through the cloth to the limit of its length (fig. 141).

The operative then moved the pantograph lever to the next stitch, the frame glided to its new position, and the foot pedal was once more depressed. The second set of pincers advanced thrusting the needles through the cloth, the first set of pincers nipped the needles' tips – and so the process was repeated throughout the entire vertical length of the design.

The embroidery began at the top of the frame which was gradually moved upwards as each part of the work was completed, the rows of needles and nippers remaining always at the same level. The frame was a little wider than the row of needles, and some 30cm high. When all the fabric had been embroidered on, it was removed, and replaced by a new piece so that the embroidery could begin again.

In the absence of non-human power, the Jacquard could not be applied to the handmachine, even though on contemporary silk-weaving looms sets of warp-selecting cards were operated by a foot treddle. A second operative was needed, continually hand-threading needles to replace those where the thread was used up. Even after the invention of a mechanical needle-threader in

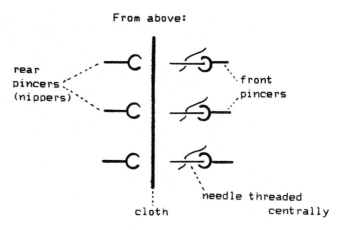

141 *Three pairs of pincers, seen from above. The opposing pairs of front and rear finger-pieces pass the needles back and forth through the cloth between them.*

1880 the frequent change-over of needles still had to be done by hand.

All machine-embroidered laces are costed by the number of stitches needed to make the design, since this determines the number of frame and needle movements required, the amount of thread needed, and the time consumed. A large handmachine could work 10,000 stitches a day, and smaller ones 2,000 to 3,000. When an especially large run of a particular design was required, a second frame and a second set of pincers and needles could be mounted above the first, and worked from the same pantograph. On the other hand, for a small run of some specially commissioned design, it was advantageous to use a smaller machine with something between 15 and 40 needles. Such machines occupied little more space than a treadle sewing machine, and their work could be of high quality since the small frame size meant that the fabric was held absolutely steady.

The initial use of the handmachine was for copying the white embroideries, on lawn and muslin, that were so popular in the 1830s and 1840s, and some of which were associated with the Appenzal area of north-eastern Swit-

140a *The handmachine (handstickmaschine) as drawn for patent no. 5788 in 1829. On the left, the tracer above* C *communicates the design via levers* D *and* F *to the double frame* I *which holds two widths of cloth. The intermediate lever* E, *on the pantograph, and the counterbalancing weight, are omitted. The bar* OO *holds the pincers, or finger-pieces, on its inner side.* b *An 1869 handmachine (Adolphe Saurer, Switzerland).* c *A twentieth-century handmachine, 1908 (Saurer).*

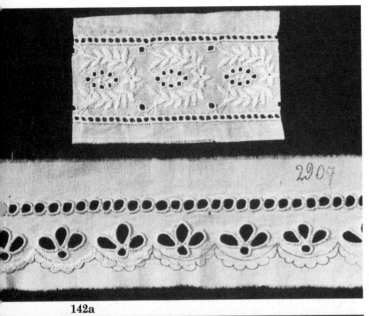

2907

142a

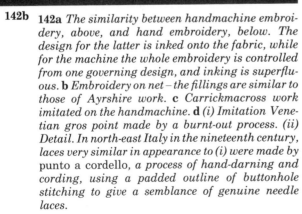

142b **142a** *The similarity between handmachine embroidery, above, and hand embroidery, below. The design for the latter is inked onto the fabric, while for the machine the whole embroidery is controlled from one governing design, and inking is superfluous.* **b** *Embroidery on net – the fillings are similar to those of Ayrshire work.* **c** *Carrickmacross work imitated on the handmachine.* **d** *(i) Imitation Venetian gros point made by a burnt-out process. (ii) Detail. In north-east Italy in the nineteenth century, laces very similar in appearance to (i) were made by* punto a cordello, *a process of hand-darning and cording, using a padded outline of buttonhole stitching to give a semblance of genuine needle laces.*

zerland near to Zurich and St Gallen. For hand Appenzal work the outline of the pattern had first to be printed on the cloth using brass strips embedded in wood. Although such outlines were unnecessary on the handmachine which could not see them, they were sometimes added afterwards to perfect the illusion of hand-embroidery (fig. 142a).

The original embroidery, made on a woven cloth, was without holes, and so was not a lace. By the 1860s additional implements known as *borers* were added which could separate the threads and force their way through to produce a series of holes, which

230

could be embroidered around, as in broderie anglaise or hand-eyelet work. Finer implements could be used to imitate many of the stitches of drawnwork of the delicate type found in Ayrshire work (fig. 142b). Both these forms of embroidery can be regarded as belonging to that marginal area in which lace and embroidery merge together, where they can with equal appropriateness be referred to as 'embroidered laces' or 'openwork embroideries'.

The handmachine could imitate even the buttonholed scallops of hand-embroidery, and was adept at feather-stitching. It could embroider not only on lawn, but also on net, making a patterned holey fabric which could not be denied the name of lace. Because of the small diameter of the needles, a small-meshed bobbinet was usually chosen. Its needles, by passing in through one mesh and back through another, could imitate running stitch, but not to the extent of counting the meshes and getting precisely the same number between every stitch, so that it could not really approach the exquisite precision and fine decorative fillings of the best Limerick work.

It could copy muslin applique on net, though not the neatly couched outline of the real Carrickmacross (fig. 142c). It could make some sort of stab at imitations of Venetian gros point, though work of this kind required extensive hand-finishing, and was proportionately expensive (fig. 142d). It was involved in some of the early experiments in 'aetzing' or the making of 'carbonised laces', a process in which the base fabric on which the embroidery occurred was degraded after the design was complete, so that only the embroidery stitches were left, making a lacey openwork.

The handmachines were also known as Swiss machines (*métier suisse*), and in their day were popular and profitable. Small numbers were exported to New York and New Jersey in the 1870s and 1880s, and larger numbers (two or three thousand) to Germany and Poland. By 1908 there were 16,000 machines in the St Gallen area of Switzerland. By that time, however, its particular type of embroidered lace was passing out of fash-

142d *(i)*

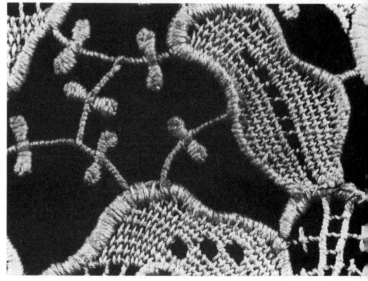

142d *(ii)*

ion. Even its surface embroideries, by their slowness, were becoming uneconomic. A few machines known as handlooms, were still operational in Nottingham in the 1930s, for the firm of John Jacoby who died in 1954. But no new machines have been built in the last 80 years; many have been scrapped and, in the 1980s, even Switzerland retains only a few not more than 10 metres long. Like the old Stocking Frames, and the Bobbinet machines, Europe can no longer afford them.

The reason for the handmachine's eclipse was not only the rise to dominance of the patterning twist-net machines, but also the

143 *The obstreporous fashions of the 1880s* (The Queen*, 1885).*

144a *A deep flounce of Schiffli embroidery on net, imitating the Belgian needle lace point de gaze.* **b** *Detail, showing the typically fuzzy appearance of Schiffli embroidery, and the zigzag blatt stitch which encircles the motifs.*

evolution of a new type of embroidery machine, bigger, faster, cheaper, and powered by steam. In the late 1880s, as the Schiffli began to emerge as a formidable power, it threatened not only the commercial viability of the handmachine, but that of the entire twist-net industry, and most notably the Leavers.

II. *Schiffli* (Le métier à fil continu à vapeur Schiffli)

The Schiffli products can provide, from a distance, an admirable illusion of handmade laces, though they cannot, at close quarters, give any simulation of hand embroidery. In the 1880s, however, verisimilitude was not what fashion required: grossness was replacing subtlety, and impact had triumphed over

detail (fig. 143). 'The heavy productions of Plauen are much in vogue,' wrote Hénon of the year 1899.'

The Schiffli could use borers, in a similar way to the handmachine, to produce openwork embroideries in broderie anglaise style. It could also embroider on net, using needle or bobbin lace designs, and so give the appearance of a handmade lace with a net, or reseau, ground (fig. 144).

It was however the development of a special technique for making guipure laces, using a degrading process, which brought the Schiffli in one bold leap to the top of the fashion market. Experiments in this field had begun in 1879, and all sorts of ingenious methods were devised for disposing of the backing fabric, once the embroidery was completed, as is shown by the following patent abridgements:

144b

4143. Renals, J., [*Steiger, J.*]. Sept. 26. 1881.
Embroidery with ground fabric destroyed. – The fabric on which the embroidery is formed may be composed of animal fibres and the embroidery thread of vegetable fibres. The animal fibres are then dissolved away by a solution of caustic soda or potash, and the embroidery is washed in clean water. Paper may be used as a base and removed from embroidery made with threads of coloured vegetable or animal fibres by a rubbing process. When the cloth for receiving the embroidery is formed of vegetable fibres, it may be destroyed by steaming or burning, the embroidery thread being prepared by solution of tungstate of soda or sulphate of ammonia to resist the action.

7931. Krüsi, J. June 30. 1885.
Lace. – Relates to a method of producing lace from embroidery. The lace is produced by remov-ing the ground on which the embroidery has been produced. This may be done by first treating the ground fabric with dilute acid, then embroidering it in any usual way, and afterwards putting it in a hot room where the ground thread falls to pieces and the lace is left. Instead of treating the ground fabric before embroidery, the thread &c. that is used in producing the embroidery may be treated with ammonia or some other alkali, and after embroidery the whole is treated with dilute acid which removes the ground while the protected embroidery remains.

8491. Buhlmann, J. G. April 30. 1895.
Lace making. – Lace-work and trimmings are made by embroidering on a fabric which is after-wards destroyed. The fabric may be cellulose material, such as cotton or paper, stiffened with starch, and treated with solution of magnesium or aluminium chloride or other metallic salts produc-

233

145a

145b

145a *The lengths of embroidered fabric, guipure on acetate, as removed from the Schiffli frame (Charles Farmer, Mapperley).* **b** *Similar pieces after the backing acetate fabric has been dissolved. The bands of embroidery are linked together for ease of handling during the burnt-out process (Charles Farmer).*

ing acids when heated; or solution of phosphoric or other acid may be used. Or a woollen fabric may be used, stiffened with starch, and soaked in a caustic alkali solution. In either case the fabric is destroyed on heating the work to 150° or 200°C., by superheated steam or otherwise. The material used for the embroidery is protected by soaking it in a solution of paraffin in benzene, or glycerine in water, or other suitable substance.

17,070. Dalichow, B. Aug. 1. 1902
Carbonized fabrics. – Relates to a process, having the effect of carbonizing, in which a material embroidered upon can subsequently be removed, the embroidery only being left. The material, after having been bleached with chlorine by a dry process, is moistened with a solution of chloric acid of about 1° or 2° Bé. After being dried, it is embroidered upon and then heated to a temperature of 60° to 80°C. The material, which is thus

rendered brittle, can then be removed by brushing, the embroidery only being left.

Yet other patents were recorded in 1888, 1890 and 1905. The idea running through all of them was to dispose entirely of the background fabric while leaving the tightly interlocked embroidery stitches unharmed so that they could, by themselves, form a durable lace. The general term for the various procedures was aetzing, from the German *aetz*, meaning corrosive. The English equivalent is burnt or burnt-out or chemical or, sometimes, 'Swiss embroidered guipure laces' a name later abbreviated to 'guipures' (fig. 145).

The Schiffli machine, like the hand-machine, was not an English invention,

46a

but belonged to the north-east corner of Switzerland. St Gallen, along with Plauen near the Erzegebirge Mountains, were from the very beginning the main centres of production, and they remain so to this day.

As far as it is possible to give credit to one individual, the Schiffli regarded as the invention of Isaac Groebli in 1863, though its concept owed much to the lockstitch sewing machine developed in America in the 1830s to 50s, as well as to the Swiss handmachine which in principle it strongly resembled. The Schiffli differed from the handmachine in having its needles threaded at the tip instead of centrally; in having only the outer end of each needle sharpened; in having two sets of

146a *A Schiffli imitation of the eighteenth-century needle lace known as 'reseau Venise', showing the wide range of fancy effects that can be produced from very limited basic stitch types.* **b** *An equally credible reseau Venise design, here with the Schiffli embroidery burnt out and then stitched to bobbinet: (i) part of a long streamer, the lower part seven inches wide; (ii) detail of the reverse side showing the net cut back.* **c** *A Schiffli imitation of a 'point lace', photographed over a blueprint. Note the precision with which the machine has copied the appearance of at least five distinct types of button-hole stitch.*

146b *(i)*

235

146b *(ii)*

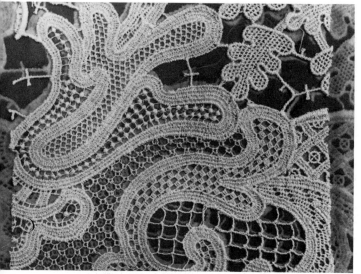

146c

threads, one in the needles, the other on shuttles (*navettes*, or in Swiss-German *schiffli*) a feature from which the machine derived its name; in having both sets of thread extremely long instead of in short lengths, so that it was sometimes referred to as the continuous thread machine (*métier à fil continu*); and in having the threaded tip of the needle penetrate the cloth only far enough to loop around the shuttle thread before withdrawing again.

Since its needles do not go entirely through the fabric, as in the handmachine, the Schiffli's stitches are far less versatile, being restricted to a lockstitch. However, by the use of varied arrangements, tensions and threads, a wide range of decorative effects can in fact be produced (fig. 146). The frequent use of a different thread for the needles, and for the shuttles, gives Schiffli embroidery a right and wrong, or face and reverse, side which is helpful in identification.

The Schiffli, being a power machine, worked first by steam and later by electricity, could become considerably larger than the entirely human-operated handmachine. By the early 1900s Schifflis were up to 13 metres long and 3 metres high. Each machine could embroider simultaneously on up to three frames, placed one above the other, and several machines could be controlled by a single design-operative, moving the lever of a pantograph.

Such a pantograph was exactly similar to that employed in the handmachine, consisting of a ×6 enlargement of the design with every stitch marked, and a lever moved in progression from one stitch position to the next, thus controlling the horizontal and vertical swings of the embroidery frames. The operation however was much more demanding since the rhythm of movement was not that of the worker who could go at his own pace, fast or slow, at will. Instead he was forced to follow the rhythm of the power-driven engine shaft which drove the needles back and forth, piercing the cloth and withdrawing again. Without a moment's faltering or hesitation, the frames had to be moved between each needle thrust, for if frames and needles moved together, instead of alternating, cloth or needles or both would be torn or broken; if the frame failed to move when it should, or moved in the wrong direction, the entire design would be destroyed. Thus the sequence of movements:

needle bar – frame – needle bar – frame

had to be as rigidly complied with as the equally vital sequence in the Leavers machine:

148a

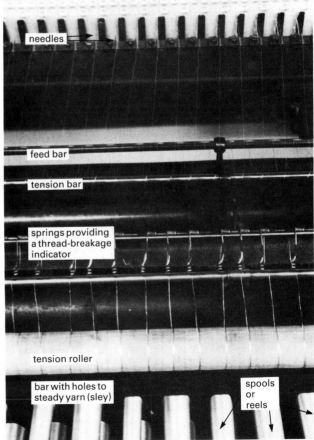

fabric being embroidered

needles →

feed bar

tension bar

springs providing
a thread-breakage
indicator

tension roller

bar with holes to
steady yarn (sley)

spools
or
reels

148b

147 *A 1970s Schiffli machine showing the two-tiered frames making identical designs. Each frame has its own set of thread-spools and needles (Saurer).*

148a *The front of the Schiffli machine which embroidered the net for the Princess of Wales' wedding train. The narrower ($4\frac{1}{2}$ inch) edging below was for the bridesmaids' dresses (Roger Watson, Nottingham).* **b** *The course followed by the thread between the spool and the needle. The tension and feed bars are sometimes referred to as straining bars.*

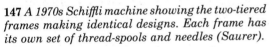

bobbin motion – guide bar throw – bobbin motion

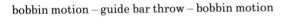

Goldenburg, writing in 1904, says, 'The Schiffli, or power machine, has a capacity nearly 8 times greater than the handmachine, and can work 15,000 to 18,000 stitches per day, against 2,000 to 3,000 on the handmachine'[2]. He continues,

To offset this advantage the Schiffli is much more expensive, and is of delicate and complicated construction, easily got out of order, and costly to repair. Until a comparatively recent date, the Schiffli was not considered as a competitor to the handmachine, its work being inferior in quality

148c

148d

and confined to simple patterns. At present, however, it is generally conceded that the goods produced by it are already superseding the latter to some extent. It is predicted that the Schiffli, operated by power, will ultimately supply all the embroidery in the low and medium grades.

The machine and its parts As shown in fig. 147, the cloth or net to be embroidered on is stretched usually on two large frames placed one above the other, and geared to move horizontally or vertically over short distances by variable cams. Thus shuttle and needle threads can interlock in a different position with each needle bar movement.

As the machines became longer, the huge size of the frames began to pose their own problems: the great spread of fabric became a prey to its own elasticity, and was to some extent stretched and distorted by every thrust of the fairly thick needles, causing the pattern to become, in time, noticeably irregular. Moreover the enormous length of the needle bars could be upset by the slightest

changes of temperature, irregularities of the floor, or even vibration, again with disastrous effects on the alignment of the embroidery. In spite of this, Saurer in 1977 developed an enormous 21 metre-long machine, with 1,500 needles. This operates very successfully today at the Forster Willi factory in St Gallen.

When the embroidery is to be on a bobbinet or a Raschel net, the less firm qualities can be supported on the frame by an acetate or other disposable backing, which prevents distortion during manufacture, and is easily removed afterwards.

The disadvantage of two frames working from one pattern source is that they must produce identical designs. Colour however can be varied: that of either the backing net, or of the embroidery threads themselves, can differ between the frames, as long as the thread and fabric textures remain the same.

The upper and lower needle bars run the full width of the front of the machine. The blunt bases of the needles are fixed into the bars, in such a way that they can be quickly replaced if they should break, or by a finer or coarser needle should the pattern require it. They have only one plane of movement, backwards and forwards, and are placed at regular intervals apart, for example one inch, though this can be extended to two or more to accommodate a broader pattern. They must, in short, be a sufficient distance apart that each completed design, entirely worked by a single needle, does not overlap the next. All the needles are threaded by hand.

In the twist-net machines, the completed lace was passed upwards on to a cloth roller. In the Schiffli the maximum size of the work produced is the size of the frame, for example 4 to 6 metres in height. The embroidery is begun at the top of the cloth or net, and patterning occurs simultaneously from every needle right across the width. Edgings are thus made crosswise of the machine, not vertically as is usual in Leavers. The 'length' of each band of edging is therefore equal to the width of the frame – say 10, 15 or 21 metres. However, bands will be made one below the other, and can be subsequently joined, so that considerable yardages can quite easily be obtained.

The thread supplying each needle is held on a spool (fig. 148a). Before reaching the needle's eye it passes over a tension roller, a feed bar and a straining bar so that it can slide quickly and smoothly as the needle makes its rapid stabs, while at the same time there is sufficient tension to prevent any loose thread accumulating around the stitches (fig. 148b,c).

The shuttles lie at the back of the machine, one opposite each needle. Their angle of movement is a slanting one, directed towards the protruding needle tip as each stitch is made. This obtuse angle gives more stability than a strictly right-angled one, providing slight friction and retardation which prevents the shuttles from rattling around (fig. 148d).

Aetzing, boring and blatt Boring means making a circular hole in the fabric, by means of a line of sharp-pointed borers fixed on a rack below the needle bar. When the pattern requires borers, the rack is advanced, and

when the needles have tacked around the circumference of the circle, to prevent fraying, the borer thrusts through the centre, separating and ripping the threads, and the raw edge is then properly sewn. The extent of the thread breakage will vary with the looseness or compactness of the weave. With net it is likely to be minimal, but where there is sufficient to present an untidy appearance, the retraction of the borers is followed by the advance of the stupfel, the sharpened edges of which shear off the torn ends. The size of the hole will vary according to how far and how often the long stiletto point goes into the cloth, and this can be regulated to small, medium or large (fig. 149).

148c *(opposite) Detail of the embroidery process: the needles are synchronised stitch by stitch, each working the same pattern.* **d** *The back of the machine showing the angle of the shuttles.*

149 *Reverse of a Schiffli embroidery showing different sized holes made by varying penetration of the cloth by the same borers.*

149

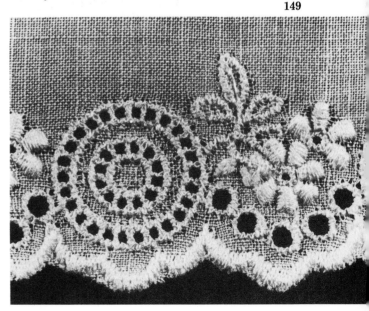

150a *Embroidery on net: the woman's shawl is made of long running stitches.* **b** *A burnt-out lace imitating Irish crochet: the ground copies faithfully the appearance of handmade crochet stitches illustrated in* Everylady's Journal *in 1912; the leaves show 'loft'.*

Although, as already mentioned, the Schiffli is limited to one basic stitch, the lockstitch, a considerable variety of effects is possible by altering the density or direction of the stitches. Steil stitch, for example, is produced by a narrow zigzag of lockstitches, and is frequently used to border the holes in imitation broderie anglaise. Blatt is a similar, but broader, zigzag. A running stitch is produced by the catching down, at intervals, of a single line of thread over the surface – but this thread can follow all sorts of shapes, and can be considerably elongated by a repetition of the jump stitch process in which the patterning device moves without making a stitch, that is without the thread being caught down. If this is done two or three times, a single long straight stitch appears (fig. 150a). A combination of the zigzag and running stitches, sometimes built up on each other to give 'loft' (fig. 150b), results in such exotic effects as French dot, wiggle stitch, pico, roseli, snorkel, vermicelli, bean, geflect fill, chicken scratch, mocca and steffels.[3]

Aetzing, or corrosion, was originally based on the chemical difference between animal fibres such as wool and silk, which are made of protein, and plant fibres such as cotton or linen, which are cellulose. The early processes of removal tended to be rather violent and not always to the good of the workers. Most commonly, now, it is the solubility of acetate rayons in acetone which is exploited, though hot air methods for blasting away a pre-treated fabric, or even placing the whole thing in water heated to 90 degrees centigrade, are also practised. This last method requires caution since it may result in differential shrinkage between the net, and the embroidery threads. In the acetate, and hot water, methods, the entire extent of fabric is immersed as a whole, since this makes for ease of handling during the finishing processes. The bands of lace can then be separated by hand-cutting of the cotton linking thread (see fig. 145b). Scalloping of the net laces is done by putting them against a sharp blade.

Making the pattern: Jacquards and pantographs The early Schifflis, like the handmachines, depended on a pantograph for their patterning (fig. 151a), although in conjunction with external power this posed problems of human fallibility as well as human endurance.

The replacement of the pantograph by Jacquard automatic patterning dates from about 1895, and is attributed to Arnold Groebli. The pantograph is now only used in training establishments, so that the work can be done in slow motion; or in some factories for the punching of the Jacquard strip (fig. 151b).

Since the function of the Jacquard is to move the frames for a specific distance, horizontally and vertically, each movement can be adequately controlled by a single line of holes or blanks. Separate cards such as are used on the twist-net machines are therefore unnecessary. Instead, a long continuous band of stiffened paper is used. On this, each line registers the co-ordinates of a single stitch position. Such a strip, or band, is known in Switzerland as a 'punch-card'. There is a series of ratchet holes down each side which engage with teeth on a spool so that the strip is constantly moved on (fig. 151c). When the vertical repeat has been completely punched, the ends of the strip are joined to make a circle, just as is done with separate cards.

Although the Jacquard band is still used, the method of punching it can now be computerized. This again helps to eliminate human error, since as a cursor is passed stitch by stitch over the ×6 drawing of the design, the pressing of its buttons causes the position of that stitch to show up on a screen, so that its accuracy or otherwise can immediately be determined. All the stitch-positions are stored in the computer's memory, and when they are complete the computer punches the tape.

Since every single line represents the position of a stitch, a pattern made up of a sequence of 600 stitches will require 600 lines, a pattern of 1,500 stitches will need 1,500 lines, and so on. The holes on the strip must be punched in such a way that they cause the frame(s) to be moved with absolute precision through the correct distance to the point

151a

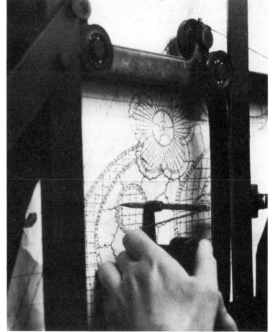

151b

151a *Part of a pantograph design showing how the points where stitches will be made are marked out (Charles Farmer).* **b** *A × 6 draft used for punching the Jacquard band or strip: pressing the button with the thumb, as the tracer touches each stitch position, will cause a hole to be punched in the appropriate position on the strip, via a series of cams. A similar sort of action originally drove the pantograph which moved the frame(s) (Charles Farmer).* **c** *Part of a Jacquard band showing the ratchet or peg holes (Charles Farmer).*

where the next stitch is to be made.

The representation on the card of the movement to arrive at that point, is an arithmetical calculation, involving a complex but logical attribution of values to hole-blank combinations. For purposes of

242

151c

assessment, the Jacquard strip is regarded as divided longitudinally into three parts: a left side controlling horizontal movements, a right side controlling vertical movements, and a middle part to deal with special effects such as the use of borers and stupfels, scalloping, speed and tension (fig. 152a):

Leaving aside special effects, the permutations of holes and blanks on each side can be given values, and arranged to cover every possible interval from 1mm to 171mm (6½ inches) inclusive. Thus:

Horizontal: (a) 2 blanks and 1 hole = plus quantities;

(b) 2 holes and 1 blank = minus quantities.

If the resultant total is a plus quantity, movement of the frame will be to the right; if it is a minus quantity, movement of the frame will be to the left. (This is occasionally reversed, but for any particular design it will be constant.)

Vertical: (a) 2 blanks and 1 hole = plus quantities;

(b) 2 holes and 1 blank = minus quantities (fig. 152b, c).

Note that the vertical values are in reverse order. When the final total is plus, movement of the frame will be up; when the final total is minus, movement of the frame will be down. These values can be tabulated, for the horizontal movement:

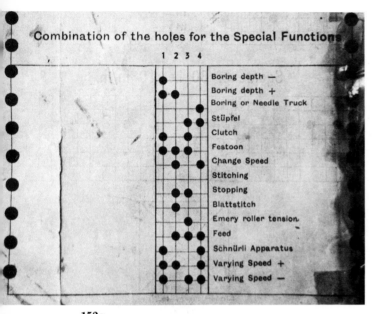

152a

Punching	I	II	III
H-B-B	+1	+7	+49
B-H-B	+2	+14	+98
B-B-H	+3	+21	+147
B-H-H	−1	−7	−49
H-B-H	−2	−14	−98
H-H-B	−3	−21	−147

H = hole.   B = blank.

152a The central special-function area of the Jacquard band. **b** The horizontal and vertical frame movement areas of the band. **c** Key to the position values of holes and blanks on the Jacquard band.

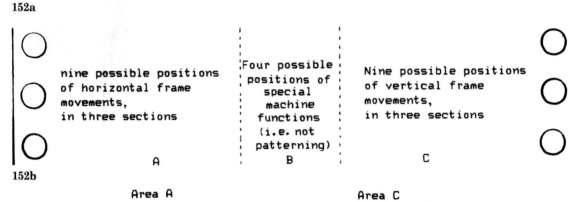

152b

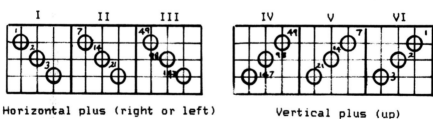

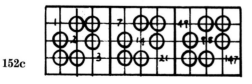

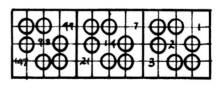

152c

and for the vertical movement:

Punching	IV	V	VI
B-B-H	+49	+7	+1
B-H-B	+98	+14	+2
H-B-B	+147	+21	+3
H-H-B	−49	−7	−1
H-B-H	−98	−14	−2
B-H-H	−147	−21	−3

Using this information as a key, any required horizontal or vertical stitch position can be accurately represented in a single line, allowing nine hole positions along the left, and nine along the right of the strip. To take an example:

Suppose the next stitch is to be made at a position 4mm to the right and 57mm up from the previous stitch. On the left side of the strip the values must total +4, and on the right side of the strip, +57. The line on the

card representing the position of the new stitch, will look like fig. 153.

Fig. 154 shows part of a theoretical Jacquard strip, and an analysis of a few of the lines.

A stitch, for the Schiffli, is usually defined as the point where the thread is caught down to the cloth by a needle movement. The maximum theoretical size, as we have seen, is enormous. In fact such large displacements are likely, if at all, only when the thread forms a 'float' linking one part of the design to

153 *The band punched for a frame movement of 4mm to the right and 57mm up from the previous needle position.*

154 *Part of a theoretical Jacquard band, and an analysis of the values it represents.*

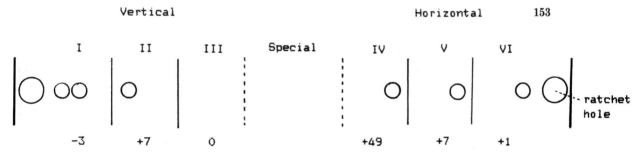

153

Vertical
I II III Special Horizontal IV V VI

−3   +7   0   ratchet hole   +49   +7   +1

Movement: 4mm to right (or left in some machines)

Movement: 57mm up

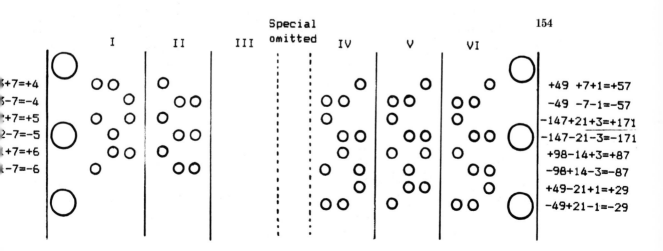

154

Special omitted

I II III IV V VI

+7=+4
−7=−4
+7=+5
−7=−5
+7=+6
−7=−6

+49 +7+1=+57
−49 −7−1=−57
−147+21+3=+171
−147−21−3=−171
+98−14+3=+87
−98+14−3=−87
+49−21+1=+29
−49+21−1=−29

movements, as in other lace machines, are geared so that they are always completed within the same brief and unvarying limit of time. The frame is counterbalanced by a large spring which prevents wobble during movement.

Compared with the Jacquard of the Leavers and Curtain machines, the whole system is extraordinarily simple. Instead of thousands of threads to be individually controlled, there is just a rectangular frame, and two possible directions. The width of the Jacquard strip is only 14cm, the number of the hole/blank positions limited to 22 (9 horizontal + 4 special effects + 9 vertical), and the 22 selectors occupy a single row.

Compared with the Leavers machine, it is an easy matter to change the design, involving only the removal of one Jacquard band, and its replacement with another. In Leavers, on the other hand, the number of separate threads per repeat can run into hundreds, and each will have its own individual sequence of movements, so that a change of pattern involves a complete dismantling of the previous set-out, the removal of the web, the emptying of the bobbins, the pricking out and threading of a new sley, and the threading of every guide bar individually and by hand right across the machine.

Any necessary repair work to the finished lace is done by a domestic sewing machine, such as an electrically operated Singer which works on the same lockstitch principle as the Schiffli itself, the thread being carefully selected to match the lace. The damaged part is mounted on a round or rectangular frame (sometimes known confusingly as a pantograph) and moved under the needle to follow the original pattern so that the missing parts are filled in.

Schiffli laces All are recognisable by the very closely-worked lockstitches which impart an appearance of fuzziness to the finished product, though when the stitches are small and the thread fine a magnifier may be needed to see the effect.

A number of types of lace can be distinguished, according to whether the embroidery is on cloth, on net, or on disposable fabric:

155 *The single line of selector pins facing a row of holes and blanks on the Jacquard (Charles Farmer).*

another. As part of the actual construction of a motif, stitches must be compact enough to give in the finished product a firm and pleasing effect. The maximum size for the design repeat is governed by other considerations, namely by the amount the frame can swing, horizontally and vertically. In large machines, this is seldom more than six inches, but in newer 5 or 10 metre models, the lightweight frames can move as much as 24 inches (600mm), so that quite enormous patterns can be created, such as the huge multi-coloured chrysanthemums embroidered on black bobbinet in Japan.

The Jacquard strip moves on at a steady and rapid pace, synchronising with the pulse of the machine and the backward and forward needle drives. The strip faces the back of the machine, and a single row of selector pins probes the holes, automatically assessing the pluses and minuses, and swinging the frame horizontally or vertically the distance required, via racks and worms (fig. 155). These

1. Embroidery on cloth (broderie anglaise or Madeira work). Borers are used to pierce the cloth and make a series of larger or smaller holes which are then worked around with blatt stitch.

2. Embroidery on net. Cotton bobbinet is most satisfactory, but bobbinets of synthetic yarn, or Raschel nets, or even patterned Leavers laces can also be used (see ch. 5). Two types of embroidered net can be distinguished:

(a) Net laces. Initially these copied the designs of bobbin and needle laces with a hand made mesh, such as point de gaze (see fig. 160), or of Brussels appliqué which hadhandmade motifs stitched to bobbinet.

(b) Needlerun. A thick cotton, silk or rayon cord, threaded through the needles is circled round and round on the surface of the net and held in place by cotton shuttle threads which chain-stitch on the reverse. The cord does not duck in and out of the meshes in the manner of hand-needlerun, or of the handmachine (fig. 156).

156 *Schiffli needlerun on an edging*

3. Burnt-out (chemical, aetzed) laces. The background fabric of the embroidery is dissolved away, or otherwise removed, leaving only the embroidery stitches to form the lace:

(a) Guipures. Initially these copied the designs of handmade laces in which the motifs were linked by legs, or bars, such as Irish crochet, Venetian gros point, reticella, coralline, Brussels duchesse, Rosaline and Honiton. In the twentieth century, as with other machine laces, imitations of the handmade diminished (fig. 157a–f).

(b) Macramé. Thicker thread such as 24/2 cotton was threaded through thicker needles, and the pattern built up in a padded manner. Neither the technique nor the result bore any resemblance to handmade macramé, except for the appearance of three-dimensional ridges. It was mainly a furnishing lace (fig. 157g).

4. Appliqué work. The frame is spread with net overlaid with a fine cotton batiste, velvet, or other fabric, and the two layers are stitched together in accordance with the

selected design. When the run is completed, the work is taken off the frame, and the excess overlying fabric cut away by hand, leaving just the motifs attached to the net (fig. 158). In a sophisticated variation of this process, the fabric to be applied is first decorated with embroidery, then the whole thing remounted on the frame over a layer of net, and the work completed as before. The enormous amount of hand-finishing, and consequent high price, is possible only during periods of extensive *haute couture* demand. The attachment of fabric to net on the Schiffli is by blatt or steil stitch. In similar work done on the handmachine, stemstitch is used; on the Cornely, chainstitch; and in handmade Carrickmacross, a couched cord.

5. Cut fabrics. After a sheet of cloth, or net, has been embroidered, some of the plain areas around the design are cut away, creating a

157a *(i)*

157a *(iii)*

157a *(ii)*

157a *(i) 'New Guipure Galon, Paris only': Paris was a shade of ecru. Imitations of Irish crochet were among the first burnt-out laces made by the Schiffli. Here, they are created 'nose to nose' so that they can easily be snipped apart to be stitched to garments as 'incrustations'. (ii) Schiffli Irish crochet with handmade roses added. (iii) Detail.* **b** *Venetian gros point: this was the basic lace imitated by the more luxurious Irish crochets, and therefore a natural for Schiffli imitation. The raised work, or loft, is made on the machine.* **c** *(i) An imitation of seventeenth century reticella. (ii) Detail, showing the angles of movement possible for the stitches, even making a semi-circle.* **d** *Brussels guipure laces were also copied. (i) and (ii) Duchesse, and detail. (iii) Rosaline.* **e** *An imitation of a Russian bobbin lace.* **f** *An Edwardian godet with a non-imitative art nouveau design, of fritillary.* **g** *Schiffli macrame, named from its heavy raised texture.*

157b

157c *(i)*   **157c** *(ii)*

157d *(i)*

157d *(ii)*

157d *(iii)*

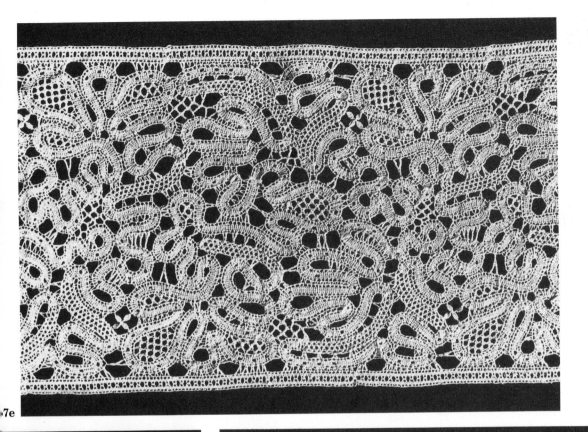

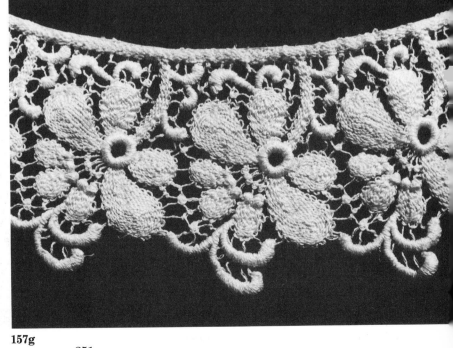

157e

157f   **157g**

251

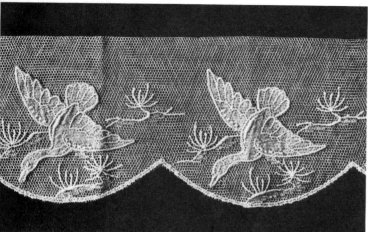

159a *A Richelieu-work effect in which strands of cloth are enclosed by embroidery, with large empty spaces left between them.* **b** *Fragments of cloth making the leaves of a burnt-out guipure.* **c** *A fine muslin fabric has cut-out circles surrounded with 'macrame' and filled with crochet-style fancy work.*

159a

kind of delicate silhouette against a background of space, something in the manner of Richelieu work (fig. 159a).

6. (a) A complex melange of lace guipure, embroidery on net, and cut fabric (fig. 159b) requires not only embroidery in two stages, but a great deal of hand-finishing. The guipure areas are first established, by embroidery on acetate. The whole thing is then remounted as a sandwich between net and satin, and the layers stitched through to make a coherent whole. Subsequently the acetate is degraded, the net and satin trimmed away over and under the guipure, and then the net and satin cut separately in their predestined areas.

(b) Manila lace. Silk, muslin or nun's veiling is treated as in (5), and selcted spaces are then backed with net, or with decorative stitches in burnt-out style (fig. 159c).

7. Raised petals. These are added to embroidered net, giving a three-dimensional effect. The original idea was to imitate the raised rose petals of the needle lace point de gaze, but all kinds of novelty effects can be produced in this way, in spite of the labour involved. The petals had first to be embroidered on the machine, washed, stiffened with size, and cut by hand, then stitched to the appropriate places either by hand or using a single-needle sewing machine (fig. 160).

159b

159c

Fashion rang the changes on all of these. Eyelet holes for example were in demand in the 1950s and 60s, burnt-out laces in the 70s, and embroideries on net – especially imitating nineteenth-century Brussels laces – in the 80s. Effects 4, 5, 6 and 7 were for a long time obsolete, but are now being revived at prestigious factories such as that of Forster Willi of St Gallen, catering for exclusive models by Dior, Balmain, Patou, Ricci and other high-fashion houses.

One effect which the Schiffli could not produce was that of darning, or weaving, which could only be made by needles passing entirely through the fabric, and back again, as they do in the handmachine. Its nearest approach was the catching down of the needle threads at regular intervals and alternating points by the shuttle threads (fig. 161).

Historically, the manufacture of guipure laces was associated particularly with St Gall (Switzerland), and of net laces with Plauen (Saxony). By 1892 their factories were already exporting to America, and to England, in spite of fierce competition from the Leavers machines. Hénon in that year wrote of the 'very pretty novelty lace, a kind altogether new, special and unknown till then' for which J-A Jahn of Plauen had registered a patent. It was an embroidery on fancy net, subsequently treated by a chemical process. It was to be called *dentelle fin de siècle* (end of the century lace). Hénon continues:

At that time there were in Plauen and St Gall 32,000 embroidery machines, of two kinds, the new continuous thread machines, and the older *primitif* handmachines, the former costing 4,000 francs, and the latter between 2,000 and 2,400. The articles which the new machines were producing were so exquisite that the manufacturers were keeping the buyers waiting three months or more for the completion of their orders. By the chemical process a sort of lace with brides, and decorative effects, was created which imitated very well Irish and Venetian guipures. Several manufacturers at Calais intended to import some of the new machines. Meanwhile they were restricting their Leavers patterned laces to those which the machines of Plauen and St Gall found it difficult to deliver.[4]

160 *Raised petals of cloth, stitched by hand to a Schiffli copy of point de gaze.*

161 *Schiffli 'darning': the short stitches do not pass over and under the longer ones as in true darning, but simply catch down running stitches at regular intervals.*

162 *A Barudan multihead machine, with tape and card reader, 1982 (Geoffrey E. Macpherson Ltd, Nottingham).*

Nottingham resisted the importation of embroidery machines until after 1900. By 1917 England had 850, compared with over 30,000 in their place of origin. It was still a damaging blow to the Leavers industry, not as a superior product but as a more versatile one.

Both Leavers and the Schiffli had problems in making 'shaped pieces', for example large collars and parasol covers, since they could only be made by considerable cutting and rejoining which was labour-intensive and expensive, and so dependent on a favourable market. The problem was to some extent overcome by the smaller embroidery machines, which will be considered next.

III. Multiheads

The Multihead machine looks like several sewing machines joined together side by side. It acts like the Schiffli in the sense that the fabric to be embroidered is stretched on a frame which is moved automatically under the needles by Jacquard or electronic control. The frames are flat instead of upright (fig. 162), and the planes of movement are thus from side to side, and forward and back.

One machine of this type is the Barudan, which can have up to 24 'heads'. These, depending on number, can be set between 132.5 and 440mm apart. Each head has five needles, every one with its own thread-supply, the five being often of differing colour, texture or lustre. One needle at each head is operative at a time. As it moves rapidly up and down it penetrates the fabric, and its loop connects with a shuttle, making a lockstitch. It can work at a speed of 600 stitches per minute, compared with the usual 200 for the Schiffli[5], and it can switch automatically from one needle to another according to the program.

Alternating with the stitches are movements of the frame (here called a pantograph) carrying it to the required position beneath the needles. It can be moved up to 12.7mm at a time in any direction parallel to its sides. The frame can hold one large piece of fabric, approximately 2.8m by 85cm for the 24-head machine, or proportionately smaller for machines with fewer heads. Alternatively, separate frames with their own piece of fabric can be placed beneath each needle. They will still work in unison, every needle doing the same thing at the same time.

The distance between needles determines

the maximum size widthways of the repeat. In the Barudan multihead it can be up to 44cm. In the Schiffli it is usually 132.5mm, and a special machine intended for the sample working of Schiffli designs is manufactured to this specification.

The frame's movements were formerly controlled by a Jacquard and selector pins, but electronic patterning has considerably speeded up the embroidery process, and there is a standard 64,000 stitch memory, which can be increased up to 160,000 stitches if required. 64,000 stitches would give a motif approximately 6 inches square, depending on the fineness of the thread, and the closeness of the work.

The Multihead also has the advantage of being able to embroider directly on to shaped pieces of fabric and so can make collars etc without a lot of cutting and rejoining (fig. 163). Its lace-making potential has yet to be realised. It does little embroidery on net, which needs a very fine mesh if the stitches are not to fall through the holes. Borers exist, but have to replace some needles, and because of the way the heads are set up the work is less straightforward than on the Schiffli. Burning out designs to make guipures is not yet practised, because of lack of demand and incentive.

IV. Bonnaz and Cornely

While the modern Multipoint may be regarded as having developed by a diminution of the Schiffli machine, the Bonnaz and Cornely were inspired both by hand-tambouring and by contemporary inventions in the field of sewing machines.

The first real attempt at embroidering by machine is described in a patent registered to John Duncan in 1804 (no. 2769). It was for 'machinery for tambouring upon cloth .. using a large number of barbed needles or hooks at the same time'. Each needle was to produce the same pattern

by moving the needles horizontally or vertically at the requisite times in front of the cloth, or by moving the cloth in front of the needles or hooks. The latter plan is preferred by the patentee, and is

163 *An asymmetrically-shaped collar which can be embroidered easily on the multihead, but only with difficulty, or wastefully, on the Schiffli.*

effected as follows: The cloth is stretched in a vertical position between two cylinders placed parallel to each other in an oblong frame, which slides freely up or down at pleasure, in another frame, and the latter slides freely to and fro horizontally, carrying the first frame with it. Thus, either a vertical or a horizontal motion may be communicated to the cloth; and when both are communicated at the same time, the cloth moves in an oblique direction. By these means, every rectilinear or curvilinear figure may be produced, and, consequently every pattern required

164a

164a *A Bonnaz hooked needle with a length of thread looped over it.* **b** *Cornely embroidered machine for chainstitch work, c.1900.* **c** *A Cornely machine for attaching two kinds of braid, c.1905. The handle beneath can alter the direction of the fabric movement ((b) and (c) from Charles and Pagès).*

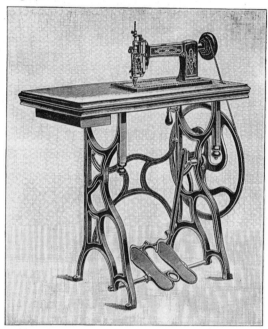

164b

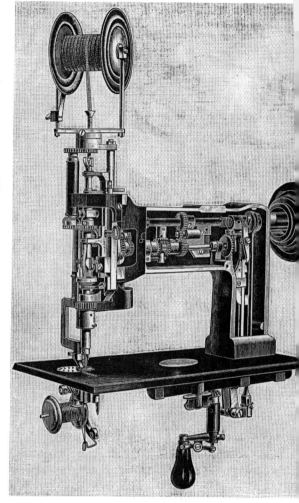

164c

a remarkable anticipation of twentieth-century developments.

Nothing more appears to be known of this early machine, although Maria Edgeworth, *c.*1810 mentioned 'a worked [embroidered] muslin cap done in tambour-stitch by a steam-engine'; and later when Harry and Lucy exclaim at the speed of their mother's hand-tambouring, she replies 'You think I go on quickly, but all that I could do in a day could be done by a steam engine in an hour'.[6] The Watt steam engine had been patented in 1769, and applied to the workings of textile machinery, with variable success, from the late eighteenth century.

Duncan's second plan, of moving the cloth in front of the needles, anticipated the handmachine of 1828. Another feature of the handmachine, the double-pointed needle, had been anticipated even earlier, in 1755, by C.F. Weisenthal (patent no. 701) for the working of

fine thread into muslin after the manner of Dresden needlework by means of a needle with two points, which needle is to be used for holding it with the fingers in the middle, so as not to require turning.

The first patent for a satisfactory sewing machine was registered to Thimonnier in

1848 (no. 12060). It could work at a speed of more than 200 stitches a minute. But Thimonnier was opposed by reactionary forces, his machines were smashed and, after several attempts to re-establish his surviving machine, which he carried around with him on his back, he died destitute. Thimonnier's was a chainstitch machine, which used a needle in the form of a small hook (fig. 164a). It had a thread-carrier which looped the thread around the needle beneath the fabric, and a nipple which held the fabric firmly down as the hook with its loop of thread was pulled back through it – a procedure very similar to tambour work done by hand.

In 1863 a patent for the Bonnaz machine (no. 2544) was registerd by William Clark, on receipt of a communication from Antione Bonnaz. Modifications made were in the needle, which could be put in and out of action instantaneously, without stopping the motion of the machine; and in the design which could be embroidered without the cloth 'requiring to be turned round to follow the contour of the said design', by altering the direction of the thread feed.

The Bonnaz machine used only one needle and one thread. The inventions of M. Cornely in the 1870s perfected and added to it, culminating in the production of the Cornely machine of a style very similar to that still in use today (fig. 164b, c).

There were several forms of the Cornely, some with two or three needles and thread-sources, and between them they could produce a variety of effects: lockstitch to attach beads or sequins (paillets) to a net ground; couching stitch (fig. 165a) to attach a fine bourdon cord to the design outline of 'Alençon' laces made on the Pusher and Leavers machines; moss stitch with loops of thread like towelling; and of course chainstitch.

Today the machine most commonly used is Cornely A. It has a single hooked needle which, as it works, constantly dips down through a hole to bring up the thread. The source of the thread is a large spool under the machine. Varied colour effects in an embroidery can only be achieved by changing the spool. Formerly foot power was used, through

165a

165a *A cut-out squirrel oversewn with couched bourdon cord.* **b** *Vermicilli work in black silk thread, like strands of handmade crochet stitches meandering over the net.*

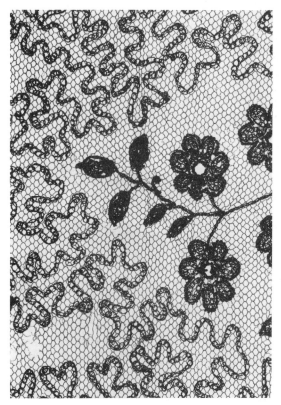

165b

257

166 *Swiss curtain samples worked by the Cornely machine, second half nineteenth century:* **a** *A net guipure. The design is made of net with all the filling stitches of the leaves and blossom worked by hand.* **b** *A fabric appliqué on net.* **c** *A fabric guipure. The raised work around the flower centres is of handmade crochet.*

167a *A worker embroidering in satin stitch on the Courteix (Charles and Pagès).* **b** *A corner of a large curtain with a huge flowing embroidery in chainstitch, reputedly made for the Paris Exhibition of 1904.*

166a

166b

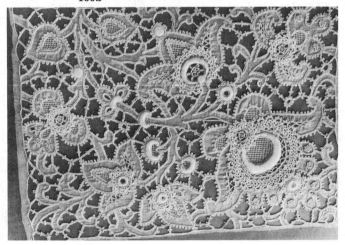

166c

167a

a treadle; now the machines are electrically operated, with the pedal acting as an accelerator providing speeds of up to 1200 stitches a minute. The net, or the cloth, is held firmly in a small frame which is moved by a handle just beneath the platform. As a safety device the handle must be pulled down a little before being turned.

A drawing of the design is first made, on a firm tracing paper. A series of small holes is then pierced round the outline by means of a stencilling machine. The rough edges left by this process are smoothed away, so that the holes do not become blocked. A lubricant such as pig fat is mixed with powdered charcoal and rubbed through the stencil holes on to the fabric to show where the lines of stitching are to be embroidered. The tracing paper is then cleaned, and can be used again, up to 20 times. Later, dry cleaning gets rid of the fat on the cloth.

In the technique of muslin appliqué, popular both for fashion and for curtains in the second half of the nineteenth century, and still in use today, the cloth with its printed design is tacked onto a net backing, and the Cornely chainstitches along every line, fixing fabric and net together. The excess fabric is then cut away by hand, leaving the cloth design appliquéd onto the net. Even more elaborate effects were produced as late as the 1950s, for example the creation of bars of

167b

thread in guipure style around parts of the pattern, needlerun fillings to the flowers, longstitch oversewing to make raised centres, and even crochet work embellishments (fig. 166). Now, however, orders are not big enough to cover the extra cost.

Much of the work is still carried on in the homes of outworkers. A single motif is embroidered at the factory as an example for them to follow, but many stages are involved, and the laces travel back and forth between home and factory, often over a three-month period, before the products are finally ready for marketing. They are therefore not cheap.

Net insets put into a woven fabric are in a sense a reverse of muslin appliqué. In this technique, small pieces of net are stitched to the back of the fabric, then the cloth cut away over them so the net is revealed. Nylon bobbinet is now most commonly used. Scalloped borders, if firm enough, can be trimmed semi-mechanically by pulling the cloth against a device known as a 'pull-cutter', which is simply a sharp blade held in a safety-frame. The work is still muscle-powered, but much quicker than scissors.

Chainstitch itself can be embroidered at various tensions, the looser form being known as *fluderstich* or vermicelli work (fig. 165b). It is indistinguishable from chainstitch made by hand, except for the length of thread used. By hand, not more than a metre is practicable, so there are frequent endings and startings, the new threads often beginning with a knot. For the Cornely, the longer the thread the better, since every interruption of the work costs time and money. Separate small motifs are therefore not economic for the machine to embroider, and strands of chainstitch tend to coil over the net and each other almost endlessly.[7]

Rarely, the Cornely works on a disposable fabric which is later burnt-out.

A third machine, the Courteix, invented in the first decade of the twentieth century, was a modification of the Cornely which took up Duncan's first option spelt out in 1804. The patterning was brought about not by the movement of the fabric under the needle, but by the movement of the needle over the fabric (fig. 167a). The advantage of this was that it enabled large pieces to be embroidered more easily – entire dresses and even bed covers could go under the needle, and swirling designs could be produced which covered the whole fabric (fig. 167b).

Summary of 18th and 19th century patterned machine lace developments

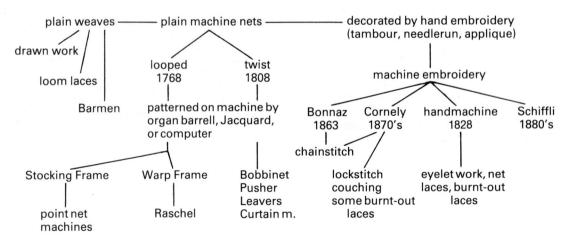

260

IX

Loom- And Other Woven-Laces

The term 'loom laces' appears in writings of the seventeenth and early eighteenth century – bought by Pepys, prohibited by import restrictions, priced in millinery accounts, listed among laces of the American colonists, and recorded from Germany, Scotland, Spain and Finland. Not once is there any indication of what they looked like or of how they were made.

This is a not unfamiliar situation in the world of lace, except that the naked names of most handmade laces have long since been clothed by tradition in generally acceptable garments.

Many examples of woven laces survive, but whether all, or one special group, were the loom laces of those years, we have no way of being certain (fig. 168). If weaves are to be called laces they must have sufficient holes or openwork in them, and they should be slender. The patterned gauzes fit most comfortably into this category, especially since some silk gauzes, hand-embroidered in running-stitch, are a recognised lace known as buratto (Venetian spelling *burato*). The increasing heaviness of patterned gauze weaves used for table linen may well form a cut-off point where lace becomes simply a patterned-weave fabric with openwork.

There are a number of other weaving techniques which could conceivably produce a woven, or loom, lace, and some can be mechanized, so that they will all be listed briefly here, even though it seems likely that to copy their involved and variable intertwining would be for a machine extraordinarily difficult.

1. *Warp twine*. A plain gauze is, in lace terms, a plain net made by a crossed-weaving technique, that is, by the crossing of the warps each time the wefts pass through them. The addition of patterning can be done in many ways, most easily by interspersing the gauze ground with blocks of plain or twill weave so that it has the appearance of solid designs set in an openwork ground. More subtle variations are achieved by twisting adjacent pairs of warps in different directions, or linking them by varying tensions into slanting strands (fig. 169). Such laces,

168 *The lady on the left darns a knotted or woven net, stretched on an embroidery frame; the one in the centre works with a needle and thread; on the right a small table-loom may be producing loom lace – see the likely-looking piece in the basket on the floor (from* Neues Model-Buch, Anderer Theil, *Nuremberg, c. 1689. The title page, engraved by Furst).*

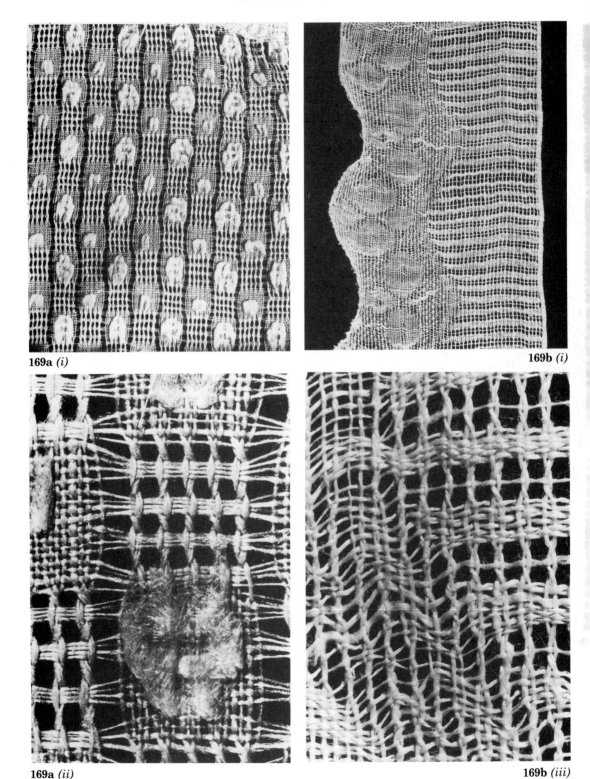

169a *(i)*

169b *(i)*

169a *(ii)*

169b *(iii)*

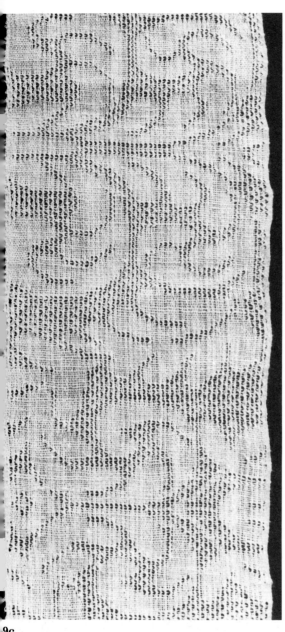

made in linen, are known from manufactories in the Tønder area of Denmark, and recorded in 1775 and 1787. For a time they flourished, but by 1812 only six machines remained, producing slightly under 1,000 metres a week, their output being progressively reduced by the importation of German gauze-woven laces. These were cheaper on two counts, the lower cost of labour and their slacker texture resulting from the smaller number of threads per unit width. These gauze laces, known locally as *jøde-kniplinger* (Jew laces) from being sold by pedlars, were used on peasant kerchiefs and caps, and on household linen; but in the more prosperous times of the 1840s and after, they were displaced by the prettier Tønder bobbin laces (Mygdal). Laces from the Carelian area of Finland, now in the USSR, consisted of plain-weave portions like linen-stitch, with a few twisted warps providing an openwork effect at intervals.

2. *Weft twine.* In this variation the warps lie straight, and a pair of weft threads, carried across them, twist between each end, or single warp (fig. 170).

3. *Weft wrap.* Even plain weaves can be converted into openworks on the loom by suitable thread manipulation. For example weft wrap is a slow and laborious wrapping of selected wefts tightly around small groups of warps and wefts (fig. 171) so that in a very complex manner, a holey fabric is created, which can look remarkably similar to drawnwork, ie an embroidered lace in which a plain weave is turned into lace, after it has left the loom, by thread deflection or withdrawal and the use of oversewing.

170 *Weft twine: pairs of wefts twine around single warps.*

9c

169a *(i) Blocks of warp twine alternating with blocks of plain weave, part of a baby's bonnet, early nineteenth century. The regularity of the patterning may indicate Jacquard control. (ii) Detail.* **b** *(i) and (ii) Varied gauze effects made by hand manipulation of warps and wefts. (iii) Detail of (i). Eighteenth century.*

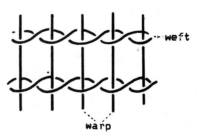

263

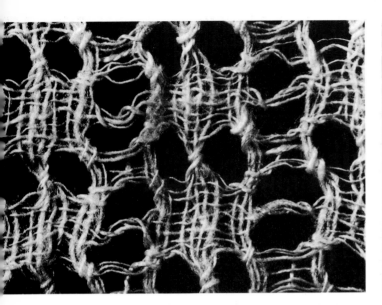

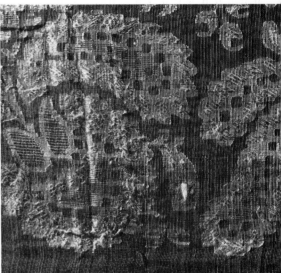

171 *Weft wrap: a fabric made by this very tedious technique, early nineteenth century.*

172 *Wrapped warp, a sketch of the technique. The resultant fabric is rather heavy to be called a lace.*

173 *Though not a true Madras muslin, this Jacquard-woven gauze gives an adequate representation of the technique. The reverse side, here, shows the multiple clipping which has taken place at every border of the patterned areas.*

4. In *wrapped warp*, wefts are again wrapped round the warps, but now in an upward or downward direction, binding them together in groups of two or three[1] in such a way that they are interspersed with plain weaves, forming a kind of guipure background to the patterned areas (fig. 172).

5. In *Madras muslin*, a patterning weft is incorporated in an otherwise uniform gauze weave. This heavy weft is caught between the warp twists in the patterned areas, and so is held tightly in place. In between, it is carried across the surface as floats, and these have to be cut back once the lace has left the loom. The large amount of hand-clipping increases its cost, and at the same time the fabric is rendered to some extent unstable by the multitude of loose ends (fig. 173).

6. *Lappet weaving* looks similar to Madras muslin but is made differently, and may sometimes be worked on a loosely-textured muslin instead of on gauze so that it is non-holey and not a lace. The thicker patterning threads are, here, additional warps, introduced at intervals, and made to pass for short distances parallel to the wefts, but across the surface, so that they are only caught down at each end of their horizontal run. At the next pick (weft passage) they turn back again, and are once more caught down by the weft. The fabric is woven face side downwards, so that the resulting effect is similar to shadow stitch. Since the patterning threads are warps, they will float from one area of design to the next in a vertical direction, and the amount of clipping is considerably less than in Madras muslin (fig. 174).

7. *Mock leno* gives the superficial appearance of a gauze weave, but the lacey effect is achieved by an interweaving of warps and wefts in small blocks with spaces between, and not by any sort of warp twine. Mock leno

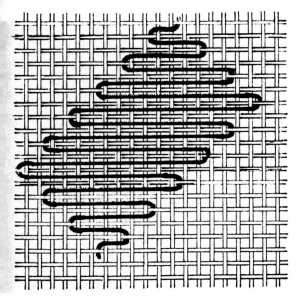

174 *Lappet weaving, showing the underlay or shadow-stitch effect on the reverse of the fabric as the warp patterning thread is carried across the back.*

175 *A fragment of mock leno weave. The openwork effect is caused by the spacing of the warps, and the irregular picks of the wefts, not by any twining process.*

is often used to provide the appearance of a mesh ground in large-scale designs as on tablecloths or dress fabrics (fig. 175).

8. In *plain weave openwork* (fig. 176) the wefts weave across only a few warp ends, repeatedly turning back on themselves to leave longer or shorter vertical slits through which light can shine. This technique, resembling the kelim weave, was known in eighteenth century Spain as Spanish stitch, Moorish weaving, loom-made lace, or red de telar[2]. This latter term, literally 'loom net' is in sound not unlike the radexelo recorded in the fifteenth-century Sforza inventory, which is sometimes interpreted not as a weave but as reticella, a handmade lace of early origin compounded of embroidery, needle and bobbin influences.

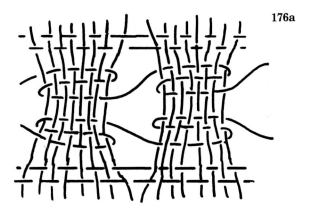

176a

176 *Plain weave openwork, or* radexelo. **a** *The threads are spaced out, and would form a loosely textured openwork.* **b** *A modern version of the work, called 'Spanish lace'.* **c** *Detail of a bed valance, eighteenth century.*

265

176b

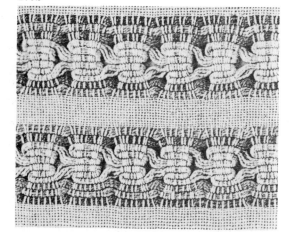

176c

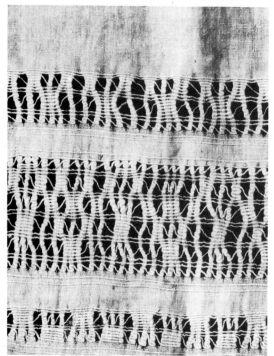

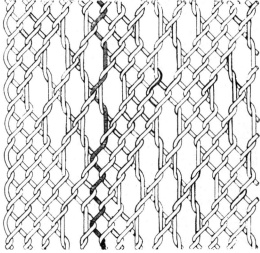

178a

All the above forms, nos. 1 to 8, are clearly specialized weaves, using both warps and wefts in a variety of ways. An interesting development appears when weaves become mixed with knots, as in *knotted weft wrap*, or *warp bundle*. The warps are still stretched on a loom, but the wefts tie them with overhand knots into bundles as they pass by (fig. 177). This technique provides a link with macramé where the fabric is made of threads hanging like isolated warps and knotted among themselves. If, alternatively, the knotted wefts are considered in isolation, as a horizontal sequence, they must appear as loops made one after the other, of a shape and in a manner not dissimilar to that of the buttonhole-stitch work which makes the needle laces.

In *sprang* only warps are used, fixed at both ends as on a loom. In the absence of wefts the openwork is made by twisting the threads together in the central area, the fabric thus being constructed in both an upwards and a downwards direction at the same time.

In *warp-plaiting* long warps are left hanging from the woven linen when it is taken off the loom. It may then be lightly twisted (twine-plaiting or twining, fig. 178a) to produce an open effect not unlike the straight down fender or Mechlin net made at one

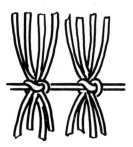

177 *A sketch of a knotted weft wrap, perhaps a forerunner of buttonhole stitch openworks.*

178a *Twine-plaiting, perhaps a forerunner of bobbin laces.* **b** *(i) Warp ends are plaited in groups of three to strengthen and decorate the towel borders, c.1830. (ii) Detail.* **c** *(i) A Hedebo towel end with the threads crossed and twisted in groups of four. (ii) Detail, showing the diagonal-thread effect and simulated torchon ground, c.1830.*

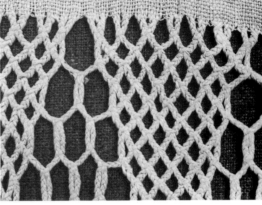

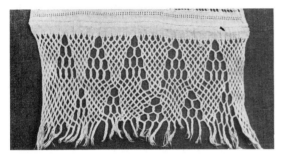

178b *(i)*

178b *(ii)*

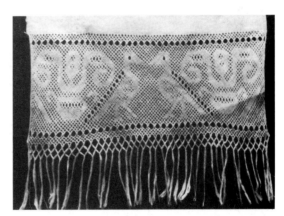

178c *(i)*

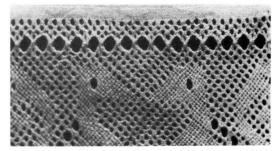

178c *(ii)*

time on the Bobbinet machines (see p. 87). Alternatively, the warps may be taken in groups of three across the width of the fringe and plaited together in an interlacing manner (fig. 178b). Even more interesting is the practice in some Scandinavian countries, especially in the Hedebo area of Denmark to the west of Copenhagen,[3] of taking the threads four at a time (two pairs) and twisting and crossing them in a manner entirely similar to the basic movements of bobbin lace-making except that the direction is reversed, that is, the twist is left over right, and the cross right over left.[4] A remarkable facsimile of the wholestitch and mesh ground of a bobbin lace is thus produced, though without using bobbins, with the threads being worked horizontally in sequence – although the final effect is diagonal, with all the threads behaving equally instead of being distinguished into workers and passives, and with none of the pinholes to be expected in bobbin laces (fig. 178c).

This chapter illustrates how the loom-woven group, harking back to pre-history and archaic methods of weaving, is sufficiently amorphous to form a potential genesis from which all the highly specialized thread manipulations known as lace could over the centuries have evolved into their many forms, both manual and machine-made.

Glossary

Note: machine terms sometimes have quite different meanings from the same words applied to handmade laces. The glossary is restricted to terms used in the text. Where definitions apply specifically to particular machines or laces, the following abbreviations are used: SF, Stocking Frame; WF, Warp Frame and other warp-knitting machines except the Raschel; R, Raschel; Bo, Bobbinet (including Old Loughborough, Circular, and Plain Net); P, Pusher; L, Leavers; LC, Lace Curtain; Ba, Barmen; HM, Handmachine; S, Schiffli; C, Cornely; Lo, Loom laces.

Aetzing (pronounced etzing; German = caustic). Refers to burnt-out laces (*qv*). A process in which the backing fabric of a machine embroidery is dissolved or corroded away, leaving only the stitches, which hold together to form a lace (HM,S,C).

Alençon a lace with raised outlining cords around a design of flower clusters, formalised, in a fine Ensor net ground. It has the superficial, not technical, appearance of an Alençon lace made by hand. (P,L).

All-overs lace 36 inches wide, or more, with a repeating design, patterned all over like a dress fabric (mainly L).

Angel lace lace made as bands (*qv*), linked by lacers, on a warp-knitting machine.

Appliqué an attachment of two layers of fabric, the lower a bobbinet, the upper a woven fabric or another net, or handmade motifs. The first two may be stitched to the bobbinet by any of the embroidery machines, or by hand; the third is always hand-stitched.

Back edge/selvage/seaming edge the straight side of an edging, equivalent to the footing in handmade laces.

Back motion the swing of the carriages towards the back of the machine (Bo,P,L,LC).

Back of the lace the reverse, or textural back of the lace as worn.

Back warp reverse or Z-twist warp threads used to supplement the front (right, or S-twist) warps.

Band narrow edgings, insertions or galloons made vertically on the machines, and joined by lacers during manufacture.

Bar ground mesh or net grounds controlled entirely by cams acting through the two or three guide bars, without Jacquard intervention (LC).

Barmen a circular braiding machine modified for the production of openwork fabrics (lace), copying mainly Le Puy, torchon and cluny bobbin lace designs.

Barred lace the ground of the lace is made not by a mesh or net but by bars or legwork, sometimes called brides. Examples: Bruges, Honiton, Venise etc (*see also* Guipures).

Bars the metal strips, wider than the machine itself, which carry the longitudinal threads. They control the patterning by deflecting the threads short distances to the right or left of the starting point. They may be several hundred inches long (Bo,P,L,LC). *See also* Guide bars.

Beading/ribbon holes lace with slots or small holes for threading tapes or ribbons through.

Beam (a) vertically stretched threads, additional to the warp threads and used mainly for liners, lacers and patterning (gimping). The beam threads are wound on separate rollers, so that each is usually involved only once in a pattern repeat, and they work independently of each other, under Jacquard control (Bo,P,L).

(b) synonymous with roller, for example, warp beam = the roller holding the warp threads.

Bearded needle a needle with a long reflexed tip. When the beard is closed by the presser bar forcing it into a groove, a knitted loop can be passed over the needle's head (SF,WF).

Binche a machine lace with a fancy net ground, or fillings (L).

Bishops net a mesh with a cross at either end, characteristic of bottom bar work (L).

Blonde a machine lace in glossy silk, pale gold or black, light in weight, the simple designs in heavier thread enclosing spaces. The ground is often an Ensor net (L and Traverse Warp)

Bobbin (a) a thread holder of circular form, some $1\frac{1}{2}$ to 2 inches in diameter, but laterally compressed to $\frac{1}{10}$th inch or less. In Bobbinet machines in general, the brass bobbins – sometimes called *brasses* – are held in and moved by carriages of steel. In the Barmen, the bobbins are tall spools carried by spindles which can glide rapidly along sinuous tracks on a running surface.

(b) the bobbin thread may be abbreviated to 'bobbin'.

Bobbin fining a Leavers technique in which heavy weighting of the warp threads pulls them straight, and stretches the bobbin threads outwards around them to take a zigzag form in the finished lace.

Bobbin lace/bobbin made a lace made by hand using stick-like bobbins with the thread wound around their necks, the lower shaft acting as a handle.

Bobbinet/bobbin net a net made of paired bobbin and warp threads twisted together. At the upper end of every mesh the bobbin threads cross each other and proceed in opposite directions taking a diagonal (traversed) course towards the right and left sides of the web. There are two-twist, three-twist and four-twist variations.

Bobbinet-Jacquard an old name for the Pusher machine, (*qv*).

Bobbinet machine (a) used specifically of the Plain Net machine, working on the same principle as Heathcoat's Old Loughborough (1809), with both bobbins and warps working in pairs to make a two-twist, or similar, bobbinet (Bo).

(b) used generally of all the derivatives of the original machine, though working with a single set of bobbins, and with many additional sources of thread supplementing the warps (Bo,P,L,LC).

Bolt see *Comb*.

Bonnaz a single-needle embroidery machine developed in the mid-nineteenth century.

Bottom bars (a) single: a set of (guide) bars situated in the lower part of the machine, with front warps threaded through them so that they control the formation of the net ground, leaving all the top bars free for patterning.

(b) double: similar bars threaded with reverse warps. Both (a) and (b) lie below the top (patterning) guide bars, and work though stump bars. They have their own Jacquard cylinders, and may number up to 800. *See also* Stump bars.

Bourdon cord the heavy yarn used to outline the design in laces where such emphasis is needed. It can be couched on by hand, or by the Cornely machine.

Braid as made on Braiding machines. Flat or tubular tapes made by interlacing (plaiting) three or more strands so that they cross each other in a diagonal manner.

Brass see *Bobbin*.

Breadth see *Band*.

Brise bise a 'break-breeze' net curtain designed to cover the lower half of a sash window (see fig. 109).

Broderie anglaise a cotton fabric perforated by a pattern of holes embroidered around to prevent them fraying (HM,S).

Brown/grey lace dirty lace, as it comes off the machine, prior to finishing.

Burnt-out/chemical lace lace formed entirely of embroidery stitches, the backing fabric having been removed by some chemical means (HM,S,C).

Cams circular wheels of uneven circumference, along which a small truck rides, following the swells and hollows, and transmitting its deflections via levers to the movable parts of the machine, for example comb bars, some guide bars.

Carcase the iron body of the machine, formerly made by frame-smiths. The delicate parts concerned more directly with thread movements are called the *insides* (*qv*).

Carriage the steel frame which holds the bobbin. By a spring it regulates the thread release. A broad blade below slots into the comb and enables it to swing rapidly between the front and back of the machine. The horizontal extent, or width, of pattern is measured in terms of carriages, eg an 80-carriage set-out.

Catch bar the heavy bars at the back and front of the machine which lock with the nibs, or ears, of the carriages to rock them back and forth along the comb slots.

Chantilly a light lace used for high quality flouncing. Formerly of silk or rayon, in black or white, with an extensive basket and floral design, heavier at the lower edge, which is often deeply scalloped.

Chemical lace see *Burnt-out lace.*

Circular machine/Circular Bolt m./Circular Comb m./Circular Rotary m. etc a name used for the Plain Net machine *c.*1820–1920. Paired bobbins and warps make a twist net. It is basically an enlarged and improved version of the Old Loughborough.

Clawker the ratchet which turns the porcupine causing the web to rise on to the work roller.

Clips the cut ends of the floats of the thick threads or liners which are put in to outline the design while the lace is being made. The floats are later clipped wherever pattern units are separated by areas of net ground (L,R).

Closed loop in warp knitting the threads cross at the base of the loop.

Cloth roller/work r. as the lace is made it is wound onto this roller until it is full, 40 to 100 yards.

Cloth/clothing/gimping the design part of the lace where the patterning threads work, as opposed to the ground where they do not.

Cluny (a) small oval body having a woven appearance imitating the leaves, or *points d'esprit ovales*, of bobbin laces.

(b) an imitation of a bobbin lace of the same name, characterised by the presence of numerous clunys, often in a wheel formation (L,Ba).

Coffin net see *Craquele.*

Comb a series of brass blades separated by slots, like the teeth of a comb, but forming an arc of a circle, and providing a short track in which the carriages can swing. Bo: two carriages per comb; P,L,LC: one carriage per comb.

Comb bars the heavy steel bars from which the comb blades project. They lie across the width of the machine, one at the back, and one at the front. The blades are welded to them in two-inch segments.

Combination/nips a Curtain machine technique in which weighted spool threads bind adjacent warp threads together, giving the effect of a barred or guipure ground.

Cornely an embroidery machine which can work with a single needle, or with several needles, embroidering bridal veils etc with chainstitch designs, or with muslin appliqués.

Count/lea the thickness (diameter) of a staple yarn such as cotton. It represents the number of 840-yard hanks needed to make up a pound weight, or 500 grams (*Textile Terms* p. 224). The higher the number, the finer the thread. Now being replaced by the metric tex system. *See also* Denier.

Course a horizontal row of knitted loops (SF,WF,R).

Craquele/crackly/crazy/coffin net an irregular fancy mesh, sometimes coffin-shaped, or like crazy paving.

Crochet machine a warp-knitting machine with the latch needles placed horizontally.

Cross-band/crosswise lace made across the width of the machine so that separation into flounces is by cutting the warps.

Curtain machine/Lace Curtain m./Lace Furnishing m. a variation of the Bobbinet machine, with its own arrangement of auxiliary threads on spools, and its own special Jacquard patterning device, making use of interceptors. *See also* Jacks.

Cut down a colloquial term for the destruction of the vertical threads following a failure of synchronisation between right-left guide bar movements, and back-front bobbin swings, so that the sharp-edged carriages collide with the warps, tearing and mangling them (Bo,P,L,LC).

Cut-outs/incrustations small designs that can easily be cut apart and stitched to underwear etc. In Leavers, and in Schiffli embroidery on net, the surrounding ground is cut away. In S. guipure incrustations are embroidered 'nose to nose' with an easily severed cord holding them together during finishing.

Cut-ups stockings etc cut out of a plain fabric instead of being shaped on the machine (mainly WF).

Dawson's wheel a special cam, invented *c.*1790, to control a limited range of repetitive movements, even simple patterning, on the machine. First used on the SF to automate openwork knitting, it is still used on twist-net and other machines to control basic right-left movements of the warp guide bars.

Denier the thickness of a filament yarn such as silk or nylon, it represents the weight in grams of 9,000 metres of yarn. The higher the number, the coarser the thread. *See also* Count.

Dog the jointed arms holding the bar of ticklers used to transfer stitches, in the same course, from one needle to another, ie horizontal stitch transfer (SF).

Draft/draught the enlarged plan representing a single pattern repeat in terms of each guide bar movement at every bobbin motion (L); in LC, in terms of spool thread movements; in Ba, in terms of twists and crosses; in R, the movements of the guides in relation to the horizontal row of needles, plotted per course; in S, the positions of interaction of needle and shuttle threads making a stitch through the fabric, in relation to frame movements brought about by the Jacquard cards.

Draw thread see *Lacer*.

Drawing off the accumulation of the finished lace or net around the cloth roller (Bo,P,L,LC,R).

Droppers sets of six or seven steel rods with shaped graded heads which by their interposition between the driving blade and the buffer control the rise or fall of the Leavers guide bars.

Duchess(e) a barred lace with narrow tape-like bands forming the design, and imitating the bobbin laces Duchesse and Honiton.

Embroidered net a lace formed by embroidery on a plain net ground (HM,S,C); or a plain net embroidered by hand with a running stitch or by tambour work.

Ensor net a hexagonal meshed net characteristic of many Leavers laces. There is no cross at the end.

Entering the threads threading the thousands of warp and beam threads one at a time through the sley and guide bars, by hand.

Eyelet hole/oilet (a) a combination of stitch transfer and tuck stitch (SF); (b) pelerine stitch: a sinker loop is raised, and stretched over two needles in the following course. This may be repeated in the next course, increasing the size of the hole. An extension of this technique to involve the whole fabric is the basis of single press point net. (c) broderie anglaise (*qv*) is also sometimes called eyelet hole work (HM,S,C).

Face the front of the lace, as worn. The inner side of the lace as worn is called the *reverse*.

Fall the horizontal movement of guide bars and threads in a direction opposite to a rise (*qv*). In L, the fall is to the left of the machine, by spring action. In R, the fall is to the right by means of a chain, Jacquard cards or computer control.

Fall plate a metal plate on the Raschel machine causing the formation of a flossing effect with heavy laying-in yarn, so that a prominent design appears on the textural front of the fabric, caught only at its right and left edges to knitted pillars.

Filament yarn made of fibres of great length eg several miles (silk, rayon, synthetics).

Filet (a) by hand, a square-meshed knotted ground decorated by darning or running stitches.
(b) by machine, a copy of the visual appearance of (a) using other techniques, and without the knots.

Filling-in the technique which produces the dense appearance of the pattern areas in a lace.

Fining/warp fining the appearance of shallow zigzagging threads filling in the clothing or design of the lace between two or three straight bobbin threads. In Leavers centre gimp the front warp may make two-gait throws in opposite directions on alternate motions. When a reverse warp is present, this pillars while the front warp throws. *See also* Bobbin fining.

Finishing the conversion of the brown or grey lace which leaves the machine into the form in which it is displayed by the retailer. Finishing includes washing, bleaching, dressing, mending, scalloping, clipping, and winding onto cards.

Floats liners, or sometimes patterning threads, lying across the surface of the fabric, not being part of its structure, and linking two or more motifs together. They are clipped away after the lace has been taken off the machine.

Flossing an overlay of thick patterning threads, originally of floss silk, caught only at their right and left extremities to the lace fabric, so that they form a conspicuous mass on the face.

Flounce/flouncing made widthwise, eg 216 inches wide, of the machine, and between 12 and 54 inches vertically. Mainly L.

Framework knitters workers on the SF, and the earlier WF's.

Front/front edge the free border of a lace edging or flounce, equivalent to the heading of a bobbin lace.

Front motion the swing of the carriages from the back to the front of the machine.

Full motion two carriage swings, from front to back of the machine, and return.

Furnishing machine see *Curtain machine*.

Gait the position at the inner ends of the comb blades where the longitudinal warp and beam threads stand during a bobbin motion, ie the inter-carriage position; or, the distance between two adjacent comb blades. Warp and beam movements are described in terms of gaits eg a six-gait throw, from comb blade 1 to comb blade 7, across six comb spaces.

Galon/galloon a lace scalloped along both sides.

Gauge a measure of the fineness of the work produced by that machine, expressed as the number of specified parts per unit width. In L, the number of carriages, or points, per half-inch, thus 16-gauge means 32 carriages per inch; SF, the number of needles per 1½ inches; LC, the number of carriages per inch. With the Bobbinet machine, it is better to specify the number of points, or combs, per inch since the carriages are paired with two in every comb space. WF, number of needles per inch; R, number of needles per two inches. Alternatively, for both weft- and warp-knitting machines, the number of needles per cm. In all cases, the higher the number, the finer the work.

Gauze/leno weave a warp twine in which the warps are twisted in pairs at each pick.

Gimp/gimping the solid part of the design, or clothwork, or the threads making the clothwork. Patterning threads may thus be called gimp thread, and the process of patterning, gimping. In Leavers, the gimps derive from the beams; in LC, from the spool threads. In double gimping, successive patterning threads make 3-gait throws so that they overlap (fig. 103c). In L, when patterning effects are produced by front warp threads instead of by beams the action is called warping, or warp fining, not gimping

Godet a triangular lace inset often used to flare a skirt or a dress.

Go-through a type of Leavers machine, invented 1835, in which the front and back catch bars swing with the carriages, following them through with every motion.

Grecian net similar to bobbin lace honeycomb stitch. Each larger hole of the net has several smaller holes around it.

Grenadine a silk yarn, and lace, made of tightly twisted singles, tightly plyed.

Grey lace see *Brown l.*

Ground the openwork background of a lace design. It serves to join the gimpings together, and may be a net, or barred.

Guides perforated pieces of metal which carry their threads to where they are required, step by step, during the formation of the design. In the Raschel they circle around the needle heads; in twist-net machines they are moved right or left to new gaits.

Guide bars the long thin strips of metal which hold the guides. In Leavers they are called top bars when a bottom bar system is in operation. All movements are to the right or left widthways of the machine, and over a small number of gaits. Simple repetitive throws are controlled by cams; more complex and variable ones by a Jacquard apparatus. The guide bars lie in the well of the machine, immediately beneath the inner ends of the back and front comb bars. The maximum number is that which, placed as closely as possible together, completely fills the two inch well.

Guipure in handmade laces, a term used particularly after 1850 for any lace with a barred, instead of a net, ground. In machine laces, used mainly of 'Swiss embroidered guipure', or burnt-out, laces in contrast with embroidered nets made by the same machines (mainly S).

Hand-Circular, Hand-Leavers etc machines worked by hand and foot with no source of external power such as water, steam or electricity.

Handmachine an embroidery machine worked manually and able to imitate with great exactness white embroidery done by hand.

Held stitch on the SF, a stitch not knitted in a particular course, the old loop being retained and carried up into the next course, while the knitting thread passes behind it.

Hole a mesh. A plain net may be defined as 10-point 15-hole, ie 20 meshes per inch widthwise and 15 meshes per inch vertically.

Incrustation a small medallion of lace stitched on to, or sometimes inserted into, underwear, stockings, blouses etc.

Independent/independent beam a Leavers technique in which no warps are used, both ground and clothing being made by the interaction of beam and bobbin threads, the clothing often looking as if it is woven. Each beam thread is moved independently of any other beam thread, hence the name.

Inlay threads see *Laying-in threads.*

Insertion narrow lace bands, straight along both sides, to be inserted into a cloth or garment.

Insides the delicate inner parts of the machine such as carriages, bobbins, combs and guide bars, needing precision manufacture and formerly constructed by clock-makers.

Jacks/interceptors in Curtain machines thin bent wires which can enter between adjacent vertical spool threads, interrupting their cam-controlled right-left shogs, and causing a hole to appear in the clothing.

Jacked ground in the Curtain machine, a mesh or combination ground which is too complex to be controlled simply by cams, and requires Jacquard intervention. It allows adjacent threads in one guide bar to behave differently, which is impossible in a bar ground.

Jacquard a patterning device making use of a series, sometimes thousands, of punched cards, the holes and/or blanks being allocated specific values which determine which threads are moved, and to what extent. The precise details vary with different machines and are described in the appropriate chapters. An endless paper band arranged in a big loop, or chains, or computer programming, can be used instead of cards.

Journeyman a skilled, itinerant framework-knitter.

Kat stitch a net made of hexagonal-shaped meshes with a small triangle projecting outwards from each side.

Knitting (a) weft: a single thread is carried horizontally, or weftwise, the fabric being knitted by courses (SF).

(b) warp or vertical looping: as many threads as needles are arranged vertically from spools above, and the fabric is knitted along wales (WF,R).

Knop a fancy stitch used in weft-knitting. Held and tuck stitches are coincided to form a raised prominence.

Knot an old SF term for partial stitch transfer, a needle loop is stretched over two needles in one course. Knots, in the usual sense of tied threads, are not made by lace machines.

Lace on the machines a patterned fabric as distinct from a net which is uniformly plain, or uniformly patterned with tiny spots or sprigs.

Lace stitch see *Stitch transfer*.

Lacer/draw thread a disposable or easily removed thread which temporarily laces together adjacent bands during manufacture and finishing. It is intended to keep the web firm and to make it more convenient to handle.

Landing Bar an earlier form of Leavers machine in which the swing of the catch bars above the comb was supplemented by back and forth landing bar movements below the comb. Landing bars were

dispensed with in the Go-through, and this form of the Leavers machine is now obsolete.

Lapping (a) the right-left movements of knitted stitches (SF,WF,R). (b) the circling (underlap and overlap) guide movements carrying the threads around the needle heads to make the loops (WF,R). (c) the right-left movements of guide bars on twist-net machines, where it is also called throwing or shogging.

Lastex thin strands of natural rubber wound around with cotton, wool, silk or rayon to make an elasticated yarn. Developed by the U.S. Rubber Co in 1925.

Latch needle a needle with a small hinged latch which can be brought up to cover the needle hook during loop formation. The latch is a substitute for the long beard which has to be pressed into a groove. R, and some weft-knitting machines.

Laying-in threads threads which pass over the lace surface in the pattern areas and are held down by the knitting threads (R,WF).

Leavers a twist-net machine with a wide range of techniques producing quite distinct patterned laces, and able to copy with amazing precision the appearance of many handmade laces.

Legwork see *Barred lace*.

Liner/corder a heavy thread outlining the design unit, or clothing. It may be worked on the machine (L and R); run in by hand later (mainly P); or couched on by the Cornely machine, (some P and L).

Locker a mechanism for propelling the carriages back and forth along the comb slots in Plain Net machines.
(a) single locker: a single toe, tab or tail projects downwards from the middle of the carriage slide, and is biffed at every motion by the locker bar immediately beneath it. Now obsolete.
(b) double locker: there are two toes, one at each extremity of the carriage slide. Two locker bars with double blades rock through a small arc hitting each toe in turn, and shooting the carriages back and forth.
(c) roller/rolling locker: seven or eight projecting toes mesh with four fluted rollers beneath the combs, like cog wheels stretching across the entire width of the machine. This gives far greater power as the rollers turn, enabling the machine to work more rapidly.
The action of the locker bars below the combs is supplemented by the driving bars above.

Loop net R: laying-in threads are held by the pillar threads for several courses, then lap across to the next wale and back, to pillar again. L: the front warp throws in a 3-1 2-1 manner, in the centre gimp technique.

Lycra an elasticated (elastomeric) man-made fibre developed by Du Pont in 1958. The yarns and fabrics made from it can stretch and spring back again like natural rubber.

Macramé a heavy guipure with over-stitching, giving the impression of padded embroidery (S).

Madras net a bar ground, generally unstable, and poor quality (LC).

Malines a light single-warp Leavers lace of cotton, or cotton and silk mix, with liners, and a fine net ground, late nineteenth century.

Maltese copies of Beds Maltese, or of the original silk bobbin lace of Malta, often with numerous clunys and raised spots (L,Ba).

Manufacturer the finisher and entrepreneur who prepares the lace for retailing and also acts as an agent between the consumer and the lace factory.

Marking stitch partial stitch transfer (SF).

Marquisette a square-meshed Raschel net made with one guide bar knitting, or chaining, and one or two bars with laying-in threads making lapping movements over a variable number of wales at variable intervals, though usually every third course (R).

Mechlin/Mecklin (a) a type of net made on WF machines, early nineteenth century.
(b) a lightweight straight-down net with a diamond-shaped mesh, made in cotton or silk. Its simple structure enabled it to be made without Jacquards, by cam-controlled bars, on a modified Leavers machine.

Milanese a solid (non-openwork) warp-knit fabric, not to be confused with Milanese bobbin lace.

Motif/object a design particle, a distinct part of the clothing.

Motion a single carriage swing from front to back, or back to front, of the comb bars. Half, or single, motions = one direction; full motions = both directions, ie back to the starting point. The vertical extent of the design repeat is measured in terms of the number of single motions needed to complete it, eg a 128-motion set-out. The total lace produced is measured vertically in multiples of for example 1920 single bobbin motions (= racks). *See also* Rack.

Multihead/Multipoint machine an embroidery machine with a row of between 6 and 24 heads each with about 5 needles threaded with differently coloured or textured yarns that can be swung into position automatically as required.

Muslin (a) a colloquial term for clothing which shows single fining (single muslin) or double fining/double gimping (double muslin) (L).
(b) a translucent woven cotton fabric.

Needle (a) upright and horizontal: paired needles on the LC machine which react to the Jacquard cards and motivate the jacks to intercept, or not intercept, the spool threads.
(b) *see also* Bearded needle, Latch needle.

Needlerun (a) a Schiffli technique consisting in the attachment of thick threads or cords to the surface of the net, often in the form of spiral coils, to make a design.
(b) the running in of a liner by hand to accentuate the design, see *Liner*.
(c) hand-embroidery of designs onto plain net, using a running or darning stitch, and a counted mesh technique.

Net a light openwork fabric consisting of regular repetitive meshes, and made by weaving, knitting, knotting or twisting.
(a) plain net: every mesh identical, and traversed (Bo).
(b) fancy nets: the meshes may be irregular or decorative, and the net uniformly spotted or chenilled.
(c) the mesh background of laces, imitating the reseau of handmade laces eg ensor, bishops, loop, Val, point de Paris etc.

Net-inlay threads non-knitting threads, lapping from right to left within the ground (R).

Net-pillar threads knitting threads which form chains of loops along individual warps in the ground (R).

Nottingham the main centre for machine lace manufacture of all kinds in the UK. Machines themselves are also made there.

Nottingham lace any machine lace made in the Nottingham area, but thought to have been used first of bobbinets decorated by hand-needlerun in the second decade of the nineteenth century.

Objects the ornamental pattern areas of a lace, especially when representational eg leaves and flowers. *See also* Cloth.

Oilet see *Eyelet*.

Old Loughborough Heathcoat's 1809 Bobbinet machine.

Open loop the threads do not cross at the base of the knitted loop (WF,R).

Organ barrel a perforated cylinder which can control the movements of selected threads and so bring about automatic patterning. First used by Robert Frost *c.*1769 on the SF.

Organzine a silk yarn spun into singles with 12–15 turns per inch, then doubled or even trebled with 8–10 turns per inch in the opposite direction.

Outworkers workers outside the factory area and usually in their own homes, either working rented machines, or embroidering plain nets, or running in liners.

Patent nets a variety of nets made on the SF and WF machines *c.*1790 to 1830. They, and the machine modifications which made them possible were patented, hence the name.

Patterning threads known as gimps, from beams (L), or spools (LC); also laying-in threads (R).

Pelerine stitch the sinker loop is raised and stretched over one or two needles in the next course. This is the basis of both single and double press point nets.

Pillar/pillaring the spiral twining of one vertical thread around another (L,LC); knitting a single row of loops along an isolated warp (WF,R).

Pin machine a form of the SF, producing single-press point net.

Platt/platt net/platting machines (a) an impression of plaited strands imitating the plaited sides of the bobbin lace grounds known as Mechlin or droschel. (b) platt goods included Leavers bobbin fining laces such as Binche, cluny and duchesse.

Point (a) the semi-sharp projections attached to the back and front point bars which, working alternately, continually enter the net or lace web, compacting the threads after the bobbins, warps, and possibly others, have intertwined, on the twist-net machines. In plain nets they help to form the bobbin thread cross. The points are equal in number to the combs, and to the carriages in all except the plain net machines, where the carriages are paired. The gauge of the machine is therefore often expressed in terms of points eg 10-point gauge.
(b) ticklers, on that variant of the SF used to make point net. They were specially designed to pick up the sinker loops.

(c) ticklers used for stitch transfer of needle loops were also sometimes called points (SF).

Point de Paris a kat stitch or wire ground, the meshes like six-point stars; used for plain nets, and also as a ground for patterned laces (Bo,L).

Point d'esprit spotted nets, named after the French term for such spots, known as tallies in English bobbin-made Bucks laces which have a similar ground (Bo). Similar spots made in Leavers nets or laces are associated with ensor net and the independent beam technique.

Point net/point net machine the first commercially successful machine net, made with points on the SF and marketed in two forms, single press and double press. Obsolete *c.*1830 (SF).

Presser bar a bar used in bearded needle SF's and WF's to depress the beards into the grooves so that loops can be passed over their heads to make a new course.

Purls/picots single or double thread loops long the front edge of the lace band, or along the legwork of the ground. During manufacture special support threads are needed, which must later be withdrawn.

Pusher machine a form of bobbin-net or twist-net machine with a single tier of inverted carriages, its products characterised by a traversed net, an added liner, and clothwork looking like half-stitch.

Quality L and R: the number of inches of lace per rack; LC: the number of full motions per three inch length of lace; Bo: the sum of the number of holes per inch width plus the number of holes diagonally in a one-inch square. For L and R a low number is good quality, for LC and Bo, a high number.

Quarter a quarter-yard, or nine inches. Web-widths, and machine-widths are often expressed in this way. A 20-quarter machine would be 180 inches wide.

Quillings narrow breadths of net or lace gathered into small cylindrical folds and stiffened to resemble a row of quills. Worn about the head and shoulders *c.*1813–1835. Used also of ribbons.

Rack (a) the length of net or lace produced by 1920 single carriage motions (L), or 1440 single motions (LC), or 480 courses (WF,R).
(b) SF: that length of net which contains 240 holes measured vertically.
(c) after 1832, the length produced by 1440 single motions on the Circular or Plain Net machine or, 240 holes measured diagonally (in

effect 240 half-holes each equivalent to six motions = 1440).

(d) used as a basis for piece-work pay, it is a much fairer method than direct measurement, since by compressing the web sideways after it leaves the machine, its length can be at least doubled, while the number of motions are recorded as the lace is made.

Raschel a warp-knitting machine using latch needles mounted vertically.

Ribbon holes a lace with slots in it for threading tape or ribbon.

Rise the opposite of fall (*qv*). The horizontal movement of guide bars and the threads they hold, brought about by automatic patterning-control. In L the rise is to the right, by means of driving blades and a dropper system. In R the rise is to the left.

Roller locker see *Locker*.

Rotary using external power such as water, steam, electricity. Hence Circular Rotary, Leavers Rotary etc.

Round hole mesh (*mailles rondes*) an imitation of the round-meshed Valenciennes ground.

Run-in a comparative figure expressing the amount of yarn consumed in producing a unit length of fabric eg on R. machines.

Runners the 'needlerunners' who added liners, or who embroidered plain net by hand.

Schiffli an embroidery machine working on a two-thread (needle and shuttle) lockstitch system, developed commercially in Switzerland and Germany during the 1880s.

Set-out the individual threading of warp and beam threads, through the sley and guide bars, for any particular design repeat. The width is measured in carriages, and the height in bobbin motions (L).

Shog/throw/throwing off the right-left movements of the patterning or gimp threads across a number of gaits between the carriage motions (twist-net machines) or a number of wales (SF,WF,R). *See also* Lapping.

Shuttle (a) the case enclosing the yarn holder (S).
(b) the twist-net machine carriage (rare).

Sinker loop in weft-knitting the part of the thread between wales, or between the bases on the needle loops, joining them together horizontally.

Sley/holey board a blocked-in wire mesh in which holes can be bored for the passage of warp and patterning threads for the set-out required. The

sley helps to prevent friction and tangling of the threads against and with each other (all twist-net machines).

Spools elongated thread holders. Used especially of the LC machine where all the patterning threads are commonly on spools arranged on a top board, and a bottom board, sometimes 1,000 or more of each. Such spools are approximately equivalent to the beam threads of a Leavers machine.

Spots/spotted net small throws of thread over a very limited area to produce a series of regularly arranged dots over the net, in imitation of handmade tallies, or *point d'esprit carrées*. Raised spots may occur on patterned areas, giving a three-dimensional effect – they are sometimes faked by the creation of small domes using an embossing press.

Square net a square-meshed ground, especially on the LC machine (filet), and the Raschel (marquisette); also an eighteenth-century SF net.

Staple yarn made of short fibres which have to be spun together to be of use eg cotton, linen, wool. Filament polyesters may be artificially broken into short staples and spun to increase their resemblance to natural fibres. Usual lengths $1\frac{1}{2}$ to 12 inches.

Stitch transfer (a) full: a loop is transferred from its own needle to the adjacent needle, which now holds two loops (sometimes called lace stitch or eyelet holes).
(b) partial: the needle loop is stretched over the adjacent needle without being removed from its own (also called a knot or marking stitch).

Stocking Frame a weft-knitting machine worked manually to manufacture plain-knit hosiery etc. The first machine to be modified for the production of net and lace.

Store a lace curtain central to the window like a blind; *Rideaux* are paired curtains.

Straight down the bobbin threads pass vertically down the lace or net, instead of diagonally across it as they do in bobbinets, thus giving the impression of straight parallel lines (L,LC).

Stump bars a set of four guide bars punched at four-gait intervals so that between them they hold all the reverse warps. They lie in the well, with the top guide bars used for patterning, and their aim is to give absolute uniformity to the net ground – which must then, of necessity, continue through the design (fig. 104). This latter can be prevented by the addition of large numbers of bottom bars (*qv*) which can hold the warps individually and so allow independence of movement for the formation of fancy nets, or to make the ground stop when the pattern begins. Although all the bottom bar threads pass also through the stump bars, the large holes in the stumps – sometimes two gaits wide – allow the warps to 'float' into different positions, while preserving the basic regularity required of a ground.

Swiss lace (a) embroidered laces made on the S or HM.

(b) lace of two densities made on the LC machine. The middle (Swiss) bar, fed by bottom board spools, makes light V-ties; the back bar, fed by top board spools, uses heavier yarn. In two-gait work the spool thread throws to the adjacent pillar and back; in three-gait work it throws to the next pillar but one, ties and returns, so that threads overlap.

Tattings Narrow widths of net patterned with thicker threads, popular in the 1830s.

Technical v. textural fronts and backs the technical front is the side of the lace facing to the front of the machine as it is made, ie technical = position as made, textural = position as worn. In Raschel and LC, but not in L, the textural back is the technical front, and vice versa.

Thick threads/T threads a general term for liners, lacers and sometimes back and front threads, which are thicker than the net and patterning threads.

Throw see *Shog*.

Ticking a line of tiny holes, also called a line of net. It may be between the front edge and the purls of a lace band, or around the clothwork (gimping) especially in imitations of handmade Valenciennes.

Tie in the Lace Curtain machine, the binding of a gaiting spool thread to a vertical warp thread by a bobbin thread. Single tie: the Swiss, or middle, guide bar throws once on every full motion – it may then tie or pillar. Double tie: the Swiss bar throws twice on every full motion, to the left on the back motion and to the right on the front motion.

Tier a row of bobbin carriages. Single tier = one carriage per comb space (P,L,LC). Two tier = a pair of carriages per comb space, one behind the other (Bo).

Top bars the general name for the guide bars in the well of the machine, as distinct from the bottom bars (*qv*) which are placed lower down.

Torchon a lace of geometric design worked at a 45°

angle. Characteristic features are fans, spiders and half-stitch diamonds. The bobbin lace form is copied by L and Ba.

Traversed net/traversing A diagonal movement of threads across the web: (a) the paired bobbin threads pass diagonally across the net, one set to the right and the other to the left. On reaching the selvage, or turnagain, the two sets travel back in the reverse direction (Bo).

(b) a similar effect can be produced with a single tier of carriages and a set of pushers acting on individual carriages (P).

(c) in Leavers Lyons technique, repeated guide bar throws in the same direction on consecutive bobbin motions result in a diagonal or traversing thread effect over a limited distance. This is especially obvious when adjacent bar threads are constantly thrown in opposite directions.

(d) sometimes used as synonymous with shog (rare).

Traverse Warp a machine invented by John Brown in 1812. The warps traversed diagonally while the bobbins lay straight. The product was similar to Heathcoat's two-twist bobbinet.

Tricks In the Curtain machine, a series of small metal partitions to preserve the spacing of the jacks as they are moved forward or backwards to intercept, or avoid, the spool threads.

Tuck presser/tuck stitch a loop is knitted, but not passed over the head of its needle so that it remains there, and is joined by the loop of the following course. Tuck stitch is sometimes a mis-press but, when made deliberately, the formation of the new loop is suppressed by an additional presser bar, or tuck presser. As long as this continues to operate in the same wale, the old loops will continue to be carried up vertically into the next course.

Tulle a fine silk two-twist bobbinet; or a similar-looking warp-knitted net with hexagonal holes. *Tulle uni* and *tulle double*: literally single and double silk net. Used initially of the point nets of the Stocking Frame, but later in France for the two-twist bobbinet.

Twelve-motion shift the bobbin exchange which takes place at the completion of every row of meshes on the Bobbinet machine. By a combination of comb bar and point bar movements, a front carriage at one side slips into the back comb, and a back carriage of the other side slips into the front comb. This is possible because there is always one more warp than there are carriages, ie the threaded area begins and ends with a warp and, all the way between, bobbin and warp threads alternate.

Twisthands workers on the twist-net machines (*qv*).

Twist net/twist-net machines all nets, traversed or untraversed, made by the twisting together of warp and bobbin threads; and the general name for the machines which produce them (Bo,P,L,LC).

Valenciennes/Val an imitation of the bobbin lace of that name, with no liner, and a diamond-shaped (*maille carrée*) or round-shaped (*maille ronde*) mesh. Also used to specify other laces of similar texture with a diamond-shaped mesh.

Venise an imitation of the seventeenth century Venetian needle lace (S,HM). Some forms were very deceptive, but the name was also used in the twentieth century for guipures with a raised effect, even when there was no design similarity to the original.

Wale (a) a vertical line of loops (SF,WF). The term 'sinker wale' is sometimes used for the sunken line of threads between the needle loops, where the sinker loops lie.
 (b) L: a vertical line occupying the space between adjacent pillars.

Warp (a) the roller which holds all the warp ends, often two or three thousand.
 (b) the warp ends or warp threads themselves, vertical threads primarily concerned with net formation (Bo,P,L,LC).
 (c) in Leavers, single warp means the front or S-twist warp only is present; double warp means the reverse or Z-twist warp is also present.
 (d) in the Barmen a static thread, or threads, arising from immobile pillars at the perimeter of the machine, and appearing as rigidly straight supporting lines in the lace.
 (d) in loom laces the warp as in normal weaving.

Warp fining/warping see *Fining.*

Warp Frame initially an attachment to the SF to convert it from weft to warp knitting. *See also* Knitting.

Warp lace lace made on the Warp Frame and its successors such as the Raschel. Patterning is achieved by variable knitted cross-connections between the wales, or by laying-in threads which do not themselves knit but, being passed across the knitted pillars, bind them together.

Web the entire width and length of the lace or net fabric as it accumulates on the machine.

Weighting tackle a system of adjustable springs at the left or bottom end of the Leavers or other twist-net machines, which adjust the tension in individual warp and beam threads.

Well the space, approximately two inches wide between the inner ends of the front and back combs, which houses the horizontal-running guide bars threaded with their vertical warp and beam or spool threads. (Bo,P,L,LC).

White lace cotton lace, associated primarily with machines.

Wire ground see *Kat stitch*

Work roller see *Cloth roller.*

Working width the maximum width (right to left) of web that can be made on a particular machine. In Leavers and others, the total carcase width is considerably more since there is the entire Jacquard apparatus extending to the right, and all the weighting tackle to the left.

Yak a heavy furnishing lace in cotton or wool, imitating the wool torchon lace of the second half of the nineteenth century.

Yarn the bulk cotton, silk, wool etc purchased for use on the machines. Also used as synonymous with the individual threads mounted as warps, beams, bobbins etc.

Notes

(Where only the author is given, see Reading List for details)

Chapter 1, pages 11–29

1. Henson, p. 13
2. *Twelfth Night*, Act II, scene 4
3. Fiennes, p. 22
4. and 5. Timbs, *William Lee and the Stocking Frame*, p. 127
6. Henson, pp. 12–14
7. Aubrey, *Brief Lives*, Penguin, 1982, p. 264
8. 'Needle-making in Aix-la-Chapelle', *The Illustrated Exhibitor*, vol. 2 July 1852, p. 86
9. Felkin, p. 33
10. Felkin, p. 50
11. Felkin, p. 51
12. Webster, 'Nottingham', *The Technical Educator*, vol. 2, pp. 278–9
13. Wells, p. 129
14. Felkin, p. 63
15. Henson, p. 53
16. Henson, p. 221
17. Felkin, p. 67
18. Henson, pp. 61–6
19. Felkin, pp. 68–71
20. Felkin, pp. 48–9
21. Felkin, p. 110
22. *Guinness Book of Records*, 1984
23. King, H. *Before Hansard*, Dent, 1968, p. 82
24. Fewkes, p. 6
25. Wells, p. 57
26. *Textile Terms and Definitions*, 1975, p. 70
27. Ferguson, p. 1
28. Porter, R. *English Society in the Eighteenth Century*, Allen Lane, 1982, p. 64.
29. Henson, p. 296
30. Henson, p. 315
31. Murphy, 'Hosiery and Lace' p. 88
32. Felkin p. 135
33. Henson, pp. 291–4
34. Bailey, p. 218
35. Felkin, p. 169
36. *Report of the Framework Knitters*, 1812, p. 12
37. *Transactions of the Thoroton Society*, vol. 67, 1964, pp. 77–83
38. Quilter and Chamberlain, Textbook 6, p. 48

Chapter 2, pages 30–65

1. pp. 353–5
2. Henson, p. 356
3. Felkin, p. 145
4. Felkin, p. 250
5. Exhibition catalogue
6. Ferguson, p. 33
7. Ferguson, p. 140
8. Felkin, p. 405
9. *Working Party Report*, p. 82
10. Wells, p. 181
11. p. 83
12. p. 82
13. *Knitting News*, no. 8, 1969
14. *Empire Mail*, June 1928, p. 473
15. Wheatley, p. 70

Chapter 3, pages 66–95

1. Gore Allen, p. 39
2. Felkin, p. 161
3. Felkin, p. 198
4. Felkin, p. 197
5. Patent Abridgements, p. 16
6. Felkin, pp. 245–6
7. Ferguson, p. 72
8. Fewkes, p. 19
9. Walker, pp. 3–9
10. Felkin, p. 151
11. Felkin, pp. 255–7
12. Henson, pp. 429, 437
13. p. 51
14. Ferguson, p. 51
15. Felkin, p. 423
16. Felkin, p. 426

279

17. Felkin, p. 281
18. Gore Allen, p. 203
19. Felkin, pp. 341–2
20. Felkin, p. 318
21. *Paris Exhibition Report*, 1844
22. Ferguson, p. 94
23. Felkin, p. 397
24. Gore Allen, p. 183
25. Gore Allen, p. 213

Chapter 4, pages 96–106

1. Quoted by Wardle, p. 230
2. Felkin, p. 226
3. Felkin, p. 224
4. Mahin
5. Hénon, p. 218
6. Felkin, p. 419
7. Felkin, pp. 417–8
8. Hénon, p. 219
9. Felkin, pp. 276–7

Chapter 5, pages 107–172

1. Rosatto, p. 49
2. Felkin, p. 271
3. Ferguson, p. 59
4. Felkin, p. 274
5. Ferguson, pp. 59–60
6. Felkin, p. 272
7. Felkin, p. 385
8. Bailey, p. 451
9. *Nottingham Weekly Guardian*, Dec. 8 1923
10. Evans, W.R., 'Raschel in the Nottingham Lace Industry', *Hosiery Trade Journal*, 12/63, **70**, pp. 111–3
11. Hénon, p. 593
12. Hénon, p. 590
13. Hénon, p. 416
14. Lemaire, *Silk*, p. 127
15. Lemaire, *Silk*, pp. 32–3
16. Rosatto, p. 73
17. Felkin, p. 397
18. Felkin, p. 373

Chapter 6, pages 173–201

1. Felkin, p. 382
2. Felkin, p. 426
3. Ferguson, p. 154

4. *Lace and Lacemaking*, no author or date, c.1850s, p. 31. Though the exact nature of the Swiss curtains of the first half of the nineteenth century is uncertain, it seems likely that they were very similar in structure to those of the second half (see fig. 166), but with the chain-stitching worked by hand instead of by machine
5. Felkin, p. 323
6. Felkin, p. 382
7. Felkin, p. 421
8. Palmer, p. 7
9. *Empire Mail*, June 1928, p. 473
10. *Lace Furnishings went to war*, n.d, c.1940
11. Harding, p. 1
12. *Daily Mail Exhibition* catalogue, 1908, p. 42
13. Harding, p. 16
14. Harding, p. 39
15. Harding, p. 100

Chapter 7, pages 202–225

1. Hénon, pp. 262–6
2. Palliser, p. 455
3. Charles and Pagès, p. 159
4. Caplin, p. 149
5. Diagonal wholestitch is also found in some handmade laces from southern Switzerland, and in the 1561 Zurich pattern book for bobbin laces.

Chapter 8, pages 226–260

1. Hénon, p. 583
2. Goldenburg, p. 20. Today 15m machines may work 40,000 to 50,000 stitches in an eight- or nine-hour day, but large machines and more complex designs must go more slowly.
3. Schneider, pp. 99–112
4. Hénon, pp. 419–20
5. Schneider, p. 30
6. Maria Edgeworth, *Early Lessons: Harry and Lucy Concluded*, vol. 1, 1827, p. 183
7. Communication from Maureen Holbrook, Embroiderers' Guild, South Australia
8. Charles and Pagès, p. 107

Chapter 9, pages 261–267

1. Emery, p. 215
2. Emery, pp. 84–5
3. Frøsig
4. The thick linen threads are Z-spun singles composed of a large number of fine fibrils

Reading List

Alcan, Michel, *Fabrication des Etoffes, Etudes sur les Arts Textiles dans l'exposition Universelle de 1867*, Paris, 1868, 2 vol.

Bailey, Thomas, *Annals of Nottinghamshire*, vol. 4, Simpkin Marshall and Co., n.d.

Büttner, R. von, *Dei Hakelgalonmaschine*, Württ, 1953.

Caplin, Jessie, *The Lace Book*, Macmillan, New York, 1932.

Chamberlain, John, *Knitting Mathematics and Mechanisms*, Leicester, 1926.

Chamberlain, John, *Hosiery Yarns and Fabrics*, Leicester, 1926.

Chamberlain, John, *Principles of Machine Knitting*, Textile Institute, 1975 ed.

Chapman, S.D., The Genesis of the British Hosiery Industry, 1600–1750, *Textile History*, vol. 3, 1972.

Charles, M. and Pagès, L., *Les Broderies et les Dentelles*, Felix Juven, Paris, 1906.

Cuthbert, Norman, *The Lace-maker's Society, 1860–1960*, Amalgamated Society of Operative Lacemakers and Auxiliary Workers, USA, 1960.

Daily Mail Exhibition of British and Irish Lace, catalogue, 1908.

Defoe, Daniel, *A Tour thro' the Whole Island of Great Britain*, 1724–6, Frank Cass edition, 1968, 2 vol.

Dreger, Moriz, *Osterreichischen Museums fur Kunst und Industrie in Wien*, 1910.

Earnshaw, Pat, *A Dictionary of Lace*, Shire Publications, 1984 ed.

Earnshaw, Pat, 'Machine Laces – Collectable?', *Antique Collecting*, vol. 20, no. 8, 1985.

Earnshaw, Pat, 'The Princess Charlotte (1796–1817): a knitted lace wedding gown'. *International Old Lacers*.

Emery, Irene, *The Primary Structure of Fabrics*, The Textile Museum, Washington DC, 1966.

English, W., *The Textile Industry*, Longmans, 1969.

Fabrication artisanale, La, Musée de Quebec, 1974.

Felkin, William, *History of Machine-wrought Hosiery and Lace Manufacture*, 1867, David and Charles reprint, 1967.

Fennelly, Catherine, *Textiles in New England, 1790–1840*, Old Stourbridge, 1961.

Ferguson, S., fils, *Histoire du Tulle et des Dentelles Mécaniques en Angleterre et en France*, Paris, 1862.

Ferriere, M.T., *Swiss Textiles*, 1953.

Fewkes, Jesse, *Fine Thread, Lace and Hosiery in Ipswich*, Salem, Mass., 1904.

Fiennes, Celia, *Through England on a Side Saddle in the Time of William and Mary*, London, 1888.

Fouriscot, M., *La France en Dentelles*, Puy-en-Velay, 1979.

Frøsig, Hanne, *Hedebo*, Nationalmuseet, Copenhagen, 1979.

Goldenburg, Samuel L., *Lace, its Origin and History*, Brentano's, New York, 1904.

Gore Allen, W., *John Heathcoat*, Christopher Johnson, 1958.

Grass, M.N., *History of Hosiery*, Fairchild, New York, 1955.

Half a Century of Lace, Shepshed Manufacturing Company, Loughborough, 1956.

Hall, A.J., *The Standard Handbook of Textiles*, National Trade Press Ltd., London, 1950.

Halls, Zillah, *Nottingham Lace*, 1973 ed.

Harding, Keith, *Lace Furnishing Manufacture*, Macmillan, 1952.

Hénon, Henri, *L'Industrie des Tulles et Dentelles Mécaniques dans le pas de Calais, 1815–1900*, Paris, 1900.

Henson, Gravenor, *History of the Framework Knitters*, 1831, reprinted by David and Charles, 1970.

Hills, R.L., *Cotton-spinning*, North-western Museum of Science and Industry, Manchester, 1977.

Hünlich, Hans, and Herman, Fritsche, *Das Gardinenbuch*, Herford, 1958.

Iklé, Ernest, *La Broderie Mécanique 1828–1930*, Paris, 1931.

Iklé, Leopold, *Schweizerische Landesausstellung, Zurich, 1883* (Swiss National Exhibition, Zurich 1883, Report on Group 5: Embroidery).

Lace Furnishings, through War to Peace, The British Lace Furnishings Publicity Committee, n.d. but *c.*1940.

Lace and Lace Articles, US Tarriff Commission, Report no. 83, 1948.

Lace Trade and the Factory Act, New Quarterly Review, London, 1860.

Lee, C.H., *A Cotton Enterprise*, Manchester University Press, 1972.

Lefebure, Auguste, *Dentelles et Guipures*, Flammarion, Paris, 1904.

Lemaire, Henri, *Valenciennes*, Lille, 1906.

Lemaire, Henri, *Silk, Platt Valenciennes*, Howitt, 1909.

Lewis, Peta, M. Phil., The evolution of the hand Stocking Frame in response to market forces during the period of rapid economic and social change 1715–1815, University of Nottingham, 1985.

Litchfield, James L., *Lace, the Fabric of Romance*, Federation of Lace and Embroidery Employers' Association, Nottingham, for the British Empire Exhibition, 1924.

Lowe, David and Richards, Jack, *The City of Lace*, Nottingham Lace Centre, 1982.

Macintyre Read, Malcolm, *Handframe Knitting*.

Mahin, Abbie C., 'Pusher Lace and Gauze Weaving', in *Needle and Bobbin Club Bulletin*, vol. 6, no. 2, 1922.

Mathias, P., *The First Industrial Nation*, Methuen, 1969.

McGillivray, D.A., *A Visit to Plauen*, Nottingham, 1908.

Middleton, George, 'Imitation of Handmade Lace by Machinery' in *Needle and Bobbin Club Bulletin*, vol. 22, no. 2, 1938 and vol. 23, no. 1, 1939.

Murphy, William S., ed., *Modern Drapery and Allied Trades*, Gresham, 1914.

Murphy, William S., ed., *The Textile Industries*, Gresham, 1910.

Mygdal, Elna, 'Lindt om Kniplinger', *Myt Tidsskrift for Kunstindustris*, no. 7, 1939.

Naumann, Rose and Hull, Raymond, *The Off-loom Weaving Book*, Pitman, 1974.

Needle and Bobbin Club Field Notes, Bulletin vol. 6, no. 1, 1922, New York Times.

Page, William, ed. *A History of the County of Nottingham*, vol. 2, Univ. London, 1970.

Paling, D.F., *Warp-knitting Technology*, Columbine Press, Buxton, 1965.

Palliser, Mrs Bury, *History of Lace*, Sampson Low, 1910 edition.

Palmer, G.L., *Labour Relations in the Lace and Lace Curtain Industry*, vol. 2, Bulletin of the United States Bureau of Labour Statistics, n. 399, Washington DC, 1925.

Pointon, F.P., 'The Making of Lace, one of the most intricate of Britain's industries', in *Britain at Work*, vol. 2, n.d. but *c.*1905

Porter, Roy, *English Society in the Eighteenth Century*, Pelican Social History of Britain, 1982.

Posselt, Emanuel A., The Jacquard Machine, 3rd ed. Philadelphia, 1893 (first ed. 1888).

Posselt, E.A., *Technology of Textile Design*, McGraw Hill, n.d. (first ed. 1889).

Quilter, J.H. and Chamberlain, J., *Framework knitting and Hosiery Manufacture*, Leicester, 1911–19, 6 vols.

Reisfeld, A., *Warp-knit Engineering*, National Knitted Outerwear Association, New York, 1966.

Risley, Christine, *Machine Embroidery*, Studio Vista, 1973.

Rosatto, V., *Leavers Lace*, American Lace Manufacturers Association, 1949.

Rotenstein, C., *Lace Manufacture on the Raschel Machines*, National Knitted Outerwear Association, New York, 1954.

Saurer, *Hints on Card-punching with Saurer's Punching Machine*, 1914.

Schneider, Coleman, *Embroidery: Schiffli and Multihead*, New Jersey, 1978.

Schöner, Fritz, *Encyclopädie der Spitzentechnik*, Leipzig, 1980.

Snyder, Mary E., *Lace and Lacey Weaves*, California, 1960.

Stevenson, W., *Bygone Nottinghamshire*, Frank Murray, 1893.

'Story of Lace and its Role in Today's Fashion, The', in *The Maker-up*, vol. 53, no. 1, 1965, pp. 588–91.

Stoves, J.L., *Fibre Microscopy, its Techniques and Applications*, National Trade Press Ltd., 1957.

Taylor, M., *Technology of Textile Properties*, Forbes Publications, London, 1972.

Textile Terms and Definitions, ed. Farnfield and Alvey, The Textile Institute, Manchester, 1978.

Thomas, F.M., *I. and R. Morley: a Record of a Hundred Years*, Chiswick Press, 1900.

Timbs, John, 'William Lee and the Stocking Frame', in *The Technical Educator*, Cassell, *c*.1872, vol. 2, p. 235.

Timbs, John, 'The Cotton Manufacture', in *The Technical Educator*, Cassell, *c*.1872, vol. 2, pp. 42, 106.

Varley, D.E., *A History of the Midland Counties Lace Manufacturers' Association*, 1915–58, Lace Productions, 1959.

Walker, Sophia A., 'The First American Lace Manufactures, 1824', in *Needle and Bobbin Club Bulletin*, vol. 8, no. 1, 1924.

Wanner-Jean Richard, Dr Anne, *Kuntswerke in Weiss*, Textilmuseum, St Gallen, 1983.

Wanner-Jean Richard, Dr Anne, 'Emil Nef: der Sticker an der Handmaschine', *Heimatwerk*, 1/1985.

Wardle, Patricia, *Victorian Lace*, Herbert Jenkins, 1968, reprinted Ruth Bean, 1983.

Waters, T.F., *Ipswich Mills and Factories*, Salem, Mass., 1904.

Wells, F.A., *The British Hosiery and Knitwear Industry*, 1935, reprinted David and Charles, 1972.

Wheatley, B., *Raschel Lace Manufacture*, National Knitted Outerwear Association, New York, 1972.

Willis, F.A., 'The Textile Industry: Hosiery and Lace', *History of Technology*, vol. 5, Oxford, 1958.

Working Party Reports: Lace, Board of Trade, HMSO, 1947.

Wykes, A.L., *The Working of Viscose Silk*, Heywood, *c*.1930.

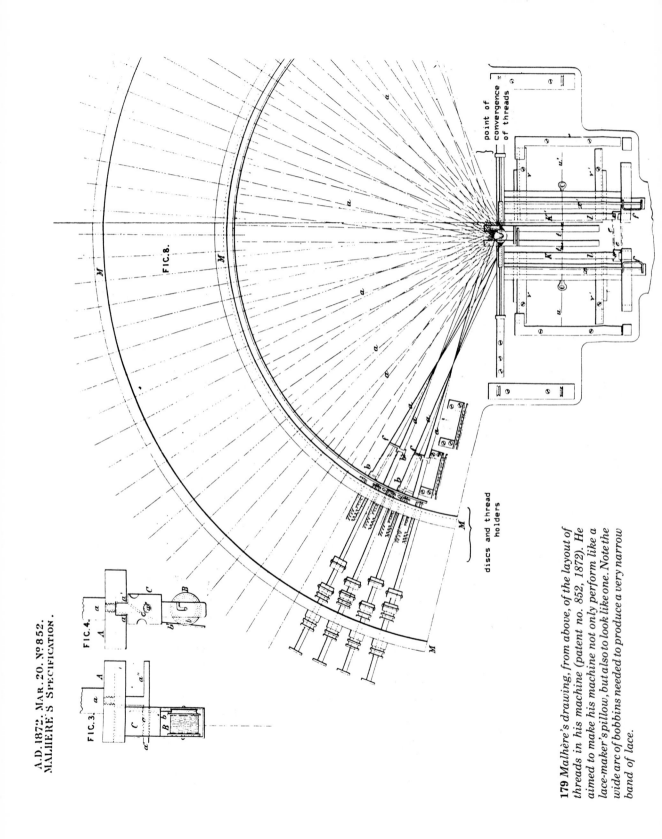

A.D. 1872. MAR. 20. Nº 852.
MALHÈRE'S SPECIFICATION.

FIG.3.

FIG.4.

FIG.8.

point of
convergence
of threads

discs and thread
holders

179 *Malhère's drawing, from above, of the layout of threads in his machine (patent no. 852, 1872). He aimed to make his machine not only perform like a lace-maker's pillow, but also to look like one. Note the wide arc of bobbins needed to produce a very narrow band of lace.*

INDEX

285